DATE DUE			

Inheriting Tradition:
Interpretations of the Classical Philosophers in Communist China, 1949–1966

Inheriting Tradition:
Interpretations of the Classical Philosophers in Communist China, 1949–1966

KAM LOUIE

HONG KONG   OXFORD   NEW YORK
OXFORD UNIVERSITY PRESS
1986

Oxford University Press

Oxford   New York   Toronto
Petaling Jaya   Singapore   Hong Kong   Tokyo
Delhi   Bombay   Calcutta   Madras   Karachi
Nairobi   Dar es Salaam   Cape Town
Melbourne   Auckland

and associated companies in
Beirut   Berlin   Ibadan   Nicosia

First published 1986
Published in the United States by
Oxford University Press, Inc., New York

Library of Congress Cataloging-in-Publication Data

Louie, Kam.
Inheriting tradition.

Bibliography: p.
Includes index.
1. Philosophy, Chinese—20th century.   I. Title.
B5231.L68   1986   181'.11   86-18266
ISBN 0-19-584046-1

British Library Cataloguing-in-Publication Data
available

Printed in Hong Kong by Kings Time Printing Press Ltd.
Published by Oxford University Press, Warwick House, Hong Kong

For Bonnie McDougall and Mabel Lee

Preface

FOR over a century, the fate of Chinese tradition in a modern world has fascinated and troubled some of the finest minds in China, and it has lost none of its allure and urgency since 1949. While Chinese writers have disagreed on exactly what Chinese tradition means, one thing is certain: the roots of this tradition are perceived to lie in the classical philosophies of the Spring and Autumn and Warring States periods (700–200 BC approximately). There is little doubt that the thinking of the pre-Qin philosophers (*xianQin zhuzi*) has formed the basis of all Chinese philosophy up to the twentieth century. The schools of Confucianism, Daoism, and Legalism, in particular, have continued to exert an influence right up to modern times. By examining their interpretations of the classical philosophers, this book looks at the way in which Chinese intellectuals grappled with the problem of the place of tradition in Communist China between 1949 and 1966.

When the People's Republic of China was created, the new government's declared aim was to establish the pre-eminence of Communism. The Party leadership, however, was well aware that the State it had just proclaimed was heir to the oldest and most resilient tradition in the world and that policies would have to be formulated regarding the treatment of that tradition. Even though many Chinese intellectuals and politicians have seen Chinese tradition as being irreconcilable with Communism—indeed, some would say it was the antithesis of modernity itself—the majority agreed with Mao Zedong's claim that 'contemporary China has grown out of the China of the past; we are Marxist in our historical approach and must not lop off our history. We should sum up our history from Confucius to Sun Yat-sen and take over this valuable legacy.'[1]

While it is a truism to say that the China of today grew out of the China of yesterday, the exhortations of authorities like Mao to preserve certain elements of the past have had profound repercussions for historians working in China. In the normal course of events, each generation of any civilization maintains and continues its cultural traditions; otherwise, that civilization ceases to exist. For centuries, the scholar-gentry class in China has conscientiously and dutifully assimilated and transmitted the Chinese heritage. After 1949, this process was facilitated by political dictate, but the new scholar-gentry class, the officials and intellectuals, had to use a totally alien ideology, Marxism, as the sole criterion for selecting those elements of the traditional culture to be retained and continued. This book is an examination of one aspect of this process of 'inheriting tradition' (*chuantong de jicheng*). It shows how scholars after 1949 have attempted to fit traditional Chinese thought into Marxist categories, so that they could argue that facets of the Chinese past could be salvaged for present use. This is to ensure that China under Marx remains Chinese (and Chinese of a kind approved by the intellectuals).

In my book *Critiques of Confucius in Contemporary China*,[2] I argued that, since the late Qing dynasty, controversies about tradition have mainly been debates about Kongzi and that the interpretations of Kongzi became progressively more critical, culminating in the anti-Kongzi movement of the early 1970s. That thesis was only partially accurate: while tradition has often been synonymous with Confucianism, the many fierce controversies surrounding the other classical philosophers in the fifties and sixties demonstrated clearly that there were other vital streams of thought and ways of life in China that were also part of tradition. The present work argues that, in the way particular traditions of the Chinese past have been singled out for praise or condemnation, Communist Chinese scholars, like their predecessors in Imperial times, are on the whole conservative[3] and élitist.

The ways in which the classical philosophers have been evaluated can best be understood in the context of the historical and ideological background of the 1950s and 1960s. Chapter 1 thus defines this historical and intellectual framework. For example, the conservatism of the majority of intellectuals is partly a reaction to the political pressures exerted on them to study and assimilate a new set of methods and values. This was especially the case when the Soviet model was an obligatory goal, so much so that many writers saw this imposition as a threat to the continuance and identity of Chinese culture itself. Chapter 1 also deals with the way in which Western philosophical and historical terminology is used in China. For example, vital concepts such as idealism, which in normal Western philosophical discourse gives the mind or spirit a more important position than matter, and materialism, which gives matter a primary position and accords to the mind or spirit a secondary one, take on political significance in China. The political connotations of historical and philosophical concepts greatly affect the way in which Chinese tradition is analysed. Chapter 2 looks at attempts to elucidate the meaning of the term 'inheriting tradition' and to devise ways in which the 'inheritance' may be achieved. Even on general questions of the meaning of philosophy and inheriting tradition, writers like Guan Feng and Feng Youlan disagreed. They were to clash even more violently in their actual interpretations of the individual philosophers.

Kongzi, the subject of Chapter 3, is the most prominent figure under consideration. Confucianism traditionally stood for respect for learning, authority, and orthodoxy. The numerous calls for the 'inheritance' of Confucian values such as *ren* and Confucian educational theory show clearly the conservative and élitist attitudes of the writers. The evaluations of the Daoists Laozi and Zhuangzi, considered in Chapter 4, are no less passionate and the arguments surrounding them contain some of the finest and fiercest polemics in philosophical analysis in the fifties and early sixties. Nevertheless, these polemics reveal that, although the conservative and radical intellectuals had opposing conceptions of Daoism, their intense interest in the subject was also an indication of the élitist nature of the debates on 'inheriting tradition' because philosophic Daoism is a way of thinking in which only the privileged can indulge. Chapter 5 presents interpretations of Mozi, which illustrate further the general snobbishness of the writers. Although Mozi's egalitarian principles make him the most 'communist' of the pre-Qin philosophers, there were very few calls to 'inherit' him. It is interesting to consider why Communist writers did not seek to elevate him to a higher position as, for example, some May Fourth radicals had tried to do. The last group of philosophers considered, in Chapter 6, comprises Mengzi, Xunzi, and Han Feizi. Their philosophies were all derivatives of the Confucians and Daoists, but they deserve examination because they served at various stages of the Communist period as convenient means by which Chinese tradition could still be studied and assimilated. The changing evaluations of these philosophers reflect most vividly the need of Chinese scholars and political leaders to 'inherit' a Chinese past: it mattered little whether that past was the orthodox one, as long as it was Chinese.

The conflicts between differing interpretations of the classical philosophers reached a climax during the Cultural Revolution; the specific nature of 'the most radical rupture with traditional ideas'[4] is briefly described at the end of each chapter. The conclusion brings out the significance of the ways in which the classical philosophers have been analysed for 'inheriting tradition'. It also points to the post-Mao analysis as a continuation and in many cases a duplication of pre-1966 ideas, thus indicating that, in a more relaxed atmosphere, a more conservative and élitist attitude with respect to tradition dominates once again.

The pre-1949 writings of left-wing historians such as Guo Moruo and Fan Wenlan are used in this book because they had a decisive effect on later works, and many were reprinted after 1949. Many of the Communist assessments can in fact be seen as continuations of ideas already outlined before Liberation. These early works, as well as some by non-Communist writers such as Qian Mu and Hu Shi, are also considered here. Apart from the standard works of the 'masters' such as Guo Moruo and Feng Youlan, other sources consulted include nearly all books and articles on the history of philosophy published after 1949. The articles discussed are taken on the whole from academic journals, although many are also from newspapers or collected works.

The variety and diversity of the sources used here do not signify an eclectic or *ad hoc* approach. Indeed, it would be rare for someone who had commented on some aspect of, say, Laozi's epistemology not to have read most of the sources on this subject. Thus, no matter where the comment was published, it is highly probable that it was read by people working on the same topic and that it thus exerted some influence. Also, the mere fact that a publication appears in China officially, no matter where, indicates a certain degree of official approval and support, and official sanctions still define the scope of academic enquiry. Sometimes, the status of the author is important; for example, what Guo Moruo or Fan Wenlan had to say was always carefully monitored. At other times, though, it was the organ carrying the article which was the important factor. For example, if an article appeared in the *Guangming Daily*, its viewpoint would be conveyed to a wide national audience.

Although I have had hundreds of discussions about this topic with people from all walks of life, ranging from Professor Feng Youlan and Professor Zhang Dainian to peasants in my village on my trips back to China since 1973 and during the time I taught at Nanjing University in 1978–9 and carried out research at Beijing

University in 1980–1, this work is in no way 'an eyewitness report', nor does it take into account the extent to which traditional customs continue to prevail in China. It is more concerned with how intellectuals have perceived and expressed their ideas about the classical philosophers in writing. Some of the more obvious implications that the ideas on inheriting tradition have had on other aspects of life such as the arts, religion, and literature have been indicated, but more detailed exploration and analysis must await further research.[5]

For the sake of consistency, the Pinyin system of Romanization has been used throughout, except for direct quotations. This causes a minor problem in that household words such as Confucius and Peking have to be Romanized into the less easily recognizable forms of Kongzi and Beijing, but this inconvenience is the price one has to pay for a consistent system of transliteration. Adjectives derived from the Chinese such as Confucian and Legalist, however, are still employed because reverting back to the original Chinese transliteration would mean that more unnecessary philosophical terms in Chinese, in this case *ru* and *fa*, would have to be introduced.

I am grateful to Mabel Lee, Tang Yijie, Bonnie S. McDougall, Louise Edwards, Pierre Ryckmans, Donald J. Munro, Toshihiko Kobayashi, Anne Louey, He Hanwei, Albert R. Davis, Ann Lau, and Anne Gunn for encouragement and advice. Some of them, of course, may not agree with all the ideas expressed in this book.

I am also indebted to Auckland University Grants Committee for a research grant.

Kam Louie
November 1985

Contents

1 Historical and Intellectual Frameworks: Mastering New Ideas for Old Problems

TRADITIONALLY, Chinese scholars belonged on the whole to an élite class of landowners and officials. Their beliefs were shaped essentially by the Confucian-Daoist classics handed down over the centuries. They rarely produced anything which went beyond the parameters defined by these classics and approved by successive dynastic rulers. To be cultured was to act in accordance with words dictated by the ancient sages. There was never any doubt that Chinese thinking, as reflected in the written word, was the one and only civilized one. Even when the presence of a scientifically advanced West was making itself felt, the Chinese were still confident that theirs was the source of all that was culturally worthwhile. It was only after repeated internal and external catastrophes such as the Opium Wars and the Taiping uprising that conscious and often painful efforts were made by thinkers of all persuasions to reassess the 'national essence' and the relative merits of East and West.

These efforts have been the subject of numerous studies in many languages, but such studies have, on the whole, been limited to the era before 1949.[1] It is often assumed that, because the Chinese Communist Party has exerted total control over intellectual life in the People's Republic of China, the question of the way in which the Chinese perceive themselves must also necessarily be monolithic and uninspired. Nothing is further from the truth. The People's Republic has probably seen some of the most anguished conflicts in arriving at a modern Chinese identity.

True, the historical and political conditions after 1949 determined the way in which intellectuals wrote. It is possible to argue, as some scholars have done about other socialist countries,[2] that the founding of the Communist regime meant that intellectuals had developed into a class which collaborated with and became part of the political leadership, interested only in strengthening their privileged positions with the help of the established ideology. However, the many political upheavals of the last thirty years, which involved opposing factions of the intellectuals, suggest that, even if this hypothesis were correct, members of this class have certainly not been unanimous in their conceptions of many fundamental issues, and the evaluation of tradition has been an issue of great contention.

Political leaders, no less than the writers, were faced in the new era with the same dilemma. They wanted to instil a sense of patriotism in Chinese people, especially in the young. Thus, almost every history text begins by exhorting the reader to study for the sake of 'correctly absorbing the rich historical heritage of our country.'[3] Yet the stated aim of the new State was to build a modern socialist ideology in China. Although the two aims were not necessarily mutually exclusive, there was no question that tensions would occur in the integration of the two into the new general programme. Although the post-1949 situation was such that only writing which was approved by the political leadership could be published, the parameters of this political acceptability were never constant. In order to understand the fluctuations in historical analysis, it is necessary to discuss the political and ideological frameworks of the last thirty years.

THE POLITICAL FRAMEWORK

Marxism Takes Command: The Early 1950s

The Communist victory in 1949 was also a triumph for the Marxist writers who, for many years, had waged an ideological battle against those of other persuasions, most significantly those such as Hu Shi who had been educated in the United States. The attack on Westernized intellectuals intensified after 1949. The outbreak of the Korean War and the subsequent 'Resist America, Aid Korea' campaign were manifestations of a conflict which lasted into the seventies. In the fifties, the cold war mentality meant that those trained in the West had to make serious efforts to remould their thinking along Soviet lines. Although movements like the 1952 'Three Antis and Five Antis' campaign were mainly political campaigns with officials the chief targets,[4] inevitably academics too had to make self-criticisms.

The first movement aimed at changing the outlook of the intellectuals came in 1952, with the criticisms against the film 'The Story of Wu Xun'.[5] The film was about an educationalist in the latter part of the Qing dynasty who had opened several schools for the poor with the help of Manchu officials. It was shown with moderate success, but in 1951 it suddenly became the target of attack by the Party. Zhou Yang, for example, criticized it as it suggested that educational reform alone could change society without revolutionary struggle, and Jiang Qing later claimed that she had in fact initiated the attacks.[6]

The criticisms made against this film heralded many of the themes of later political movements. It is interesting to note, for example, that this important academic debate, which was transformed quickly into a political campaign, was against an educationalist. In the new society, where the mind of traditional man was to be transformed into that of a new socialist man, it was important to change the whole concept of traditional education and the idea of human nature itself. By mid-1952, the criticism levelled at the film had turned into a full-fledged political campaign, filling most newspapers and journals.[7]

The major task of the Communist Party in the first few years of the new regime was to extend and consolidate its control. As part of this process, attempts were made to increase the influence of Soviet ideas and to try to reduce Western, especially American, influence. This was reflected in the study of philosophy. Universities throughout China closed their Chinese philosophy departments. Instead, professors were required to learn Marxism-Leninism. Professors in Beijing and Tianjin were reported to be spending twelve to fifteen hours a week in the study of Communist documents alone.[8]

With such a task ahead of them, it is not surprising that these professors did not produce very much that was new. Their publications show an uneven development in the first couple of years of the People's Republic. In 1949, while scholars like Feng Youlan were busy writing self-criticisms, books like Liang Souming's *The Essentials of Chinese Culture*, written in praise of traditional Chinese virtues, were still being published.[9]

On the whole, however, material that was published tended to be revised or updated versions of earlier works by writers who professed to be left-wing or Marxist. In historical studies, standard works such as Lü Zhenyu's *A History of Chinese Political Thought* and Zhou Gucheng's *General History of China* continued to exert a strong influence. In the new editions, the outlines of the old texts were generally preserved, but the authors usually added prefaces discussing the Marxist methodology which was now to be employed in studying history.[10] Besides this, prominent historians like Jian Bozan and theoreticians like Ai Siqi wrote articles setting out guiding principles for the study of history and philosophy and discussing principles for the study of such Marxist concepts as 'class struggle' in history[11] and 'dialectical materialism' in philosophy.[12] As most of the historians of thought were still struggling to master the new terminology, not to mention the new methodology, no elaborate statement could be made on the assessment of historical figures or epochs during this period.

By far the greatest emphasis in publishing in these early years lay in the printing of Marxist books, reflecting the fact that the political leaders were far more interested in propagating new ideas than in evaluating old ones. Between 1949 and 1953, over 15 million copies of works by Marx, Engels, Lenin, and Stalin, and 25 million copies of works by Mao were printed.[13]

The influence of Soviet ideas was equally important in the dissemination of Communist ideology, and Soviet intellectual trends were closely followed in China. In 1947, A.A. Zhdanov, the Soviet Party spokesman on cultural matters, made a speech in which he criticized G.F. Alexandrov for failing to stress the struggle between idealism and materialism in his history of Western European philosophy. This speech was translated and published in China a year later by Li Lisan,[14] and it was reprinted and widely distributed after 1949. Zhdanov's critique had a great deal of influence on discussions on Chinese philosophy in the next thirty years. The extent of Soviet influence in general on Chinese intellectual circles can be gauged by the fact that between 1949 and 1956 over 12,000 Soviet books were translated into Chinese, with 191 million volumes printed.[15]

The Hundred Flowers Period

By 1954, the political leaders felt confident enough to reopen the philosophy department of Beijing University, following the death a year earlier of Stalin and the relaxation of political control in the Soviet Union. However, it was only at Beijing University that a philosophy department existed at this stage. Over the next four years, tertiary teachers of Chinese philosophy throughout the country were requested to carry out a period of study there. In 1957, Wuhan and Fudan universities also reopened their Chinese philosophy departments, and others such as Zhongshan University followed soon after. Beijing University, however, continued to be the centre and focus of philosophical research in China. Most of the debates considered below, for example, took place there. Although the Chinese philosophy faculty was small, with about ten members of staff, these included such key writers as Feng Youlan, Ren Jiyu, and Tang Yijie, who later played prominent roles in discussions on the pre-Qin philosophers.

By 1954 too, the publication scene had become less strictly Marxist, and the scope for more academic debate was expanded. In the first few years of the People's Republic, there were no journals devoted specifically to history or philosophy. Articles on these subjects were published instead in journals of a general nature, such as *New Construction*. In 1954, the *Guangming Daily* began to devote regular columns to areas of academic interest. In the same year, the journal *Historical Research* appeared, followed by *Philosophical Research* in 1955. Avenues were now expanded for academics to present their ideas and to debate issues, albeit within a Marxist framework. When *Philosophical Research* first appeared, its stated aim was 'to struggle for the triumph of Marxist philosophy,'[16] but the more immediate task seems to have been to repudiate the ideas of Hu Shi, for the articles in that year were mainly devoted to attacks on Dewey's philosophy of pragmatism. This was probably the most influential theory among those who had not accepted Marxism, and Hu Shi had been Dewey's best-known disciple and spokesman in China.[17] Hu Shi was criticized on many grounds, one of which being that he had adopted a disdainful stance towards Chinese culture. Hou Wailu, one of the most influential historians of thought, accused him of having 'smeared and slandered the history of Chinese culture.'[18] The motivation for this kind of criticism seems to have stemmed more from a fear that Chinese civilization would be totally destroyed than from Marxist ideological considerations. The attack on Hu Shi was a convenient way to express a concern that some of the basic ingredients of Chinese tradition should be preserved in the new state. The emphasis on the translation and publication of Soviet books at the expense of those written by Chinese writers must have been part of those fears.

In 1956, Khrushchev denounced Stalin at the 20th Party Congress in Moscow, an event which marked China's gradual break with the Soviet Union.[19] From this time, China began to move away from the Soviet model and turned more to the task of working out its own policies and directions. In doing so, China inevitably had to turn more and more to its own past for inspiration. Another consequence of the worsening of relations with the Soviet Union was that knowledge of the Western world was no longer indirectly filtered through Soviet sources. Even this rather weak channel for outside information was gradually closed.

In the same year, Mao Zedong delivered a speech to a closed session of the State Council in which he proposed the policy of 'let a hundred flowers bloom and a hundred schools of thought contend'.[20] This slogan became the motto for academic discussion in the second half of 1956 and in early 1957. The slogan 'a hundred schools of thought contend' was first coined some two thousand years ago to describe the intellectual life of the Warring States period, so that it was fitting that, in the intellectual climate of that time, there was a revival of interest in the study of the ancient schools of thought. In fact, in the first decade of the People's Republic, the bulk of the studies completed on the classical philosophers or on the question of 'inheriting the traditional legacy' were carried out in 1956 and 1957.

Articles began to appear with such titles as 'The Critical Assimilation of Our Country's Cultural Heritage is Necessary for Socialist Cultural Reconstruction.'[21] Those who wrote urging the inheritance of traditional values were usually careful to ensure that they quoted Mao to justify their ideas. Mao had written a number of times on this topic, stating, for example, that 'we must on no account neglect the legacies of the ancients and the foreigners or refuse to learn from them, even though they are the works of feudal or bourgeois classes,' although at the same time he had warned that 'uncritical transplantation or copying from the ancients and foreigners is the most sterile and harmful dogmatism.'[22] His statement in 1938 that 'we should sum up our history from Confucius to Sun Yat-sen and take over this valuable legacy' was quoted by many writers to justify their concern with the past.[23] There was, as well, the example of the Soviet Union, which not only spoke of, but practised, the policy of inheriting the legacies of the past, where pre-revolutionary art and literature still had a place, and selected figures in Russian history were praised.

The question whether Chinese tradition could be 'inherited' in a socialist era was examined at a conference held at Beijing University in January 1957.[24] This conference raised many issues that were to be discussed in later years. Feng Youlan, Zhou Gucheng, and other prominent historians of thought maintained that some values were class-transcending and thus could be inherited, even though they might have been derived from idealist schools of thought.[25] This gave rise to the whole debate on what 'philosophical inheritance' meant and whether philosophical and moral values could transcend class. It was at this conference also that Feng Youlan argued that Han Feizi was a materialist because of his theory of the causal relationship between population growth and economics. Following this, many articles were written discussing the position of Han Feizi and the Legalists. The conference also gave rise to a series of debates on Kongzi, after it was suggested that the Confucian concept of *ren* was one of the values that transcended class. When Feng Youlan later tried to defend his role at the conference, Guan Feng accused him of being a 'modern-day Zhuangzi'. Following this, a spate of articles appeared on Zhuangzi and Daoism. This conference was thus instrumental in bringing about a revival of interest in 'the hundred schools'. Because it was held as a consequence of many academics' desire to preserve some aspects of the Chinese heritage, it is not surprising that the tone of the conference reflected just that: attempts by influential historians to preserve traditional philosophy by eulogizing the classical philosophers. The concrete discussion of the pre-Qin schools of thought which resulted from this conference will be looked at in some detail in later chapters.

A second conference on the history of Chinese philosophy, held in May 1957, saw further criticism of Zhdanov-type views. It continued to debate the relevance of the classification of philosophers as idealist or materialist to an understanding of Chinese philosophy. Hou Wailu was one of those who felt that this had created the tendency to place as many philosophers as possible in the category of materialists, 'as if it would be a glory to us that many of our forefathers were materialist. Consequently many of the idealists were presented as materialists; if this goes on, all our philosophers from Confucius to Sun Zhongshan will be materialist, but that's not the way to do scientific research'.[26] The implications of Hou Wailu's statement are interesting. His observation that Chinese academics, even before the more relaxed political climate of the Hundred Flowers, had been busy classifying Chinese philosophers as materialists because that was seen to be good and 'inheritable' was indicative of the fact that, whatever theoretical framework Chinese scholars had to work with, they were not slow to present Chinese tradition in the best light within it. Furthermore, as soon as the political controls were lifted, the non-native framework itself was questioned. Had the movement for liberalization stayed confined within the academic sphere, its continuance might have been tolerated, but it quickly spread to other areas of intellectual activity. For example, in literature, some young writers such as Liu Binyan began to produce stories which exposed aspects of the bureaucratic inertia that had set in since the People's Republic was established.[27] When this was coupled with explicit criticisms of the Party, of learning from the Soviet Union, and even of Communism itself, some Party leaders became uneasy.[28] As soon as signs of student unrest began to develop, those leaders who had initially opposed the relaxation of political control felt that their original fears had been justified, and it was not long before the liberalization movement was abruptly brought to an end.

The Drift Back to China: The Late 1950s and Early 1960s

The Party launched the anti-rightist campaign in June 1957. Although this movement was meant to suppress critics of the Party, it widened in scope to include many who had been staunch Party supporters as rightists, a label which stopped them from being effective social beings. Many university teachers, including of course many who had shown support for 'inheriting' Chinese tradition, were among those who were labelled and either removed from teaching posts or placed under close supervision. The swiftness and ruthlessness of this campaign left its mark on intellectual life for many years to come.[29]

The anti-rightist campaign was followed by the Great Leap Forward of 1958, when scholarly research gave way to the movement to promote mass culture. The idea of relying on the masses in scientific research and academic work was promoted, and thousands of poems by ordinary people, for example, were published as expressions of mass creativity. The Yan'an model, rather than the Soviet or traditional models, was followed.[30] Radical writers like Guan Feng, who was to assume importance as a Party spokesman on philosophical matters, wrote in philosophical journals about the wonders of socialist society in its constructive efforts such as building dams.[31] It was not long before schools and universities came under fire for having placed too much emphasis on ancient and classical learning. The motto for the day in historical research was 'more modern, less ancient' (*houjin bogu*). It is not surprising that in this climate the study of classical philosophy once more suffered a setback, although it was only temporary.

By 1959, there were indications that a new trend was about to emerge. A directive was issued on the handling of 'rightists' and, on 1 October 1960, many of those who had previously been labelled as 'upholders of the white flag' had their labels removed.[32] Three years of natural disasters followed the Great Leap Forward. As China faced new economic difficulties, the spirit of optimism characteristic of much of the 1950s gave way to a more sober mood. More conservative policies were followed, especially in rural areas: peasants were again allowed private plots, and collective dining halls were largely abandoned. The rejection of the Great Leap Forward policies weakened Mao's position. In the early sixties, he retreated to 'the second line', leaving administrative matters to Liu Shaoqi, who took over as head of state.[33] Liu's own penchant was for more careful planning and a greater emphasis on order, in contrast to Mao's more flamboyant style.[34]

The final break with the Soviet Union came in 1960 during the 'three hard years' when all Soviet technicians were withdrawn, taking with them the technical plans and blueprints of projects they had been working on. The break also had a direct effect on intellectuals who, whether or not they agreed with the policy of learning from the Soviet Union, had at least been able to use the Soviet Union model as a guide for carrying out their work. With this removed, there was the question of what would replace it. The policies developed during the Yan'an period had been largely discredited because of their association with the Great Leap Forward. Despite a more liberal academic climate, it was still by no means possible to advocate Western theories openly. It is not surprising then that traditional Chinese ideas again became influential.

In historical studies, the break with the Soviet Union was reflected in a number of ways. History journals no longer carried translations of Soviet works and, after 1960, Chinese and Soviet historians ceased to exchange visits. All of this was regarded by Soviet historians as crass ingratitude.[35] Perhaps the most important indication that a new trend was to be followed in intellectual activities came in a speech given by Chen Yi in August 1961. Making it clear that he was speaking not as an individual but in the name of the State Council and the Party, Chen Yi went on to give what was essentially a new theory on the relationship of 'redness' and 'expertness'. Political consciousness, redness, was to be manifested through vocational work and not judged solely in terms of political activity. The tendency to brand as 'white experts' those who immersed themselves in study was wrong. Calling for a more academic education, Chen Yi proposed that specialized schools should spend less time on politics and manual labour. Politics, henceforth, would be left largely to political schools. He stated that intellectuals could not be expected to have deep-rooted Marxist convictions: it would be sufficient if they worked with the Party. Interestingly, Chen Yi seemed to assume that a lack in Communist convictions meant a belief in ancient Chinese thought. Even his own mind, Chen commented, still contained traces of the ideas of Kongzi and Mengzi.[36] In March 1961, the *Red Flag* carried an article which called for a revival of the Hundred Flowers policy, although this time it was made clear that freedom of discussion was to be limited to academic matters and not to be extended to politics.[37] A wide range of new courses was introduced in the universities in 1961 and 1962 as part of the new spirit. While the revival of the Chinese philosophy departments in the fifties had been significant, the courses taught had been new and had been given by teachers who were themselves often uncertain of the new directions. This time, some of the courses actually corresponded to individual professors' interests and specialities. In 1962, Beijing University added such courses as 'Historical Sources for Chinese Philosophy' given by Feng Youlan and 'General Introduction to Chinese Buddhist Philosophy' taught by Ren Jiyu.[38]

The new Hundred Flowers spirit was also reflected in the holding of a great number of academic conferences and seminars in the universities. Whereas, during the Great Leap Forward, students and laymen with practical experience were called on to give papers, experienced teachers and research workers were now given these roles. An important conference held in Shandong in 1962 to commemorate Kongzi, for instance, was attended by some of the finest scholars in the country.[39] The return to a more 'nationalist' interpretation of history was the result of both a more relaxed political atmosphere and a moving away from the Soviet and Yan'an ways of thinking. The rejection of both lines of thought left a vacuum that tradition began to fill. Significantly, Liu Shaoqi's *How to Be a Good Communist* was republished in 1962.[40] Later allegations that Liu's espousal of self-cultivation (*xiuyang*) had its roots in traditional Chinese concepts and was Confucian in nature, though politically motivated, were by no means without substance.[41]

History and Philosophy as Political Tools

These changes inevitably invited opposition from those who saw the purity of the socialist cause as more important than economic planning or academic debate. After Mao issued his call 'never to forget class struggle' in the second half of 1962,[42] China began to show signs of increasing politicization and polarization. The Socialist Education Movement was launched in the countryside, followed in 1963 by a nation-wide campaign to 'learn from Lei Feng.' Increasing emphasis was placed on class education. It was felt that the young knew little about the exploitation of the old society, so that students in schools and universities were encouraged to take part in compiling 'four kinds of histories', of village, commune, factories, and families.[43] This brought the emphasis on history back to the recent past. A number of intellectuals came under attack for theories they had put forward in the previous few years. Mao, who in the early sixties had remained to some extent in the background, now came to the fore again. In 1965, he decided to escalate the political struggle.

Some of the opposition to Mao had been expressed in the form of historical allegory, a time-honoured Chinese device. In November 1965, the *Wenhui Daily* in Shanghai published an article criticizing the play *Hai Rui Dismissed from Office*,[44] in which a just official who sided with the peasants in their fight against a local bully was dismissed from office. The play was performed soon after the Lushan conference of 1959 in which Peng Dehuai had disagreed with Mao's policies and been dismissed.[45] The similarities between these two dismissals were too obvious for Mao's liking. Besides being a historian, the author of the play, Wu Han, was also deputy-mayor of Beijing. It was unlikely that he would have written in this way without having some support within the Party. The fact that the article criticizing the play had to be published in Shanghai showed that Mao felt he had little control in Beijing.[46]

At a talk in December 1965, Mao claimed that 'the crux of *Hai Rui Dismissed from Office* was the question of dismissal from office.... Peng Dehuai is Hai Rui.'[47] On 27 December, the *Beijing Daily* published Wu Han's self-criticism of the play, in which he explained his 'error' in academic rather than political terms.[48] This was along the same lines as a report drawn up under the instructions of the Central Committee and issued in February 1966. At Beijing University, several debates were held concerning the question of Wu Han's play. At a meeting on 1 April, Lu Ping, the Party Secretary of the University, chose to view the question again as an academic one. He explained that, under his guidance, some of the teachers and students of the Department of Law had looked through 1,500 books and read 14 million characters of material on the question of Hai Rui, and had come to the conclusion that Hai Rui's orientation and methods had been correct.[49] A week later, the Party committee presided over by Lu Ping issued instructions to criticize Wu Han, but it was too late for them to avoid the coming storm. A group of teachers and students had already put up a wall poster asking why the Cultural Revolution had been suppressed within the university. On 16 May, the Central Committee of the Communist Party issued a second report which, it was later alleged, had been largely written by Mao.[50] For the first time since 1949, the extent of the intra-Party struggle was brought out into the open. The new report argued that the earlier one had covered up the serious nature of the struggle. Among the intellectuals criticized, Wu Han and Jian Bozan, both established historians who had written in favour of traditional Chinese values, were mentioned by name.

Thus, again, a social upheaval that was to develop into near civil war was initiated by a seemingly academic question of historical interpretation. That Wu Han was instrumental in bringing this about is significant in the context of cultural inheritance, since he was one of the main exponents of 'inheriting' traditional morality. This will be further discussed in the next chapter. Wu Han's political disgrace, of course, meant that what he advocated in the historical and philosophical realms would also be dismissed. Conversely, those whose views clashed with his, like Yao Wenyuan and Guan Feng, enjoyed a meteoric rise in their political fortunes.

At the end of July, Mao returned to Beijing from a provincial tour aimed at enlisting support for his policies. On 5 August, the *People's Daily* published a big character poster which he had written, headed 'Bombard the Headquarters', in which he praised the first poster put up at Beijing University.[51] Three days later, the Cultural Revolution was formally adopted as Party policy when a sixteen-point document was issued in the name of the Central

Committee to guide the new movement.[52] On the grounds that students should be able to participate in revolutionary activities, schools and universities were closed down. Red Guards organized long marches which took them all over the country. They launched attacks on 'the four olds'—old culture, old ideology, old customs, and old habits—which were to be replaced by the 'four news'.[53] Mao Zedong Thought was to be the standard against which all thought and actions were to be judged. To achieve this, study groups were organized among the whole population. Needless to say, such a social and political climate meant that any talk of inheriting the cultural heritage was denounced outright. Indeed, for about four years in the second half of the sixties, nothing at all was published on the classical philosophers.

'Philosophy is no mystery',[54] proclaimed the title of a widely distributed pamphlet. Even peasants were encouraged to study and write philosophy. 'Philosophy' meant Marxist philosophy as interpreted by Mao in his *Quotations*.[55] For the more sophisticated, two of Mao's most studied tracts were 'On Practice' and 'On Contradiction'.[56] Mao's writings were supposed to have helped in all kinds of endeavours from weather forecasting to cement-making.[57] Claims of practical problems solved by Mao Zedong Thought were often carried to unbelievable lengths.[58] The limitations placed on the whole concept of philosophy meant that the classical philosophers were simply regarded as irrelevant. To have written positively on them in the manner of the early sixties would have been impossible even to contemplate.

Within the universities and institutes of higher learning, teachers and researchers were frequently victimized as bourgeois intellectuals, while many administrators were removed from their posts. Even for those who were not attacked, the disruptions in the universities together with the social pressure against academic pursuits made research difficult, if not impossible. Also, the Red Guard slogan of destroying the 'four olds' made it difficult to arrive at any balanced evaluation of the past. Consequently, there were no academic works published during the Cultural Revolution proper on the classical philosophers. All the criticisms raised about the influence of tradition were directed at actual politicians of the day.

The officials within the Party who were criticized included not only Liu Shaoqi and Deng Xiaoping but also Zhou Yang and Lu Dingyi, who had both played important roles in the formulation of policies regulating academic life.[59] By mid-1967, Zhou Enlai had also come under attack. Supported by the Cultural Revolution Group, a section of the Red Guards put forward the slogan 'strike down the handful of army leaders who have taken the capitalist road.'[60] While a few generals were imprisoned and some, like He Long, actually died, the escalation of attacks on such powerful groups as the army élite and higher echelons of bureaucracy meant that even Mao's prestige could not contain the increasing opposition to the movement. Consequently, in August Mao was forced to impose limits on the movement.

As a result, Guan Feng, Wang Li, and later Qi Benyu, members of the so-called 'May 16 Detachment', were dismissed from the Cultural Revolution Group, which from this time onwards had its power reduced. This was a turning-point in the Cultural Revolution. In the late fifties and early sixties, Guan Feng had been the most outspoken and prolific critic of the pre-Qin philosophers and the idea of inheriting tradition. He had challenged Feng Youlan on virtually every major point that the latter had raised in his search for a more Marxist interpretation of traditional thought. Although he has disappeared from the scene, his thinking still pervades the philosophical world in China, as is demonstrated by the number of articles denouncing him even in the post-Mao era.[61] Whatever his political role, there is no doubt that Guan Feng is one of the most important thinkers in philosophy since Liberation.

Although they were disgraced, the approach that such writers as Guan Feng and Qi Benyu used to evaluate philosophy and history continued to be influential throughout the Cultural Revolution and its aftermath.[62] Major movements such as the campaigns to criticize Kongzi and the *Water Margin* used virtually the same jargon and methods formulated in the pre-Cultural Revolution writings of these radical thinkers. The Cultural Revolution period, though loud in its denunciations of tradition, therefore said very little that was new in its interpretations of classical philosophy.

The fates of the various participants in the polemics in history and philosophy vividly illustrate the way in which political battles were fought in the academic arena. Older and more established intellectuals such as Feng Youlan, Wu Han, and Jian Bozan, though not allied formally or working under a particular 'school' of thought, nevertheless had a common concern in their approach to Chinese history and philosophy. This is characterized by a more conservative outlook on the Chinese past in the sense that they were not happy to see the Communist era as the only one which was worthwhile and the past ignored or condemned. They were also less prepared to espouse struggle as the norm in society and were more inclined to argue for rationality and compromise.

The younger group of writers such as Guan Feng and Qi Benyu, by contrast, were basically trained in Marxism and saw Chinese history as a continuous struggle for class supremacy. This perspective was also used to view the present, so that they were prepared to 'struggle' against their opponents with increasing passion and monomania. They do form a 'school' in the sense that they follow the Leninist doctrine more dogmatically than their rivals. By the mid-sixties, they also found patronage in Mao, so that their writings were very much a reflection of a definite political faction in the central leadership.

Like the scholar-gentry in imperial China, post-1949 intellectuals are obsessed with finding a 'correct way' to govern the country. What they write therefore impinges directly on politics. Conversely, political leaders do not hesitate to make use of and meddle in their writings. This symbiotic relationship between these two groups of people means that, no matter how ludicrous some of the 'scholarly' tracts may seem to outsiders, it is also true that such tracts often carry momentous political implications.

THE IDEOLOGICAL FRAMEWORK

A prerequisite for even a basic understanding of the historical and philosophical texts written after 1949 is a grasp of the terminology and premises of Marxism, for these governed all areas of academic research at this time. While historians spent much of their time on the issues of periodization and 'historicism' to the neglect of other topics, it was believed that these questions needed to be settled before any conclusive statements could be made about any historical figure, including the classical philosophers. What follows does not pretend to be an interpretive analysis of Marxist historiography.[63] It is merely an outline of some of the major topics that Chinese historians and philosophers have debated in the last thirty years. At first glance, topics such as the periodization of ancient history or debates on 'historicism' may seem remote from the question of cultural inheritance. However, the following pages will show quite clearly the intimate relationship between them.

The Materialistic Conception of History in China

Marx's view of history is characterized by his conception of the materialistic and dialectical nature of social progression. His supporters have claimed that Marx was the first person to have 'discovered the law of development of human history.'[64] Marx criticized all earlier historians, saying that 'while the French and the English at least hold by the political illusion, which is moderately close to reality, the Germans move in the realm of "pure spirit", and make religious illusion the driving force of history.'[65] Marx therefore strongly opposed the study of ideas and attitudes which were divorced from the social conditions in which such ideas originated. In his famous second thesis on Feuerbach, he states, 'the question whether human thinking can pretend to objective truth is not a theoretical but a practical question.' He continues in the fifth thesis, 'Feuerbach, not satisfied with abstract thought, wants empirical observation, but he does not conceive the sensible world as practical, human sense activity.'[66] By 'practical' Marx did not simply mean empirical observation, but the dialectical relationship between mind and matter. This idea is expressed by Mao in his essay 'On Practice', in the dictum 'if you want to know the taste of a pear, you must change the pear by eating it yourself.'[67]

A Marxist evaluation of pre-Qin philosophers therefore required a prior analysis of their social and historical context, and a look at how their ideas were implemented in practice. As a result, virtually every discussion on the pre-Qin thinkers devotes attention to the material conditions in which the philosopher lived and the social effects his ideas produced.

When the iconoclasts of the May Fourth movement attacked Chinese tradition, their task was easier in the sense that the tradition to them was simply 'feudal' (fengjian): Chinese history was as monolithic to them as it was to the newly arrived Westerners. Even those who argued for 'the national essence' took a simplified approach, viewing the 'essence' as distinct and inseparable.

By the time Guo Moruo studied ancient Chinese society with what he understood as Marxist methodology in 1929, however, Chinese history had begun to emerge as a progression of distinct and qualitatively different epochs rather than a never-changing dynastic cycle. In fact, the word 'feudal' was no longer automatically a term of abuse, but could imply progress in the Marxist sense. This change in interpretation is closely linked to the questions of class and periodization in history.

If the nature of material and economic conditions changes dialectically from period to period, how are these changes manifested? For Marx, although ideas in history are contingent on existing conditions, there is one absolute truth about social changes which is summed up in the famous slogan from the *Communist Manifesto*, 'the history of all hitherto existing society is the history of class struggles.'[68] This axiom became the criterion on which all historical research in China was supposed to be based. This was shown most vividly in new editions and reprints of pre-1949 works which covered the whole span of Chinese history: they all carried new prefaces stressing the importance of class struggle in history.

Zhou Gucheng, for example, changed the title of Chapter 1 in his *General History of China* from 'The Era from Nomadic Tribes to Settlements' in the 1939 edition to 'Ancient China: From Man's Struggle with Nature to Sharpened Class Contradictions' in the 1955 edition.[69] Feng Youlan, who had paid even less attention to Marxist analysis before 1949, rewrote the whole of his *History of Chinese Philosophy* using class terminology.

This change in emphasis affected the way in which the pre-Qin philosophers were to be evaluated. Whereas people outside China like Tang Junyi continued to write about ancient Chinese thought without reference to class and class struggle, this was no longer possible for those who remained in China. To talk about the ideas of the pre-Qin philosophers without at least mentioning their class origins and class interests would have been regarded as ignoring the whole methodology of the Marxist conception of history. The major problem was not only that there had been very little work done before 1949 on the class membership of these thinkers, but that the very nature of pre-Qin society itself remained unclear. Most writers relied on traditional accounts based on the work of Sima Qian. While Sima Qian can rightly be regarded as the 'grand historian' of his time,[70] he was, needless to say, not very specific on the class nature of the classical philosophers. Writers had therefore to limit themselves to vague generalizations that Kongzi or the others had belonged to the upper classes. This was not very satisfactory. What the 'upper classes' constituted had to be more specifically pinpointed.

Before any specific class label could be attached to a particular pre-Qin thinker, the exact class composition of the Spring and Autumn and Warring States periods had to be ascertained. A knowledge of the mode of production of that time and hence of the periodization of ancient history is required, as different historical periods were supposed to have produced different classes. The interests of a particular class at the beginning of a certain period according to the Marxist schema might be historically and politically progressive, but the same interest at the end of that particular period could be considered reactionary. For example, if it was argued that Xunzi had stood for the interests of the landlord class, he would be judged as progressive if he had been living towards the end of the slave era, but not if he had been living in the feudal period. According to this scheme, the landlords were the new class that had formed during the decline of the slave-owners and had forged ahead to create a new economic structure, the feudal structure. This was in itself a progressive step. But as soon as they became the new rulers and their power was established, they became the new exploiters and thus reactionary. A knowledge of the mode of production can also rule out certain possibilities. For example, if Xunzi had lived in the feudal period, then he could not have been a member of the slave-owning class, as it was assumed that feudalism brought an end to slave labour as a mode of production.

Even if periodization could be established, the question still remained to which of the particular classes existing in that period a historical figure belonged. Periodization merely narrowed down the possibilities. A distinction could also be made between class membership, namely, the class to which a person belonged, and class stand, that is, the class whose interests he represented. Both are relevant to an overall assessment of a historical figure. The two are normally thought to coincide, but exceptions are possible, particularly at points of transition between one historical period and another. Marx stated in the *Communist Manifesto* that

in times when the class struggle nears the decisive hour, the process of dissolution going on within the ruling class, in fact within the whole range of old society, assumes such a violent glaring character, that a small section of the ruling class cuts itself adrift, and joins the revolutionary class, the class that holds the future in its hands.[71]

Elsewhere, Marx implied that this small, fluid section tended to be intellectuals, people who saw the changes occurring in society and so joined the oppressed but triumphant class. In the modern Chinese context, of course, this supposedly fluid nature of intellectuals has been alluded to many times by political leaders like Mao Zedong and Zhou Enlai in the Party's search for ways of using them. The same descriptions have often been used to praise or blame the pre-Qin philosophers. Whatever the class composition of that time, it was unlikely that any of the philosophers under discussion would have been members of the oppressed class, for all of them were at least literate and had been teachers or leaders of men. Thus, in order to argue that they were good men whose ideas had relevance in modern times, many critics argued that they were the section that had cut itself adrift from the ruling class. What exactly was this ruling class, and whom did its members join? The debates on periodization attempted to give more concrete and specific details about the classes of that time.

The Periodization of Ancient Chinese History

While Marx analysed European society in detail, he did not write about ancient China at all. His intriguing statement that 'in broad outlines Asiatic, ancient, feudal and modern bourgeois modes of production can be designated as progressive epochs in the economic formation of society' only adds confusion to the dilemma whether Chinese society had the same structure as ancient European society or whether it was special and should be treated separately.[72] The fact that by 'Asiatic' Marx probably meant Indian made the task of analysing ancient Chinese history even more difficult for Chinese historians.

For Marx, the question of the historical development of different countries was a theoretical one which needed research and investigation. However, with the establishment of socialism in the Soviet Union, the Soviet leaders needed to argue the universality and applicability of communism for all countries to support their own position. A unilinear scheme of development that proposed that all societies should pass through the stages of primitive communism to slavery to feudalism to capitalism and finally to socialism was a dogma which was imposed throughout the Communist world by the time Stalin exerted control over the international Communist movement.[73]

By the time Guo Moruo wrote his *A Study of Ancient Chinese Society*, in 1929, the Stalinist view was predominant. In the preface to his book, Guo Moruo explained that he had written the book to repudiate those who believed that China had a unique 'national essence' and consequently a different pattern of development from other countries. His book was intended to supplement Engels' *The Origin of the Family, Private Property and the State.*[74] 'His [Engels'] methodology was used as a guide. Apart from using the American Indians and Europe's ancient Greece and Rome as examples because he knew them, he has not mentioned ancient China once.'[75] After examining such ancient texts as the *Book of Changes* and the *Book of History*, Guo Moruo came to the conclusion that the Western Zhou period had been the only period of slavery in Chinese history. Other left-wing historians such as Deng Tuo and Li Maimai quickly joined in the quest to discover the true nature of ancient Chinese society from this Marxist perspective.[76]

The debate on periodization was to continue and intensify over the next forty years. In 1949, Guo Moruo changed his original periodization scheme, this time including the Qin as well as the Zhou dynasties in the slave era,[77] and revised it further in 1950.[78] Of all the periodization schemes formulated after 1949, Guo Moruo's 1950 scheme was the most important. It became more and more the accepted scheme for historians working on the pre-Qin period and, in the early seventies, it was taken as the only correct scheme by all historians writing on pre-Qin thought.

Guo Moruo was prompted in 1950 to revise his earlier scheme after reading a report by the archaeologist, Guo Baojun, on the archaeological finds in the Shang tombs at Anyang, in which over two thousand people had been buried alive as sacrifices for the dead. Guo Baojun had remarked that, after excavating two Zhou tombs, only six such bodies had been found, so that compared to the Shang dynasty, the difference was quite considerable.[79]

The fact that some evidence of human sacrifice had been discovered in the Zhou tombs, however, was enough for Guo Moruo to revise his concept of the dividing line between the slave and feudal periods. Although Guo Baojun had stated that slave burial had declined by the Zhou period, Guo Moruo argued that there was not enough evidence to support this. As the tombs discovered from the Shang dynasty were those of emperors, they could not be directly compared to the Zhou tombs, which were of lesser personages. His new theory held that both the Shang and the Zhou were slave societies, that the end of the slave period should be placed between the Spring and Autumn and Warring States periods.[80]

In this article, Guo Moruo departed from his original methodology in which he used Engels' anthropological concepts to analyse slave society. Instead, he took his definition of a slave society from Stalin: 'Under a slave system, the basic relations in production are such that the slave owners own the means of production and the producers. These producers are the slaves whom the slave-owners could buy, sell and slaughter like domestic animals.'[81]

In stressing how cruelly the slaves were treated, it was possible to argue that anyone who defended the ideas of a slave-owning class defended not just a philosophical stance but barbarity as well. This naturally had repercussions for the assessments of the pre-Qin philosophers.

The periodization of ancient Chinese history was probably the biggest historical issue to be discussed in the fifties, with over two hundred articles published on the subject.[82] Another scheme which was highly influential was proposed by the veteran historian Fan Wenlan, who believed that the feudal period began with the Western Zhou.[83]

Among the supporters of this scheme was the influential historian Jian Bozan, another Beijing University professor who was attacked by the radicals in the early sixties.[84] One of Fan Wenlan's arguments rested on a quotation from the *Mengzi*, where Kongzi was supposed to have remarked, 'Was he not without posterity who first made wooden images to bury the dead?'[85] Fan Wenlan coupled Kongzi's opposition to the use of images as burial objects with his advocacy of adherence to the Zhou rites to infer that the custom of human sacrifice must have disappeared by the Zhou dynasty.

Guo Moruo, in reply, gave a very different interpretation of Kongzi's opposition to the use of burial objects. He believed that, before the slave period, first straw and then wooden objects had been used in funeral rites and that it was only with the beginning of the slave era that they had been replaced by human beings. According to Guo, that was the reason why Kongzi cursed the first person to use images as burial objects.[86]

This exchange underlies the general pro-Confucian bias of historians because both Fan Wenlan and Guo Moruo accepted without question the traditional belief that Kongzi had opposed human burials. The quotation from the *Mengzi* 'Was he not without posterity who first made wooden images to bury the dead?' could easily mean that Kongzi was in favour of human burials and cursed the person who made wooden images as substitutes. Besides, Mengzi in whatever context would want to present Kongzi in the best light. It would seem that, as they lived at approximately the same time, comments made by the classical philosophers about each other would be reliable primary source material. This assumption, however, is untrue, because the classical philosophers sometimes belonged to the same school and sometimes to antagonistic schools so that what they said about each other may be neither reliable nor accurate. This difficulty caused many problems for the historians working on the pre-Qin philosophers.

Another topic considered important in the determination of a correct periodization scheme was the question of the land ownership patterns in ancient China. Again, the documentary evidence used came basically from the *Mengzi*. Mengzi had stated that, before Zhou, fields were divided into nine squares, with eight on the sides and one in the middle, thus forming the shape of the Chinese character *jing* (well). This was called the *jingtian*, or the well-field system of cultivation. Mengzi saw this as the ideal agricultural system, believing that the surrounding eight squares were privately owned, with the middle one publicly owned and the yield from it serving as taxes.[87] While most writers in the past and even after 1949 accepted Mengzi's description of agricultural formations, they disagreed about whether the divided fields had been privately and individually owned.

Guo Moruo discussed this problem in the article in which he propounded his final periodization scheme. First of all, he agreed with Mengzi that this kind of agricultural system had in fact existed in the days before the Spring and Autumn period. He used as evidence characters and symbols from the oracle bones which suggest that, in the Yin dynasty, even before the writing system was fully developed, something in the nature of a well-field system was already in operation.[88] However, Guo argued that, quite contrary to the utopian state that Mengzi had thought it to be, this system was further evidence that the Yin dynasty, unlike the time when Mengzi was living, had been a slave society. He believed that, in fact, the whole well-field, together with labouring slaves, was bestowed by the emperor on the lords to work. The lands belonging to the emperor were not those surrounding the one in the centre, nor were they the central ones, but all the land which was outside the well-field proper.

This land, which belonged to the lords, that is, the slave-owners, could be said therefore to have been private land. According to Guo Moruo, the lords began to make their slaves reclaim more and more of this 'private' land and thus became more and more powerful at the expense of the central rulers. Thus, something resembling feudal states was beginning to emerge by late Zhou times. This fits in well with the periodization scheme that Guo Moruo had proposed. By mistaking a well-field system as humane and one which rulers should strive to achieve again, Mengzi was seen to have been utopian. Whether this utopianism was a genuine wish to return to what he saw as a more equitable agricultural system or a reactionary historical stance is a central problem in assessing the historical role that Mengzi played.

Fan Wenlan did not discuss the well-field system and its relevance to his periodization scheme at any length. He seems to have accepted the traditional view that the land was divided into public and private sectors and that was as far as he went in relation to the division of the land. He did, however, quote some classical poems where the farmer prays for rain to fall on his land after it had fallen on public land as evidence that the peasant really possessed land of his own.[89] Fan also believed that land ownership passed from father to son and that this hereditary system operated from the emperor right down to the ordinary peasant. Fan's perceptions and explanations of the ancient system of land ownership and political structure are closer to traditional ones. His understanding of feudal, for example, is very close to the original Chinese concept of *fengjian*, which literally means to enfief and establish, signifying land or power bestowed upon the lords by the emperor. However, Fan's description did not state whether these lords were slave-owners or not, thus making it difficult for historians to conclude whether the Zhou dynasty was a slave society or feudal. One historian, for example, remarked that the social system of Zhou as described by Fan Wenlan, far from being feudal, also fitted in nicely with descriptions provided by Marx and Soviet historians when they talked about the Asiatic mode of production.[90]

Apart from the classifications proposed by Guo Moruo and Fan Wenlan, there were numerous other minor schemes and proposals put forward, with some historians following Soviet theories that slave society lasted right into the Han dynasty.[91] No scheme, however, was able to produce any evidence capable of settling the argument conclusively. It was only in the early seventies that Guo Moruo's scheme was generally accepted in China, and this was by fiat from above rather than from convincing argument. And as soon as the political support this scheme enjoyed was removed, it was challenged again.[92]

The Uses of History

The question of periodization was the focal point of discussion throughout the fifties, reflecting the official belief that the development of China conformed to a universal Marxist pattern. The amount of time and effort spent on the periodization question in history was a symptom of the increasing rigidity of historical analysis. The Chinese past was forcibly made to fit an unproven pattern of historical progression that Soviet theoreticians had formulated. While all historians felt obliged to write according to the fixed formula, many must have felt that the whole exercise was artificial and tedious. The problem with such a rigid progression of history, too, is that, according to Stalinist periodization, each epoch is supposed to be better and more advanced than the last, not only materially but also in terms of social organization: the Communist epoch and the proletarian class are raised as perfect models to which all other epochs and classes can be compared. This means that a historian was obliged to find shortcomings in any period in Chinese history or any historical figure, and the further back one goes in history, the more defects there logically should be. These implications did not entirely suit historians who have viewed Chinese history as rich and glorious and the ancient philosophers such as Kongzi and Laozi as sages for all time. In the early sixties, when relations with the Soviet Union were already very strained, a more nationalistic history emerged. Wu Han voiced the view that Chinese feudal history should be looked at more sympathetically when he wrote in 1961 that 'I have asked children for comments and they said that with dynasties which were all corrupt, it is difficult for us to love our country though we try to.'[93]

The suggestion that Chinese history should be examined without preconceptions as to the relative merits of different classes was couched in terms of 'historicism' (lishi zhuyi). Briefly, this means that a historical figure should be judged by the social conditions operating at the time this figure was living, and not by criteria which are operating at present. Jian Bozan, the most famous exponent of this theory, stated in 1961 that peasants in the feudal era 'should be treated in the spirit of historicism, and their image should not be created after the model of the modern proletariat.'[94] By implication, intellectuals such as the pre-Qin thinkers who served the ruling classes should not be judged too harshly, for they were only doing what was appropriate for that time. This theory thus softens the kind of class analysis which states that only the modern proletariat was praiseworthy and all the great philosophers of the past were defective, a thesis which many historians abhorred.

In 1963, another historian, Ning Ke, sparked off a minor debate on 'historicism' when he wrote on the dilemma that historians faced in trying to combine historicism with class analysis. He pointed out that while 'historicism' and class analysis should both be employed in historical analysis, overstressing historicism could lead to a restoration of ancient things. He went on to say, however, that if too much emphasis was placed on class analysis, this could lead to an interpretation of history which was too mechanistic and over-simplified.[95]

In this article, Ning Ke pointed to the uneasiness historians felt about condemning outright people from the ruling classes of the past. At this stage, the trend in historical studies to glorify peasant leaders was still relatively new. Most heroes of the past traditionally came from the ruling classes, like the pre-Qin philosophers. By evaluating them in a positive light, there was the real likelihood of a restoration of ancient values and moral systems. However, simply to denounce them as members of the ruling classes would also be unsatisfactory to historians who cherished the past, not only because it would be too mechanistic but because it would mean denouncing much of recorded Chinese history. When these values suddenly had to be changed, tremendous problems were created for historians. Opponents of Ning Ke argued that the problem arose because Ning Ke failed to draw a distinction between 'bourgeois historicism' and 'Marxist historicism'. They held that 'we must uphold the Marxist class viewpoint, conquer the "class viewpoint" of mechanistic materialism, uphold Marxist historicism and oppose bourgeois historicism.'[96] It was not really clear, however, just what the differences were between 'bourgeois historicism' and 'Marxist historicism'.

Nevertheless, the political situation after Mao's call 'never to forget class struggle' in 1962 became increasingly favourable for the proponents of class analysis. Under the weight of criticism, Ning Ke was forced to modify his position. In 1964, he wrote again on this topic, this time stating that 'only by standing on the platform of the proletarian class can there be true and genuine historicism, and also only then can the principle of historicism be applied thoroughly.'[97]

Moreover, the view that an individual could perhaps make compromises in the actual class struggle and the theory that a member of the exploiting class could sometimes take the side of the exploited class were repudiated. This was important in evaluations of the pre-Qin philosophers since it removed the most common argument used to defend them. Despite his willingness to go all the way with his critics, Ning Ke's ideas on 'historicism' were still attacked, together with those that had been put forward by Jian Bozan.[98] By the mid-sixties, a group of younger and less well-known historians such as Qi Benyu were becoming highly radicalized, so that to them class struggle was the only permissible criterion to look at any aspect of history. Thus, the plea by more moderate historians such as Wu Han and Jian Bozan to see the Chinese past more sympathetically was savagely ridiculed.

In 1966, it was alleged that, in talking about Marxist analysis in history, Jian Bozan had not placed enough stress on class struggle because he had also insisted on 'historicism'.[99] The campaign to criticize him was given added support when Mao referred to him as 'going from bad to worse.'[100] The fact that Mao joined in the debate meant that it could no longer remain an academic exercise but that it had become a highly political issue. Mao's intervention effectively put an end to 'historicist' views.

The attacks made on historicism were part of a call for a more rigid class analysis of history and a demand for the use of a proletarian orientation in historical studies. This meant that many of the analyses of pre-Qin philosophers made in the fifties and early sixties were no longer feasible. From a strictly theoretical standpoint, if a proletarian orientation was to be adopted, then the whole of Chinese tradition had to be condemned. Since there was no proletarian class in Chinese history, there could be no justification for arguments about inheriting tradition. This problem was partly resolved by Mao earlier when he regarded the peasantry in China as the revolutionary vanguards.[101] This substitution of the peasantry for the proletariat leads to other theoretical difficulties, but at least it opened up the possibility of salvaging part of the tradition.

Closely connected with the debate on 'historicism' was the

theory that there were in fact good and benevolent officials among members of the ruling classes in the past. This was again put more systematically by Jian Bozan in his 'theory of concessions', in which it was claimed that members of the ruling classes sometimes made concessions to the peasants in Chinese history. Jian Bozan wrote in 1961 that 'after a great peasant war, the feudal ruling class made a concession to the peasants to a certain extent in order to restore feudal order. But it is not the case they made a concession after every peasant war'.[102] At a time when sections of the Chinese leadership were beginning to feel uneasy about the softening of class rhetoric in the Soviet Union, such views of course were not welcome.

Qi Benyu, Lin Jie, and Yan Changgui, who had become members of the powerful group that advocated a cultural revolution, attacked Jian Bozan's theory, accusing him of advocating the theory of concessions as early as 1951.[103] In order to negate Jian, it became necessary to take a black and white approach to history and to insist that the ruling classes had never made any compromises with the peasants. Quoting Lu Xun's 'Madman's Diary' the younger historians insisted that

in reality, there has never been any 'policy of concession' in history. If we open the *Twenty-four Histories*, 'in between the lines, the whole book is covered by the two words "eat men"'. How could there have been a 'policy of concessions' given to the peasants by the ruling classes?[104]

When Lu Xun wrote 'Madman's Diary', he was attacking the whole of Chinese tradition. In quoting Lu Xun in this context, these critics on the eve of the Cultural Revolution were also making clear that Chinese tradition as exemplified in the *Twenty-four Histories* was totally evil and not to be inherited. This tendency to negate traditional culture continued right up to the early seventies.

The 'juxtaposition' of history for political purposes,[105] or the use of history as allegorical comments on contemporary events, is a time-honoured device in China. In the Communist period, the use of history to comment on the present, whether intentional or interpreted thus by others, was also popular and significant. Mao Zedong himself, when commenting on the play *Hai Rui Dismissed from Office*, remarked that 'Peng Dehuai is Hai Rui.'[106] He attacked the play, not so much because it used history for political purposes, but because it was used to criticize himself. As the Cultural Revolution progressed, the use of history as a political tool became even more pronounced. In the anti-Kongzi movement, for example, it was clear to readers in China that at least at the beginning of the movement, Zhou Enlai was under attack.

This use of history as allegory is known in Chinese as *yingshe* (reflective) history: history which casts shadows on contemporary events. In the post-Mao era, this type of history came under intense criticism.[107] Ironically, the use of history for political allegory is in a sense a good example of cultural inheritance: using things past for the present.

The Philosophical Limitations: Materialism versus Idealism

Traditionally, Chinese philosophy has been concerned mainly with political or moral philosophy. Even with the introduction of Buddhism and the subsequent development of neo-Confucianism, the search for an inner goodness in man, whether it be *ren* (benevolence) or *cheng* (sincerity), was a manifestation of the search for a moral being. This is particularly true of the pre-Qin philosophers. Kongzi, Mengzi, Mozi, Xunzi, Han Feizi, and even the Daoists Laozi and Zhuangzi, were chiefly concerned with how to find a sage and moral man for the correct government of society. This is in contrast to early Western philosophy, which was more speculative. Even when Socrates was discoursing on the immortality of the soul, for example, he was interested in whether the soul was material or spiritual, while others like Democritus were searching for the basic elements of matter.

The methodology and aims of traditional Chinese and Western philosophies are thus very different. As Marxism is in the Western tradition of philosophy, the attempt to integrate it with Chinese philosophy was a difficult task which occupied much of the modern Chinese scholars' time. Many Chinese scholars would argue that this was not really a fruitful line of work, indirectly expressing resentment at the fact that it was Chinese philosophical traditions that were placed under a Western microscope and not vice versa. Whatever the misgivings, the turn of historical events in the last fifty years meant that this work had to be done, and with Marxism as the tool, whether the Chinese historian liked it or not.

Like other schools of Western thought, Marxism is concerned with solving metaphysical and ontological problems. At the same time, however, it is supposed to be a programme for political and moral action, for it claims to be not only a philosophy but a force which will eventually liberate the world. Marxists also consider their philosophy to be in contrast to 'all previous materialism',[108] which is said to have been mechanistic and naïve because it did not take the subjective mind into account. Thus, Lenin claimed that

materialism, in full agreement with natural science, takes matter as primary and regards consciousness, thought and sensation as secondary, because in its well-defined form sensation is associated only with the higher forms of matter (organic matter), while 'in the foundation of the structure of matter' one can only surmise the existence of a faculty akin to sensation.[109]

While such philosophical investigation may seem purely academic and harmless, Lenin already referred to philosophers he was opposed to as 'reactionary',[110] a strong term of abuse in Marxist political jargon. Metaphysics is thus not simply philosophy, but a political stance.

In his work on historical materialism, Stalin also submitted that since materialism was scientific and social laws and historical development were knowable through this science, then the proletariat must necessarily follow this materialism;[111] that is, materialism was not only a philosophy, but also a political force. This view became the dogma for studying the history of philosophy after Zhdanov's speech defining the parameters of philosophy came to be generally accepted in both the Soviet Union and China. This speech was delivered in 1947, ostensibly to review a book on the history of Western philosophy by Alexandrov. Zhdanov attacked the book for not stressing the struggle between materialism and idealism as the driving force in philosophy. He defined the history of philosophy as 'the history of the struggle between materialism and idealism.'[112] The fact that the speech was delivered as an attack on a historian of thought by a Party theoretician was also significant as it meant Party thinking was to dictate academic research.

Chinese Party theoreticians closely followed this method of defining and investigating the history of philosophy. Ai Siqi's widely studied textbook on Marxist philosophy, for example, had in a chapter headed 'The Two Opposing Armies in the History of Philosophy' a description of the interaction between idealism and materialism.[113] From being a metaphysical problem, therefore, the relationship between idealism and materialism became a political question, the working class being represented by materialism and the oppressors by idealism. This view reached such extremes that, when Yang Xianzhen, the professor of philosophy at the Central Party School, gave a series of lectures on materialism to cadres, he began his lectures by saying: 'Why should we study materialism? Because if we depart from it, we will commit mistakes. It is dangerous and reactionary to depart from it.'[114]

With such dogmatic conceptualizations of materialism and idealism, it is not surprising that materialism and idealism featured prominently in discussions on the question of cultural inheritance and that idealist and materialist were used as synonyms for bad and good in the evaluations of the pre-Qin philosophers. It was necessary and sufficient to prove that a philosopher was idealist for his ideas to be dismissed. In the same way, if it were possible to prove that a philosopher's ideas were materialist, this was tantamount to an argument that they could still have a place in contemporary society. Such an arbitrary and trite distinction between idealism and materialism often trivializes philosophical investigations, and because of the political import of these labels, many of the debates and interpretations were naturally politically motivated, and this also was an obstacle for objective scholarship.

While attaching importance to the distinction between idealism and materialism, Leninist-Marxism argues that it is not enough in itself to explain the world. Matter continually changes dialectically, and there exists a dialectical relationship between mind and matter, so that 'sensation is indeed the direct connection between consciousness and the external world; it is the transformation of the energy of the external excitation into a state of consciousness.'[115] The argument is that matter gives rise to ideas and that ideas in turn put matter into motion. This will transform matter, which in turn gives rise to new ideas *ad infinitum*.

The way in which dialectics can be interpreted in terms of class struggle is most clearly seen in Mao's depiction of the metaphysical and the dialectical outlooks as 'two opposing world outlooks.'[116] This categorization was particularly important in the study of the Daoists, whose cryptic sayings could be construed as dialectical. This will be examined more closely in the following chapters, but one debate on dialectics should be looked at now because it highlights how this question can become political and how, like the debates on history, it became another factor contributing to the Cultural Revolution.

In May 1964, two students at the Higher Party School wrote an article in the *Guangming Daily* which suggested that 'two combines into one' was the fundamental process in dialectics.[117] The source of this interpretation was traced to their teacher, Yang Xianzhen. Not long after, Yang himself wrote to defend this position, pointing to the Communist and Nationalist alliance during the resistance war against Japan as an example of the law of 'combining two into one'.[118]

Critics were quick to declare that Yang Xianzhen erred in saying that 'combining two into one' was more fundamental than 'one divides into two'. They quoted Mao Zedong that 'the unity of opposites is conditional, temporary and transitory, and hence relative, whereas the struggle of opposites is absolute'[119] to substantiate their attacks.[120] This criticism of Yang coincided with the worsening of relations with the Soviet Union, when any suggestion that two should merge into one was not welcome. Articles began to appear saying that Yang's theory was capitulationist.[121] It was also argued that Yang's ideas were opposed to the view put forward by Mao that class struggle was absolute. Saying that two combines into one was said to be similar to arguing for the extinction of class struggle.[122]

This controversy had consequences for the interpretations of the pre-Qin philosophers. What Yang Xianzhen had argued for was, in its distaste for extremes, similar to the doctrine of the mean (*zhongyong*) advocated by the Confucians. The Daoists Laozi and Zhuangzi had also indicated the integration of opposites in their writings.[123] Thus, the criticism of Yang Xianzhen was an indirect way of banishing the positive evaluations of traditional concepts such as the doctrine of the mean. Yang and his views were disgraced. Both, however, were to be rehabilitated after the Cultural Revolution, and the concept of 'combining two into one' became popular again.[124]

The humiliations suffered by such thinkers as Wu Han, Jian Bozan, and Yang Xianzhen were concrete manifestations of the radicalization of thought on the eve of the Cultural Revolution. This extremism was characterized by stressing non-compromise, struggle, and, most importantly, breaking with the past. Conversely, when these intellectuals were rehabilitated in the post-Mao era, a softer and more sympathetic approach to Chinese tradition became possible again. These people, by their changing fortunes, illustrate in no uncertain terms how heavily assessments of traditional thought are dependent on political expediencies.

Because historical and philosophical investigations were so intimately linked to political aims and policies, it was inevitable that truth would become, in the end, a political stance rather than a position arrived at by true premises and valid arguments. With such an approach, evidence was often sought to substantiate beliefs already held. Philosophical expositions were thus reduced to subjective interpretations. This did not mean that original work was not produced. Some interpretations of the classical philosophers such as Guan Feng's work on Zhuangzi did show some insights which were new, but the acceptance of the idea that every pursuit was to serve political ends meant that even these essays were marred by their deliberate polemical style. If the older scholar cherished any one aspect of tradition, the younger ones felt almost obliged to attack it. This polarized writers even further. The idea that non-compromise was an ideal on the part of the radical writers, too, further exacerbated disagreements between themselves and the more established scholars, so that a 'two-line struggle', if it had not already been in existence, was certainly created by the beginning of the Cultural Revolution.

2 Cultural Inheritance: Definitions, Methods, and Criticisms

THERE is no established Marxist position on the question of the inheritance of tradition. In the *Communist Manifesto* itself, there is the famous statement:

The Communist revolution is the most radical rupture with traditional property relations; no wonder that its development involves the most radical rupture with traditional ideas.[1]

However, the *Manifesto* also states that

when people speak of ideas that revolutionise society, they do but express the fact, that within the old society, the elements of a new one have been created, and that the dissolution of the old ideas keeps even pace with the dissolution of the old conditions of existence.[2]

While Communism aspires and claims to create a new society, it cannot but evolve from those that preceded it. In the case of China, the paradox of having a modern socialist superstructure supported by a 'feudal' economic base is very pronounced. While professing to be socialist, China is nevertheless a society with a long and enduring tradition; and the conditions which sustain the existence of old ideas are very far from being dissolved. Thus, the question of the place of traditional ideas is inevitably a major issue. In a sense, too, this dilemma is not a new one. Late Qing reformers like Liang Qichao,[3] the May Fourth writers,[4] and modern philosophers like Liang Souming all faced the question of how to deal with a world that is being reluctantly transformed.[5] It is a problem faced by all modern Chinese intellectuals, and they deal with it in very different ways.

THE CONFERENCE OF 1957

In 1957, scholars working on intellectual history gathered for the first time in Beijing and held a conference which aimed at finding a definitive answer to the question of Chinese tradition. The debates at this conference and the papers which were published immediately after it are of intrinsic interest. More importantly, an exposition of these debates is absolutely essential for an understanding of the evaluations of the pre-Qin philosophers. For while all modern Chinese historians are aware that tradition has a place in present-day China, this was the first time that a national conference had been held to deal specifically with the question of how to treat the philosophical heritage. The more important papers from this conference and subsequent statements were published as *A Symposium on the Problems of the History of Chinese Philosophy* in the same year. The ideas expressed in this book were to influence philosophical investigations for the next two decades.

Zhdanov and Chinese Philosophy

After 1949, China 'leaned' so heavily towards the Soviet Union that, for some four years,[6] all study of the history of Chinese philosophy practically ceased. In the universities, there were no courses in this area until 1953. What little was written followed closely the line set down by Zhdanov; that is, the history of philosophy is the history of the struggle between idealism and materialism. Feng Youlan, for example, began his article written in 1950 for the Soviet *Encyclopaedia* by declaring that 'the history of Chinese philosophy, like that of European philosophy, is a history of the struggle between materialism and idealism. The history of this struggle is a reflection in the ideological sphere of the class struggle in different periods of Chinese history.'[7] Even with such a simple definition, there was still very little written in the next few years. Perhaps the definition was so simple that it frightened the majority who did not know the terminology. In any case, everybody was busy studying the new ideology.

The lack of research into classical Chinese philosophy was also partly due to the political movements at the beginning of the 1950s, when it was deemed necessary to denounce old customs and morality. Since there were as yet no definitive statements on which of the classical philosophers were materialists and which were idealists, it was impossible even to begin to carry out research without first facing this question. It was a difficult area for scholars, who could not have helped but be aware that they too could be labelled idealists because of their training. As Zheng Xin, the Kantian scholar, confessed at the 1957 conference: 'We were materialists and yet we were also idealists: in public we were materialists, but in our private bookrooms we were idealists; in politics we were materialists, but in academic thought we were idealists.'[8]

If those involved with Western philosophy felt the pressure to view philosophy in terms of idealism and materialism to such an extent, those engaged in Chinese philosophy must have felt it even more. With the spirit of the Hundred Flowers, complaints had begun to emerge at the conference that after Liberation, 'a rich and colourful philosophy had been changed into something which was lacking in content.'[9]

Arguments were presented in 1957 which suggested that Zhdanov's definition was not suited to the study of Chinese philosophy. For example, it was postulated that Western philosophy 'sought knowledge' while Chinese philosophy 'sought action,' so that 'if the two philosophical traditions are not suitably distinguished, and we foist the methods used by Western historians of philosophy to categorize and evaluate Western philosophy onto the history of Chinese philosophy, then of course we will not get a true picture of Chinese philosophy.'[10]

Because the Hundred Flowers movement meant that different ideas and the urge to study Chinese philosophy could be expressed more openly, scholars like Zhang Dainian of Beijing University began to argue that, even in ancient China, there had been a branch of learning which bore similarities to Western philosophy. The rationale given for this claim was not very convincing. What was really at issue was the desire on the part of some historians of thought to construe Chinese classical philosophy in such a way that it would be possible to study it using Marxism. This was, in fact, the line of argument presented by Zhang Dainian.[11] Some people even claimed that, since Marxism had taken root and blossomed in China so quickly, this surely meant that it was compatible with the Chinese cultural tradition.[12]

It is not surprising that even those most averse to Marxist ideas should welcome the assertion that Chinese philosophy could be studied by Marxist methods. While the Hundred Flowers movement ostensibly encouraged diverse opinions, it was understood that Marxist ideology was still to guide all thought. Thus, to assert that it was possible to study Chinese philosophy with it was a prerequisite for any attempt even to start studying classical philosophy at all. However, while some writers like Zhang Dainian were quite happy to say that there was little difference between Western and Chinese philosophies, the fact remained that classical Chinese philosophy was more concerned with ethics than with metaphysics and epistemology. The application of Zhdanov's definition to Chinese philosophy was therefore not an easy one.

Ren Jiyu's expression of dissatisfaction with applying Zhdanov's definition too rigorously was fairly representative of the general feeling. He gave three reasons why he thought this definition was inadequate for a study of Chinese philosophy. First, if only the struggle between idealism and materialism were examined, the philosophers' social and historical outlook would be neglected. This was especially true in the history of Chinese philosophy where the struggle between idealism and materialism had not been so obvious. Secondly, Zhdanov in his 1947 speech had not paid enough attention to the struggle between dialectics and metaphysics. This was important because in Chinese philosophy in particular there were many dialecticians. Thirdly, Zhdanov did not give idealism its proper place in history. He only commented that idealists served the exploiting classes. This was too simple as idealism had played a very important role in the history of philosophy. Ren Jiyu confessed: "In my own work on the history of philosophy in the past, I have onesidedly stressed the struggle between idealism and materialism, and neglected the fact that they interacted with and influenced one another, so that idealism actually enriched materialism."[13]

By 1957, many scholars were quite eager to 'liberate idealism'.[14] He Lin, who had been criticized severely in 1953 and again in 1955 for suggesting that idealism had some good points, took advantage of the relaxed environment to press his case again. At the conference, he pointed out that the struggle between idealism and materialism was different from political and religious struggle. The relationship between idealism and materialism, he said, 'is not one between a revolutionary and counter-revolutionary. It could even be said that sometimes it is a relationship between teacher and student, or between friends.'[15]

This analogy was one which was quoted throughout the fifties and sixties. As an example, He Lin referred to Marx, who claimed to have been Hegel's student when Hegel himself was considered a 'dead dog' in the Western philosophical world.[16] For people like He Lin, whose philosophical training had been Western in orientation, the distinction between political and philosophical investigation of course was a valid one. What he failed to take into account, however, was that in Marxism, as understood by the Party leadership and Party theoreticians like Ai Siqi, politics and philosophy were intricately bound, and to state explicitly that the two were different was after 1949 regarded as heresy.

He Lin was thus once again criticized, albeit this time more gently. Guan Feng explained that, in history, it was possible that materialists and idealists might have been friends on a personal level, sharing political outlooks or not working out their political beliefs in detail. However, this did not mean that there was no struggle between idealism and materialism as such. Guan stated that the struggle between idealism and materialism was one of 'life and death'.[17] Thus, while Guan Feng was prepared to make a distinction between ideological conflicts and human struggles, it was quite clear that even on the basic issue of the definition of the history of philosophy, he had already disagreed with the older scholars. Later on, he was to disagree with philosophers like Feng Youlan on the analysis of the individual pre-Qin philosophers on virtually every point.

Even so, Guan Feng's views were not at this stage radical enough to escape criticism. Deng Chumin challenged Guan Feng's admission that idealists and materialists could have been friends as people. He claimed that many philosophers had been either put in gaol or executed for political reasons whether or not their beliefs were openly stated or consciously held. He gave as examples the Polish astronomer Copernicus, whose theories had been suppressed by the Church, and the Italian philosopher Bruno, who was burnt at the stake in Rome for continuing to propagate Copernicus' theory.[18]

It should be noted that all the cases cited by Deng Chumin of materialists who suffered for their alleged political beliefs were Europeans and that he did not even bother to prove that they had really been materialist or that the reason for their suffering was because of their belief in materialism, and not, say, their religious beliefs. Because Marx, Engels, or Lenin had analysed or at least mentioned most of the major philosophers or philosophical schools before them, the Chinese historian was reduced to looking up, in an almost religious manner, what they had to say about a certain philosopher and to follow suit. This was the major reason why, throughout the debates on Chinese philosophy, European thinkers and not Chinese were cited automatically as models of materialism or idealism.

Because the Zhdanov line says idealism is politically unsound and materialism is politically progressive, those who adhered to this line treated anyone who deviated from it in any way as political enemies. Accusing Guan Feng of having come close to separating philosophy and politics, Deng Chumin claimed that 'all political errors are produced by wrong ideologies. This is an absolute and unconditional truth. To separate philosophy from politics and theory from practice is absolutely not permitted under the basic principles of dialectical materialism.'[19]

Guan Feng was already quite adamant about the unity of philosophy and politics, yet on the whole his writings were relatively careful and well reasoned. But it is quite clear that, in Deng's attack, neither the logic nor the dramatic examples provided by him displayed a calm or very philosophical approach. Such an approach became common in the extreme phases of the Cultural Revolution, but in the fifties, it lacked support. At this stage, few of the people involved in the debates saw each other as enemies carrying out 'life and death struggles'. This came later.

In Search of Chinese Materialism

In the fifties and early sixties, the extreme developments in the Cultural Revolution could not have been foreseen as a possible consequence of the quest for a straightforward Marxist account of Chinese thought. Many people were aware of the numerous difficulties in assessing traditional Chinese thinking with the new Marxist methodology, but they were convinced that these difficulties were surmountable, and they were anxious that this new approach should be given a chance to test itself. In the fifties, in particular, Chinese intellectuals were conscious of the fact that they were attempting to mould a new outlook, a new way of life; and most were optimistic. Zhu Bokun, a student of Feng Youlan, aptly remarked at the 1957 conference, 'if when we talk about the history of philosophy we do not clearly point out which philosopher is idealist and which materialist, then where do we differ from the history of philosophy of past bourgeois classes?'[20] There was the hope that by using the new methods of Marxism to study Chinese philosophy, the good could be separated from the bad, the materialist from the idealist. With this, it would be possible to determine what aspects of Chinese tradition were worth inheriting.

The assumption that there was a continuity of development in materialist thinking was in keeping with Zhdanov's description of the history of philosophy as the development and gradual victory of materialist thought. To talk about the inheritance of traditional philosophies, therefore, it was necessary to study the growth of materialist thought in China. Many articles and books were thus devoted to different aspects of the growth of materialism in China.[21] It was an exercise similar to that undertaken by Hu Shi some thirty years earlier when he wrote *The Development of the Logical Method in Ancient China* to try to show that China also had scientific and logical thinking in its past.[22] The quest for a materialist development in China was not an easy one. The definition of materialism itself already posed a problem. Theoretically, it was possible to argue that someone was materialist or idealist without making political or ethical judgements. In the Chinese version of materialism, however, the definition itself had political and moral dimensions built into it. In the fifties, in particular, thanks to popular but authoritative tracts on philosophy by Party spokesmen such as Ai Siqi and Yang Xianzhen, where idealism was invariably linked with the exploiters and materialism with the exploited, and where 'if you depart from materialism, you fall into the danger of making mistakes and being reactionary,'[23] the class nature of these concepts was firmly fixed. This caused a great deal of confusion to those who were not used to equating philosophy with politics.

One example which was often quoted by writers who were bewildered by this whole issue of linking idealism with exploitation was the ideology of the Taipings. It was often pointed out that the Taipings were members of the oppressed class and yet they were quite clearly idealists in their belief in God.[24] Ren Jiyu pointed to another example in 1957. His analysis of the Daoists Laozi and Zhuangzi at that stage was that they were materialists, but they obviously came from the aristocratic classes, so there was another contradiction there.[25] The problem was even more basic than that. At that time, many people had used Fan Wenlan's periodization scheme, which was closer to the traditional view of Chinese history than that proposed by Guo Moruo. By the late fifties and early sixties, however, more and more historians were adopting Guo Moruo's scheme. This meant that the different classes of different historical periods changed completely depending on the periodization scheme adopted. This difficulty of evaluating historical figures raised by Ren Jiyu is a fundamental one which nobody has answered satisfactorily. As Ren pointed out: 'It is very possible in our analysis of a thinker that when we say he represented such and such a class, in the future, history will prove that such a class did not exist at all.'[26]

The confusion over the meaning of materialism was further compounded by the accepted understanding that, before Marx, there was no genuine and thoroughgoing materialism. It has always been claimed by followers of Marx that, in historical and political thought, Marx was the first person to have recognized that the economic mode of production was the motive force in history. In this respect, therefore, Marx was the first materialist and all philosophers before him were idealists in varying degrees. Thus, when Zhdanov defined the history of philosophy as a struggle between idealism and materialism, this struggle was seen mostly as a metaphysical and epistemological one because, politically, all philosophers before Marx were said to have been idealists anyway. This interpretation was of course not the complete picture, but it was a view many people worked from, and Feng Youlan, in outlining this view, argued that it was inadequate.[27]

These limitations must have been particularly felt in the study of Chinese philosophy, which was after all Feng Youlan's own speciality. Traditionally, Chinese philosophers did not on the whole engage in metaphysical and epistemological debates as much as their Western counterparts. When the writers talked about cultural inheritance in the fifties, they emphasized the inheritance of the historical, political, and moral outlook of traditional philosophers and more or less ignored their metaphysical and epistemological speculations. True, the 'metaphysical materialism' of the ancient Chinese philosophers such as their cosmological and ontological outlooks were often analysed, but such analyses mostly served as preludes to praising or condemning their 'ethical materialism'. The most urgent task in the fifties was seen to be to determine which of the classical philosophers still had a place in present-day society. To say that Marx was the first person to have been truly materialist in his historical and political thinking would mean that few, if any, of the classical Chinese philosophers would have been acceptable as models to emulate in the fifties.

Feng Youlan remarked in his article 'Two Problems Concerning the Study of the History of Chinese Philosophy', which was written a few months before the 1957 conference but which set the tone for it, that while it was true that before Marx philosophers and social scientists did not explain social and historical development in terms of changes in the mode of production, some writers did use factors such as population variations or geographical environments to explain it. These writers could have been depicted as mechanistic or naïve materialists. However, Feng Youlan commented, 'Why should they be regarded as idealists? I have asked many people this, and I have never been able to get a satisfactory answer.'[28] The confusion over the various uses of the terms 'idealism' and 'materialism' was thus employed by Feng Youlan as another step in his overall argument that traditional Chinese thought could be 'inherited'.

To illustrate the complexity of the problem, Feng Youlan referred to Han Feizi and Mozi. According to Feng Youlan, Han Feizi had explained social progress and decay in terms of population changes. While this explanation was not totally adequate, it was still fundamentally different from explaining social changes by using idealist concepts such as 'the Will of Heaven'. The alleged materialism of Han Feizi was taken up by others in 1957 as a theme for debate on the materialism and idealism issue, though Feng Youlan did show that idealism and materialism were not absolute all-embracing terms and that, if it was possible to say that a philosopher was idealist in some respects and materialist in others, one should be able to find elements of materialism throughout Chinese intellectual history. Again, Feng pointed out that while it was generally agreed that Mozi was an idealist because of his religious attitudes he could also be seen as materialist because his social role was progressive.[29] Debates surrounding these inconsistencies in the interpretations of Mozi will be examined more carefully in Chapter 5.

The Theory of 'Abstract Inheritance'

Having established that idealists had some good points, that idealism and materialism could exert mutual influence, and that the Chinese classical philosophers had materialist strands in their thinking, the next step for those who wanted to preserve tradition was to assert that much of classical philosophy was acceptable. The final implication, of course, was that this philosophical heritage should be given a place in Communist society. Some scholars were therefore consciously or unconsciously writing directives for correct behaviour in contemporary society. To establish guidelines on the inheritance of one's tradition was in post-1949 China no longer simply an academic exercise. By claiming a role for themselves in determining actual behaviour, an area for which the Communist Party claimed complete responsibility, academics were inviting reciprocal political interference.

Since as far back as Imperial times, Chinese intellectuals have themselves also been policy-makers.[30] Although Feng Youlan tried to make a distinction between the roles of the ruler (*jun*) and the teacher (*shi*) in Chinese history,[31] Tang Yijie in reply provided many counter-examples to show that, in fact, the two classes tended to merge.[32] Traditional Chinese thought itself provided strong theoretical justifications for philosophers to put their own theories into practice. The most famous epistemological statement made by Kongzi, one quoted often in later debates, is 'Is it not pleasing to practise what one has learnt?'[33] Mao Zedong's *On Practice*, although framed in Marxist terminology, could also be seen as a restatement of this basic principle. It is not surprising, then, that scholars like Feng Youlan tried to show how traditional philosophy could be practised in contemporary society.

A key document in the 1957 debates on inheritance is Feng Youlan's 'On the Question of Inheriting the Chinese Philosophical Heritage.'[34] He claimed that, in his earlier work on Chinese philosophy, he had placed too much stress on the abstract meaning of philosophical propositions and neglected the concrete meaning. This, he said, was of course not correct. However, he added, philosophical investigations in the early fifties had over-emphasized the concrete side of philosophical propositions and neglected the abstract.[35] Most of the examples he quoted to illustrate the difference between 'concrete' and 'abstract' came from classical Chinese philosophy.

The first is from the *Analects*. Feng Youlan explained that the concrete meaning attached to the statement 'Is it not pleasing to practise what one has learnt?' was an exhortation to study the *Book of Poetry*, the *Book of History*, the Zhou rites (*li*) and other ideas which were orthodox in Kongzi's time. In this case, Feng Youlan claimed that the specific content of this statement was meaningless in the new society and should be discouraged, but that the abstract principle of practising what one had learnt could still be utilized.[36] However, some propositions had only concrete meanings. Kongzi said, 'Doesn't it make one feel good to have friends (*peng*) coming from afar?'[37] Some scholars have interpreted the character for friend (*peng*) as phoenix (*feng*). If this were the case, Feng Youlan argued, then the statement would have very little abstract meaning. A further example is again from Kongzi, who said: 'Love the people (*ren*) well and use them (*min*) in a timely way.'[38] Here, Feng Youlan went on, some scholars have interpreted *ren* as meaning only people from the ruling classes. If this had been the case, then the concrete meaning should be criticized, but the abstract meaning of loving people should still be inherited.

Feng Youlan also quoted Mengzi to argue that this method of abstract inheritance had already been employed in the history of Chinese thought, even if unconsciously. Mengzi had professed that 'everybody can become a sage like Yao or Shun.'[39] Feng Youlan remarked that the concrete meaning of this statement when Mengzi made it had no progressive significance, as being a sage in those days simply meant following closely the feudal ethics of that time. However, the idea was taken up by Wang Yangming,[40] who added to it the notion of innate goodness in man (*liangzhi*). The concrete meaning of this innate goodness, however, was still feudal ethics. But the abstract meaning of this proposition implied that, since everybody had that sageness in him, then all men were in essence equal. Feng Youlan concluded: 'Historical fact showed this to have been the case. The Wang Yangming school was later able to develop into a left-wing school such as that of the Li Zhi type ... Later on Huang Zongxi,[41] who had a very democratic spirit, also inherited from Wang Yangming.'[42] In the same vein, Feng Youlan claimed that the traditional concept of self-cultivation (*xiuyang*) was incorporated by Liu Shaoqi in his book *How To Be a Good Communist*, where the central theme was self-cultivation.[43]

In another illustration that was to be used again and again in later debates, Feng Youlan also quoted Marx as an example. He claimed that his method of abstract inheritance was really not particularly special or new because Marx, Engels, and Lenin had all agreed that Hegel had a 'reasonable inner core' from which they had inherited. When Marx talked about 'putting Hegel on his head', it was quite obvious that Marx believed that there were abstract concepts and methods in Hegel which could be inherited.[44] This argument was so attractive that, even after Feng Youlan had been criticized and had himself renounced the abstract inheritance method, many people still argued that, if Marx and

Engels could make use of an idealist like Hegel, then the classical Chinese philosophers, idealist or not, could still be studied and made use of.

As a final example to show that there are some concepts which serve all classes in philosophical thought, Feng Youlan quoted from the *Zhuangzi*. Zhuangzi, in the chapter 'Thieves', was supposed to have made the comment that 'thieves have their own ethics (*dao*).'[45] Zhuangzi was here ostensibly quoting from Bandit Zhi who, though a wrongdoer by Confucian standards, none the less had his own code of behaviour. Zhuangzi's point was that ethical principles (*renyidaode*) were like weapons: they could be used by anybody, and whoever commanded them would be served by them. In other words, Feng Youlan's final point was that ethics does not have a class nature. It was to be a theme that he would take up again and again later when he analysed each of the pre-Qin philosophers individually.

Debates Surrounding 'Abstract Inheritance'

Feng's article 'On the Question of Inheriting the Chinese Philosophical Heritage' immediately aroused tremendous interest, both sympathetic and critical. Many writers at the 1957 conference and afterwards accused him of rehashing the methodology and sentiments outlined in his 1939 work, *New Rational Philosophy*.[46] Feng's attempt in this work to abstract and 'inherit' the good points of past philosophers, especially neo-Confucians, was severely criticized by people like the Fudan professor Cai Shangsi in the early fifties.[47] In support of these critics, Ai Siqi stated at the conference that it was necessary to follow Mao's directive on inheritance in 'On New Democracy' and not some principle of abstraction.[48] For example, in the case of 'Is it not pleasing to practise what one has learnt?', Ai Siqi believed that the reason why this proposition could still be applicable was 'not because it had an abstract meaning, but because it had ingredients of materialist epistemology.'[49] Thus, the verdict from this authority was still that materialist ideas alone could be absorbed in the new society.

Another prominent Party theoretician, Hu Sheng, similarly claimed that materialists should only inherit from materialists. He did add, however, that in some instances materialists could inherit the good points of idealism, by utilizing the written sources of idealists provided that they were corrected, transformed, and developed, so as to be in conformity with objective laws.[50]

These criticisms reveal the extent to which, in the more liberal period of the Hundred Flowers, theoreticians who were mainly responsible for providing the general guidelines for studying philosophy continued to follow the Zhdanov definition of the history of philosophy. For both Ai Siqi and Hu Sheng, idealism and materialism had by definition all the evaluative and emotive connotations that made them such politically charged terms. They could not admit to the division of philosophy into independent disciplines. If a concept were idealist, it necessarily served the oppressors politically and morally. These critics were accurate in their perceptions, since, as became increasingly apparent, Feng Youlan, and others like him, were chiefly concerned with the inheritance of traditional ethics and morality. The inheritance debate became progressively centred on ethics so that, by the early sixties, it was the major issue under discussion.

At this stage, however, Feng Youlan, in his reply to Hu Sheng, continued to talk about the general topic of cultural inheritance. He could hardly disagree with Hu, who had after all only insisted that he wanted to follow Mao Zedong. Feng Youlan, in turn, pointed out that, while he agreed that traditional thought must be analysed, criticized, and transformed before it could be used for socialist construction, the question remained how this was to be done. He claimed that his essay was concerned with the 'how' part of inheritance, and not with 'what' one should inherit. Feng went further, saying that if Hu Sheng (and others, such as Yang Zhengdian, who accused Feng Youlan of devising a method which would just lead back to idealism)[51] was afraid of the term 'abstract' because it sounded too much like idealism, then he would be quite happy and ready to substitute other terms for 'abstract' and 'concrete': general and specific, following the usage of Engels in *Feuerbach and the End of Classical German Philosophy*.[52]

Feng Youlan was thus, at this stage, quite prepared to change the terminology to save the method. Whatever terminology he substituted for the original one, however, the method remained vulnerable to criticism. Indeed, whatever its objective, it was doubtful if such a simple criterion could be proposed for sifting such a long and durable tradition as that of China. Not only was

Feng Youlan attacked by Party theoreticians, but his colleagues in Chinese philosophy also expressed reservations. Zhang Dainian said of this method that it 'was close to a metaphysical outlook.'[53] Zhang himself did not offer an alternative method for cultural inheritance except to repeat the often quoted and rather vague dictum that 'we should inherit the scientific and democratic thinking of past philosophies.'[54] In another article in 1957, however, he did make the point that, in the realm of morality, different periods in history have some common elements. To argue this point, Zhang Dainian was able to rely on both traditional and Marxist conceptions of primitive society as classless. Thus, the morality of primitive society was also classless and belonged to the labouring people. Zhang believed that this was the morality which was passed from generation to generation.[55] While this essay is not detailed or carefully argued like Feng Youlan's, its tone is definitely conservative in its appeal to preserve parts of tradition and it could be seen as supporting Feng's method. It was also the first article which argued that traditional morality could be inherited and not just philosophical concepts.

Another Beijing University professor, Tang Yijie, wrote in support of Zhang Dainian's suggestion that the morality of the labouring people should be inherited. In reference to Feng Youlan, however, Tang observed: 'Our duty is not to find a morality with a "general meaning" which serves all classes. We should inherit the morality of the labouring people.'[56] Again, although Tang Yijie criticized Feng's method as being inadequate, he did not attempt to devise a more appropriate method of his own.

This lack of concrete guidance on the 'how' part of cultural inheritance was the major problem in this whole question of inheritance. It was quite clear that the method proposed by Feng Youlan would arouse opposition from many people, if for no other reason than the fact that it was Feng who had advocated it. But no other alternatives were suggested. The whole idea that rules could be worked out for inheriting a cultural tradition was an artificially imposed one anyway. Perhaps there never could be any one correct method. It is a truism that cultural and social events progress in a causal manner; that is, events follow one another. But it is questionable whether this causal progression can be externally imposed by formula.

If China had not come under Communist rule, where academic

and cultural matters like all other aspects of social life were to be controlled by political policies, traditional thinking might have been allowed to dissolve naturally with the advent of modernization. But the tight ideological control exercised by the central government after 1949 and the Communist rhetoric of building a totally new society provoked some intellectuals into defending this tradition, albeit using a Marxist terminology. Most were willing to compromise, making vague references to the fact that since 'dialectical materialism' had taken root in China so easily, this must mean that elements of the Chinese tradition were compatible with Marxism, and that the two should be integrated. Mao Zedong's works were often quoted as examples of a successful integration of Chinese tradition and Marxist thought.[57] But these were only indefinite generalizations and did not specify the 'what' or 'how' aspects of cultural inheritance.

Apart from the method proposed by Feng Youlan, the whole debate seemed to go round in circles: while numerous generalizations were made, nothing very concrete was resolved. Guan Feng, who subsequently formulated concrete ways of approaching this problem, through his observations regarding the pre-Qin thinkers, made a very apt analogy at the 1957 conference. Philosophical development is like the development of a man from childhood to adulthood. Looking back on one's own intellectual development, one can see both immaturity and achievement. To use any one single criterion to measure that past, however, would make an overall appreciation of it impossible, and it is not certain what such a criterion would achieve in terms of that total life. Guan Feng proposed then to go beyond the confines of trying to find 'good things' in Chinese tradition.[58] This was good advice, but it left the problem unresolved: was the Communist revolution part of that natural growth of China, or was it a 'complete rupture with tradition?'

In these debates of 1956 and 1957, Xiao Jiefu, from Wuhan University, was the only writer to quote from the *Communist Manifesto* that the Communist revolution 'involves the most radical rupture with traditional ideas.'[59] In the context of the Hundred Flowers, when tradition was undergoing a limited revival, Xiao Jiefu's was not a very loud or important voice, nor was it at that time the voice of the majority. By the time of the Cultural Revolution, however, this kind of call was the only one heard.

FROM THE ANTI-RIGHTIST CAMPAIGN TO THE CULTURAL REVOLUTION

Guan Feng's Criticisms of Cultural Inheritance

The 1956–7 debates on the proper direction for philosophical investigations in a socialist country never reached a definite conclusion. The spirit and relative freedom of the Hundred Flowers quickly gave way to the more rigid political atmosphere of the anti-rightist campaign, the rectification movement, and the Great Leap Forward. By late 1957 and early 1958, the only voices heard were those from the Left. In 1958, the philosophical community concentrated its efforts on the denunciation of Feng Youlan's 'abstract inheritance'. This was a time of 'more present, less past (*hou jin bo gu*)', so Feng Youlan's attempts at finding a way to inherit the classical past were certainly not appreciated. In emphasizing the present, the Yan'an model devised by Mao Zedong was emulated.[60]

In philosophy, Guan Feng denounced the attempts to 'soften' research and to revive traditional thought in the first issue of *Philosophical Research* of 1958.[61] In the same year, he wrote a series of articles vehemently attacking the 'revisionist philosophy' of the previous two years. These essays were collected together and published in book form in the same year,[62] an indication of their importance in the eyes of the leadership. As his article in *Philosophical Research* set the tone for research both in the Great Leap Forward and more significantly in the Cultural Revolution, it deserves detailed consideration.

Guan Feng labelled the 1957 conference revisionist because, according to him, it 'revised' the basic principles of philosophy as defined by Marxism (which for him meant Zhdanov's views) by obscuring the two-line struggle between idealism and materialism. The conference had also 'revised' the Marxist principle that 'before the appearance of Marxism, there was no materialist outlook' by trying to show that some of the classical philosophers had been materialists. Furthermore, it 'revised' the Marxist principle that philosophy was class-based by asserting that some philosophical propositions transcended class.[63]

Guan Feng first attacked the proposals put forward by He Lin and Chen Xiuzhai.[64] In a fashion which was typical of this kind of critique, he began by quoting Engels, who had mentioned that philosophy was divided into the two great camps of materialism and idealism. If this principle were to be taken as an absolute truth, then it was relatively easy to refute He Lin, who had tried to find 'unity' between the two. Guan Feng alleged that, by doing this, He Lin had confused the issue and obscured the demarcation line between idealism and materialism. He also claimed that He Lin had tried to oppose the Zhdanov formula 'materialism equals correctness and idealism equals error' by saying that it was metaphysical.[65] According to Guan, materialism and idealism did not share any common elements whatsoever. To He Lin's claim that there were aspects of similarity between the two, he replied, 'Can materialism and idealism have similar aspects? Then I would like to ask: are these common elements materialist or idealist?'[66] Such rhetorical certainty of the mutual exclusiveness of and antagonism between idealism and materialism meant that there was little possibility of compromise under this kind of framework. There was little attempt at appraising He Lin's argument from He's perspective. The premises Guan was working from were completely different, and his criterion for rejecting an argument here was not to look at the internal logic of his opponents but to reject the premises altogether.

Guan Feng then proceeded to attack the two central essays written by Feng Youlan during the debates of 1956–7. In the first essay, 'Two Problems Concerning the Study of the History of Chinese Philosophy,' the stated purpose was to discuss the area in which the struggle between idealism and materialism had developed. Again, Guan Feng was more interested in Feng Youlan's premises than the soundness of his arguments. Guan Feng was of the opinion that, in fact, the real motive of the essay had been to discover whether there had been a materialist outlook before the advent of Marxism. He stressed that, while Feng Youlan was correct in saying that some ancient philosophers had not used such concepts as 'god' or 'Will of Heaven' to explain changes in society or the causes of the universe, yet they almost always tried to find the causes of social development outside society itself, 'that is, they tried to explain social transformations by looking for causes in Nature. This must necessarily result in fatalism.'[67] In regard to Han Feizi, who had made laws (*fa*) the deciding factor of social change, Guan Feng concluded that, if he seemed materialist in explaining individual problems of history, these were exceptions in a system which was largely idealist.

After Guan Feng was disgraced, in particular during the anti-Kongzi movement of the early seventies, Han Feizi was raised to the status of being a true materialist. By then, the Legalists were regarded as being beyond reproach and were effectively used to glorify a particular stream of traditional Chinese thought. But Guan Feng was not so sentimental about any facet of Chinese philosophy. He firmly adhered to the belief that Marxism was the sole philosophy which expressed truth as revealed in historical materialism. He insisted, too, that there could be no compromise between Feng Youlan's position and the maxim that 'there was no historical materialism before the appearance of Marxism.'[68] The absoluteness of his assertion meant that there was no possibility of interpreting classical Chinese philosophy in a favourable light. To find materialism in Chinese thought, one would have to look to the current era, that is, at the thought of Mao Zedong.

Guan Feng's final assault on the conference held at Beijing University was on the inheritance method proposed by Feng Youlan. Guan claimed that the 'abstract inheritance' method devised by Feng Youlan amounted to yet another 'revision' of the class nature of philosophy espoused by Marxism. Guan denied that there were any philosophical concepts which served all classes and could thus be inherited in an abstract manner. He quoted Feng Youlan's own example of Zhuangzi's descriptions of Bandit Zhi's 'ethical code' (*dao*). Guan Feng said that *dao* was a distinct entity. There was the *dao* of the sages, the *dao* of robbers, the *dao* of the bourgeois and proletarian classes, and so on: 'That is to say, in class society, *dao* has a class nature, and there is no such thing as a *dao* which is abstract and beyond class.'[69]

As for the 'discrepancies' that some people had pointed to—that some progressive classes of people such as the Taipings had been idealist in their thinking while others who belonged to reactionary classes such as Laozi and Zhuangzi had been materialist in theirs—Guan Feng's answer was that these might not have been discrepancies at all. What was needed perhaps was further research to show their conformity to Marxist logic. He said further that many people had placed Zhuangzi in the materialist camp but had not given sufficiently convincing evidence and that he himself did not regard the case as proven.[70]

At the end of this article, Guan Feng adopted the role of an authoritative Party spokesman. He warned:

It is one thing for a researcher in philosophy to deviate unconsciously from the basic principles of Marxism; but revisionism in the methodology of the history of philosophy is another. The latter is a thousand times more serious than the former—if not more.[71]

Thus, it was already evident that the first tentative and timid attempts by some older historians of thought to use what they understood of Marxism to portray sympathetically traditional Chinese philosophy was anathema to those who held a strong belief in orthodox Marxist ideology.

Guan's extremism is clearly shown in his statement that

in ancient philosophy, there was not and could not have been anything good and ready-made which could be taken over and used now and which is not already found in Marxist philosophy (or something similar to this philosophy). This is not only true of the history of idealism, but also of materialism and dialectics before Marx. Marxist philosophy is the only scientific philosophy.[72]

The belief that Marxism contained all the good points of past philosophies and was self-sufficient made it pointless even to raise the topic of cultural inheritance.

As well as the criticisms raised by Guan Feng above, another major objection to the abstract inheritance method was that it was nothing more than a repetition of Feng Youlan's 'new rational philosophy' (*xinlixue*). This objection was voiced when the method was first proposed, but no systematic study or detailed analysis of it was then made. Wu Chuanqi, another left-wing critic who first coined the phrase 'the method of abstract inheritance' (*chouxiang jicheng fa*) to describe Feng Youlan's methodology, alleged in early 1958 that this method was not simply a 'continuation' of the 'new rationality' but a 'copy' of it.[73] He quoted from Feng Youlan's *New Rational Philosophy*, which made a distinction between the 'real sphere' (*zhenji*) and the 'existential sphere' (*shiji*): 'The real sphere is everything that has being, and it could also be said to be the essence of things; the existential sphere refers to things which actually exist, and it could also be said to be the natural manifestation of things.'[74] To Wu Chuanqi, 'the so-called concept of "general meaning" is no more than the "real sphere" of *New Rational Philosophy*.'[75]

The criticisms directed against Feng Youlan in 1958 were on the whole based on these points raised by Guan Feng and Wu Chuanqi. With politics turning more and more to the extreme left, the criticisms intensified into something of a minor campaign. Feng Youlan's colleagues and students in the philosophy department at Beijing University held meetings and discussion groups to criticize him.[76] Many wrote articles criticizing him for his inheritance method, following Guan Feng's lead in calling it 'a major revision of Marxism–Leninism.'[77] Although these criticisms did not go beyond the points raised by Guan Feng and Wu Chuanqi, they did become more and more rigidly political in their denunciations and less and less academic. Some of his students accused him, as a professor of the philosophy department, 'of leading the department away from a place which trains Marxists who could be red and expert into a place which could only train bourgeois philosophy workers who are divorced from production and proletarian politics.'[78]

'Abstract Inheritance' Re-emerges

By the second half of 1958, Feng Youlan had himself made numerous self-criticisms. These self-criticisms, however, were composed in such a way that they were basically re-statements of what others had said about him. Feng followed his critics so faithfully and was so intent on agreeing with all the scorn that they had poured on him that it almost seemed as if he were ridiculing his critics by parodying them. As well as agreeing that his abstract inheritance method was based on his *New Rational Philosophy*, for example, he went further and claimed that his new method was more deceitful than his *New Rational Philosophy*.[79]

In early 1959, when the political climate became more relaxed again, Feng Youlan had another rapid change of mind, suggesting that the 1958 self-criticisms were the result of political expediency rather than a genuine change of heart. In relating the circumstances leading to the appearance of his abstract inheritance method in 1956, Feng described his desire to express his true feelings whenever the political situation permitted:

All latent and hidden things lie in wait for the right opportunity for them to come out into the open. After the 'Hundred Schools Contend' policy was announced in 1956, all latent and hidden things felt that 'spring was in the air' and were ready to begin wriggling. My own thinking then also came out into the open, and became 'one of the Hundred Schools'.[80]

By likening his own thinking to that of a subterranean worm

or insect, Feng Youlan was presenting a rather poetic image of a pathetic old scholar working in a changed society. Alternatively, it could be seen as a damning statement of an authoritarian society that drove intellectual thought underground. The quotation comes from a review of his work over the forty years prior to 1959.[81] This review is a remarkable document if for no other reason than that it is an autobiographical sketch of an active participant in the most momentous changes in Chinese thought from the May Fourth movement to the first ten years after Liberation. Because Feng Youlan had just been the butt of criticism, the outline was phrased in the form of an explicit denunciation of his past 'idealist philosophy' as well as an intellectual autobiography. Yet, by stating his own thoughts in his own words in the course of narrating his past thinking, it in fact amounts to a self-justification. Meanwhile, the radical leftist thinking of the Great Leap Forward was so short-lived that, by the time Feng Youlan added a postscript to his memoirs in 1959, he was confident enough again to go on the offensive, albeit in an oblique manner. The postscript was headed 'Queries and Seeking Advice'.[82] Although 'seeking advice' (*qing-jiao*) sounded polite enough, there was little doubt that the tone connoted a challenge, especially as it was addressed by a famous and respected professor to his younger colleagues. After quoting from Lenin, who had said that idealism overstated and over-developed certain peculiarities of certain aspects of knowledge, Feng Youlan went on to say that

the belief that an idealist philosophy is a completely subjective fabrication of an idealist philosopher and has no basis whatsoever in the objective world is not entirely correct. The origins of philosophical epistemology are of secondary importance compared to the origins of class, but it has its own independent nature, and we cannot neglect it completely. It is here that I cannot fully comprehend the criticisms that some comrades have made about the *New Rational Philosophy*. The class origin of the 'spheres' of the *New Treatise on the Nature of Man (Xin yuanren)* was to serve the reactionary Nationalist clique of that time.[83] I have already mentioned this above, but as to its epistemological origins, I think it has grasped some special characteristics of life. I think that these special characteristics have become increasingly prominent after Liberation.[84]

What he meant by this was that, after Liberation, 'everybody is a proletarian, and everybody serves the proletarian class ... using the terminology of the *New Treatise on the Nature of Man*, the sphere that everybody has now reached is a moral sphere.'[85]

And so, although Feng Youlan theoretically agreed that morality served class interests, he 'queried' the interpretation that the only function of philosophy was to serve class interests. What he implied, of course, was that the debates on philosophical inheritance in 1957 had some value and that, since there were no more classes after Liberation, the class-transcending parts of morality of the past could be inherited. The claim that after Liberation everybody had become members of the working class was an echo of a shift in policy in the Soviet Union. After the death of Stalin, the idea of class struggle in a socialist society was played down considerably. The ideological break with the Soviet Union was already at this stage imminent, and Feng Youlan's statements were soon subject to renewed criticism. Although this essay, together with one which he wrote criticizing his *New Rational Philosophy*,[86] ostensibly dealt with his own past theories both before and after 1949, they were in reality a continuation of the inheritance debate. By going along with his critics in denouncing his *New Rational Philosophy* and *New Treatise on the Nature of Man*, what Feng Youlan did effectively was to revive interest in his former philosophical systems. Also, it did not take much discernment to see that Feng Youlan was really defending his thinking, as he outlined his ideas in each article very carefully before criticizing them; and the attacks he made on himself were such faithful repetitions of what others said about him that it was hard to believe he took them seriously. Furthermore, the only times that he differed from his critics were when he ventured to disagree in the form of queries and seeking advice. Not surprisingly, many of his critics were not satisfied with his self-criticisms, least of all Guan Feng.

In his 'exposé' of the basis of Feng Youlan's thought, Guan Feng claimed in 1959 that Feng Youlan had inherited the worst of idealist thinking in China's philosophical heritage, namely, the sophistry of Gongsun Long and the defeatism of Zhuangzi.[87] Guan Feng concentrated on Zhuangzi, saying that he represented the despair of the class to which he belonged, the slave-owning aristocracy, who were rapidly dying out in Zhuangzi's time. In the same way, Feng Youlan's *New Rational Philosophy* represented the thinking of the comprador class in China, which was also quickly disappearing from the historical stage. Feng Youlan's thinking was put in such a bad light that it was said to have been worse than that of Zhuangzi.

Guan Feng's attack of Feng Youlan as a disciple of Zhuangzi led to a series of articles in philosophical circles on the thinking of Zhuangzi. The discussions on Zhuangzi lasted throughout the whole of 1960 and into early 1961 and were a direct outcome of the dispute on cultural inheritance. By late 1961, discussions on Zhuangzi had in effect petered out, but the question of inheritance was still not resolved.

In September 1961, Feng Youlan published an article in *Philosophical Research* on the meaning of the Confucian concept of *ren*.[88] In this article, Feng Youlan again raised the topic of inheritance, this time substituting another term for his idea of 'abstract inheritance'. He quoted directly from Marx and Engels to justify his stand:

For each new class which puts itself in the place of one ruling class before it is compelled, merely in order to carry through its aim, to represent its interest as the common interest of all the members of society, that is, expressed in ideal form: it has to give its ideas the form of universality, and represent them as the only rational, universally valid ones. The class making a revolution appears from the very start, if only because it is opposed to a class, not as a class but as the representative of the whole society; it appears as the whole mass of society confronting the one ruling class.[89]

Feng Youlan used this quotation to argue that the concept of *ren* was universally valid and had not simply been put forward by the newly arisen feudal class to deceive the people.[90] This concept was obviously very similar to the 'abstract ideas' which he had put forward during the Hundred Flowers period, except that now he expressed his views by quoting from the Marxist classics.

Apart from this article, Feng Youlan began to incorporate these ideas in the first volume of his *New History of Chinese Philosophy*, published in 1962. Here, he used the 'form of universality' to explain *ren* and other classical philosophical concepts, thus creating the impression that many ideas were not created for a particular class but for the whole of society.[91] Because the book was a general textbook rather than an article in an academic journal, its influence was more widespread, as it was studied by the general reader as well as those involved in philosophical research.

The Rift Widens: 1962–6

In 1962, the year that Feng Youlan's *New History of Chinese Philosophy* appeared, Mao Zedong had also announced his call to the people that they should 'never forget class struggle'. Although many people at this stage ignored the call, some did not. Guan Feng and Lin Yushi in early 1963 published a paper they had given at the October 1962 conference on Kongzi in Shandong. In this article, they criticized those who had neglected class analysis in their discussions on Kongzi.[92] After the appearance of this article, an intensified attack was launched on Feng Youlan's new method of the 'form of universality'. Lin Jie, another left-wing critic who later rose to prominence in the Party machine, claimed that Feng Youlan had deliberately misinterpreted the *German Ideology*, which had in fact 'stressed that the form of universality was false and not genuine.'[93] Other left-wing critics also warned that the form of universality as outlined in the *German Ideology* was false the moment it was conceived and that anyone who quoted from the Marxist classics should do so carefully.[94] These criticisms were not without substance. If Feng had wanted to use Marxist thinking to promote his own ideas, he had not done so very convincingly, for the passage he quoted was out of context, as Fang Keli was quick to point out. Fang provided the passage from the *German Ideology* immediately before the one Feng Youlan quoted:

If now in considering the course of history we detach the ideas of the ruling class from the ruling class itself and attribute to them an independent existence ... if we thus ignore the individuals and world conditions which are the sources of the ideas, we can say, for instance, that during the time that the aristocracy was dominant, the concepts honour, loyalty, etc., were dominant, during the dominance of the bourgeoisie the concepts freedom, equality, etc. The ruling class on the whole imagines this to be so.[95]

It was thus clear that Feng Youlan had deliberately or unconsciously distorted Marxist methodology—no wonder, then, that critics accused Feng Youlan of 'hypothesizing the existence of the non-existent' when he tried to assert the existence of *ren* as a class-transcending concept.[96]

However, it is one thing to say that abstract ideas do not and never did exist as material substances but, in attacking Feng Youlan's attempt to revive traditional ideas in socialist China, some critics went to the other extreme and claimed that such ideas as equality and freedom did not exist even as ideas in history and that they were merely illusions.[97] Marx never denied the reality of ideology in history as a real social force, and later Marxists like

Lenin and Mao relied on ideology in transforming the material world in their actual practice. It was one thing to say that ideas had no existential content, but it was another to say that as such they were mere illusions to be banished from historical studies or the present world. By exaggerating their claims in their attempts to prove Feng Youlan wrong, the critics were 'shooting arrows where there are no targets,' widening the gulf between the moderates and themselves.

At the same time that Feng Youlan was trying to revive respectability for the concept of *ren*, an even more heretical and daring attempt to revive this notion was taking place in the south. In early 1962, Liu Jie, an elderly professor at Zhongshan University, published an article entitled 'The Problem of the "Unity between Heaven and Man" in the History of Chinese Thought.'[98] The article began,

Of the works that treat the question of Chinese thought according to Marxism-Leninism, there is already the great work *A General History of Chinese Thought*,[99] which can act as a model for us. It has gathered a whole new collection of sources and provides an excellent basis for a new path in the study of the history of Chinese philosophy. It has made a great contribution and its line is correct. My article, however, is an attempt to look at the question of the history of Chinese thought from another angle. This is the theory of 'the unity between Heaven and Man' (*tian ren he yi*).[100]

Liu made no pretence that his theory was Marxist and left out class analysis altogether. By the 'unity between Heaven and Man', Liu Jie referred to the theory that the aim in traditional Chinese thought, be it Confucian or Daoist, was to find a way to harmonize the activities of man and nature; that is, the classical philosophers' main concern was to discover a method of making man content to obey the natural laws of heaven (nature). This theory was not an original one, but it was in direct opposition to the current tendency to classify each philosopher as materialist or idealist depending on which class he served, and where struggle rather than obedience was stressed.

A few months later, Liu Jie wrote another article which was even more provocative, entitled 'Kongzi's *ren* Only Theory.'[101] The title itself was a challenge to the prevailing attitudes on class analysis. In saying that the theory espoused by Kongzi was based solely on *ren* (*weiren*), Liu Jie ignored completely and deliberately the criteria of idealism (*weixin*) and materialism (*weiwu*) as the only important 'isms' that a philosopher could espouse. He treated *ren* as a combination of all the traditionally positive qualities such as *li* (rites) and *zhong* (loyalty). While acknowledging that Kongzi's thinking originated in the feudal period, Liu Jie nevertheless asked, 'What harm is there in using it in modern times?'[102] Thus, Liu expressed even more strongly than Feng Youlan the view that some traditional values, though rooted in feudal times, were nevertheless above class and could still be worthwhile today. This was something his opponents were quick to point out and to criticize.[103]

When Marx observed that 'the philosophers have only interpreted the world, in various ways; the point, however, is to change it,'[104] he was referring mainly to Western philosophers. In China, however, especially in pre-Qin times, philosophers had not been so speculative, and many were in fact already politicians who had tried to put their thinking into practice. This was true to some extent also in modern times. Those who took part in these debates would have been fully aware of the implications of their declarations. Thus, the proposal for a class-transcending concept derived from classical times was no mere academic exercise, given all the political backlash that the academic debates of the Hundred Flowers had caused only a few years earlier. By the same token, the critics who poured so much scorn on it were not doing it purely out of academic interest either. Indeed, it is difficult to dignify much of the discussion on both sides as scholarly. One was an excuse to sustain the traditional heritage, while the other was to make sure that such values were looked at critically and denounced as lies and illusions.

Without doubt, many left-wing critics were hopeful that a new modern society would be created as a result of the Communist revolution, one which would have shed all the vestiges of feudalism which had typified Chinese society for some two thousand years. They were afraid that finding in ancient philosophy sayings which were still applicable today was tantamount to 'putting the basic principles of Marxism–Leninism under the names of ancient people who lived some two thousand years ago, making the thoughts of the ancients very similar to those of Marxism–Leninism.'[105] If this objective could be achieved, it was thought, then the continuation and elevation of tradition would be greatly enhanced at the expense of those who wanted drastic policy changes.

The way in which philosophical debates were intricately bound to politics became even more evident when Wu Han, author of *Hai Rui Dismissed from Office*, took up his pen to defend the position that traditional ethics could and should be inherited. In 1962, Wu Han wrote two articles on morality, both declaring that ethical values in feudal society were still relevant in the new socialist China. In the first article,[106] after quoting from Engels' *Anti-Duhring* that the morality of any period is the morality of the ruling class of that period, Wu Han concluded that, if one were to inherit any moral teachings from the past, they would have to be those of the ruling classes anyway. Specifically, he named the Confucian concept of loyalty (*zhong*)[107] as one which could be useful in the new State and should be inherited. He observed, in the second article, 'regardless whether a morality is feudal or capitalist, the proletarian class can absorb certain aspects of it.'[108] Coming from Wu Han, this of course did not go unnoticed, and many people wrote and asked how this was to be done. Wu Han did not give a very definite answer, except to say that it should be done 'critically'.[109] The vagueness of this position left considerable room for criticism. By the end of 1965, nearly forty articles had been published on this topic, most of which were repetitions of arguments put forward earlier denouncing Feng Youlan. For example, Guan Feng and Wu Fuqi, whose joint article was probably the most scholarly, repeated the contention that, while the proletariat might sometimes borrow terms from feudal or bourgeois ethics, the content of such terms should be different. For example, loyalty in the old days meant loyalty to the landlord class, whereas in a socialist country loyalty implied loyalty to the state and the people.[110]

The involvement of Wu Han channelled the debate on cultural inheritance more into the moral arena and it also pointed to the fact that the debate was beginning to impinge on policy-making in the political sphere. Even at the level of discussing how to approach the teaching and research of traditional philosophy, it was becoming obvious that factions were forming, and that if a 'principal contradiction', to use Mao Zedong's terminology, could be picked out, it was a contradiction between those who wanted to proceed slowly and thus preserve some aspects of that tradition and those who were eager to 'break completely' from what they perceived as a tradition that had impeded progress for two thousand years.

In his attempt to 'inherit' the Chinese philosophical tradition, Feng Youlan and other conservative writers tried to do so by quoting at length from Marx and Engels. The fitting of Chinese tradition to Marxist categories was further given support by other established historians such as Wu Han and Jian Bozan. But the policies their essays implied were not ones espoused by Mao Zedong and his group. In their writings, the radicals such as Guan Feng, Qi Benyu, and Wu Chuanqi denounced not only Chinese tradition but those who favoured a return to a particular type of that tradition. In the 1950s, when the controversies were mainly centred around the 'inheritance' issue, some scholars such as Zhang Dainian and Ren Jiyu seemed to have remained 'neutral' in the political polemics and others, including Yang Rongguo and Zhao Jibin, were relatively silent. But as the confrontation between radicals and conservatives became more bitter and irreconcilable, historians were forced to take sides.

When historians such as Jian Bozan made the point that the Chinese past should be excused in terms of 'historicism', it seemed a reasonable plea. But to claim from this that the past should be 'inherited', as Feng Youlan and Wu Han did, was to provoke all those feelings which since the May Fourth era had seen that past as the greatest obstacle to China's modernization. It is not surprising that Guan Feng found support in the top leadership.

Although in the fifties China had not yet formally broken with the Soviet Union, tensions were already being felt. Using the Yan'an rather than the Soviet model to cure the nostalgia for the past expressed in the Hundred Flowers made it easier to label both the 1957 conference and what it stood for and later the Soviet Union as revisionist, although the two things were very different. The conference was the first major attempt by scholars in the People's Republic to define philosophy in such a way that classical Chinese philosophy—the core of traditional Chinese thinking—could be sympathetically studied. Although Guan Feng's savage attack on the conference lapsed with the quick demise of the Great Leap Forward, his thinking was to be more systematically worked out in his later analysis of the pre-Qin philosophers. That 're-visionist', a modern political term, had been used to describe the conference meant that the political nature of research in Chinese philosophy was made explicit. Revisionism became the term which included all unacceptable thinking during the Cultural Revolution.

This was the first time that anyone had written in detail about what it meant.

It is significant, too, that it was Guan Feng who launched the attack on the conference. At the conference, most of the major speeches were made by people who either were members of Beijing University or had had associations with it in the early fifties when philosophy teachers throughout China had been called to do in-service training at the newly reopened department at Beijing University, the most prestigious and established institution of higher learning. Most of the participants were also trained primarily in the history of Chinese philosophy. Guan Feng, however, had no formal ties with Beijing University. He lectured at the Shandong Party School and had been primarily trained in Marxism. His association with Beijing was through Chen Boda, who was the editor-in-chief of the Party journal *Red Flag*. Guan Feng was one of the sub-editors. At this stage, Chen Boda was still very close to Mao Zedong and had personal access to him. Guan Feng was thus able to keep in touch with the highest organs of political power, although he was based in the provinces. In this light, it is easy to see why he was able to write on philosophical matters with an air of authority.

In August 1966, Guan Feng, together with other radical writers such as Qi Benyu and Lin Jie, worked formally under Chen Boda in the Cultural Revolution Group to carry out political struggles against their rivals.[111] They were thus thrust into a power struggle which was really 'life and death' for many of them. Guan Feng, Lin Jie, Wu Chuanqi, and others were imprisoned in September 1967 as 'ultra-leftists'. While many would say they deserved such tragic ends because they had engineered the Cultural Revolution, the ease with which this group was silenced showed that the patronage they enjoyed was a matter of expediency on the part of the political leaders.

3 Orthodoxy Upheld: Kongzi and Traditional Ethics and Education

OF the pre-Qin thinkers, Kongzi has without doubt been the single most important influence on traditional Chinese thought to the extent that, in China, 'traditional' is often synonymous with 'Confucian'. To denounce tradition, it was necessary to 'strike down the Kong family shop' (*dadao Kongjia dian*).[1] In the same way, when historians talked about inheriting tradition, they were in many cases talking about inheriting Confucianism. This point will become evident when the interpretations of Kongzi are compared to those of the other philosophers. While the Daoists, Moists, and Legalists have sometimes been condemned, none has aroused as much feeling in contemporary scholars as Kongzi.

PERIODIZATION AND CLASS

The new methodology adopted after 1949 emphasizes the class membership and class affiliation attributed to Kongzi. Traditionally, of course, this would not be pertinent to a study of the history of philosophy. In the minds of many scholars now, no doubt, there is still the belief that the philosophy of an individual has nothing to do with his class and that, in fact, the greater a philosopher, the more his thinking transcends historical limitations placed on him. Thus, Feng Youlan and Liu Jie argued repeatedly that Kongzi's *ren* was really class-transcending. Be that as it may, Marxist methodology depended primarily on class analysis, and the scarcity of traditional material on this topic did not deter almost all historians after 1949 from spending time looking at Kongzi's class background when studying him.

As with all the other pre-Qin philosophers, the source which was considered most reliable for a biographical account of Kongzi, apart from the *Analects*, was Sima Qian's biography.[2] Kongzi, in this account, held a number of positions, ranging from minor official to prime minister.[3] Indeed, it could even be argued that he had spent much of his life unemployed. Also, among his students, there were people from many economic backgrounds, so that conceivably he associated with people from very different classes. It is therefore possible to place him in almost any pre-capitalist class, especially since before the Cultural Revolution there was no accepted Marxist periodization of early Chinese history.

In fact, in the early 1950s, there was a great deal of confusion over the use of class analysis and periodization. Many historians were happy to give evaluations which were close to traditional ones, stating that Kongzi had been a member of the gentry class (*daifu*, *shi*, and so on). However, traditional historiography did not include a slave period in China's past. Thus, those who continued to give traditional accounts ignored Marxist periodization in practice, even if they gave lip-service to it. Yang Xiangkui pointed out this anomaly as early as 1953 when he referred to the *Essentials of Chinese History*, edited by the prestigious Chinese Historical Association. While it acknowledged that the question of the nature of society in the Spring and Autumn and Warring States periods had not been settled, it nevertheless went on to state that Kongzi had upheld the feudal system. Yang observed:

If Kongzi had not been living in a feudal society, then he could not have been an upholder of the feudal system. One can see that the editors of the *Essentials of Chinese History* have basically accepted that society in the Spring and Autumn period was a feudal one.[4]

While in the May Fourth era it was fashionable to attack tradition as feudal and to maintain that Kongzi's philosophy represented the feudal past, 'feudal' in this sense really implied all the negative aspects of 'traditional' life from the pre-Qin slave burials to Qing dynasty foot-binding. With the advent of Marxist historiography and the appearance of Guo Moruo's 1950 periodization scheme, however, it was possible to argue that, in being feudal, Kongzi had in fact been progressive. Indeed, Guo Moruo went so far as to say that Kongzi had been a revolutionary who had supported attempts to overthrow the slave system, citing examples which he claimed showed that Kongzi had been willing to assist the rebels of his time.[5]

Guo Moruo, however, had a tendency to exaggerate when it came to talking about personalities, whether historical or living. While Kongzi was lauded by many writers in the highest possible way in the fifties and early sixties, none went so far as Guo Moruo's romanticized version of Kongzi as an anarchist revolutionary. Neverthelesss, Guo's sources for his argument, like his periodization scheme, were used extensively by other writers.

Another commonly accepted interpretation of Kongzi's class affiliation was provided by Fan Wenlan. Although his periodization meant that Kongzi lived in feudal times, he acknowledged that the Spring and Autumn and Warring States periods had been a time of great social change. According to Fan, although the whole period was feudal, it was nevertheless a time of the decline of the clan system and the rise of the family system.[6] Kongzi was a member of the scholar-gentry class (*shi*). The description given to this class by Fan Wenlan and others who followed him is very much like the vacillating middle and petty bourgeoisie described by Mao Zedong in his analysis of Chinese classes.[7] They belonged neither to the upper aristocracy nor to the lower working classes, but fluctuated in between, and their class interests vacillated accordingly. Fan Wenlan believed that Kongzi had belonged to a more progressive wing of that 'class' and that he had fought on behalf of the new landlord class against the old clan system by introducing concepts such as *ren* and *li*.

This line of reasoning was closer to traditional accounts, too, in suggesting that Kongzi had been responsible for integrating and propagating all the ideas before him, as embodied in the principle of the 'golden mean' (*zhongyong*). A number of historians expressed the same idea in different ways. Some, for example, believed that Kongzi had stood on the side of the feudal *junzi* class. Generally translated as 'gentlemen', the concept of *junzi* is also akin to that of a scholar-gentry class. It was said that Kongzi had tried to reach a compromise between the aristocracy and the people through such techniques as the rectification of names (*zhengming*).[8] Using this, Kongzi was supposed to have admonished the feudal lords to carry out their duties according to their allotted positions (names) and not to overstep their roles. This was supposed to have limited the power of the lords so that the peasants could not be over-exploited.

Such ideas about Kongzi were already held by these and other scholars before 1949. On the whole, they did not contradict the orthodox view that Kongzi had made a great contribution to ancient culture and that his historical position was high. The theory that although Kongzi had been a thinker who represented the feudal aristocracy he still worked for the common good was thus voiced in journals such as *History Teaching*,[9] ensuring that it was an idea which influenced school curricula.

These scholars were also orthodox in their agreement that Kongzi had lived in a time of great social change, but that his time was nevertheless part of the feudal period in China. However, it has already been noted in Chapter 1 that, during the fifties, Guo Moruo's periodization scheme gained greater acceptance while the others were gradually abandoned. Moreover, although Fan Wen-lan's periodization scheme fitted in better with the traditional view of ancient history, it had not really been as carefully researched as Guo Moruo's, and, strictly speaking, was not as Marxist in orienta-tion. Hence, the class analysis based on this scheme was rather vague. The classes of *junzi*, *shi*, or *daifu* that Kongzi was said to have belonged to were not really economic classes in the Marxist sense, but rather different ways of describing the scholar-gentry.

Both Guo's and Fan's interpretations of Kongzi were still largely sympathetic. The 1950s was still a period when intellectuals were respected, and the scholars as a whole still saw themselves as mem-bers of an intellectual class in a period of tremendous social change, just as Kongzi had lived in a transitional period of history. An equally positive approach to Kongzi was given by Feng Youlan. While the writings of both Guo Moruo and Fan Wenlan were highly influential, they were basically historical. Feng Youlan's discussion of Kongzi focused more on his philosophical thought. Adopting Guo Moruo's periodization scheme, Feng had already argued that Kongzi, though a member of the aristocracy, had tried to bring about social reforms which would serve the whole people by instilling new meaning into the old Zhou rites and that he had represented the newly emerging landlord class.[10] This was a very common point of view in the fifties. In the first of a series of articles he wrote on Kongzi in 1960, Feng Youlan again re-stated the theory that Kongzi had been a representative of the slave-owning class but that he had changed his stance and become instead a spokesman for the new landlord class.[11]

The implications of these statements are clear. China in the fifties and early sixties was entering a new period in its history, an era which found parallels in Kongzi's time. If it could be shown that Kongzi's thinking was created as part of, as well as an agent of, that change, then aspects of it must be applicable in the present new society, and thus should and could be inherited. This was in fact argued by many, especially in the field of education, which will be discussed later. Feng Youlan, who had many times con-fessed that before 1949 he had served the landlord and comprador classes that had declined and all but disappeared after 1949, must have realized the implications for the present when people claimed that Kongzi, another teacher, had also come from and served a reactionary class, but was able to change his allegiance and join the victorious class. Many other older academics must have gone through the same process of self-doubt and self-justification.

But this kind of thinking was inevitably challenged. Although Marx made allowances for a small section of the ruling class to drift away from its original class and join the ranks of the oppressed, this was seen by orthodox Marxists as an exception rather than as a general rule.[12] It is certainly not in the mainstream of class analysis to say that members of a certain class switched and changed at will. If Kongzi had lived in a slave society and belonged to the slave-owning class, he would have to have been exceptional to want to give up all the privileges that his class enjoyed in order to create a new system. Although some people like Feng Youlan argued precisely the point that Kongzi was exceptional and had foresight in joining the victorious class, many who saw him as a member of the slave-owning class believed instead that he had wanted to keep the slave system intact.

KONGZI: A SLAVE-OWNER MENTALITY?

In fact, even the writers who agreed on a particular periodization scheme still had different opinions on Kongzi's class origin. He was variously seen as a member of the slave-owning ruling class, a member of the feudal ruling class, a revolutionary, a reformer, or one who had risen from the ranks of the poor.

Yang Rongguo and Zhao Jibin were foremost among those who argued that Kongzi had been a member of the slave-owning class who had tried to prevent slave society from falling into decline. This was a view they had already expressed in the forties.[13] Yang Rongguo argued that Kongzi had tried to destroy the three powerful Lu families, Jisun, Mengsun, and Shusun, because these families represented a threat to the rule of the slave-owning aristocracy. He interpreted Kongzi's execution of Shaozheng Mao in the same way.[14] Zhao Jibin's analysis was more textual. He analysed the meanings of the terms used in the *Analects* and concluded that, when Kongzi said '*ai ren*' (usually translated as 'love men'), he actually meant 'love the class of slave owners'; that is, in the time of Kongzi, *ren* (men) had signified the slave-owners while the slaves were referred to as *min*.[15] Yang Rongguo and Zhao Jibin continued to promote this point of view throughout the fifties and sixties. Even in the early sixties, when the prevailing climate was one of praising tradition and Kongzi, there were some important adherents to this view. By the Cultural Revolution and the anti-Kongzi campaign, this was the only view which was officially acceptable.

Some scholars, including Ren Jiyu and Guan Feng, argued that Kongzi had not only oppressed the slaves but tried to suppress the newly arising feudal forces that challenged the old Zhou aristocracy. They cited as evidence Kongzi's hatred of the three Ji families who had usurped the rites traditionally reserved for Zhou princes. Kongzi had even urged his other students 'to strike the drum and attack' his student Ran Qiu, because he had helped the Ji family. Guo Moruo had argued that this incident showed that Kongzi was a rebel because he was prepared to attack the ruling families. By interpreting the whole episode as one in which Kongzi was trying to suppress those who did not observe the Zhou rites therefore, Ren Jiyu made an indirect attack on the kind of argument put forward earlier by Guo Moruo. Ren Jiyu concluded that there was no factual evidence to support the view that Kongzi was sympathetic to the rebels.[16]

Critics like Ren Jiyu and Yang Rongguo also cited Kongzi's opposition to the inscription of legal codes on to tripods, arguing that he therefore opposed an attempt by the newly arising Legalist forces to overthrow the old Zhou system of rule by rites. The notion that Kongzi had opposed the Legalist strategy to change the political system proved to be a significant one in contemporary shifts of historiography. Kongzi was seen here as opposing a new form of government and a new breed of people, the Legalists. It was thus later argued that, far from being an offshoot of Confucian ideology, the Legalist doctrine was from the very beginning opposed to Kongzi. This interpretation accorded well, too, with the Zhdanov definition of the history of philosophy as one which was full of struggle and not one of mutual influence and support. The 'line struggle' idea was basic to the Cultural Revolution ideology and this was one reason why this interpretation became so fundamental in the analysis of the Chinese philosophers in the aftermath of the Cultural Revolution.

The interpretations of the struggle between the Confucians and

Legalists also made manifest the problem of using historical data to fit a 'Marxian dress'.[17] While the sources had merely stated that Kongzi had opposed the inscription of legal codes on to bronze tripods, one could make any interpretation of this fact as long as the Marxist terminology was preserved. Some historians, for example, while agreeing that Kongzi had been a member of the slave-owning class, reversed the argument and claimed that he was a progressive member of that class because he had opposed the legal codes which had been oppressive. Kongzi's preference for government based on virtuous conduct rather than law is interpreted as an indication that he was sympathetic to the slaves.[18]

Other examples of almost arbitrary interpretations of terms and events occurred frequently in the debates on Kongzi. One example which was often quoted was again provided by Guo Moruo in the early fifties:

When Gongshan Furao was holding the territory of Bi in an act of rebellion he invited Kongzi to join him. Kongzi was inclined to go. Zilu was annoyed and said, 'Indeed you cannot go! Why must you go and see Gongshan?' Kongzi replied, 'Could he have invited me without some reason? If anyone will employ me, may I not make an Eastern Zhou?'[19]

Guo Moruo took this passage to mean that Kongzi had been prepared to help the rebels. Guan Feng and Lin Yushi, however, gave it an entirely different interpretation. They pointed out that Gongshan Furao had in fact rebelled against the Ji family, which had already incurred Kongzi's wrath for usurping the Zhou rites. If Kongzi had been willing to support rebellions against the Duke of Lu, perhaps an argument could be made for saying that he was a revolutionary rebel. As it was, he had only been prepared to help to suppress representatives of the newly arising landlord class, a regressive step.[20]

Guo Moruo did not answer this criticism, but a number of people joined the debate. Some contended that Kongzi had been indebted to the Ji family, because he had begun his official career with them. They quoted Sima Qian that 'growing up and working as a keeper of the granaries for the Chi (Ji) family he measured the grain fairly, when he was keeper of the livestock the animals flourished, and so he was made minister of works'.[21] From this, it was argued that it was unlikely that Kongzi would have opposed his benefactors.[22]

Other interpretations were placed on Gongshan Furao's rebellion. Tang Yijie, for example, argued that, although Kongzi had originally been a member of the slave-owning class, he had worked on behalf of the landlord class. Tang Yijie claimed that Kongzi had become progressive because of his ambitious nature. This was illustrated by his question, 'If anyone will employ me, may I not make an Eastern Zhou?' Tang believed that, when Kongzi saw that the slave-owning class was collapsing, he had aligned himself with the more progressive landlord class then rising in power.[23] Thus, any episode from Kongzi's life could be construed in completely different ways. Often, the interpretations were means to preconceived conclusions, and as a result they were frequently arbitrary.

Historians also frequently simply asserted rather than reasoned out their case in their interpretations of basic terminology from the *Analects*. For example, Feng Youlan disagreed with Guan Feng and Lin Yushi when they used Zhao Jibin's distinction between the classes *ren* and *min* as denoting the slave-owners and slaves.[24] Feng Youlan argued that, rather than denoting a particular class in the Spring and Autumn period, *ren* (men) had been an all-embracing term:

For example, those people living in the cities were called '*guoren*'; those living in the rural areas were called '*yeren*'; the aristocracy was called '*daren*'... If *ren* had only denoted the slave-owning aristocracy, the '*yeren*' must denote the barbarian aristocracy ... this is not possible.[25]

In answer to this, Guan Feng and Lin Yushi simply stated that there had in fact been 'barbarian aristocrats' in the sense that there were slave-owners who lived in rural areas.[26] Judging from his later writings, though, their argument seems to have had little effect on Feng's views. Nevertheless, Feng Youlan did agree that Kongzi had been a member of the slave-owning class. As the debate continued, those who argued that Kongzi had been a member of the slave-owning class and that he had worked for the interests of that class seemed to gain ground. This was not surprising, considering that Guo Moruo's periodization scheme was also gaining more general acceptance. Logically, to say that he lived in a slave period and belonged to the upper class would imply that he was a member of the slave-owning class, unless one were to adopt Guo Moruo's romanticized version of him as a rebel, that is, a renegade to his class.

It is interesting to note here that whilst the younger historians such as Guan Feng and Tang Yijie were by no means sympathetic to Kongzi, their assessments of him were in fact not as negative as those made by some of the older critics like Yang Rongguo and Zhao Jibin. Guan Feng, in particular, would have been aware of the political use of historical interpretations. Why did he not denounce Kongzi totally? It was not because Guan denied the existence of completely negative characters in history. To him, Zhuangzi was the pre-Qin villain who was totally reactionary. He claimed that, right after Liberation, the most sinister malaise confronting intellectuals was the escapism of Zhuangzi and not the 'false benevolence' of Kongzi.

Historically, the strength of Confucianism has not lain in its philosophical profundity or its poetic appeal. Daoism, especially the *Zhuangzi*, has been more important as a philosophical and poetic inspiration. As Balazs points out, the strength of Confucianism lay in its ability to perpetuate a vast bureaucracy, the biggest and most durable in the world. In the fifties, the newly formed bureaucratic class was just beginning to extend its base, and problems concerning the bureaucracy did not come under scrutiny until the late fifties.[27] Before that time, this was not yet seen as a major social problem. In this sense, Guan Feng was perhaps correct in concentrating his attacks on Zhuangzi rather than on Kongzi. During the Cultural Revolution, when it was felt that the bureaucracy was again becoming too unwieldy, Kongzi once more became the target of leftist ire.

The pre-Cultural Revolution period was still a time when academics were trying out the new tools of Marxist terminology and methodology. Class analysis was new to many, and periodization to some seemed ridiculous as a basis for philosophical analysis. Even so, the analyses of Kongzi made in the fifties were quite different from those of the early sixties. After ten years of Communist rhetoric and re-education in the fifties, most scholars by the sixties were more confident in their use of Marxist techniques, and it was taken for granted that class was the most important factor in evaluating a thinker. Some historians like Tang Lan had become so adept at using class analysis that in discussing Kongzi they could reject both Guo Moruo and Fan Wenlan's periodization schemes and create their own.[28] Tang Lan, however, also believed that Kongzi had worked for the good of the common man.

By the sixties, class analysis was regarded as being of such paramount importance that it was no longer possible to write about

Kongzi and ignore class altogether, as the well known idealist scholar Xiong Shili had done in 1956[29] during the Hundred Flowers period. By the 'second Hundred Flowers' of the early sixties, those who wanted to examine Kongzi without reference to class analysis had to argue such a stand explicitly. Feng Youlan's 'abstract inheritance' and 'universal forms' were already being criticized for indirectly dispensing with class analysis. Liu Jie, too, was accused of having argued that

Kongzi was the saviour for all times, the embodiment of the truth and the divine. With Kongzi's concept of *ren*, all problems of the world can be solved. Things such as Marxism-Leninism, the theory of class struggle and the method of class analysis can be dispensed with.[30]

It was one thing to say that tradition could be inherited in a socialist state, but quite another to argue that class analysis could be dispensed with. At this juncture, writers in favour of inheriting tradition had reached a point of no return. As indicated in the last two chapters, the academic debates on the pre-Qin philosophers and cultural inheritance had begun to spill over into the political arena. Increasingly, Kongzi as a historical figure was no longer the issue. By 1964, very little mention was made of him. Articles began to appear stressing class analysis and class struggle in history, and the philosophical debates focused on the 'two combines into one' controversy raised by Yang Xianzhen.

FROM MATERIALISM TO ETHICS

Class as a concept in the history of Chinese philosophy only became paramount after the establishment of Communism in China. Traditionally, the most important facet of Confucianism was its ethics. The debates about Kongzi's class were in reality an elaborate prelude to debates on the validity of his moral doctrines in modern-day China. For those who were favourably inclined towards his ethics, what little Kongzi said about the material world was quoted as evidence that he had been materialist. Because being materialist in the Zhdanov dichotomy was equivalent to being politically sound, this was one way to argue that he had worked for the class which was historically progressive, so that it was possible to extrapolate from this the praiseworthiness of his ethical principles. Many writers thus preface their appraisals of

Kongzi's ethical principles with a few comments on his materialism.

Because Kongzi made no statements on metaphysics as such, implications were drawn from the limited observations he made about the existence of ghosts and a few comments on cosmology. Fan Wenlan, for example, used Kongzi's statements that 'While you are not able to serve men, how can you serve their spirits? While you do not know life, how can you know about death?'; and 'Respect the spirits but keep them at a distance' to support his view that there were elements of materialism in Kongzi's conception of the world.[31] Other writers in their quest for materialism in Kongzi used the same statements and the same doubtful deductions to arrive at similar conclusions. Another saying which was often quoted was 'Does Heaven speak? The four seasons pursue their courses and all things are continually being reproduced, but does Heaven say anything?' This was taken to mean that Kongzi had adopted a pantheistic outlook, laying the foundation for the development of materialistic and atheistic strands of thought.[32]

The tenuous nature of these arguments can be seen in the fact that the same quotations were used by many who wanted to prove the exact opposite. For example, Ren Jiyu remarked that, although some people believed that these quotations showed the beginnings of atheism, 'in reality, Kongzi openly admitted the existence of ghosts. His statement "It is obsequious for a man to sacrifice to a spirit not belonging to him" ('Wei zheng', *Analects*) shows that he only opposed sacrificing randomly'.[33] In line with his general condemnation of Kongzi's thinking, Ren Jiyu concluded that Kongzi had been an idealist.

Like the discussion on Kongzi's class, therefore, the approaches to his philosophical premises were very *ad hoc*. Conclusions, rather than logically arrived at, were categorical statements dependent on the particular bias of the critic. In a sense, this is understandable as Kongzi's philosophy is not as speculative as early Western philosophy. The purpose of asking whether or not he was a materialist was really to decide if his ethical theory was inheritable or not. Before the Cultural Revolution, it was generally argued that, since he had lived in a period when materialism was just emerging from an idealist mould, it was reasonable to assume that his thinking contained elements of both. This belief, though common, was also very tenuous.

Allied to this claim was the suggestion that, in his advocacy of *ren*, Kongzi had discovered the nobility of man, enabling him to inject a new humanity into the old rites. This was the most common assessment of his ethics before the Cultural Revolution and one of the most common arguments put forward for saying that he had made an unparalleled contribution to Chinese civilization. Of those who held this view, Guo Moruo again offered the most unorthodox exposition. His interpretation of Kongzi as a revolutionary enabled him to render *ren* in such a way that it encompassed such concepts as serving the people, even to the point of self-sacrifice. He believed that Kongzi, in using *ren*, had discovered humanity in the slaves, the common people of his time, and that this recognition of their human qualities had been behind a movement to liberate them.[34]

Other writers in the early fifties, including Du Guoxiang and Ji Wenfu, also interpreted *ren* as meaning benevolence extended towards the common man.[35] Ji Wenfu's article, written in 1953, contended that because Kongzi had advocated the use of *ren* his ideas should still be inherited in a socialist society. While this line of reasoning was implicit in a number of other articles, Ji Wenfu seems to have been the first to state it explicitly. He wrote that the good in Kongzi should be inherited in the same way that 'Marx was able to separate and absorb the rational inner core from the mysterious outer coating of Hegel.'[36] He believed that, with the discovery of human nature in all men, Kongzi had been able to break through the confines of aristocratic thought to display the beginnings of a democratic spirit.

Ji Wenfu continued throughout the fifties to hold this high opinion of Kongzi, referring to him in 1958 as 'the cock whose crow brightened the sky.'[37] There was thus a current of thought throughout the fifties which saw Kongzi's thought as being applicable to contemporary China, with some historians contending that the spirit of such Confucian concepts as the great commonwealth (*da tong*), the five constant virtues (*wu chang*), and personal cultivation (*xiuyang*) could be inherited and practised in a Communist society.[38] As indicated earlier, these moral precepts were not advocated simply in the universities and school textbooks, but by the highest political leaders and propaganda organs in the country.

Besides indicating the importance of Kongzi for Chinese philosophy, Zhu Qianzhi went even further to argue that Confucian values had influenced the great seventeenth and eighteenth century thinkers in Europe. As evidence, he referred to the fact that these thinkers had spoken positively of Kongzi, and he claimed that their writings on love and democracy reflected the kind of teaching advocated by Kongzi.[39] No stronger claim could have been made for the value of Confucian teaching than to suggest that Marx had been indirectly influenced by Confucianism and that Marxism was therefore a descendant of Confucianism. Zhu invited others to debate with him on this issue, but the argument seems to have been too farfetched to have evoked any response.

Of the pro-Kongzi voices, however, Feng Youlan's was again the most detailed and 'philosophical'. He had of course in the early fifties already made observations about the benevolent nature of ren,[40] but his most significant contribution to the evaluations of Kongzi came in 1957 at the conference on the treatment of Chinese philosophy at Beijing University. One illustration he gave for his method of 'abstract inheritance' was Kongzi's ren. Feng Youlan claimed that, if Kongzi had only advocated ren to urge people to 'love the class of aristocratic men,' then one should eschew the concrete aspect of ren because it belonged to a different age. However, one should retain the abstract notion of 'love men' by the use of 'abstract inheritance' because this abstract principle was applicable to all ages.[41]

Feng Youlan found many supporters who elaborated on his ideas,[42] as well as many critics who attacked them.[43] In reply to the critics who warned that there could not be love that transcended class, Feng Youlan quoted an extract from Mao Zedong:

As for the so-called love of humanity, there has been no such all-inclusive love since humanity was divided into classes. All the ruling classes of the past were fond of advocating it, and so were many so-called sages and wise men, but nobody has ever really practised it, because it is impossible in class society.[44]

This quotation has usually been used to demonstrate that class-transcending love is impossible. Feng Youlan, however, insisted instead that, while it had never been 'practised', this did not mean that it was impossible to advocate ren as an abstract concept, or that class-transcending love could not exist. With this kind of sophistry, Feng was able to continue to claim that, when Kongzi talked about 'ai ren', he had meant a love that was above class.[45]

In claiming that Kongzi had preached progressive ethical principles, Feng Youlan took into account the possibility that the ruling class could use fine-sounding phrases to deceive the people. In anticipating this objection to his method, he argued that when a class was in the formative stage, the universal characteristics of its thought were not entirely false, whereas when a class was on the decline, its thinking was on the whole deceptive. He referred to the slogan 'liberty, equality, and fraternity,' claiming that when the bourgeoisie first used it to combat the feudal classes, they had not used it to deceive, whereas in contemporary times, it had become a deceptive slogan.[46] Since Feng believed that Kongzi belonged to the feudal landlord class at its formative stage, he was able to argue on this basis that Kongzi had proposed his ethical principles with some sincerity.

To scholars who wanted to show that academics in socialist China could utilize old concepts in a new way, the notion that Kongzi had been able to modify the Zhou rites (*li*) so that the benevolent nature of *ren* could be rejuvenated as a moral principle was certainly an attractive one. The central argument put forward by those who thought that Kongzi's ethics could and should be 'inherited' was precisely that he had departed from the old Zhou rites (*li*) by advocating the primacy and application of *ren* as 'love men' (*ai ren*). In the fifties and early sixties, there were few voices which were critical of Kongzi and this interpretation. Of the dissenting voices, Zhao Jibin's was one of the most important. He had already interpreted the character *ren* (men) in the expression '*ai ren*' as the slave-owning class. Naturally, this had important implications for interpretations of Kongzi's *ren*, which had always been translated as benevolence, or 'love men'. By saying that, in advocating *ren*, Kongzi was simply urging his fellow slave-owners to love and support each other, Zhao Jibin implied that Kongzi in fact did not want to depart from the Zhou rites at all. On the relationship between *ren* and *li* then, Zhao believed that *li* was still the primary concept in Kongzi's ethical theory, with *ren* subordinate to it.[47] Thus, the supposed 'new invention' *ren* made by Kongzi was seen by Zhao Jibin as merely a derivative of the old Zhou rites (*li*), so that Kongzi was not as revolutionary as some people made out.

In 1962, Zhao Jibin went further in his thesis that Kongzi had been reactionary in his moral teachings by examining another important definition of *ren* found in the *Analects*. This was restraining oneself and returning to the rites (*ke ji fu li*).[48] The standard interpretation of this phrase, one which Feng Youlan had adopted, was that it meant to cultivate oneself and return to idealized ways of behaviour. Zhao Jibin, however, claimed that this reading was based on later views put forward by neo-Confucians such as the Cheng brothers and Zhu Xi, rather than on the sayings of Kongzi himself.[49] He also condemned this interpretation on the grounds that it took the meaning of the words at face value. Analysing each character of '*ke ji fu li*' etymologically, he concluded that by *ren* Kongzi had in fact exhorted people to observe and perform the old Zhou rites personally. This had been a retrogressive proposal, since its main purpose had been to try to reconcile the internal contradictions among the *ren* (slave-owner) class.

In the sixties, Zhao and those who were more critical of Kongzi were joined by Guan Feng and Lin Yushi. Guan and Lin agreed with the overall assessment made by Zhao Jibin, but they arrived at their conclusion by different methods. While Zhao relied on a semantic analysis, Guan and Lin used historical examples. They argued that Kongzi had lived at a time when the slave system was on the decline. Local authorities had usurped the central leadership, that is, the Zhou court, which had held power when Zhou was still stable and strong. Most of the local lords neither attended court nor paid homage to the Zhou prince. Many of them called themselves rulers in defiance of the central authorities. The transitional and chaotic nature of society then was also revealed by officials who murdered their rulers, sons who had their fathers killed, and brothers who slew each other.

According to Guan Feng and Lin Yushi, since Kongzi had represented the class whose power was crumbling, he had wanted to restore the old Zhou rites to try to preserve its rule. He had attempted to do this by defining *ren* as restraining oneself and returning to the rites and by proposing that *ren* was the highest ideal for men to follow. All the other measures that Kongzi advocated, such as the rectification of names and his opposition to inscribing legal codes on bronze tripods, were also directed to this end.[50]

Zhao, Guan, and Lin thus all agreed that Kongzi's motive for promoting *ren* was to restore the old Zhou rites (*li*). Despite this, all three writers conceded that Kongzi had been to some extent progressive for his time. Guan and Lin, for example, agreed partially with the orthodox interpretations when they said that, in using *ren*, Kongzi had brought the rites, which had been reserved for the aristocracy, down to the common people and thus could be said to have discovered 'man'.[51] Instead of claiming that Kongzi was a reactionary, they concluded that Kongzi's ethics had been reformist.

Although these critics made some concessions, Feng Youlan nevertheless found fault in their saying that Kongzi was mainly backward-looking.[52] Guan and Lin conducted a long debate with Feng Youlan on the issue of class-transcending values in the early sixties. Guan and Lin insisted in their later articles that ethical terms could not be taken out of their historical context,[53] and so they used the tenets of historicism to their advantage by analysing the class composition of Kongzi's era in order to determine what he meant by such concepts as *ren* and *li*.

Yang Rongguo, a professor at Zhongshan University, was another writer who was highly critical of Kongzi's thinking and whose views became prominent in the aftermath of the Cultural Revolution.[54] Yang, who believed that Kongzi had lived at a time when the slave system was disintegrating, argued that he had formulated the concept *ren* to keep the slaves in check. In answer to the assertion that Kongzi had 'discovered man' in his formulation of *ren*, Yang replied that 'the man discovered by him was only the declining aristocracy.'[55] To Yang Rongguo, Kongzi had advocated *ren* because it subsumed all the old moral concepts of the slave era such as filial piety, loyalty, and the rites. In advocating *ren*, Kongzi had in fact attempted to restore a crumbling social structure.

In 1962, Yang Rongguo reiterated his view that Kongzi had tried to use ethical concepts as a way to perpetuate the rule of the slave-owning class. He was more critical of Kongzi than Lin Yushi and Guan Feng. His 1962 article, however, was again largely ignored, indicating that, at that stage, his views were not popular. Perhaps as a token to the general pro-Kongzi atmosphere of that time, Yang acknowledged that Kongzi had made positive contributions in his time, especially in the field of education.[56]

Although the writings of those who were critical of Kongzi such as Zhao Jibin, Yang Rongguo, and Guan Feng did not receive as much support as those of Feng Youlan and Fan Wenlan, they were on the whole well-argued and well-researched. In many ways, too, their assessments provided a more novel way of looking at Kongzi than those of the more established scholars, and many of the arguments they put forward were to become official in the Cultural Revolution and its aftermath. One of their most significant interpretations was the postulation of a restorationist theme in the writings of Kongzi, particularly in the analysis of *ren* as a means of restoring the old rites and old values. The restorationist theme, which was to become one of the most important political issues in the aftermath of the Cultural Revolution, thus had its basis in the debates of the early sixties.

CONFUCIAN EDUCATION: THE 1950s

Before the Cultural Revolution, almost all writers agreed that the educational aspect of Kongzi's thinking above all could be inherited. Traditionally, the teacher in Chinese society was held in the highest esteem. That Mao Zedong himself had wanted to be remembered as a teacher was not simply modesty or self-effacement;[57] it was based on a tradition where one's teachers were the most highly respected and revered after one's own ancestors. In traditional political theory, the sage ruler was in fact a teacher whom others should take as their model. The greatest sage of all, Kongzi, had one attribute which all agreed he possessed: he was 'the paragon of teachers' (*wanshi shibiao*).

Publications which referred to Kongzi in the early fifties usually included at least a paragraph or two praising his contribution to education. Apart from such scattered references, no articles specifically on his contribution to education seem to have appeared until 1954.[58] This lack of interest in traditional education in the early years can be explained by the emphasis placed on creating a new educational system which would stimulate a socialist spirit and aid economic reconstruction through the training of scientists, engineers, and technicians. In education, as in other fields, the policy was to 'lean to one side,' that is, to copy the Soviet Union.

Since the beginning of this century, traditional education has been undermined by the continuous encroachment of Western ideas, so that it was Western rather than traditional ideas of education which were seen as the real barrier to constructing a new communist system. Western liberal theories on education now came under intensive attack, focusing on the theories of John Dewey, as represented by his student, Hu Shi.[59] It may have appeared that traditional concepts, which had already declined so much in importance by 1949, would simply wither away and that no particular drive against them would be necessary.

Some aspects of traditional Chinese education, such as the

emphasis on the role of the teacher, were also found in Soviet education at the time. After a radical beginning, Soviet education by the thirties had begun to reabsorb features of the traditional Russian system.[60] This change in the Soviet Union had accompanied the increased emphasis placed by Stalin on economic construction. Faced with the expectation that they should produce students of high academic standards, rather than experimenting with the education of a new socialist man, Soviet educators turned again to the old educational ideas. A similar process may have occurred in China since articles which did appear on Kongzi's educational policies coincided with the emphasis on economic construction brought about by the five-year plan of 1953–7. During this period, more emphasis was placed on training students according to their individual capabilities, a policy which was explicitly referred to in articles which drew parallels between Confucian ideas and the educational needs of China in the socialist period.

In 1954, the *Guangming Daily* published four articles which debated the question of Kongzi's theories on education and their contemporary relevance. The first was written by Xu Mengying, who argued that Confucian education encouraged people to practise benevolent government by teaching 'the ways of the *junzi*.'[61] Xu considered that Kongzi had broadened the meaning of *junzi*, so that instead of just referring to a member of the aristocratic class it involved a code of behaviour. In this way, it was not restricted to one level of society. Xu also claimed that Kongzi had stated that education should be made available to more people as a country's wealth increased, drawing a parallel with contemporary conditions in China. As socialist construction raised the standard of living in China, so Xu believed, education would be gradually extended until it became universal.

He listed three major principles of Confucian education: students should have reverence for their teachers, lessons should be reviewed, and the teacher should know the individual characteristics of the students. Kongzi was said to have taught according to the ability of each student, giving different answers to different students to the same question. Xu Mengying inferred from this that Kongzi believed that the methods and requirements of teaching meant that tuition should be on an individual basis and that teachers should set an example by being enthusiastic about learning.[62]

Xu concluded that Kongzi occupied an important place not only in Chinese, but also in world educational history. As the first person to teach privately instead of working as a tutor for the aristocracy, he made education available to a wider group of people. While Xu mentioned at the beginning and end of his article that there were good and bad points in Kongzi's educational thought, he presented only the positive features. His qualification that Confucian education had negative aspects seems to have been largely designed to try to forestall the possibility of criticism.

If so, this ploy did not succeed. Shen Yi replied that Xu had given an unbalanced view of Kongzi, making too high a claim for his achievements.[63] He claimed that Xu Mengying had

almost turned Kongzi into a modern educationalist by practically forcing the ancient teaching principles of Kongzi into formulas so that they could be fitted onto contemporary progressive educational principles such as the 'authority of the teacher', 'reviewing lessons', 'consolidation of knowledge', and 'understanding the individual characteristics of each student'.[64]

He said that, while it was correct to try to assess Kongzi fairly, it was wrong to exaggerate the claims made for him. As an example, he pointed to the quotations Xu had given to support his claim that Kongzi's students had great respect for him as a teacher. These quotations, Shen Yi wrote, indicated rather that Kongzi had encouraged a blind worship of teachers. This was very different from the modern concept of respect.

This response was followed by two articles from Chu Shusen, a teacher in an experimental primary school in Jiangsu. In the first article, Chu argued that, by claiming that Xu had wanted to apply ancient educational theories in modern society, Shen Yi had misunderstood Xu's article. All Xu had been advocating, Chu Shusen claimed, was a selective use of Kongzi's ideas in line with socialist policies, thereby critically inheriting ideas from the past.[65] He also disagreed with Shen's rejection of Kongzi's teaching principles.

Who can deny that Kongzi's teaching principles have great practical significance? We cannot, because of different times, social systems, educational aims and requirements, deny the historical place of those educationalists who historically propagated culture, thereby destroying their educational principles.[66]

To support his view, he pointed out that the writings of the seventeenth-century Czech educator Comenius and those of the nineteenth-century Russian educators Polinsky and Ushinsky were still praised in Soviet educational circles.

In his second article, Chu Shusen attempted to present a balanced evaluation of Kongzi's educational thought, listing both its positive and its negative aspects. He criticized Xu Mengying for neglecting the class character of Kongzi's 'way of the *junzi*'.[67] On the positive side, he pointed out merits which he believed Xu had omitted. He claimed that Kongzi had advocated the active pursuit of knowledge, quoting Kongzi that 'it is better to like something than to know it, and it is better to take pleasure in something than to like it.'[68] He also praised Kongzi's use of concrete examples in teaching and his understanding of human psychology.

These four articles were published between 14 June and 4 October 1954. Nothing else seems to have appeared on Confucian education until the Hundred Flowers period. This minor skirmish revealed that there was still significant support for Confucian educational ideas. All three writers had acknowledged that Kongzi had been a great educator in his time, even though Shen Yi and Chu Shusen had also offered some criticisms.

During the Hundred Flowers period, another article by Xu Mengying was published in the journal *People's Education* in February 1957. The article was intended to be the first of a series of essays on the history of Chinese education, but the rest of the series failed to appear. It was also the first article in *People's Education* dealing with traditional Chinese educational theories, although the journal had begun publication in 1950. As the most prestigious journal on education, it had, on the whole, reflected contemporary Chinese interests in education. By contrast, it had included over seventy translations of articles by Russian educators between 1950 and 1957.

The break between the Soviet Union and China, which affected education as it did everything else, can be traced back to 1956. From that period on, China began to search for independent solutions to its problems. Russian writers date the move away from Soviet educational methods to this time, acknowledging that, by the end of 1956, educational institutions in China had departed from their reliance on Soviet curricula and textbooks used prior to this.[69]

Criticisms expressed during the Hundred Flowers period revealed dissatisfaction with the extent of Soviet influence on education.[70] Mao Zedong is said to have exclaimed at a talk with

heads of provincial and municipal education departments in 1957,
'Is the Ministry of Education a Soviet Ministry of Education or a
Chinese Ministry of Education?'[71] By 1957, a writer in *People's
Education* complained:

To be an educational worker in new China and not understand a little of
Kongzi's educational thinking reveals inadequacies. Now there are some
teachers who, when talking about educationalists, seem to know a great
deal about Dewey and Makarenko (and of course this should be the case),
but when it comes to educationalists of our country like Kongzi, they
cannot say more than a few words about them. We can't call this a normal
phenomenon.[72]

In his 1957 article, Xu Mengying reiterated several points he had
made in 1954, suggesting that he had either ignored or disagreed
with the criticisms Shen Yi and Chu Shusen had made. Again,
he made no criticisms of Kongzi, claiming that his ideas were
still relevant for education.[73] This seemed to contradict the edi-
torial introduction to the article, which held that, while one should
learn from his good points, the 'poisons' of Kongzi should be
eliminated.[74]

People's Education, in 1957, also published a review of Li
Changzhi's book on Kongzi[75] and another review of Shen Guanqun's book on educational thought in ancient China.[76] Both these
books were very positive in their evaluation of Kongzi's educational theory. It seemed that there was a minor revival of interest in
Confucian ideas in the educational world. Even in the journals of
the provincial teachers' colleges, articles appeared arguing that
Kongzi had implemented 'humanist education' (*rendaozhuyi
jiaoyu*) and because of this, he was a 'great educator'.[77]

The year 1957 also saw the first book to appear on Kongzi's
educational thought since 1949. Written by Chen Jingpan of Beijing University, it was compiled from lecture notes for a course he
had given called 'The History of Chinese Education'.[78] His interpretation of Kongzi's educational ideas was also very positive. He
wrote that Kongzi had referred to two models of behaviour: the
sage and the *junzi*. Since Kongzi had said little about the sages, not
even classing himself as one, the main model was that of the *junzi*.
According to Chen, '*junzi*' for Kongzi meant those who loved and
cared for the people and who would provide them with peace and
security.[79] This was similar to the view proposed by Xu Mengying
in 1954. The *junzi* were to practise self-cultivation (*xiuyang*) on the

basis of *li* and *ren* which, Chen claimed, formed the basic content of Confucian education.[80] Chen argued that, by including the notion of *ren*, Kongzi had added a humane element to the old aristocratic rites. Although both *ren* and *li* had then had a class basis, this was simply because of the nature of the era in which Kongzi lived.[81]

Entering into the debate on whether traditional Chinese values could be inherited, Chen Jingpan argued that many Confucian ideas on education remained valuable. He justified this by the common practice of referring to Mao's statement that

contemporary China has grown out of the China of the past; we are Marxist in our historical approach and must not lop off our history. We should sum up our history from Confucius to Sun Yat-sen and take over this valuable legacy.[82]

Although Chen had acknowledged the class character of *ren* and *li*, he believed, following Feng Youlan, that these concepts could somehow be separated from their class content. Treated as abstract qualities, they could be relevant in socialist society.[83]

THE PARAGON OF TEACHERS: THE EARLY 1960s

As the fifties drew to a close then, the general tendency was to adopt a more sympathetic approach to Confucian education. This was interrupted during the Great Leap Forward, but only very briefly. Although Kongzi could never again be seen as Kang Youwei once saw him, 'the Sagely King, the Everlasting Teacher, the Protector of the People and the High Priest of the World',[84] by the early sixties there was a revival of interest in his ideas to an extent not seen in China since 1949. Chan Wing-tsit lists eighteen articles written specifically on Kongzi's educational thought between 1949 and 1963, over three-quarters of which were written in 1961 and 1962.[85] Besides these articles dealing exclusively with Kongzi's educational theories, his contributions to education were inevitably mentioned in critiques of his thought.

This revival of interest in Kongzi's ideas on education did not remain simply a matter of academic interest. Increasingly, Kongzi's ideas were being referred to in general discussions of education. This should be understood against the background of educational policy at the time. In the early fifties, the Soviet model had been the source of inspiration for educational theories. In the late fifties, this was replaced by the Yan'an model, with its emphasis on popularization and adapting education to the needs of local conditions. However, by the early sixties, both models had been discredited: the Soviet model after links had been broken with the Soviet Union and the Yan'an model because of its association with the Great Leap Forward. It is not surprising then that educators began to turn to traditional ideas as a guide.

Traditional thinking, with its emphasis on diligent study, also fitted in with current needs and policies. The Soviet withdrawal of technicians and experts in 1960 made China's need for highly trained scientific personnel even more urgent. By 1961, China had turned to a policy which stressed 'expertness' and the learning of specialized skills. In Chen Yi's speech in August 1961, students were encouraged to study, drawing inspiration from the ancients. Chen believed that:

To study a specialized subject, one should study it with concentration and absorption, even to the seemingly foolish extent of forgetting to eat and sleep. One should take an interest in one's specialized subject and be totally involved in it for eight years, ten years, or even the whole of one's life. Only then can one achieve something. All great ancient scholars had this spirit of devotion. Kongzi 'was so absorbed in reading that he forgot to eat,' Dong Zhongshu 'did not look at his garden for three whole years,' Boddhidarma 'faced a wall for nine years.' We should learn from their spirit in searching for knowledge.[86]

Chen Yi's reference to Confucian tradition as a model of scholarship was by no means isolated. In 1961, a commentator of the *Guangming Daily* also referred approvingly to the fact that Kongzi studied so hard that he forgot to eat. He quoted the first line of the *Analects*, 'study and practise often', as still being an important principle in learning. If a person practised often, he would have a great store of knowledge, but if what was learnt was not reviewed constantly it would be forgotten. The commentator argued that, through review, a student could come to understand the new, mentioning as an example that through studying Mao repeatedly one could gain new perceptions and ideas.[87] He also believed that all real scholars should learn from Kongzi's attitude of humility expressed in his words, 'Knowledge is to realize that you know something when you know it; and to be aware that you do not know something when you do not.'[88]

In 1964, a book written in a similar vein entitled *On the Spirit and Method of Learning of Our Country's Ancient Scholars* appeared. It was intended as a guide for young students. Stories from the *Analects* and other classical texts were used to illustrate the attitude of Kongzi and other ancient scholars towards study.[89]

Traditionally, Kongzi has been regarded as the first person to have made teaching a profession, an accomplishment which earned him the title of 'paragon of teachers'. In the early sixties, this was regarded by most writers as his greatest contribution to Chinese culture. Kongzi was also believed to have been the first to popularize education. It was often argued that, since Kongzi had had some three thousand students, this was proof that he had tried to spread education widely. In addition, Kongzi's 'in teaching there is no distinction of classes' and 'I have never refused instruction to anyone who brings anything more than a bundle of dried meat to me'[90] were quoted to show that Kongzi had been willing to teach the common man, an innovation in the period in which he was living.[91]

It was also argued that Kongzi's educational endeavours had been in the service of the newly arisen landlord class and that all his students, except one, had been commoners. Yan Hui, his favourite student, had come from a poor family, and Zi Lu, another favoured student, was from a barbarian tribe.[92] Even those who otherwise did not look so favourably on Kongzi, such as Tang Yijie, believed that Kongzi had advocated teaching without distinction of classes because of the unstable social situation in the Spring and Autumn period. By advocating 'in teaching there is no distinction of classes,' Kongzi had addressed himself to the task of finding talented people who could solve the urgent problems of the time. Looking at his students, Tang Yijie argued that they had in fact included talents of various kinds, which helped the establishment of feudal society. By putting an end to official education and initiating private teaching, Kongzi had made an important contribution to the progress of society in his time.[93]

Kongzi's teaching methods were also praised as progressive. For instance, Wang Xianjin listed as outstanding the method Kongzi had developed of teaching in accordance with the level of the student's knowledge and his untiring commitment to teaching. He also praised Kongzi for having compiled such texts as the *Book of History* and the *Spring and Autumn Annals*.[94]

Traditional Confucian ideas began to have an influence again in the area of teacher-student relationships. Kuang Yaming, the Party Secretary of Nanjing University, suggested that modern educators could learn from the spirit of traditional education:

The ancients thus regarded respect for the teacher as an indication of love for studies and attention to knowledge ... For his part the teacher should 'learn without ever feeling tired of learning and teach without ever feeling tired of teaching,' love his pupils and set higher standards for them. Kongzi said, 'If you love somebody, will you not work hard for him? If you are loyal to somebody will you not advise him?' ('Xian Wen', *Analects*). To be sure, the teacher-student relationship in class society, like any other kind of relationship between one man and another, bears class impressions. But it has also left behind many useful and reasonable things for us.[95]

Some of the writers who argued in favour of Confucian education tried to find parallels between Kongzi's ideas and the ideas then prevailing in China. A distinction could be made, of course, between the ideas that Kongzi had taught and the way in which these ideas had been transformed over the centuries. This was done in a number of articles which sought to show that, while traditional education as it was practised in the Qing period indeed had many failings, these represented a degeneration of Kongzi's ideas.

One of the ways in which modern educational practice differed from traditional practice was in the inclusion of physical education as an important part of the curriculum. This had come about largely because of Western influence. In the early part of this century, this had aroused intense opposition, as testified by Zhu De, who had attended a college for physical education teachers.[96] Xin Lan, who frequently wrote for the journal *New Sports*, argued that Kongzi had encouraged an interest in physical culture, but that, in later dynasties, the feudal class had distorted Kongzi's ideas by stressing only literary education and ignoring physical culture. The argument that Kongzi had been interested in sports rested on two main claims. One was that he had paid attention to his own physical health. Traditional descriptions suggest that he was very tall and strong. He liked walking in the countryside, fishing, and hunting, and was good at archery and charioteering. His refusal to use a net instead of a line when fishing and his refusal to shoot birds in their nests were cited to show his good sportsmanship. He also stressed the importance of a well-regulated life, with proper hygiene, eating and sleeping habits, and posture. He lived to the ripe old age of 73, further proof of his physical fitness.[97] The second claim lay in Kongzi's inclusion of archery and charioteering among the six arts that he taught. These were military activities, but it was argued that they could also be regarded as sport. Like other sports, they developed the body and harmonized movements and could also help to build character.[98]

In keeping with the sentiments of the time, Xin Lan called for more research into traditional Chinese ideas on sports. He claimed that, when physical education was discussed, people knew about Greece and the Olympics, and about sports in Europe, as if only Western capitalist countries had sports. He urged the Chinese to look into their own history too. While Confucian ideas on sport had been distorted by many later writers, he cited several historical figures such as Dong Zhongshu and Ouyang Xiu, who had written about Kongzi's ideas on physical education. These people, he claimed, represented the true stream of Confucian thought in physical education.[99]

Perhaps the most important area in which Confucian education seems to differ from Marxist theories of education is on the question of the relationship between study and productive labour. Mao Zedong pointed out that

Confucius never reclaimed land or tilled the soil ... When a student asked him how to plough the fields, Confucius answered 'I don't know, I am not as good at that as a farmer.' Confucius was next asked how to grow vegetables, and he answered, 'I don't know, I am not as good at that as a vegetable gardener.' In ancient times the youth of China who studied under a sage neither learned revolutionary theory nor took part in labour.[100]

Despite this, Li Yinnong tried to show that Kongzi had not looked down on manual labour. He argued that Kongzi had approved of those who loved manual labour and worked for the welfare of society. Li claimed that Kongzi had praised Shun, the sage-emperor who had fished, ploughed the fields, and made pottery, because he had laboured for the welfare of the people. Shun had used productive labour to civilize the people, and through taking part in productive labour himself had served as a model for the people to follow. There were also examples of Kongzi praising ordinary people for their love of manual labour. Kongzi was said to have extolled the virtues of a particular woman who liked weaving as a form of manual labour, despite her husband's disapproval.[101]

Examining the question why Kongzi had disapproved of his students learning farming, Li suggested that this was because he had been politically ambitious and had wanted to create a virtuous society. He had encouraged his students to develop their talents in such a way that they would be able to help him in his political goals. That he had disapproved of his students doing manual labour had not been because he looked down on it, but because he had had high political aims.

Li argued that it was wrong to criticize Kongzi and his students for not wanting to engage in productive labour. They had been living in a period of rapid social change, when political, educational, and cultural activities were most important. Those most concerned with society would have taken an interest in politics; only those with no concern for society would have failed to consider political questions. He referred to the three farmers who criticized Kongzi for not participating in productive work.[102] According to Li, they had only managed to feed themselves, and there was nothing to be learned from them. In contrast, Kongzi had left great contributions for later generations.[103]

Praise of Kongzi's ideas on education was so pervasive in the early sixties that even those who were otherwise critical of him agreed with the view that his contributions to education had been progressive. Ren Jiyu, who argued that on the whole Kongzi had been reactionary, stated that this did not take away the historical significance of Kongzi. Ren believed that, being a great educator, historian, and learned scholar, Kongzi occupied an extremely important place in ancient Chinese history and that his teachings made a positive contribution to the feudal culture and education of China.[104]

Guan Feng and Lin Yushi, while pointing out that there were inconsistencies in Kongzi's ideas on education, considered that such statements as 'by nature men are nearly alike; in practice they grow apart' had been progressive.[105] These statements were taken as an indication of a materialist strain in his thought.[106] Even Yang Rongguo, who in the forties and fifties had seen Kongzi's ideas on education as an instrument of his reactionary politics, conceded that Kongzi had popularized education and that one could still learn from his sayings 'I never tire of learning and I never weary of teaching.'[107] In the early sixties then, writers were unanimous in their opinion that Kongzi's ideas on education had been progressive and that he had made important contributions to Chinese education.

Taking the pre-Cultural Revolution period as a whole, it was quite evident that nearly all contributors to the discussion agreed that Kongzi's educational thinking should be inherited in the new socialist society. This viewpoint did not remain simply on an ideological plane. It was meant to be put into practice. This was shown by the fact that much of the debate was carried out by peda-gogues, from the primary school teacher, Chu Shusen, to the Party Secretary of Nanjing University, Kuang Yaming. There was thus a definite attempt to try to keep Kongzi's educational thought alive and active, a fact which hardly justified Levenson's claim that there was an attempt to 'museumify' Kongzi.[108] Indeed, in a China where the minds of the young were meant to be instilled with a new consciousness, the number of articles eulogizing Kongzi and traditional thought written by precisely those people who were supposed to mould the new man suggests that the conservatism of the educated was as entrenched in the fifties and early sixties as it had been in traditional times.

On the whole, the interpretations of Kongzi's ethics and educa-tional thought were less damning than the May Fourth ones. When radical thinkers like Chen Duxiu and Lu Xun launched the anti-Confucian movement, they were concerned with dismantling the prevailing social order and replacing it with one based on Western ideas such as equality and liberty.[109] In the early fifties, a May Fourth-style attack on Confucianism was made by Cai Shangsi, but his writings were essentially ignored by other scholars.[110] Most historians of thought were concerned with classifying Kongzi according to Marxist criteria of class and periodization, and whether he was materialist or idealist. Those who were critical of Kongzi such as Cai Shangsi and Yang Rongguo had been averse to Confucianism before 1949 without the use of Soviet Marxist methods.

After the formation of the People's Republic, intellectuals were co-opted into the establishment so, instead of trying to tear down the social order, they wrote to strengthen it. In actual practice, Confucian ethics stressed co-operation with the state, conformist behaviour, and a sense of moral duty. Confucian education rein-forced these values by making virtues of rote learning, blind obedi-ence, and respect for authority. Once in power, the Communist Party could benefit from such a tradition. It was thus not ac-cidental that the Party actively encouraged meetings such as those held in Shandong Province in the early sixties when Marxist methodology such as periodization and class analysis served not only to excuse Kongzi's ideas but also to glorify them.

As most of the writers had themselves belonged to a pre-1949 intellectual élite, the idea that Marxist periodization and class analysis allowed this élite to vacillate and join the more historically progressive and victorious class would have been a very attractive one. It is not surprising that the common interpretation of Kongzi revealed that he too as an educated thinker living in changing times joined the more progressive elements of his era. With the Chinese scholars' penchant for seeing the present in the past and their acceptance that Kongzi was the paragon of teachers and scholars, they would want to claim that Kongzi's teachings had a place in the new society and that his life as an educator and compiler of the classics was praiseworthy and glorious.

All this must have worried those political leaders and radical thinkers who were anxious to see a new socialist China being created quickly. Generally, it was the young who were more impatient for rapid social change, and in his desire to change the conservative Party apparatus at the beginning of the Cultural Revolution, Mao Zedong turned to the young radicals and Red Guards to achieve that task. It was not fortuitous that China's educational institutions and intellectuals were the most severely affected by the Cultural Revolution. Despite the chaos and social injustices that were concomitants of the Cultural Revolution, the radical nature of the whole movement must have seemed, to some people at least, the only way of eradicating the deeply-entrenched conservative attitudes which were so prevalent among China's educationalists and scholars. Nowhere was this conservatism more manifest than in the assessment of Kongzi's thought.

4 Escaping from Communism: Use and Abuse of Laozi and Zhuangzi

DAOISM and Buddhism have traditionally been philosophies taken up by mystics, recluses, and the religious. These two philosophies have inspired the fine arts, many poems and paintings being directly based on their mystical elements. Buddhism, though a significant part of Chinese civilization, was not cited as having any 'inheritable' qualities during the debates on cultural inheritance, partly because Buddhism is more directly a religion than any other school of thought in traditional China and partly because its origins were not considered Chinese. Accordingly, Buddhism will not be discussed in this book. Daoism, however, was the focus of a fierce debate which is intrinsically interesting as well as politically significant.

Of the native Chinese philosophies, Daoism, based on the writings of Laozi and Zhuangzi, is second only to Confucianism in the influence it has exerted on the Chinese mentality. While the other pre-Qin schools of thought considered in this book have traditionally been perceived as 'rational' and 'moral' in their approaches to life, the writings of Laozi and Zhuangzi have been seen as essays advocating freedom from conventional respectability and carefree wanderings in the transcendental realm. For the scholar-gentry, Confucianism was the doctrine which had to be learnt and practised while in pursuit of success through wealth and officialdom. Daoism complemented Confucianism in functioning as an escape valve for a highly bureaucratized society. It was common practice for those out-of-favour officials who were forced into retirement or exile to indulge in activities with a Daoist flavour such as creating poetry or paintings and sometimes even by living as recluses.

It is quite obvious that, in modern China, especially after 1949, such practices must decline. It was difficult, if not impossible, to live the life of a recluse, and mystical elements in writing and painting also came under attack. However, it was much more difficult to stop a scholar fallen from a privileged position from withdrawing into himself and becoming a Daoist with a Marxist face. Different interpretations of the *Laozi* and the *Zhuangzi* since 1949 provide some of the most revealing insights into whether Daoist teachings have continued to be used by intellectuals in such a fashion. The influence of Daoism on Chinese thinking has always been more subtle and complex than Confucianism and Legalism. In the new society, when historians and political leaders have openly advocated 'inheriting' Confucianism and Legalism, that the Daoist legacy is still cherished is only seen through the ferocity with which it was attacked.

LAOZI

In assessing any historical figure and his thinking, one is always faced with the problem of the authenticity and reliability of works ascribed to him. To go from criticizing a work which is attributed to a certain author to criticizing that particular author is a tricky and dubious business. This is especially so in the case of Laozi. The popular image of the mystic riding a black ox into the west after he had completed the *Daodejing*, though capturing some of the other-worldly aspects of 'his' teaching, has very little historical foundation.[1]

It is quite obvious that formulating a critique of Laozi the person is a much more difficult task than composing a critique of, say, Kongzi or Mengzi. Before modern, especially Marxist, historiography, Sima Qian's legend that Laozi had been a keeper of the royal archives who became a recluse was enough to satisfy both scholarly and popular curiosity about Laozi the Daoist. But with the advent of the materialist conception of history, where ideas could only be interpreted as a reflection of their materialist base, the indeterminate nature of Laozi's life and times meant that, even if the periodization debate was settled, there remained the question of identifying the man, but this was not an easy task as there is no reliable biography of him.

Thus, whether Laozi was on the side of progress or stood for the status quo or, more specifically, whether he supported the oppressed or oppressor class, was largely based on the arbitrary interpretation of individual commentators. The Sima Qian version of the *Laozi* suggests that, unlike Kongzi, Mengzi, and Han Feizi, Laozi did not seek an official appointment. The abstruseness and refinement of his writing rule out the possibility of his having been a simple peasant. The alternative is therefore that he voluntarily or involuntarily became a recluse because he was disappointed at losing his social position and privileges.

The period and location in which the book was written prove equally difficult to establish. In discussing the other pre-Qin philosophers, it is often possible to deduce the time and place in which they lived from the works. For example, in the *Analects* and the *Mengzi*, specific rulers and specific places they visited are mentioned throughout the texts. In the *Daodejing*, however, no such detail is given. It is therefore very difficult to tell exactly when the book was written.

Traditionally, it was believed that Laozi was the same person as the Lao Dan mentioned in the *Zhuangzi* (this was also related later in Sima Qian's *History*).[2] Lao Dan was older than but contemporary with Kongzi.[3] In modern historiography, this version was accepted by many influential historians such as Guo Moruo and Lü Zhenyu.[4] Lü Zhenyu claimed that Kongzi's thinking was partly influenced by Laozi, in, for example, the phrase in the *Analects* 'to repay a grudge with virtue (*de*).'[5] A great number of scholars, however, believed that the *Daodejing* was in fact written in the Warring States period, that is, after the *Analects* was compiled. Included in this group were such scholars as Feng Youlan, Fan Wenlan, and Hou Wailu. Feng Youlan, for example, claimed that the *Daodejing* could not have been written earlier than the *Analects* because its style was not in the form of questions and answers like the *Analects* or the *Mengzi*. Feng further questioned whether, historically, there ever was the person Lao Dan.[6] Some historians believed that the *Daodejing* was written even later than the Warring States period. It is also thought that it was probably compiled by not one but many authors.[7]

As the authorship of the *Daodejing* remains elusive, so does the meaning of the text itself. The terse and cryptic nature of the *Daodejing* makes any definitive interpretation of it very difficult. This fact is shown in the hundreds of translations of the book into Western languages since the first Latin translation in 1788.[8] The convenient ambiguity of the *Daodejing* lends itself to any rendering the reader sees fit. Even in pre-Qin times, Han Feizi was able to interpret the *Daodejing* to fit in with his own philosophy of material power,[9] while Zhuangzi made the *Daodejing* a Daoist classic. Among scholars in the West too there are many interpretations, with the religiously inclined, such as the missionary Blakney, seeing the *Daodejing* as a sacred scripture.[10]

With the Marxist historians, of course, the point of departure for analysing the thinking behind the text is one based on class analysis and the political role it has played in history. For example, Fan Wenlan claimed that, in encouraging people to 'do nothing', Laozi was in fact urging people to return to the life-style of primitive societies, where

people restrict themselves to remote places, and live always in extremely poor conditions. They are solitary and have nothing to do with one another. Laozi saw as harmful the important ingredients of hope and struggle which are necessary for social progress. Such thinking is that of the declining lords.[11]

This kind of reasoning was typical of those who believed that Laozi was on the side of the oppressor class. It is not a strong argument, merely superimposing a class analysis on a traditional interpretation which itself still needed to be validated. Traditionally, of course, scholars were not interested in which class Laozi represented, for this was a problem which became mandatory only after the Communist victory. Thus, when left-wing scholars like Fan Wenlan and Lü Zhenyu first wrote on Laozi's class origin before 1949, their analyses, though influential, only came as part of their general texts on the history of China and were neither detailed nor convincing.

It was not until 1959, when a seminar was organized to discuss Laozi's thinking, that Tang Yijie wrote an article devoted entirely to the question of the class nature of Laozi's thought. In this article Tang Yijie tried to establish that Laozi's thinking worked in the interests of the ruling class. Using a line of argument similar to the traditional Legalist one, he viewed the *Daodejing* as a manual for government and contended that it was 'not on how to develop oneself, but on how to maintain one's position.' Tang's analysis brought out a point similar to one made about the *Analects* by Zhao Jibin, that is, that the *Daodejing* made a distinction between 'I' (*wo*) and 'people' (*min*). According to Tang, *wo* represented the ruler and *min* the slaves. In addition, the text made a distinction between 'the sage' (*shengren*) and the people. Tang Yijie quoted several examples from the *Daodejing* which illustrated ways for the sage to rule.[12] Although Tang's argument is relatively simple, it was nevertheless one of the very few essays which actually tried to prove that Laozi worked on behalf of the ruling class instead of just categorically stating this.

Interestingly, in other articles written by Tang Yijie on Laozi, he argued that Laozi was a materialist.[13] This would have been inconceivable a few years later, when the equation of materialism with progress and idealism with reactionary politics became much more rigidly applied. However, at this stage, it was still possible to say that a philosopher was a materialist even though he stood on the side of the ruling class. Tang tried to excuse this position by saying that Laozi, unlike Wang Chong and Fan Zhen,[14] espoused a materialism which was not active and which had no fighting spirit.[15] Other historians also made the claim that Laozi was both materialist and a member of the declining aristocracy;[16] Tang Yijie, however, again made an attempt to argue this position rather than simply stating it.

Many scholars working on Laozi were not in the least interested in the problem of class background or the debate between materialism and idealism, and preferred to pay nothing but lip service to the Zhdanov formula. Gao Heng, for example, who in 1940 wrote an authoritative commentary on the *Laozi* which is still widely used today, confessed in the preface to the 1956 edition of the book, 'I had no knowledge whatsoever of Marxism, so that it could be said that my standpoint, my outlook and my methodology in interpreting Laozi were entirely wrong.'[17] However, Gao did not change the content of the book at all. He simply wrote a preface where he added a few interpretations which he considered to be Marxist. One of these was that Laozi was close to the people and hated the ruling class and the corrupt conditions of the time and he therefore attempted to lead the people back to a primitive lifestyle. According to Gao, Laozi's sympathy with the people was praiseworthy, even though his political aims should be criticized.

Although Gao Heng admitted that he did not use Marxist methods when he wrote the commentary on the *Laozi*, his subsequent failure to 'correct' his work before reprinting it was typical of much of the scholarship of the 1950s. As it was obligatory to determine Laozi's class origins, the preface did just that in an almost arbitrary manner. In fact, the idea that Laozi worked on behalf of the people against the ruling class was expressed with a certain amount of spontaneity by scholars like Gao Heng who obviously liked the philosophy of Laozi. The majority of writers did in fact argue that Laozi represented the working classes, but few could justify their belief in a convincing or detailed way.

The most important and influential writer on this topic was the

Russian historian of thought, Yang Xingshun. Though ethnically Chinese, Yang was a Soviet citizen who wrote in Russian. His writings were translated into Chinese and in the early fifties he went to China to lecture on philosophy. In his book on Laozi, which was translated into Chinese in 1955, Yang claimed that

[Laozi] was a real sage. Everything he did was for others and not for himself. He served the people. In order to realize this lofty aim, the sage did not even care about his own life. He had no personal interests. His personal interests were integrated with those of the people.[18]

Yang claimed that in the *Daodejing* Laozi exposed the hypocrisy of the ruling classes and expressed his hatred for them. Such unqualified praise was equalled only later in the early sixties when the same things were said about Kongzi, and in the early seventies when the Legalists, especially Han Feizi, were also said to have cared about the people so much that they were prepared to sacrifice themselves. Although Yang was not Chinese, his sentiments about Laozi were echoed by several important Chinese scholars whose interpretations were sympathetic to Laozi.

For example, Ren Jiyu in his *History of Chinese Philosophy* said that, in the second half of the Spring and Autumn period, when bigger states were annexing smaller ones, resulting in the insecurity of the ruling class, the power of the aristocrats was limited. Thus, many of the peasants became freemen and the common people on the whole were to some extent more independent of their former rulers. Ren Jiyu claimed that Laozi's ideas stood for these common people and their aspirations. That they had wanted to be left alone by the rulers was revealed by the fact that thinkers such as Laozi and others like him who represented them became hermits and recluses, placing their hopes on the 'sages'.[19] Thus, the passivity of Laozi which scholars like Tang Yijie saw as evidence of the despondency of a class in decline is here seen by Ren Jiyu as a positive attribute. Such completely opposite interpretations of the same attribute show the arbitrariness of evaluations of the pre-Qin philosophers.

Elsewhere, Ren Jiyu remarked that, in the history of countless peasant rebellions, many slogans adopted by the peasants such as 'Executing Justice on Behalf of Heaven' (*ti tian xing dao*) had their origins in Laozi and the *Daodejing* and that the '*dao*' in these slogans was the '*dao*' of Laozi.[20] Ren thus developed Yang Xingshun's thesis by saying that Laozi had worked on behalf of the peasants instead of saying that he had worked on behalf of the 'people'. The theory that Laozi had worked on behalf of the peasants or expressed the desires of the peasants was a common one: other authorities like Hou Wailu, Feng Youlan, and Yang Xiangkui repeated essentially the same idea.[21]

There is little doubt that, in the history of China, Daoism played an important role in the lives of the common people. Outwardly at least, the literati-gentry were Confucian gentlemen, while Daoism was practised by wandering priests and the uneducated. Creel calls this aspect of Daoism '*Hsien*' (saint) Daoism and shows that it was quite distinct from philosophical Daoism.[22] So one can surmise that the many slogans adopted by peasant rebellions which seem to have a Daoist ring were really a manifestation of this popularized version of Daoism. Thus, as well as the difficulties involved in determining exactly the author of the *Daodejing* and when it was written, scholars of the work have had to contend with the two facets of Daoism which can be quite different. It seems that, in many cases, writers such as Ren Jiyu have haphazardly drawn on both aspects of Daoism and so weaken their arguments.

If the theses put forward by Tang Yijie, Fan Wenlan, and others that Laozi represented the declining aristocracy were not convincing, theses to the contrary by Hou Wailu, Feng Youlan, and others also lacked validity. Although no final judgements were made on the class membership and interests that Laozi represented, the attempts to define them, though crude at times, did open up new avenues for research. If any conclusions are to be drawn from this debate which centred on Laozi, one could say that, numerically at least, most of the writers seemed to be saying that Laozi was on the side of the peasants against the declining aristocracy. However, there was no revival of Daoism as there was of Confucianism in the early sixties, since the praise heaped on Laozi was on the whole restrained and also because there were no systematic calls to 'inherit' the *Daodejing* as there were for Confucianism.

Laozi the Materialist

Unlike most other pre-Qin texts, the *Daodejing* does not make direct reference to modes of behaviour or knowledge, so that it is difficult to examine Laozi's ethics and epistemology. However, if one looks at the descriptions of the *dao* given in the *Daodejing*, one gains the impression that *dao* is a concept equivalent to either an intangible principle of the universe or existence itself. As such, the *Daodejing* lends itself easily to metaphysical discourse. Also, as the debates on Laozi in 1959 came on the heels of the general discussion on how to treat Chinese philosophy, in which the Zhdanov idealist/materialist dichotomy was a major theme, it was natural that attention should be focused on the idealist/materialist aspect of Laozi's thought.

At this stage, because the Soviet Union's way was regarded as the truly Marxist one, the Russian Chinese Yang Xingshun had a tremendous guiding influence on interpretations of Laozi's metaphysics, for his lectures and writings were enthusiastically received in China. His book *China's Ancient Philosopher Laozi and His Philosophy* was written for the non-specialist, so the arguments presented were not very rigorous, a feature which may have gratified many whose mastery of Marxism was not profound. His translator, Yang Chao, claimed that Yang Xingshun was the first person to have identified Laozi as a materialist.[23] In fact, this is not correct. In the thirties, Chen Boda had written two articles on the materialism of pre-Qin philosophy, one specifically on the philosophy of Laozi. Chen Boda claimed that the distinctions Laozi made between *ming* (name), *shi* (matter), and *dao* meant that he was a materialist, although in the end he held on to some of the trappings of idealism because of the limitations on him as a thinker of so long ago.[24] Chen's articles were not well-known, but more meticulous scholars must have been aware of his arguments, as his political position was such an important one.

Be that as it may, Yang Xingshun's book was certainly highly influential and his arguments were adopted by many people. Yang Xingshun claimed that, according to Laozi, everything was made up of minute particles called '*qi*' (gas, air) and that '*tian*' (heaven, nature) and '*dao*' (way, laws) gave rise to '*tiandao*', which is just another name for natural laws. Thus, *dao* is something like the *logos* of Heraclitus. Yang also claimed that *dao* was like the 'substance' of Spinoza; that is to say, *dao* was the original matter which through its *qi* formed the basis of the universe and gave rise to life and human forms on earth. This, according to Yang, was the meaning of the '*dao* gives one, one gives two, two gives three, and three gives all life' in the *Daodejing*.[25] He also claimed that the 'nothingness (*wu*)' of Laozi was not the same as the 'nothingness' of Hegel, but an expression of natural laws which were invisible.[26]

The references and analogies to ancient Greece and modern

European philosophers were presumably made for the sake of Russian readers. More important, however, is the fact that Marx, Engels, and their successors had already pronounced these philosophers to be idealist or materialist, so that a mere identification of Laozi with them was often sufficient to classify Laozi as materialist or idealist.[27] Argument by analogy is notoriously unsound, but the technique was nevertheless often used by some of the most prominent academics in China. Many critics took this lead and made comparisons of Laozi's *dao* and *qi* with various ancient Greek concepts. For example, some historians who argued that Laozi was materialist claimed that, as well as being similar to Heraclitus, Laozi's philosophy was like that of the Democritus school because his *dao* was like 'atoms',[28] while others who argued that Laozi was idealist claimed that the *dao* was really like the 'numbers' of Pythagoras, which were thought to have mystical qualities.[29] It is doubtful whether many of the historians really understood fully the concepts devised by the ancient Greeks or the modern Europeans when they made these comparisons. It would seem that these Western ideas became mere instruments of convenience to be used in controversies involving idealism and materialism.

Having established that the important concepts of *dao*, *qi*, and *tian* were essentially materialist, Yang Xingshun then went on to say that *de*, another fundamental concept in the *Daodejing*, was the material manifestation of *dao* and was therefore the substance of matter; that is to say, 'the reason why matter is matter is because it has *de*.'[30] This interpretation of the major concepts in the *Daodejing* would probably have been unacceptable to many people because it was so favourable. Because of the cryptic nature of the original text, however, any rendition is possible. The point about such interpretations at this time, however, was that they were to determine whether or not Laozi and his teachings were officially 'inheritable'.

Often, in their desire to 'inherit' a certain philosopher's thinking, writers would make exaggerated claims for the merits of that philosopher. When Ren Jiyu wrote his book on Laozi in 1956, he claimed that Laozi was 'the first spontaneous dialectician and simple materialist philosopher in the world. We should seek truth from the facts and let this truth be revealed to the whole world.'[31] He was immediately attacked for praising Laozi in such an unqualified manner by Yang Liuqiao, who remarked that at least Yang Xingshun was careful to say that Laozi had idealistic tendencies.[32]

In fact, Ren Jiyu did make this point about Laozi, but his enthusiastic appraisal of the *Daodejing* probably irritated many of his fellow academics.

Ren argued that, even with the difficulties of acquiring knowledge during his time, Laozi was able to perceive that everything had its opposite and that everything was forever changing. For this, he could be considered the first dialectician in the world. In reply to the charge that Laozi's thinking was passive, Ren argued that, in Laozi's time, people did not know how to cope with natural disasters because of the low level of scientific knowledge, so that the advice to submit to natural laws and regulations in fact implied knowledge of natural laws.[33] Such a feeble excuse was contradicted by Ren himself, who admitted that Laozi did have serious weaknesses in his philosophy because, having discovered the principle of contradictions in nature, he avoided them instead of confronting them.[34]

To the writers on Laozi then, *dao* had two aspects. It could be seen as encompassing the original substance, whether it be the *qi* or the *de*, or dialectics similar to the dialectics of Marxism. So *dao* seemed to encompass both the method and metaphysics of dialectical materialism. Indeed, Yang Chao, in his article, said that in the *Daodejing* the *dao* was both matter which made up the universe and principles which governed nature, and that these two aspects should not be confused.[35] If it were true that Laozi had elements of dialectics and materialism in his thought, no matter how simple, there was certainly some justification for calling him a great thinker for his time and, further, to say that his thinking was compatible with Marxist thought.

In the more general books on Chinese history, of course, Laozi's idealism or materialism was also mentioned, but those works were very often based on Guo Moruo's study of ancient philosophy in which he discussed the disappearance of an omnipotent God from Chinese thought.[36] For example, Hou Wailu, who saw Laozi as idealist, used statements from the *Daodejing* such as '*dao* ... the ancestor of all things,' and 'when things came together, earth and heaven were born'[37] to try and prove that because *dao* gave birth to heaven and earth, it was like the creation by God,[38] so that Laozi must be idealist. Using nearly the same quotations from the *Daodejing*, however, Feng Youlan claimed that Laozi had in fact denied the existence of an anthropomorphic god and thus was materialist.[39] These cosmological arguments were very weak, to say the least. As they appeared in general history books, they were not intended to prove definitely whether he was materialist or idealist. However, such books were important because they were very influential, affecting later discussions on Laozi's metaphysics by people who wrote specifically on Laozi like Yang Xingshun and Ren Jiyu. The majority view of such people was that Laozi was a materialist.

The Critiques by Guan Feng and Lin Yushi

Even though Yang Xingshun and Ren Jiyu had attempted to make some sort of philosophical analysis of Laozi's thought, their books were nevertheless really 'Marxist' biographies in the sense that, like other books of this kind, much discussion was devoted to extra-philosophical themes such as historical background and the historical role and significance of his life and work. As mentioned earlier, the uncertainty of the actual existence of the man Laozi makes such analysis suspect from the beginning. The reliance on this kind of analysis for a 'Marxist' approach was broken in 1959 when Guan Feng and Lin Yushi wrote an article entitled 'On the Idealist Basis of Laozi's Philosophical System' devoted to only one proposition: that the system of thought as expressed in the *Daode-jing* was in essence idealist. They claimed that it ought to be possible to examine Laozi's writings as a philosophical system and thus analyse it without reference to the social and historical background against which it was written. They observed:

Of course, it is important to analyse the period and class background in which a philosophical system is produced. Otherwise, it is difficult to make a fair evaluation of it. But this is not to say that unless this analysis has been done correctly first, we cannot judge whether this system is idealist or materialist.[40]

Like other philosophical critiques of the classical thinkers by Guan Feng, this paper was original and well argued. This fact was recognized immediately, and many articles were written by such established scholars as Feng Youlan and Ren Jiyu to attack it.

The concept singled out for analysis by Guan Feng and Lin Yushi was '*dao*'. The section on the *dao* was divided into four parts, each part on a different aspect. The analysis by Guan and Lin departed from the mainly historical analyses that had prevailed up to that time, being more philosophical and modern in the sense that it was conceptual. Because of this, critics were quick to charge that Guan and Lin had 'modernized' Laozi. One criticism, for example, was that in Laozi's time there were no concepts of space and time, concepts used by Guan and Lin in their essays.[41] Guan and Lin, however, countered that, in Laozi's time, there were concepts which were equivalent to space and time but which were expressed in different terminology. For example, '*xing*' (translated as 'form') was a spatial concept and '*jiu*' (translated as 'length of time') was a temporal concept.[42] Besides, Guan and Lin could have added that it was a philosophical system they were examining, not a historical thesis.

By way of introduction, Guan and Lin used a quotation from the chapter 'Under Heaven (*Tianxia pian*)' of the *Zhuangzi*: '*Jian zhi yi changwu, you; zhu zhi yi taiyi.*'[43] Guan and Lin took the *taiyi* in this quotation as another word for *dao* and they interpreted the passage to mean 'the *dao* is built on the unity of non-existence and existence.'[44] According to Guan and Lin, Zhuangzi was right in saying that Laozi's philosophical system was based on the assumption that the *dao* was built on the unity of *changwu* and *changyou* (non-existence and existence).[45]

If *dao* was *changwu* and *changyou* combined, then it must always exist and exist in itself, never changing. If this were true, they asserted, *dao* then must be a metaphysical concept, and so Laozi's philosophy was idealist. Guan and Lin were aware that 'some comrades would say that *changwu* and *changyou* were not confined to Laozi's thought, and that by doing this, you [Guan and Lin] are using Zhuang to explain Lao.'[46] Guan's reply to this anticipated objection was that this was only by way of introduction and that, besides, it was well known that Zhuangzi had been able to grasp the essential features of most of the pre-Qin philosophers before him. Also, it would seem that of all the pre-Qin philosophers, Zhuangzi should have been the one to understand Laozi best.

Having established, with the help of the *Zhuangzi*, the essential framework of the *Daodejing*, Guan and Lin then began to examine the first chapter of the *Daodejing* phrase by phrase, saying that this first passage was the key to the whole text. They claimed that, unlike other pre-Qin philosophical works such as the *Analects* and the *Mengzi*, where important and unimportant passages were scattered throughout, the *Daodejing* was an entire and systematic philosophical tract and therefore the first passage provided the basic theme of the whole book.

The first sentence, '*Dao ke dao, fei chang dao; ming ke ming, fei chang ming*,'[47] was interpreted by Guan and Lin as meaning that the *dao* which was just an ordinary *dao* was not the never-changing metaphysical *dao (changdao)*, so that if we were to name it, it was not a never-changing name (*changming*); that is, the *changdao* cannot be named. If the *changdao* was so metaphysical that it could not even be named, how should one proceed? Guan and Lin thought that the next sentence in the *Daodejing* was a logical step. '*Wu, ming tiandi zhi shi*; *you, ming wanwu zhi mu*'[48] (interpreted by Guan and Lin as: non-existence is the origin of the universe; existence is the mother of all things) showed that *dao* preceded universal existence. This is because both *wu* and *you* are just different names for *dao* and they are said to be the *shi* and *mu* (the origin and mother) of the universe and all things. The next sentence, '*Gu changwu, yu yi guan qi miao; changyou yu yi guan qi jiao*'[49] is interpreted by Guan and Lin as meaning only when the concept *changwu* is established can we talk about the beginning of the universe; and only with *changyou* can we see its limits. The next and last sentence in the passage, '*Ci liang zhe tong chu er yi ming; tong wei zhi xuan, xuan zhi you xuan, zhong miao zhi men*'[50] (interpreted by Guan and Lin as meaning that, although the two things *changwu* and *changyou* have different names, they are both still called *xuan* and this *xuan* is but another name for *dao*) is, according to Guan and Lin, the final logical step in the sequence. *Dao* is therefore the unity of *changwu* and *changyou*. This fundamental conclusion was what Zhuangzi pointed to, and it demonstrates the thesis of Guan and Lin that Laozi was an idealist.[51]

Even to a lay reader, though, it is fairly obvious that, although the arguments presented by Guan and Lin seem logical, the premises are quite suspect. They have taken many liberties in their definitions of the concepts used by Laozi. Terms such as *wu, you, changwu*, and *changyou*, which ordinarily evoke such mystical connotations in the minds of readers, have been very neatly rendered into modern philosophical language. One of the major criticisms against Guan and Lin was that they had modernized Laozi. This complaint, however, seems to indicate that the critics were not used to 'modern' analysis. It is hard to see anything wrong with giving a classical text a modern rendition and systematic scrutiny.

A more serious problem is the ambiguity in the *Daodejing* itself. Different ways of punctuating the text produce readings that are substantially different. For example, Guan and Lin have read the three characters *chang wu yu* as two semantic units *changwu* and *yu* and the three characters *chang you yu* as two semantic units *changyou* and *yu*. Most commentators on the *Daodejing*, however, have read these characters as complete individual semantic units *changwuyu* and *changyouyu*. According to Guan and Lin, this did not make sense as the unit *changyouyu* meant 'to have desire always', running counter to everything that Laozi stood for.[52]

With the thesis that *dao* was the unity between *changwu* and *changyou* established, Guan and Lin went on to investigate other qualities of *dao*. To begin with, *dao* was *xuwu*, which Guan and Lin interpreted as 'void', quoting extensively from the *Daodejing* to prove this point. For example, '*Tianxia wanwu shengyu you, you shengyu wu*'[53] (Chapter 40) is interpreted as saying that the ultimate source of *dao* must be *wu*, or emptiness.

They then claimed that *dao* is also timeless and absolute, in direct contradiction to views expressed by Ren Jiyu that *dao* moved in accordance with natural laws. Again, Guan and Lin cited numerous examples from the *Daodejing* to justify their argument. For example, '*Duli er bu gai, zhouxing er bu dai; keyi wei tianxia mu*'[54] (Chapter 25) is interpreted by Guan and Lin as: it is independent and never changes, it moves about and never dies; it can be the mother of the universe. The same statement was often quoted to show that *dao* 'moves about' (*zhouxing*). To Guan and Lin, however, the reverse was true: as *dao* is 'independent' and 'never dies', this meant that it is always unchanging and always moves in the same way. In other words, it is timeless and absolute.

Finally, *dao* is the originator of all things. For example, '*You wu hun cheng, xian tiandi sheng*'[55] (Chapter 25) is interpreted by Guan and Lin as: there is something (not necessarily material) which came before the universe, and '*Tianxia you shi, yi wei tianxia mu*'[56] (Chapter 52) is interpreted by Guan and Lin as: the universe has a beginning, the *dao* is the creator of the universe. Guan and Lin claimed that it was obvious from such statements that Laozi thought that *dao* created the universe.

With the above characteristics of *dao* 'established' by Guan and Lin, they then asked the rhetorical question, 'Can such a *dao* be the material atoms, material categories, or objective laws of materialism?'[57] Guan and Lin went on to negate in advance any such propositions, attempting thereby to disprove much of what had been written about Laozi until then.

For example, *dao* could not be the atoms of the ancient Greeks, as some people have suggested, because atoms, though invisible, were not empty, whereas the *dao* was. It was also not the 'apeiron' of Anaximanders because Anaximanders' 'apeiron' did not transcend space and time, as Laozi's *dao* did.[58] By using examples and explanations such as these, Guan and Lin concluded that *dao* could not be a material thing or an objective law of nature. Laozi's philosophy was in fact an 'objective' idealism describing existence objectively but idealistically.

Having established Laozi's *Weltanschauung* (*yuzhouguan*), Guan and Lin then examined Laozi's methodology, not for its own sake but to present further evidence that his metaphysics was idealist. Everyone, including those who were critical of Laozi's theories, had agreed that they were dialectical. However, Guan and Lin commented that, although Laozi talked about the opposites of things, he resolved these contradictions by having an absolute, the *dao*, just as Hegel had an Absolute. Therefore, instead of real dialectics where things evolved and changed, Laozi's methodology was circular. Thus, according to Guan and Lin, Laozi's dialectics contributed to making his metaphysics even more idealist.

The same is true of his epistemology. According to Guan and Lin, in the statement '*sai qi dui, bi qi men*'[59] in the *Daodejing* the '*dui*' should read '*sui*' (way); that is to say, by blocking (*sai*) the way (*dao*) and locking one's doors to the outside world (dulling one's senses), one could still obtain knowledge and be aware of everything. Guan and Lin said that, in the *Daodejing*, each time perception was mentioned, the subject of the action was always *dao*. Laozi thereby denied the experience of the senses, and his epistemology was thus *a priori*. Furthermore, by advocating theories which suggested that sages, like infants, relied on non-rational thought processes, Laozi denied the power of reason and instead claimed that the source of all knowledge was the *dao*. This was further proof that his metaphysics was idealist.

The final section of this lengthy and systematic discussion is on Laozi's cosmological outlook (*tiandaoguan*). Since Guo Moruo first put forward the theory that, by the end of the Spring and Autumn period, belief in a god had declined,[60] Laozi's atheism has been commonly used to substantiate the thesis that he was materialist. Guan and Lin concurred that Laozi had been a positive force in the development of philosophy in this respect and that 'in denying the existence of an anthropomorphic god and advocating natural laws, Laozi's philosophy had some materialistic tendencies.'[61] Unlike most critics, however, Guan and Lin did not stop at this platitude. They pointed out that his cosmological viewpoint was not the most important criterion in determining the metaphysics of a philosopher. Also, although it was true that in Laozi's time people were becoming agnostic, Guan and Lin claimed that those people who were doubtful of the existence of an anthropomorphic god were already by this stage power-holders and that some of them even tried to explain human affairs by looking at social relationships. This showed that even the ruling class had realized that the concept 'god' could no longer be used to help to rule the people and that some other concept had to be invented. Laozi's *dao*, seen in this context, can even be said to have been invented as a substitute for the fallen god. Thus, to Guan and Lin, there was no philosophical justification whatsoever for saying that Laozi was materialist.

Attacks on, and Counter-Attacks by, Guan and Lin

Guan Feng and Lin Yushi were relative newcomers to the field of philosophical investigation. Their article represented a treatment of Laozi which at least in appearance was more Marxist than the rest, and it gave rise to a general reassessment of Laozi. Ren Jiyu, who in his previous essays had examined the historical background and class nature of Laozi in preference to his metaphysics, wrote a reply to the article by Guan and Lin in which he claimed that they had ignored the social make-up of Laozi's time. Believing that one should not simply examine a text but see it in its historical perspective, he cited the case of Spinoza, whom, Ren said, bourgeois scholars had classed as idealist, but he added that 'fortunately, Marx saved him from the idealist camp of the history of philosophy.'[62] In other words, even if a person's philosophy had been full of 'mysterious atmosphere', it should be seen as materialist if it was progressive for its time. Leaving aside Ren Jiyu's illogical argument by the use of analogy and quoting from authority, the problem of seeing the idealist/materialist dichotomy as a descriptive or evaluative device is here clearly revealed. It will be seen later that, in fact, Guan also tried to denounce the Daoists as reactionaries who had left a pernicious legacy, but at least he had chosen to arrive at this position by first analysing that philosophy on its own terms. Ren Jiyu and others who followed the Zhdanov definition closely, however, chose to identify what they saw as Laozi's progressive role in his time and then to say that the philosophy must therefore be materialist. To support Ren Jiyu's view, other factors would have to be taken into consideration.

Ren Jiyu therefore did not attack the problem of Laozi's metaphysics directly. Instead, he argued again that the central problem in Laozi's philosophy was still his 'cosmological outlook' (tiandaoguan) and that Guan and Lin were wrong in dismissing this so lightly. He quoted again the criterion set forth by Engels that, if in a philosophical system the spirit is taken to have come before nature, then the philosophy is materialist.[63]

Whereas Guan and Lin had argued that by Laozi's time belief in god had diminished considerably, Ren claimed that this was not so. Although the word 'god' (shangdi) might not have been used, classics such as the Shijing, Zuozhuan, and Guoyu contained numerous accounts of people directing their hatred and curses at Heaven (tian), which meant they were treating Heaven as god. However, Laozi was the first person to refer to Heaven and Earth as space and to dao as the mother of all things, including god. To Ren, 'Laozi's materialism had remnants of idealism in it and so it was not pure. But at that time, there were no philosophers or philosophical schools that were more materialistic. He was the most advanced of all.'[64]

Although Guan and Lin had stated that they did not 'modernize Laozi', Feng Youlan charged all the writers with having done so because their expectations of the ancient philosophers were too high.[65] Guan and Lin again reiterated their belief that they had not forced contemporary terminology on to ancient thinkers.[66] To Ren Jiyu, however, to 'modernize Laozi' was not so much a matter of modern terminology, but of analysing Laozi's philosophy as a systematic whole in a way which Guan and Lin had done when the Daodejing was not meant to be systematic.[67]

To refute Guan and Lin effectively, however, it was necessary to debate with them on their own ground, that is, to prove either that their premises were ill-founded or that their argument was internally inconsistent. A few people actually tried to do this. For example, Zhan Jianfeng, a specialist on Moist logic, examined the statement from the Zhuangzi which Guan and Lin had taken as the key to understanding Laozi: 'Jian zhi yi chang wu you, zhu zhi yi tai yi.'[68] Guan and Lin had read this as 'Jian zhi yi changwu, (chang)you; zhu zhi yi taiyi.' Zhan Jianfeng, however, claimed that this could be read in at least five ways depending on punctuation and division of semantic units. '*Jian zhi yi "changwuyou", zhu zhi yi taiyi*,' (the *dao* is based on the eternal non-being); '*Jian zhi yi "chang", "wuyou", zhu zhi yi taiyi*' (the *dao* is based on Nature and non-being); '*Jian zhi yi "changwu", you zhu zhi yi "taiyi"*' (the *dao* is based on non-being and its principle is based on the 'extreme one'); '*Jian zhi yi "changwu", "you" zhu zhi yi taiyi*' (the reading of Guan and Lin); and '*Jian zhi yi chang, wu, you; zhu zhi yi taiyi*' (the *dao* is based on the unity of permanence and change, non-being and being, the reading that Zhan himself adopted).[69] 'It is clear,' Zhan Jianfeng concluded, 'that the readings and interpretations of these two statements are very diverse. How can Comrades Guan and Lin use them as evidence?'[70]

As poetry, or as inspiration in philosophical thinking, these passages are highly suggestive, but they do not offer a basis for systematic or definitive analysis. Hu Quyan, for example, questioned the division of the words '*chang wu yu*' and '*chang you yu*' by Guan and Lin into the separate entities '*changwu yu*' and '*chang-you yu*.' He maintained that Laozi was concerned with the problem of desires and that one should adhere to the more commonly accepted reading of '*changwuyu*' and '*changyouyu*'.[71]

Without agreement even on the reading of the *Daodejing*, there was little likelihood of a unanimous verdict on Laozi. Throughout Chinese history, there have been hundreds of different interpretations of the *Daodejing*. Post-1949 interpretations were made even more complex because the metalanguage of Marxism was relatively new to many of the commentators. Guan and Lin, who were primarily trained in Marxism, adopted an approach that was apparently more Marxist, but their attempts for the most part were not appreciated.

Interestingly, the assessment by Guan and Lin of Laozi's position in history was expressed in terms that were not totally negative. They claimed that Laozi's was the first idealist philosophical system in China which was rational and formal. As such, it performed some progressive as well as regressive functions. Zhou Jianren was much more negative about the historical role played by Laozi. He denounced the influence of Laozi as 'reactionary', saying that Laozi's attitudes would be harmful for the construction of the new society.[72]

Apart from these scattered references, however, there was very little actual discussion on the inheritability of Laozi's philosophy.

This was in sharp contrast to the discussions on other pre-Qin philosophers like Kongzi and Zhuangzi. Ren Jiyu had tried to argue that Laozi's philosophy was a valuable heritage not only for China but for the whole world,[73] but there was no concrete discussion as to how to 'inherit' him. Considering that Daoism was one of the main pillars of traditional Chinese thought, this omission seems anomalous, especially when it was at this time that the question of cultural inheritance was in the mind of nearly every writer on philosophy. However, the 'inheritance' issue was in fact raised in subsequent debates on Zhuangzi. Guan had already hinted at this in his article on Laozi,[74] and it was not long after the seminars on Laozi that he published his book on Zhuangzi.

Although the discussions on Laozi lack the passionate intensity that characterizes many of the writings on Kongzi and Zhuangzi, there are a few significant features which are more pronounced than the interpretations of the other pre-Qin philosophers. The analyses made of the *Daodejing* illustrate very clearly the arbitrary way in which academics arrive at 'proofs'. First of all, the indefinite nature of classical Chinese is most obvious in the *Daodejing*, so 'proofs' are often made solely on an acceptance of orthodox interpretations or a matter of political expediency.

Laozi's philosophy has traditionally been seen as embodying the principle that there are no absolute truths apart from the *dao*. From this, some Marxist historians claim that it is dialectical, which many people saw as another word for compromise or 'combining two into one'. No wonder, then, that in the fifties the Soviet Chinese writer Yang Xingshun and his followers in China praised it so much. At that time, relations between the Soviet Union and China were good, and intra-Party strife in the Chinese Communist Party was not yet apparent, so the notion of compromise was still acceptable. Yang Xingshun and Ren Jiyu were therefore not challenged. But, by 1959, when Guan Feng and Lin Yushi wrote on Laozi, the Sino-Soviet split was imminent and the conflicts within the Chinese Communist Party were becoming sharper and more irreconcilable. Laozi was therefore interpreted more unfavourably.

As well as the political implications of the analysis by Guan and Lin, it is interesting to note that established historians such as Feng Youlan had accused them of 'modernizing' Laozi. Guan and Lin treated the *Daodejing* as a philosophical system, and to many writers who were used to talking about ancient Chinese philosophy as part of Chinese history, 'modernizing' the classical philosophers was seen as being unfair. For those who wanted to 'inherit' it, presenting a philosophy as part of a historical process permitted them to say that the system of thought under scrutiny had been progressive in its day, although it might not meet modern standards. The disadvantages of such an approach are many. For Daoism, the historical approach means its proponents often confuse philosophic Daoism with popular Daoism, and 'philosophical' analyses often read like lives of saints and their wonderful legacies. This, of course, was also an inevitable outcome of research which took as one of its aims the idea that some aspects of the past should be 'inherited'.

ZHUANGZI

If it was difficult to arrive at a definitive assessment of Laozi, the case of Zhuangzi was not to be any easier. The *Zhuangzi* contains many internal contradictions, and much of the work consists of fables and allegories. To treat it as a philosophical text is no easy task. Although the early commentators Xiang Xiu and Guo Xiang have interpreted the text in such a way as to give it coherence and to find in it inspiration for their own philosophies,[75] most later writers have been selective in what they took from the *Zhuangzi*, using it either for their artistic and literary pursuits or for their political actions.

Before 1949, left-wing historians in general considered the *Zhuangzi* to be a text revealing the author's despondency in the face of rapid social and political change.[76] For example, Guo Moruo argued that Zhuangzi had attempted to be other-worldly because the latter objected to the corruption and decadence prevailing during his time. As a result of trying to disengage himself from involvement in worldly affairs, a 'crafty philosophy' (*huatouzhuyi zhexue*) evolved. 'For over two thousand years, this crafty philosophy, the ultimate magic weapon of the feudal landlord class, was in fact cultivated by Master Zhuangzhou's school.'[77]

Guo Moruo concluded that Zhuangzi's philosophy encouraged people not to participate in politics and society. This view was a commonly accepted one. Non-participation in political and social activities is of course unacceptable to Communist ideology, so even before 1949, left-wing critics registered their distaste for

Zhuangzi's thinking. However, although these critiques exerted an influence in the People's Republic, they were not written as part of a conscious evaluation of Zhuangzi. This came later. The debate on Zhuangzi's influence on present-day China and his 'inheritability' took place shortly after the articles on Laozi in the late fifties.

The debates on Zhuangzi were also a direct result of the discussions on cultural inheritance a few years earlier. When Feng Youlan was attacked for his method of abstract inheritance in 1958, he wrote self-criticisms not only of this method but also of his past philosophy, which it was claimed had given rise to his idea of abstract inheritance. Thus, in one article, he analysed his pre-1949 books such as *New Rational Philosophy (Xin lixue)* and *New Treatise on the Nature of Man (Xin yuanren)*.[78] Guan Feng immediately responded to this article, saying that Feng Youlan had not really criticized his own philosophy and accusing Feng Youlan of having inherited Zhuangzi's idea of absolute freedom of the mind and spirit. According to Guan, the 'universal realm' (*tiandi jingjie*), which was the central concept of the book *New Treatise on the Nature of Man*, was directly influenced by the *Zhuangzi*. To Feng's claim that his philosophy differed from Zhuangzi's, Guan retorted that 'if there were any differences, then Feng's philosophical system was even more reactionary and degenerate.'[79] In a further defence, Feng Youlan wrote another article entitled 'Queries and Seeking Advice' saying that, although his 'universal realm' might have been mysterious and so idealistic, it was a case of objective idealism rather than subjective idealism;[80] that is, it existed independently of man's mind. However, Guan Feng attacked him again, saying that, no matter how one looked at it, this 'realm' was still false.[81] Feng Youlan continued to disagree with Guan Feng in a later article he wrote with the same title,[82] this time defending not only his interpretation of the *Zhuangzi* but his idea of abstract inheritance as well.

Zhuangzi's influence was not restricted to the field of philosophy. In November 1959, *People's Literature* published a poem by Guo Xiaochuan called 'Gazing at the Starry Sky'. In this poem, Guo Xiaochuan described his feelings of insignificance in looking at the firmament: all the roads and bridges together in the world did not amount to one small section of the Milky Way.[83] Although in the second half of the poem the poet spoke of the glories of the socialist revolution and how human life, though finite, could still conquer space by sending a rocket among the stars, the poem was still deplored by many as lacking in socialist spirit.[84] Guan Feng immediately attacked it also as an example of the complete nihilism and subjective idealism of Zhuangzi. He said, 'A great battle and a bold and heroic ambition is overtaking the whole of China. Yet the author of "Gazing at the Starry Sky" is crying out a completely different tune.'[85] This tune, of course, according to Guan Feng, was Zhuangzi's in that it expressed longing for such nebulous concepts as freedom of mind and spirit. To Guan Feng, this kind of individualistic desire was detrimental to the progress of socialism in China. It is in the light of these political connotations that the debates on Zhuangzi should be seen.

The Authorship of the Zhuangzi

The problem of the authorship of the *Zhuangzi* is particularly complex, even among pre-Qin texts. Although the existence of a historical figure called Zhuangzi is not in question, the book which bears his name shows evidence of multiple authorship. Of the fifty-two chapters mentioned in the *Hanshu*, only thirty-three are extant, grouped into three main divisions, 'Inner Chapters' (*nei pian*), 'Outer Chapters' (*wai pian*) and 'Miscellaneous Chapters' (*za pian*). The 'Inner Chapters' form a reasonably coherent whole, while the 'Outer Chapters' and 'Miscellaneous Chapters' contain passages that often conflict with the general line of thought of the 'Inner Chapters'.

The 'Inner Chapters' include the more 'transcendental' passages such as 'Carefree Wanderings' (*Xiaoyaoyou*) and 'Equality of Things' (*Qiwu lun*). These chapters evoke the image of the Daoist who is reclusive and elusive. The 'Outer and Miscellaneous Chapters' (which are collectively known as the *waiza pian*), which include chapters such as 'Bandit Zhi' (*Dao Zhi*) and 'Thieves' (*Qu qie*), portray Zhuangzi as being much more active socially, even to the point of angrily denouncing those in authority. Although non-co-operation with the aristocracy is consistent with Daoist philosophy, the passive nature of the 'Inner Chapters' makes them quite different from the 'Outer and Miscellaneous Chapters'. It is therefore essential for assessments of Zhuangzi to identify which sections of the *Zhuangzi*, if any, were written by him and which, if any, were written by his followers. The traditional attribution of the 'Inner Chapters' to Zhuangzi and the remainder to later Daoists was accepted by most writers after 1949.[86]

The debates on Zhuangzi in the late fifties and early sixties revolved around three distinct evaluations by Guan Feng, Feng Youlan, and Ren Jiyu. Their assessments of Zhuangzi ranged from Guan Feng's wholesale denunciations of him as a reactionary idealist to Ren Jiyu's appraisal of him as a materialist whose ideas should be inherited. These evaluations depended very much on which chapters of the *Zhuangzi* they took to be authentic.

As in the evaluations of Laozi, the most original interpretive work on Zhuangzi was carried out by Guan Feng (this time without Lin Yushi). He began by stating his reasons for thinking that the 'Inner Chapters' were written by Zhuangzi. First, Guan reasoned that the philosophy expressed in the 'Inner Chapters' formed a systematic whole, revealing a pessimistic outlook typical of the survivors of a declining slave-owning class. As Guan Feng took the end of the slave period as being between the Spring and Autumn and the Warring States periods, then the *Zhuangzi* could not have been written after the Warring States period.

Secondly, according to Guan Feng, the style of the 'Inner Chapters' is characteristic of Warring States writing. For example, in 'Equality of Things', much of the argument was pitted against the Hundred Schools spirit of the Warring States. Also, there was no mention at all of events after the death of Zhuangzi, whereas in the 'Outer and Miscellaneous Chapters' such events were referred to. Thirdly, the 'Inner Chapters' form a systematic whole, whereas the 'Outer and Miscellaneous Chapters' are heterogeneous in style and ideas, pointing to the possibility of their having been written by a number of people. Fourthly, Guan Feng believed that the division into the 'Inner Chapters' and 'Outer and Miscellaneous Chapters' itself gave some indication of authorship. It would be logical for the core of a philosophy to be contained in the 'inner' chapters and further expositions by disciples to be the 'outer' and miscellaneous ones. Guan cited the *Huainanzi* and the *Mengzi* as examples which were also divided into internal and external parts with the inner parts being the more authentic.

As further evidence, Guan listed the different editions of the *Zhuangzi* from the Han to the Qing, pointing out that the inner seven chapters were always seven in number but that the outer ones had varied a great deal, showing that the 'outer' chapters had been altered. Finally, Guan quoted from the Japanese Kōzanji edition of the *Zhuangzi*, which contained an epilogue written by Guo Xiang, claiming that the passages he had deleted came from later writers and abounded in the mysterious and the strange. Guan Feng inferred that such types of writings were, in fact, generally found in the 'Outer and Miscellaneous Chapters', showing that these were the ones that had been changed.[87]

Guan Feng also quoted from Sima Qian's biography of Zhuangzi, which states that three of the 'Outer and Miscellaneous Chapters' were not written by Zhuangzi as the only evidence against his thesis. Sima Qian had stated that 'Zhuangzi had written the "Fishermen" (*Yufu*), "Bandit Zhi" (*Dao Zhi*), and "Thieves" (*Quqie*) to vilify the Confucians, and to illuminate Laozi's teachings.'[88] Guan Feng commented that Sima Qian, having suffered the most humiliating form of punishment in the hands of the Confucianist Han Court, used every means possible to belittle the Confucians. He therefore attributed the three chapters which directly attacked Kongzi to Zhuangzi himself rather than a mere disciple.[89]

Guan Feng went into great detail in his attempt to prove that the 'Outer and Miscellaneous Chapters' were not written by Zhuangzi.[90] He wanted to prove that there was one systematic philosophy which could be properly called Zhuangzi's. This was to be found in the 'Inner Chapters'. As the addition of the 'Outer and Miscellaneous Chapters' would make much of Guan Feng's analysis of the 'Inner Chapters' inconsistent, he was determined to prove that Zhuangzi was not the author of the 'Outer and Miscellaneous Chapters'.

He divided the 'Outer and Miscellaneous Chapters' into six groups on the basis of style or content:

Group 1: 'Joined Toes' (*Pianmu*), 'Horses' Hoofs' (*Mati*), 'Thieves' (*Quqie*), and 'Free and Easy' (*Zaiyou*). These could not have been written by Zhuangzi because in the 'Inner Chapters' the most basic thinking was one of nihilism and denial of truth and falsehood. In these four pieces, however, there is a strong sense of what is right or wrong and what is moral or immoral.

Group 2: 'Heaven and Earth' (*Tiandi*), 'Heaven's Way' (*Tiandao*), and 'Heaven's Movements' (*Tianyun*). Guan Feng believed that these were written by the Song Yin school,[91] which had been quite prominent in the Warring States period. He listed several reasons for his belief. In these three pieces, the most fundamental concept was Heaven (*tian*), but for both Laozi and Zhuangzi, it was *dao*. *Tian* or *tiandi*, however, were important concepts for the Song Yin school, suggesting that these pieces belonged to this school of thought.

Group 3: 'Engraving the Will' (*Ke yi*) and 'Cultivating the Personality' (*Shanxing*). These two pieces were written in a very clumsy style which made it obvious that they were not written by Zhuangzi.

Group 4: 'Autumn Waters' (*Qiushui*), 'Ultimate Joy' (*Zhile*), 'Access to Life' (*Dasheng*), 'Trees in the Hills' (*Shanmu*), 'Tian Zifang' (*Tian Zifang*), 'Knowledge Wandered North' (*Zhibeiyou*), and 'Gengsang Chu' (*Gengsang Chu*). These seven pieces were grouped together because Guan Feng believed that they had the same ideology as the 'Inner Chapters'. He went through each chapter and showed how all of them developed and expounded ideas and concepts already contained in the 'Inner Chapters'.

Group 5: 'Bandit Zhi', 'Abdicating the Throne' (*Rang wang*), and 'Fisherman' (*Yufu*). Guan believed that these were written by the Yangzhu school of the late Warring States period. Quoting from various sources such as the *Mengzi*, the *Han Feizi*, and the *Guanzi*, Guan Feng argued that the basic outlook of the Yangzhu school was one of egoism (*weiwo*), which was aimed at saving oneself and then possibly the world. This differed from the avoidance principle of the Daoists, and because these three chapters also espoused the principles of egoism, Guan Feng thought it reasonable to conclude that they were written by the Yangzhu school.

Group 6: Others. Although the chapter 'Under Heaven' espoused the same ideology as the 'Inner Chapters', Guan Feng accepted entirely the conclusions reached in Tan Jiefu's study of it which claimed that it was a combination of two other works not by Zhuangzi, the *Hui Shi* and the *Huainanwang*.[92] Guan made no further analysis of this himself. As for the rest of the chapters from the 'Outer and Miscellaneous Chapters', Guan dismissed them as being so incoherent and unlike the rest of the *Zhuangzi* that it was unnecessary to discuss them.[93]

Feng Youlan, whose analysis of Zhuangzi's thought was a great deal more flexible and who did not put Zhuangzi strictly into either the materialist or the idealist camp, said that the two chapters 'Carefree Wanderings' and 'Equality of Things' were historically the most influential.

When we are discussing Zhuangzi, we should dispel the notion that the Inner, Outer, and Miscellaneous Chapters are different and use instead these two chapters as the basic ones. If the spirit of any other chapter is in accord with these two, then it could be used to clarify Zhuangzi's thinking.[94]

Feng Youlan maintained that the division of the *Zhuangzi* into the Inner, Outer, and Miscellaneous Chapters was an artificial one imposed by Guo Xiang and that, although Guo Xiang's is the only extant edition now, there must have been many different versions in the past, so that one could not be absolutely certain which in fact were the Inner and which the Outer. Feng added that, even at the time these works appeared, people were not clear about the authorship. He quoted as an example Qin Shihuang's wish to meet the author of the *Han Feizi*, thus showing that, even though he was a contemporary, he had no idea who the author was.[95]

Feng Youlan's reasons for choosing 'Carefree Wanderings' and 'Equality of Things' as the only chapters clearly attributable to Zhuangzi were simple. He quoted a passage from the chapter 'Under Heaven', which he believed succinctly summarized Zhuangzi's thinking:

Associate only with the spirit of the Universe and scorn the myriads of material things (*Du yu tiandi jingshen wanglai, er bu aoni yu wanwu*). Though living a worldly existence, rise above the level of right and wrong (*Bu qian shifei, yi yu shi suchu*).[96]

Feng claimed that the former sentence expressed the same idea as 'Riding on the path of the Universe and the transformations of the six elements, it is possible to roam the Infinite (*Cheng tiandi zhi zheng, yu liuqi zhi bian, yi you wuqiong*)'[97] in the 'Carefree Wanderings' and that the latter summarized the relativist thinking behind 'Equality of Things'. Feng Youlan added that the passage under consideration was the key to understanding Zhuangzi because it clearly revealed a philosophy which advocated avoiding problems in the world and which was relativist. This, in fact, did represent the traditional view of Zhuangzi. Feng's eclectic approach, while lacking in rigour, meant that he could be flexible in selecting those passages from the *Zhuangzi* which he considered to be consistent with Zhuangzi's thought.

Ren Jiyu, the last of the representative writers on this topic, 'reversed the verdict' (*fan'an*) on Zhuangzi by arguing that the 'Inner Chapters' were not written by Zhuangzi at all, but were forgeries which appeared at the beginning of the Han dynasty and which should be disregarded in order to reveal the real essence of Zhuangzi's thought, expressed in the 'Outer and Miscellaneous Chapters'. In recognition of his departure from orthodoxy, Ren Jiyu began by arguing that the traditional view was incorrect.

He listed three reasons generally used by traditional scholars to argue that Zhuangzi wrote the 'Inner Chapters'. One was that the seven chapters formed a consistent whole and that the style of these chapters also seemed to suggest that they were written by one person.[98] Ren argued that, even if this were true, there was no reason whatsoever to assume that this person was Zhuangzi. Such a rebuttal by Ren Jiyu is weak, to say the least. A second reason given traditionally was that the 'Inner Chapters' were written in so poetic a style that no one but Zhuangzi could have written them.[99] Ren argued that this reason was invalid because, unless it was already known that Zhuangzi had in fact written in a style similar to that of the 'Inner Chapters', the argument was based on false assumptions. Lastly, the most popular reason was that 'in the past people did not doubt it, so now there is no need to doubt it either.'[100] This, according to Ren Jiyu, was naturally no argument.

Of the reasons provided by Ren Jiyu, only the first was really accepted as legitimate by Guan Feng and others. However, it seems rather pointless to say that the 'Inner Chapters' may not have been written by Zhuangzi but by, say, a Mr X. While it would be interesting to have some knowledge of this historical person, what is really at stake is his ideas, not his name. For Ren Jiyu, then, it was more relevant to prove that in fact Zhuangzi had written the 'Outer and Miscellaneous Chapters' and that there was positive proof that he did not write the 'Inner Chapters'. Ren Jiyu proceeded to do just that, citing the same passage as Guan Feng from Sima Qian's *History*. Whereas Guan Feng had interpreted this passage as indicating that Sima Qian did not like the Han Court and its Confucian courtiers, Ren Jiyu argued instead that, as these three chapters did not belong to the 'Inner Chapters', Zhuangzi could not have been the author of the latter.

The *Xunzi*, which was more or less contemporary with the *Zhuangzi*, claims that 'Zhuangzi was obsessed with Heaven and knew nothing about Man' (*Zhuangzi biyu tian er buzhi ren*).[101] Asserting that Xunzi's critiques of the pre-Qin philosophers were generally accurate, Ren Jiyu interpreted the statement on Zhuangzi as meaning that Zhuangzi only knew about the natural order of things but did not pay enough attention to the subjective nature of man. As the 'Inner Chapters' were full of discussion on the subjective nature of man, Ren concluded that they could not have been written by Zhuangzi.

Ren also observed that it was only after the Spring and Autumn period that chapters of books were given titles; before that, chapters were usually referred to by the first two or three characters from the text. As the 'Inner Chapters' had proper titles, whereas the 'Outer and Miscellaneous Chapters' had headings of the latter kind, the 'Outer and Miscellaneous Chapters' probably preceded the 'Inner Chapters'. Furthermore,.

The separation of passages into the inner and outer began in the Han dynasty. Thus, the *Zhuangzi's* 'Inner Chapters' must have been the result of editing in the Han dynasty. Its seven chapters could be called the work of the Later Zhuangzi school to be distinguished from the philosophy of Zhuang Zhou.[102]

If Zhuangzi did not write the 'Inner Chapters', then who did? Ren Jiyu postulated a resemblance to Han prognosis (*weishu*) texts, so that it was possible that it was written by remnants of the slave-owning classes which still existed at the beginning of the Han. This Later Zhuangzi school stressed relativism, sophism (*huatouzhuyi*), and nihilism. Because its pessimistic and passive nature did not suit the Han rulers after an initial period, it was suppressed in favour of Confucianism.[103] Interesting as Ren Jiyu's arguments were, none of them were irrefutable, as Zhang Dejun showed.[104]

In this debate on the authorship of the *Zhuangzi*, the most convincing arguments put forward were those of Guan Feng. As his was also the orthodox interpretation, he had of course two thousand years of scholarship on the *Zhuangzi* to help him to argue his case. Neither Feng Youlan's nor Ren Jiyu's attempts to refute Guan's essays were very successful, and the arguments they put forward to support their own classifications were much less rigorous than his.

Zhuangzi: Progressive or Reactionary

Without agreement on basic texts, discussions on Zhuangzi as a historical figure were bound to be confusing. The 1959 discussions on Zhuangzi rapidly degenerated into personal attacks that at times became quite bitter. The language used by the participants about each other was certainly more impolite than that used in previous philosophical discussions. This intensified debate evolved because the nihilism and non-cooperativeness of Zhuangzi's philosophy were seen to be manifest in each Chinese even today. Necessarily, then, discussions on the inheritability of Zhuangzi became directly connected to personalities involved. While, before, no one had been accused of being a modern-day Laozi or Han Feizi when these philosophers were discussed (Kongzi only became a central figure for debate later), Feng Youlan and the poet Guo Xiaochuan were said to have revealed in their thinking a trait which was definitely Zhuangzian.

All the participants of the debate took it for granted that Zhuangzi lived in the Warring States period around the third century BC, a time when the slave system, according to Guo Moruo's scheme, was a thing of the past. Although there was more information on the family background and life of Zhuangzi than Laozi, this information was ambiguous and scanty enough for there to be very different interpretations of his class background and historical role.

Guan Feng's identification of the real Zhuangzi was orthodox, but his interpretations certainly were not. He claimed that Zhuangzi was a representative of the once powerful slave-owning class and that his reclusive attitudes were those of a disappointed, disillusioned person who had lost all hope of regaining a position of power. Unlike Laozi's philosophy, which apparently was not particularly influential in modern and contemporary China, Guan Feng saw Zhuangzi's philosophy as having had a very strong influence even up to the present. A dominant trait embodied in Zhuangzi's thought, according to Guan Feng, was his Ah Q spirit, that is, the claim to 'spiritual victory'.[105]

Thus, the progression from Kongzi to Laozi to Zhuangzi fitted neatly into Guo Moruo's periodization scheme. Kongzi, who had lived at the end of the Spring and Autumn era, had seen the collapse of the slave society and had tried his best to prevent this from happening. Laozi, coming after Kongzi, saw that the slave society had almost completely collapsed, and his had been its swan-song. By the early Warring States period, when Zhuangzi came on the scene, slave society was a thing of the past and there was no hope of reviving it. What Zhuangzi did was to retreat into his mind and invent a philosophy of moral victory in a world which to him was utterly chaotic and immoral.

At a time when the slave-owners were in effect finished economically and the world of the slave-owners was gone forever, many intellectuals joined the ranks of the newly arisen landlord class. Yet Zhuangzi refused to attach himself to the landlords and he also refused to attach himself to the peasants.[106]

Presumably, this meant that Zhuangzi was more reactionary than Kongzi and Laozi, as the latter were living in times when intellectuals were not certain which class was gaining supremacy. To Guan Feng, Zhuangzi was the ultimate reactionary.

This neat progression of the history of thought which Guan Feng formulated for the pre-Qin era depended entirely on the validity of Guo Moruo's periodization scheme. Guan Feng himself was aware of this when he remarked that the study of the history of thought could help the 'periodization' problem, that is, research into the superstructure could help to determine the economic base. Conscious of possible heterodoxy, he pointed out that 'when treating this problem, historians of philosophy should not passively wait for the scientific conclusions of general historians because they are afraid of making mistakes.'[107]

Looking at the interpretations of Zhuangzi's class background that were made at that time, however, few writers were afraid of making mistakes in determining the class that Zhuangzi belonged to. Feng Youlan, for example, agreed with Guan Feng in saying that Zhuangzi's pessimistic and nihilistic views were those of a declining slave-owning aristocracy.[108] He also agreed with Guan Feng on the 'spiritual victory' mentality of Zhuangzi.[109] However, he qualified his denunciations of Zhuangzi by saying that, under certain historical conditions, Zhuangzi's philosophy could have had an opposite effect from its original intent and therefore in fact had a positive influence:

The target of Zhuangzi's ridicule and the people whose positions his philosophy threatened at that time were members of the newly arisen landlord class. This class was then progressive, and its opposition was reactionary. But after the Qin and Han dynasties, the two opposing classes changed their characteristics by becoming the opposite of what they had been. The feudal landlord class became reactionary after it achieved power, so that that which had ridiculed and threatened it had to a certain extent a positive significance.[110]

Thus, Feng Youlan believed that, although Zhuangzi's philosophy might have been reactionary for the Warring States period, it had become progressive by the Han dynasty.

Tang Yijie challenged this contention by saying that

in the early part of the Han dynasty, the thought of Huangdi and Laozi (Huang-Lao school) had been used as the ruling ideology,[111] but there were no indications that the thinking of Zhuangzi had been used at all.

The main reason for adopting Huang-Lao thought was to revive and to a certain extent to develop production. The core of Huang-Lao thought was to ask rulers not to interfere too much with labourers, and this suited the demands of a feudal society which had just been established after many years of warfare.[112]

Tang went on to say that Zhuangzi's ideas were self-deceptive, and that, as far as the people were concerned, the consequences of Zhuangzi's ideas were even worse, because they encouraged people to become more passive in the face of class struggle. Hence, the thinking of both Zhuangzi and Kongzi was adopted by the ruling classes in both the slave and feudal periods. Feng Youlan was therefore wrong in his reasoning that Zhuangzi's thought could become progressive in certain situations.

The accusation that Zhuangzi's thinking encouraged people to be passive and so meekly submit to tyranny was a very common one. Some people who tried to defend Zhuangzi did so not on his political or social theory, but on the basis of his philosophical thought. Ren Jiyu was perhaps the most representative of these. As early as 1957, Ren said that people only saw the passive element of Zhuangzi and neglected the most valuable aspect of his thought, namely, his materialism. Ren agreed that Zhuangzi came from the declining slave-owning class, but added that, by the time Zhuangzi lived, this class was living in poverty so that they understood how the poor felt.[113] This argument was similar to that put forward by those who argued that Kongzi had lived among the poor and had thus evolved a philosophy which had helped the lower classes.

Ren did not change his assessment of Zhuangzi's class nature in 1961. He claimed that Zhuangzi did not act as a member of the declining aristocracy, but as an intellectual. As Marx and Mao had said that intellectuals did not belong to an independent class, this gave Ren Jiyu room to argue that Zhuangzi need not have worked on behalf of the slave-owners. As he pointed out, 'If too much attention is paid to the class origins of the pre-Qin philosophers, then 90 per cent of them could be said to have come from the declining aristocracy.'[114] In those days, peasants lacked the material conditions for producing their own philosophers. They therefore had to rely on thinkers who were from other classes and whose ideas represented their interests. Because of this, such thinkers naturally would have traces of the thinking of the class from which they had originated.

Like his opponents who claimed that Zhuangzi had come from and had represented the ruling class, Ren Jiyu had no reliable documentary evidence to back up his arguments. Ren Jiyu's choice of the 'Outer and Miscellaneous Chapters' as the only chapters which were authentically Zhuangzi's meant that his argument that Zhuangzi represented the masses could be amply supported by textual evidence. For example, Ren quoted the chapter 'Bandit Zhi' where the bandit cursed Kongzi for his hypocritical talk of morality and for not doing any physical labour.[115] Ren believed that Zhuangzi's denunciation of those who did not do any physical labour as being the true bandits indicated that his sympathies lay with the working masses against the rulers. Quoting from other parts of the 'Outer and Miscellaneous Chapters' such as the 'Horses' Hoofs', Ren added that Zhuangzi 'opposed exploitative and oppressive cultures and pointed to the hypocrisy of the morality of the rulers who mouthed benevolence and righteousness all the time.'[116]

Although some people pointed out that Zhuangzi's opposition to the ruling classes did not mean that he stood for the peasants but was only a manifestation of his nihilistic and reclusive attitudes,[117] Ren Jiyu continued to push his case. His third article on Zhuangzi was devoted entirely to Zhuangzi's class background. From arguing that Zhuangzi was sympathetic to the labouring masses, Ren Jiyu went on to say that Zhuangzi's thought reflected the interests of the small peasants. He also argued that, unlike the later hermits who used this method only as a political ploy, in Zhuangzi's time, there were genuine recluses who did not join the ruling class not because of 'sour grapes', but because they sincerely detested the exploitation of the oppressor class.[118] He concluded that this 'individualism' current in Zhuangzi's time was progressive because, at that time, advocating self-sufficiency meant in effect opposing exploitation and oppression by other people.

The evaluations thus far of Zhuangzi by the major critics, though radically different, do not seem to have been directed against one another. There was no debate as such, and apart from Tang Yijie's direct reply to Feng Youlan, the writers seemed to have been talking at cross purposes. Even at this stage, however, it was fairly clear that the disagreements had implications which went beyond mere academic exchange. To a Chinese scholar accustomed to reading the past into the present, Feng Youlan's theory that while Zhuangzi's thinking might have been reactionary in the last days of the slave era because it was used to ridicule the ruling class but that after the new society was firmly established it could have been used to criticize the newly established ruling class had obvious implications for the present. Feng Youlan had already been attacked before for his theory of 'abstract inheritance'. In the debates on Zhuangzi, his defence of Zhuangzi in the face of the vehement attacks by Guan Feng could only mean that both he and Zhuangzi were to be subjected to even more severe attacks.

Zhuangzi: Materialist or Idealist?

The early left-wing critics of Zhuangzi such as Guo Moruo, Hou Wailu, and Lü Zhenyu all seem to have agreed that Zhuangzi was idealist in his outlook. Given that most people used the 'Inner Chapters' as the basic text, this was inevitable. However, these evaluations were only part of more general histories of philosophy. Like the evaluations of Kongzi and Laozi, more thorough analysis of Zhuangzi in a 'Marxist' framework did not come until several years after 1949.

In 1957, Ren Jiyu devoted an entire article to trying to prove that Zhuangzi's philosophy was materialist. He began by observing that Zhuangzi had inherited the philosophy of Laozi. As Ren Jiyu had earlier expressed his conviction that Laozi was a materialist, he naturally went on from here to say that, as both Laozi and Zhuangzi belonged to the same school, Zhuangzi was also materialist. Quoting from 'The Great Master' (*Dazhongshi*), he claimed that Zhuangzi's definition of *dao* was very similar to that of Laozi:

The *dao* is irrational and yet rational. It has no action and no form. It can be given but not accepted. It is attainable but invisible. It is its own source and its own root. It existed from the very beginning, before Heaven and Earth. It gives spirits and gods their divinity, and it begets Heaven and Earth.[119]

Ren says that three points can be made about this passage: that *dao* was a material substance which was infinite temporally and spatially, that it was more basic and more everlasting than gods or spirits, and that, though not perceivable, it was the basis of all material existence.[120]

Using further examples from the *Zhuangzi*, Ren also claimed that Zhuangzi did not use the supernatural to explain the natural, showing that he was an atheist. Ren went as far as to say that to Zhuangzi man was so insignificant in the natural order that there was no way that man could control Nature and that Zhuangzi was thus a 'captive' of Nature. Ren recognized that this was in fact fatalism but, instead of denouncing it as such, Ren claimed here that fatalism meant that Zhuangzi had been correct, because he repudiated the idea of a god and was anti-superstitious.[121] Ren suggested that, although Zhuangzi's materialism was not thorough, his fatalism should still be considered only as a shortcoming in an otherwise materialist conception of the world. Also,

[Zhuangzi] came into contact with the principles of dialectics. He saw that everything was developing and changing; but he dared not face contradictions and tried to avoid them instead. He recognized that in the process of getting to know something, one should try one's best to avoid being subjective and biased, but then he put the matter aside and did not affirm anything at all.[122]

Ren was thus prepared to admit that, despite the basic materialism of Zhuangzi, he lacked a genuine understanding of dialectics and he denied the existence of any truth at all, and in this way had fallen into absolute relativism. This theme was to be taken up later and greatly expanded by those who were critical of Zhuangzi.

Although many astute observations were made in this period about the idealism of Zhuangzi,[123] the most thorough investigation and certainly the most influential came again from Guan Feng. Having already argued that only the 'Inner Chapters' were written by Zhuangzi and that the rest were later forgeries, Guan Feng proceeded to analyse the 'Inner Chapters' chapter by chapter in a book entitled *Translations, Explanations and Critiques of Zhuangzi's Inner Chapters*.[124] In an accompanying article to this book, he attacked Zhuangzi's philosophy, asserting that those who wished to claim that Zhuangzi was a materialist had supported their arguments with sentences taken out of context. His own method was to take the 'Inner Chapters' as an integrated systematic whole and to analyse this formally in much the same way as he had done with the *Daodejing*.

In his discussion on Laozi's metaphysics, the focus was on the meaning of the central concepts themselves, but Guan Feng was more interested here in looking at the structure of the system that Zhuangzi had devised. Other scholars such as Tang Yijie and Yang Xiangkui had attempted to look at the composition of Zhuangzi's *dao*,[125] but not Guan Feng. He began by postulating that Zhuangzi's system was built on the skeletal structure '*youdai-wuji-wudai*'.[126] Briefly, '*youdai*' meant that everything in the universe had something to depend on: its existential self or existential counterpart. By reaching the stage where the 'self' or 'counterpart' became just a part of the universe (*wuji*), where there were no more opposites, however, one could reach the state of '*wudai*', that is to say, the absolute spirit '*dao*'. By saying that the absolute *dao* could exist even in one's own mind therefore, Zhuangzi's idealism was subjective, that is, even worse than the objective idealism of Laozi.

According to Guan Feng, the idealism of Zhuangzi was more despicable than that of the subjective idealism of Western capitalist idealism or the idealism of Mengzi. The subjective idealism of the bourgeois philosophers in the West and of Mengzi was outward-looking, and both sought the material world. Zhuangzi's, however, sought absolute freedom within one's own mind. It saw everything as being empty, life as a dream. To Guan Feng, such a philosophy bred nihilism, the Ah Q spirit, sophistry, and pessimism. It was an idealism which therefore had no redeeming features at all.

Guan Feng claimed that each of the 'Inner Chapters' revealed different aspects of this system. The first chapter, for example, revealed that everything, from the great albatross to the little turtle-dove, had to depend on the wind to soar into the air (*youdai*). Only by getting into one's own mind, without having to rely on anything at all, could absolute freedom (*xiaoyaoyou*) be achieved. This chapter thus talked of the philosopher's aim. Chapter 2, 'Equality of Things', was on epistemology. Zhuangzi believed that, only by destroying the difference between the self and things beyond the self, i.e., *wuji*, could true knowledge be reached. Guan Feng's analysis of the other five chapters followed the same lines, coming always to the conclusion that Zhuangzi must have been an idealist.

Guan Feng attempted to prove that Zhuangzi's methodology was relativistic rather than dialectical and that this gave rise to a view of the world like that of an ostrich with its head in the sand. Zhuangzi held that, since everything could be viewed from opposite standpoints, there was no fixed truth. For example, the living think that death is the negation of life, yet the dead think the same of life.[127] Again, Zhuangzi once dreamt that he was a butterfly. When he woke up, he did not know if he was Zhuangzi who had dreamt he was a butterfly, or a butterfly dreaming he was Zhuangzi.[128]

Sympathetic critics like Ren Jiyu said that Zhuangzi recognized that all things had an opposite and that we should thus avoid biases.[129] However, to Guan Feng and most other commentators, the denial of objective truth was equivalent to idealism. Marxism states explicitly that the world is knowable through practice,[130] and Zhuangzi's philosophy was in direct contradiction to this in its denial of the possibility of knowledge.

'The Sage King' (*Yingdiwang*), the last of the 'Inner Chapters', concludes with a story about Hundun (according to Guan Feng, another name for chaos, Zhuangzi's most perfect state). Hundun, the central emperor, was very good to the kings of the south and north seas, who decided to repay his kindness. They observed:

'Everybody has seven apertures which are used for seeing, listening, eating, drinking, and breathing. Hundun is the only person without any. We will try and open up seven apertures for him.' They thus opened up one aperture each day. On the seventh day, Hundun died.[131]

To Guan Feng, this summarized the whole philosophy of Zhuangzi. It was a philosophy which advocated complete lack of knowledge about the world as being the perfect state of existence. Guan Feng's explanation for such a negative attitude to the world was that, in Zhuangzi's time, the slave system had entirely failed, so that Zhuangzi believed 'that the time he was living in was one where Hundun had already died. He had lost all hope of returning to the Hundun (chaos). This reflected the sorrow of the declining slave-owning class.'[132]

Few writers argued with Guan Feng's devastating criticism of Zhuangzi. Although Feng Youlan later wrote an article modifying his own position, he did not disagree with Guan Feng, but sought 'to go deeper'.[133] Feng thought that the structure built up by Guan Feng, namely, *youdai-wuji-wudai*, should be modified. He argued that Zhuangzi believed that, after achieving the state of absolute freedom (*wudai*), the sage (*shengren*) would still return to his own self, thus 'relying' on himself; that is, the final stage should still be 'something to depend on' (*youdai*).[134] However, Feng Youlan concluded by saying that Zhuangzi's philosophy was one of 'muddling through the world' (*hunshizhuyi*), much the same as Guo Moruo's description of it as 'sophism'. In the end, Guan's assessment was the accepted one, although to people like Ren Jiyu who worked from different sources anyway that acceptance was only temporary.[135]

By 1961, the received verdict on Zhuangzi was Guan Feng's. Guan, in 1959, had criticized Feng Youlan for being influenced by Zhuangzi and, in 1961, Feng admitted the charge. Almost in parody, he remarked, 'I absorbed completely the rotten, reactionary aspects of Zhuangzi's philosophy.'[136] He even gave an example of a friend and colleague who had also been influenced by Zhuangzi in his futile attempts to run away from the Communist take-over of the country.[137] This example points to an important reason for the bitterness engendered by discussions on Zhuangzi. There is no doubt that, when many older intellectuals were confronted by the Communist victory and forced to abandon their former academic pursuits, they retreated into their own inner selves. In the debates on inheritance and the idealism/materialism controversy during the Hundred Flowers period, many actually admitted to having done this. In traditional China, Daoism had always provided the means of this internal escape and Zhuangzi provided the most poetic expression of it.

Although the point was not made explicitly, both the older and the younger writers were aware of the potential subversiveness of Zhuangzi's teachings. Traditionally, the subversiveness of Daoism has been tolerated mainly because it seldom threatened the state. It was, for many, a convenient escape mechanism from the predicament of being a Confucian scholar-official whose observance of all the suffocating social norms must have often been psychologically frustrating and intellectually stultifying.[138] In providing such an essential social function, Daoism served the state as well as those who cherished it. Without Daoism, the life of the scholar-official would undoubtedly have been a much more shallow and colourless one. This explains why, emotionally, Chinese intellectuals have always felt such a strong allegiance to it and why Guan Feng's attack on it, though original, was marred by outbursts which were out of all proportion to the topic under consideration.

If scholars in the past have depended on Daoism as a form of intellectual escapism, they have at least regarded it as a true liberation for the mind to wander in the Infinite. Guan Feng's assertion that this was as self-deceiving as Ah Q's 'spiritual victory' and that the *dao* was an empty crutch on which they had in fact depended when they thought they were free must have dismayed many. Avenues to Western and Soviet ideas were closed or being closed by 1959 and Confucianism had also been attacked in the Great Leap Forward. It was understandable that those who did not embrace wholeheartedly Maoist Marxism would need some form of intellectual and spiritual solace. This explains the slight resurgence of escapist thinking such as Guo Xiaochun's 'Gazing at the Starry Sky'. Guan Feng's savage attack on Daoism would seem logically to force thinkers to turn to Communism because all other channels, including the one for taking flight, were 'banned'.

It is not surprising, then, that Guan Feng's position was adopted as correct. The debates on Zhuangzi finished in late 1961 and early 1962. By that time, the political situation was moving towards the extreme left. As Guan's own position tended that way, it was to be expected that his view would triumph. In fairness though, Guan's position was also the most logically argued and most detailed one. Again, this is not surprising. Guan had adopted the orthodox view of the 'Inner Chapters' as the authentic text for analysing Zhuangzi and his evaluation of Zhuangzi as a philosopher at odds with the world was also a commonly accepted one. He thus had two thousand years of scholarship to draw on to support his arguments.

It is unfortunate that, by linking Zhuangzi directly with Feng Youlan, the debate had begun on a personal rather than an academic note. Although, at this stage, political differences were still couched in terms of scholarly exchange, those who were sympathetic to certain classical philosophers were starting to be given the same labels as the philosophers themselves. This trend developed to such proportions that, by the anti-Kongzi campaign of the early seventies, current political figures were said to have been embodiments of the pre-Qin philosophers.

5 Disinheriting a Neglected Tradition: Mozi in a Continuing Minor Role

MOST scholars agree that Confucianism and Moism were antagonistic schools. Writers as different as Guo Moruo, Yang Rongguo, and Hou Wailu have employed the term 'Kong-Mo' in their works to illustrate the opposition between these two schools.[1] The *Huainanzi* states that 'Mozi studied under the Confucians, and accepted Kongzi's methodology,'[2] so that Moism has been regarded as a development of Confucianism. However, since there has been little other evidence to support this argument, and there is much suggesting that Mozi was hostile to the Confucians, the weight of opinion has been against it. One of the chapters in the *Mozi* is unambiguously entitled 'Against Confucians'.[3] Furthermore, the philosophical foundations and methodology of Moism are very different from those of the Confucian school, as this chapter will indicate. In contrast to the Daoists, who only opposed the Confucians indirectly through such means as parables and insinuations, or the Legalists, whose Confucian and Daoist ancestry has been universally acknowledged, the Moists were the most direct and consistent opponents of Kongzi in classical times.

This is also borne out in the history of the two schools. Before the Qin dynasty, according to Han Feizi, both the Confucian and Moist schools were considered 'illustrious schools' (*xian xue*)[4] but by the Han dynasty, Moism had declined so much that Sima Qian only wrote Mozi's biography as a brief addendum to the biographies of Mengzi and Xunzi.[5] In the Han period, of course, Confucianism had already become the dominant philosophy in China. Nevertheless, the Daoists and Legalists were still given more attention than Mozi, showing that, even at this early stage, the rise of Confucianism meant the demise of Moism. Since then, Mozi, whose teachings directly challenged the Confucians in his time, never regained the status of being an 'illustrious philosopher'.

In the May Fourth movement, some radical writers attempted to revive the neglected tradition of Moist teachings to replace the Confucian tradition they tried to destroy. But this was only a half-hearted affair and it did not get very far. If traditional scholar-officials were drawn to the intellectual snobbery of philosophic

Daoism and élitist statism of Confucianism, the explicit Communist aim of creating an egalitarian and non-exploitative society should mean that if any indigenous intellectual tradition were to be revived, Moism would be a top-ranking candidate. This in fact was not the case. Moist teachings have seldom been cited in the cultural inheritance debate, either favourably or unfavourably. Nevertheless, the reasons for this neglect are illuminating in the context of the question of the place of tradition in present-day China.

MOZI: COMMONER OR FANATIC?

While the exact dates for Mozi are not definite, scholars before and after 1949 have agreed that he lived at approximately the same time as Kongzi, and that he was perhaps a few years Kongzi's junior. This was based on Sima Qian's brief description: 'Mozi was a member of the gentry (*daifu*) from the state of Song. He was good at defensive warfare and was thrifty. He lived around the same time as Kongzi or after him.'[6] Despite this description, some writers believed that Mozi came from the state of Lu.[7] Such slight differences of opinion on the life of Mozi were merely stated and they never developed into the kind of heated controversies that surrounded the lives and times of Laozi and Zhuangzi.[8] There was also little debate on the authorship of the *Mozi* itself. It was generally agreed that the book represented the thinking of Mozi, even though it might not have been written entirely by him.

In comparison to the Daoists, whose social positions were obscure, or the Confucians and Legalists, who either were members of the aristocracy or had held high positions, Mozi and his followers were distinguished by their insistence on leading humble and hard-working lives. They wore coarse clothing and condemned music, indicating that they did not belong to the cultured élite. By his own admission, Mozi was a 'base person' (*jianren*).[9] Despite Sima Qian's account that he was a member of the gentry (*daifu*) then, the prevalent view among modern scholars was still that Mozi had belonged to the lower classes.

Even before class analysis was first used, the traditional view of Mozi was that he had been a member of the working populace. Indeed, the traditional disdain the literati had for physical labour may partly explain why Mozi's was never a 'popular' philosophy.

However, to say that he came from the lower classes is like saying Kongzi had come from the ruling class: there is simply insufficient evidence.

In exploring the question of the exact nature of the class Mozi had come from, Yang Rongguo in 1946 stated that Mozi had come from the lowest possible class and that Mozi was in fact a slave. He argued that '*mo*' meant 'ink' and that in the old days, 'there was a punishment called "ink punishment". This was such that the face of the criminal was cut with a knife, and black ink was used to fill the wound, so that an ink scar would remain.'[10] Also, Mozi's given name was Di. According to Yang Rongguo, *di* meant the feathers of a bird used in the hats worn by slaves. However, Yang Rongguo did not argue this position in any detail, but cited as evidence research by Qian Mu.[11]

If Mozi had been a slave, as was the claim, there remained several incongruities that required justification. Although Mozi was supposed to have led a very hard and frugal life, he was still literate and had many followers. He was able to travel from place to place seeking audience with kings. While the ancient Greeks and Egyptians had had literate slaves who also sometimes acted as advisers, they had normally been captured in warfare or kidnapped. One could, of course, argue that Mozi might have been a slave who had been captured. If so, what was his original class?

Compounding the problems this question raised was the uncertainty of the periodization schemes. If Kongzi had lived in a time of transition, as most people seem to have agreed, and Mozi came after Kongzi, then was his time also one of transition from slavery to feudalism or was the transition complete? With all these problems, it is little wonder that, although Mozi had advocated egalitarian ideals such as sharing out wealth and working for the good of the common people, it was difficult to conclude that he had been a slave. In fact, Yang Rongguo was the only Communist writer to put forward this claim. When, in the 1950s, the periodization issue was becoming clearer and Guo Moruo's scheme was gaining acceptance, Yang Rongguo also changed his stance slightly and claimed that Mozi 'could have been a slave'[12] or perhaps a free artisan.

By 1956, when Ren Jiyu wrote his book, *Mozi*, the observation that Mozi had suffered an 'ink punishment' was denounced as propaganda by 'running-dog scholars such as Qian Mu.'[13] After this, the idea that Mozi might have been a slave was generally dismissed for no better reason, it seems, than that nobody wanted to be a running dog of a running dog. Ren Jiyu himself was not very definite about the class membership of Mozi, saying that he had been a *shi* who was an artisan and who expressed the desires of the small handicraftsmen and ordinary labourers. Ren made the point that, unlike the Confucians, the Moists did not disdain physical labour, and he also contrasted the way the Moists 'wore coarse clothing and ate simply' with the Confucians, especially Mengzi, who had 'several scores of chariots and several hundred followers when they went around trying to get food from the ruling lords.'[14] Ren Jiyu's views were fairly typical of those who wrote about Mozi at this time.

The belief that Mozi belonged neither to the ruling class nor to the lowest labouring classes was based on the statement from the *Mozi* that 'Mozi did not have the concerns of the aristocracy (*jun*) above or the worries of the peasants (*nong*) below.'[15] If he was regarded as a *shi* this would place him in the same class as the Confucians and Daoists. In fact, in most history texts, nearly all the pre-Qin philosophers were described as being members of the *shi*, especially if the writers were unsure of their exact class. However, as the last two chapters have indicated, to say that a thinker was a *shi* is like saying he was an intellectual. The meaning of this term is so vague that in the Marxist class framework it confuses rather than clarifies.

Some attempts were made in the early fifties to define the *shi* class that Mozi belonged to more exactly. According to the chapter '*Lu wen*' in the *Mozi*, Mozi was also a carriage craftsman.[16] This was used as evidence to support the claim that he was a member of the *shi* class which had just emerged from the craftsman class and now was engaged in political activities. Zhang Dainian explained that, by the end of the Spring and Autumn period, the *shi* class had split into three sections:

Some had become members of the landlord class; their representatives were the Confucians. Some had become recluses, and were closer to the peasants and participated in agricultural labour; their ideological representatives were the Daoists. Apart from that, a section of the craftsmen rose to become the *shi* and participated in political activities; their ideological representatives were the Moists.[17]

This identification of Mozi as having belonged to a politically active branch of the artisans was slightly more specific than most of the analyses of his class, which simply stated that he was a member of the *shi*. However, Zhang Dainian also stated that Mozi was close to the peasants and that as well as representing the peasants, he also represented the ruling class.[18] Mozi was therefore seen as representing every possible class at the same time. Such a contradictory conclusion reached by one of the most respected professors at the most prestigious university in China was typical of much of the use of class analysis at that time.

Considering that Mozi was supposed to have been one of the first philosophers in Chinese history to perceive class differences,[19] the haziness and general paucity of analyses of his class membership and class interest were indicative of a lack of interest in Mozi, especially when compared to the huge amount of material on Kongzi and the Daoists. This vagueness could perhaps be understood in terms of the rigidity of the Zhdanov-type analytical framework which the writers felt obliged to adopt. For, to follow strictly class analysis and periodization, Mozi either had to belong to the ruling class and thus be a slave-owner or landlord, or had to be a member of the exploited class, that is, a slave or peasant. The idea that he could have been a slave or peasant seemed ludicrous in view of the fact that he was so knowledgeable and accomplished. Yet to say that he was a slave-owner or landlord would contradict much of his thinking and his life-style and so the vagueness surrounding his class status remained.

In fact, the best analyses of Mozi were those which contrasted him with Kongzi, a method which was traditionally used. Zhao Jibin, who had carried out extensive research on the class nature of Kongzi, listed several reasons why the Moists were what the Confucians would call the '*xiaoren*' (the common people). Although Mozi himself did not call himself a *xiaoren*, what Kongzi in the *Analects* referred to as characteristics pertaining to the *xiaoren* were precisely those qualities that Mozi had advocated. For example, the Moists promoted the idea that one should work for profit (*li*), criticized those in the upper classes, rejected fate (*fei ming*), and advocated productive labour.[20] In an article published in 1963, Zhao Jibin reiterated this contrast between Mozi and Kongzi. He claimed that the difference between Mozi and Kongzi was that the former wanted to change society by revolutionary means whereas the latter wanted to do it by reformist means. As Kongzi represented the aristocracy (*junzi*) and Mozi the common people (*xiaoren*), Kongzi was said to have wanted to preserve the status quo of aristocratic rule, so that his motto was 'to transmit and not to create' (*shu er bu zuo*) whereas Mozi's motto was 'to transmit and also to create' (*shu er qie zuo*).[21] According to Zhao Jibin, Mozi used '*zuo*' to refer to creative activities. Kongzi, however, simply wanted to inherit what was in the *Book of Poetry*, the *Book of History*, and the *Book of Rites*, without himself creating anything new which might threaten the status quo. By contrast, because Mozi was acting from the tangible needs of his time, he was much more prepared to change drastically the existing social structures.[22]

Thus, by arguing that Mozi and Kongzi were political enemies who stood for opposing class interests at the end of the Spring and Autumn period, it was possible to deduce something of his loyalties by using the huge amount of class analysis already made of Kongzi. As Kongzi was said to have worked for the *junzi*, which in general have been seen to represent the aristocrats, Mozi was therefore opposed to the ruling aristocracy. He was a *shi*, which was the same as most of the other classical philosophers. However, he belonged to the lower strata of this class, as he was also a *xiaoren*. This meant that he was close to the *min* (slaves or peasants, depending on the periodization scheme used) although he himself was not one. It was generally agreed that 'although we do not completely agree on the meaning of *xiaoren*, there is no doubt that it is lower than the *junzi* and higher than the *min*.'[23] Of all the important classical philosophers then, Mozi was seen to have been closest to the ordinary people.

As he himself had said that he was a base person (*jianren*), it seems reasonable to expect that Mozi's thinking would be evaluated highly and thought suitable for 'inheriting'. But in fact, this was not the case. Mozi, in advocating a hard-working and frugal style of life denounced 'unnecessary' luxuries such as the arts as represented by music (*yue*). The debates surrounding this, though limited, furnish some of the reasons why Mozi's ideas were not proposed for inheritance.

The pre-1949 edition of Yang Rongguo's study of Mozi made no mention of his condemnation of music.[24] However, in the later editions, Yang Rongguo claimed that Mozi was against the arts because in Mozi's time, music and the arts were Confucian and enjoyed only by the aristocracy.[25] Guo Moruo, however, argued that, if Mozi had opposed music and the arts because they prevented people from engaging in production, this would be reasonable, but as he had opposed all music, it was obviously not just a case against waste, but against enjoyment itself. 'His opposition to music was not simply an opposition to music, but it was completely against all the arts. It was anti-culture.'[26] Guo Moruo argued that people should have a cultural life as well as engaging in production and that culture might even improve productive labour. He concluded that Mozi was only interested in helping the rulers to exploit people by depriving them of cultural enjoyment. To Guo Moruo, Mozi was working in the interests of the ruling class in every possible way.

The opposing viewpoints put forward by Yang Rongguo and Guo Moruo were to provide the basis for a minor debate in the *Guangming Daily* in the early sixties. Jin Zhong, who wrote the first article, claimed that Mozi denounced music only because he thought that music would disrupt production and not because he thought that music was not beautiful to listen to. Jin Zhong quoted from the chapter 'Against Music,'

Mozi therefore denounces music not because the sound of big bells, rolling drums, zither and pipes is not beautiful; not because the sight of carvings and ornaments is not pleasing, not because the taste of fried and broiled meats is not delicious; not because...[27]

It was thus reasonable to assume that Mozi did have an aesthetic sense, unlike the Daoists, who, according to Jin Zhong, thought that the arts only dulled the senses.

Jin Zhong concluded that Mozi had condemned music because he was waging a battle against the ruling classes in all areas, including the artistic field. His claim was disputed by Li Chunyi, who, echoing Guo Moruo, argued that Mozi was against music and the arts because he was only interested in immediate profitability and that anything which did not produce immediate material results was considered wasteful and therefore evil.[28] Because of this, Li thought that Mozi did not appreciate the real nature of music and the arts, which when used properly could lead to social action. In fact, both Jin and Li were in agreement that 'Mozi's mistake did not lie in his totally negating the arts, but in his under-estimation of the social function that the arts perform.'[29]

Even if Mozi was correct in pointing out that the only people who could enjoy the arts in Mozi's time were the ruling classes, it was doubtful whether such a view would be welcome. The attacks on Mozi's appreciation of the arts are important as they help us to

understand why he was so neglected in discussions of cultural inheritance. From its inception, the Communist Party has placed
great value on the arts. Not only has it controlled the practice of
the arts since 1942, but many of the Party leaders have theorized
extensively on the relationship between the arts and social action.
This tendency became even more pronounced during the Cultural
Revolution and when Jiang Qing's 'model revolutionary operas'
later appeared. Another reason is the intellectual, cultural, and
social snobbery of the academics themselves: there was no reason
for 'cultural workers' such as Guo Moruo to want to belittle the
fine arts or underestimate their social function. These considerations partly explain why, even though his class credentials were
the most acceptable of the pre-Qin philosophers, Mozi's thinking
did not arouse much interest in terms of cultural inheritance.

MOZI: FRIEND OR FOE OF THE WEAK?

Like Kongzi, Mozi had a large following while he was alive. Some
writers pointed out, however, that the two groups were very different. To begin with, the followers of Mozi were of mixed background, many coming from the lower classes, whereas Kongzi's
students were from the middle or upper strata of society and were
eager to become officials.[30] Moreover, the relationship between
Mozi and his followers was not a Confucian teacher-student one,
but more like a brotherhood or an independent army: discipline
was strict and personal relationships were comradely. Mozi's followers were prepared 'to go through forests of knives and fire' to
finish tasks assigned to them.[31] Also, unlike the Confucians, the
Mozi school had its own regulations rather than the traditional
rites and codes of the Zhou dynasty.

In this brotherhood, there was one supreme leader (*juzi*), whose
position was similar to that of a modern-day general. To illustrate
the strict discipline of this school, many writers quoted the story of
the *juzi* Fu Huang, whose only son had committed murder. The
king of Qin wanted to pardon him because he was an only son, but
Fu Huang would not give his consent and had his son executed.
According to Moist laws, murder was a capital offence without
exception or extenuating circumstances.[32]

When contemporary historians wrote about this episode, they
inevitably praised the Mozi school for its strict discipline. One

significant feature of this episode which they failed to mention, however, was the fact that, when ordering his only son's execution, Fu Huang deprived himself of descendants, a serious transgression in traditional Confucian ethics. The historians' praise for discipline and loyalty rather than for the basically anti-Confucian stance of the Moists, who did not value the sanctity of the family, is indicative of the values they approved. In a Communist society, discipline and loyalty are still paramount, whereas anti-Confucianism, with its stress on having descendants, may or may not be a virtue.

Mozi was generally seen as having fought for justice for the poor and the weak. Again, the aims of his organization were very different from those of the Confucian school, who on the whole sought political power as advisers to the rulers. One chapter from the *Mozi* which is frequently quoted to show that Mozi worked tirelessly for the benefit of the weak and oppressed is the '*Gongshu pian*'.[33] Briefly, this chapter relates how, when Mozi heard that Gongshu Ban had helped the king of Chu to design ladders to attack the state of Song, he walked for ten days and ten nights to the state of Chu. After much effort, he succeeded in convincing the king of Chu that the state of Song was not worth attacking because it was poor and lacking in resources. He demonstrated the defensive weapons he had designed to repulse those of Gongshu Ban and they proved to be totally effective. Finally, he stated that he had already sent his followers to defend the state of Song in case Gongshu Ban had him killed to prevent him from going there. The king of Chu finally desisted.

This story was recounted in Lu Xun's *Old Stories Retold*[34] and, as many critics have pointed out, Lu Xun preferred Mozi to all the pre-Qin philosophers. This was in keeping with the general May Fourth spirit, which was anti-Confucian but pro-Mozi. In the Communist period, many writers were also impressed with this episode, whole chapters being devoted to discussions of it. For example, Ren Jiyu prefaced his book *Mozi* with this story, adding that 'in order to realize his ideals, Mozi dared to conquer difficulties from which others shrank. He even risked his life to quench flames which were about to flare up into a war of aggression'.[35] Even in general books which were not particularly pro-Mozi, this story was used to demonstrate Mozi's opposition to military aggression and his strong sense of justice.[36]

Mozi's anti-militarist stance was not, of course, founded on this story alone. One chapter in the *Mozi* deals specifically with the subject 'Against Offensive Warfare'.[37] Under normal circumstances, one would expect the pacifist tendencies of Mozi to be looked at approvingly. In traditional analyses, there certainly were no attacks on it. One would expect, therefore, some discussion on how to inherit this aspect of Mozi, yet this was not the case. The praise accorded him was couched in terms of his sympathy for the weak and his sense of justice, not his anti-militarism as such. In the controversies on Mozi, the main point at issue was always whether his stance against offensive warfare was really defensible in class terms.

In the *Ten Critiques*, Guo Moruo indicated that Mozi had only proposed non-aggression because he was working on behalf of the ruling class, and warfare meant damage to property that belonged to the ruling classes.[38] Like his insistence that Kongzi was an anarchist revolutionary, Guo Moruo's theory was an extremely unorthodox and far-fetched one. Yet this interpretation was taken very seriously after 1949 and the debates conducted on Mozi were partly centred on these points.

Zhong Lei, a relatively unknown writer, in an article published in the *Guangming Daily* in 1961, claimed that when Mozi talked about non-aggression he was actually working on behalf of the exploiting classes. This was really a restatement of Guo Moruo's claim. Zhong Lei, however, gave several reasons to substantiate his point of view and hence extended Guo Moruo's argument. He claimed that, when people quoted from the '*Gongshu pian*' to show Mozi's non-aggression, they did not examine the real reasons why Mozi had wanted to stop the king of the state of Chu from attacking the state of Song.[39] Zhong Lei gave three reasons for Mozi's action. First, the state of Chu had a small population and a war would deplete that population even further. Secondly, the battle might not have ended in victory for Chu. Thirdly, the state of Song was poor, so it was not profitable to attack it. If, Zhong Lei reasoned, the state of Chu had had a large population, if success had been a certainty, and if the state of Song had been rich, Mozi might have considered it worth attacking. Thus, the non-aggression of Mozi was not based on the principle of not causing suffering to the people, but on the principle of benefit that one could expect to derive from the exercise. To Zhong Lei's way of thinking, in Mozi's time, benefit was basically benefit in material terms. Zhong Lei went further and argued that as in those days the

common people were in fact slaves without property and the propertied class were the rulers, it was this élite class which had most
to lose from warfare. Mozi was therefore, in fact, working on
behalf of the rulers when he proposed non-aggression.

Published in the *Guangming Daily*, this article reached a wide
audience. While, in 1961, the political situation was relatively relaxed, it was still extraordinary that this old and unorthodox interpretation of Guo Moruo's should find its way into such an important national daily paper. It is especially curious that this happened
at a time when interpretations of Kongzi were increasingly orthodox and traditional. It may be explained partly as a reaction to the
belief that the Soviet Union was becoming revisionist. While there
were as yet no border clashes, the feeling that the two most powerful countries in the world were hostile could not have been very
comforting either to the political leadership or to the intellectual
élite. Thus, non-aggression, while not openly attacked, was understandably dismissed and in its place it was suggested that all countries, even poor ones, should always be prepared for war. The
Guangming Daily received over forty letters commenting on
Zhong Lei's article, but the editors declared that they 'would not
in the near future open a discussion on this topic.'[40] Considering
the huge amount of material published on Kongzi at this time, the
editors' decision displayed a reluctance to 'open up' this particular
stream of Chinese tradition. Like all newspapers, the *Guangming
Daily* was a propaganda organ for the Communist Party. It was,
moreover, aimed at intellectuals. That it was unwilling to discuss Mozi, even though there was an interest in him among the
'masses', indicates that the Party was prepared to encourage a
revival of certain aspects of Confucianism but not Moism.

However, the paper did publish two letters, presumably because
they were the most representative and the best written. One reader, Zhang Dehong, accused Zhong Lei of having been much too
extreme in his criticisms of Mozi. He claimed that, although slaves
had no material possessions themselves, the slave system had
already started to crumble and the feudal period had already begun. This meant that, by the end of the Spring and Autumn period,
new classes such as self-employed artisans (with which Mozi had
often been identified) had begun to emerge. Such people did have
things like tools which belonged to them. Although these possessions did not amount to much, they certainly meant a great deal to
the people who owned them, so that when Mozi advocated non-

aggression, he was also thinking of these people and of ways of protecting their rights and property.[41]

These arguments, of course, are dependent on the correctness of Guo Moruo's periodization scheme. It is interesting to note, too, how some critics were so ready to denounce Mozi because they believed that he had worked on behalf of the slave-owning class. And yet, those who argued that Mozi had worked on behalf of the people were more concerned about establishing that he did not represent the slaves. It made sense to say that the thinking neither of Kongzi nor of the Daoists represented the slaves, but why was it not possible for Mozi to have worked on behalf of the slaves? Later, especially in the anti-Kongzi movement of the early seventies, figures like Bandit Zhi were said to have represented the slaves despite the fact that his eloquence, like Mozi's, made it unlikely that he was a slave. At this stage, however, it seemed that because Qian Mu had proposed the theory that Mozi was a slave no mainland historian wanted to be associated with it.

Furthermore, the confusion over the periodization issue led to muddle-headedness in other areas of analysis. For example, Zhang Dehong concluded his article by saying:

Since Mengzi accused Mozi of having ideas which were 'deviant', and 'Mozi's universal love meant having no fathers,' and that 'such people can only be called animals,'[42] can't these accusations be used as counter-evidence to show that the Moists were in direct opposition to feudal morality?[43]

If Zhang Dehong agreed that Mozi had lived between the slave and feudal periods, then how could he imply that Mozi's ideas were more progressive than feudal ones? This kind of confusion is a result of the rigid adoption of the Marxist periodization scheme, which views history as a linear development and denies the possibility of a 'progressive' ethics in an 'unprogressive' period. The confusion was made worse when historical analysis was mixed up with the question of cultural inheritance.

If the idea that history has a fixed progressive pattern is adhered to too closely, then any war which would 'push history forward' could be justified. Some of the analyses of the Gongshu Ban episode in fact reached this conclusion. In saying that Mozi had argued for non-aggression from the standpoint of the slave-owners, Zhong Lei was implying that the success that Mozi had in dissuading the king of Chu from invasion was a retrogressive step.

This kind of argument 'can use class analysis to justify any act. Another reader, Lü Lizhuo, pointed out this problem in his reply to Zhong Lei:

History proves that, in the internal struggles of the ruling classes, it has always been the labouring people who suffered and were massacred. At that time, the state of Chu was about to attack the state of Song. Mozi, who was living among the people of the lower classes, started from the standpoint of the will of the people and practised what he preached, thereby enabling the people of Song to avoid the disaster of a war, and the massacre of a battle. No matter how one puts it, this was progressive.[44]

Lü Lizhuo also stated that Zhong Lei was mistaken in saying that Mozi would have advised the king of Chu to attack if the state of Song had been prosperous. Mozi used this argument to appeal to the king's greed because Mozi knew this kind of reasoning would work and not necessarily because it was his own point of view. As Mozi had a reputation as a brilliant strategist, this is a plausible defence.

In accordance with the editors' decision, no more articles on Mozi appeared in the *Guangming Daily*, and Lü Lizhuo's useful distinction between means and ends was not discussed further. As the analysis of philosophy became more politicized, what was said was taken very literally, and means and ends in political analysis and action merged to become one single question.

UNIVERSAL LOVE AS UNREALISTIC IDEALISM

Apart from his theories of non-aggression, which have been used often to show the willingness of Mozi and the Moists to endure hardship for their beliefs, another aspect of Mozi which received attention was his idea of love. The central concept in Mozi's theoretical framework is *jian'ai* (usually translated as 'universal love'), which performs a similar function to Kongzi's *ren* philosophically. *Jian'ai* has traditionally been recognized as meaning loving all people, but has been almost totally neglected in comparison with the numerous studies and interpretations given to *ren*. The traditional hostility to Moism arising from Mengzi's statement that the Moists 'have no fathers' has been maintained throughout history, where the dominance of Confucianism spelled the death of Moism. With the establishment of the People's Republic and its ostensible opposition to Confucianism, one would expect a different reception to *jian'ai*. This was, in fact, not the case, and the traditional contempt for Mozi's 'universal love' continued, though for different reasons.

Before 1949, some left-wing writers like Yang Rongguo did in fact interpret *jian'ai* as loving the masses. This was contrasted with Kongzi's *ren*, which was said to have advocated that the aristocratic class should unite together and only love people within that class.[45] In a reference to Guo Moruo's claim that Kongzi's concept of *ren* meant that the latter had discovered man (*ren*), Yang Rongguo stated instead that 'for the idea that man was the real creator of history to be discovered, one had to wait until Mozi proposed the classless *jian'ai*. Therefore, the real "discoverer of man" was not Kongzi, but Mozi.'[46] He concluded that Mozi's *jian'ai* was in fact classless love and that the other elements of Mozi's thought such as non-aggression came from this concern for the ordinary people.

Such analysis was common to many who were sympathetic to Mozi before 1949. Yang Rongguo spoke of love in class terms, but other interpretations spoke of love in terms of humanity. In Western writings that have been influenced by traditional and modern Chinese interpretations on the subject, the usual interpretation is also that Mozi had advocated universal love and that this was a proposal both original and great for his time. Burton Watson, for instance, says:

This is a noble and original ideal indeed, especially when we consider the strife and hatred that characterized the society of Mo Tzu's time. Here at last is a man who dared to look beyond the hierarchical and geographical divisions of feudal society to a view of all mankind united in fellowship and love.[47]

This line of reasoning has some major flaws when seen in the Chinese Marxist framework. The first is the assumption that all pre-modern Chinese history is feudal. The second is that the ideal of universal fellowship and love is a praiseworthy one. The statement that Mao Zedong made in Yan'an in 1942 about the impossibility of universal love in class society had been taken as an indisputable truth in the fifties. Therefore, Yang Rongguo had to change his position after Liberation by saying that Mozi's *jian'ai* had a flavour of class compromise.[48] Thus, a concept which in traditional and modern China was considered good came to be interpreted as something which had no basis in reality in class society.

Because of Mao's doctrine that there could be no universal and classless love, writers who might otherwise have been positive about *jian'ai* began to evaluate it in less enthusiastic terms. For example, Ren Jiyu, who had been so eager to eulogize Mozi's non-aggression (*feigong*), regretted that such a progressive notion had to be based on what he saw as an idealist ideology of *jian'ai*. He added that, because non-aggression was based on *jian'ai*, Mozi was not able to grasp the real causes of war and thus could not eliminate them.[49] Ren Jiyu arrived at this conclusion by adopting Mao's position that any talk of universal love must be idealist. Thus, although Ren was prepared to inherit Mozi's non-aggression, the philosophical basis of his thought was criticized, and there was no question of its being adopted for present-day use. This meant that even those who were most enthusiastic about Mozi were compelled to negate his thinking as idealist.

In order to make *jian'ai* acceptable, it would have to be shown that it was based on class love rather than universal love. Few attempts were made in this direction and most writers preferred to say instead that, because Mozi had lived in a class society of so long ago, what he advocated was in fact for the good of the ruling class. Hou Wailu, however, concluded that Mozi had referred to two different types of people in his chapter on *jian'ai*.[50] As well as meaning 'universal', the term *jian*, according to Hou Wailu, had connotations of being benevolent, fair-minded, and progressive. *Jian* had a negative counterpart in the *Mozi*, namely *bie* (usually translated as 'partial', 'different', and so on). Thus, *jian* described the class of people that stood for progress and reform while *bie* described those who were conservative. In the *Mozi*, terms such as *jianjun, jianshi* and *biejun, bieshi* abound, referring to two types of people in positions of power.[51] Hou Wailu quoted extensively from the chapter '*Jian'ai*' to substantiate his argument. For example, Mozi posited a hypothetical situation to illustrate the differences between *jianshi* and *bieshi*. Suppose there are two men: one of them maintains partiality (*bie*) and the other universality (*jian*). The believer in partiality says:

'How could I possibly regard my friend as myself, or my friend's father as my own?' Because he views his friend in this way, he will not feed him when he is hungry, clothe him when he is cold, nourish him when he is sick, or bury him when he dies. Such are the words of the partial man, and such are his actions. But the words and actions of the universal-minded man are not like these. He will say, 'I have heard that the truly superior man of the world regards his friend as himself, and his friend's father as his own. Only if he does this can he be considered a truly superior man.' Because he views his friend in this way, he will feed him when he is hungry, clothe him when he is cold, nourish him when he is sick, and bury him when he dies. Such are the words and actions of the universal-minded man.[52]

To Hou Wailu then, Mozi's *jian'ai* was not simply a vague notion of universal love, but an ideal for the transformation of social relationships and also an ideal for rulers. Naturally, this division of society was in no way Marxist. Hou Wailu made no claims that it was a materialist/idealist division or that it should be inherited in modern times. Instead, he claimed that, although such a notion was not yet in existence, it was a 'courageous idealism' (*yonggan de lixiang zhuyi*),[53] that is, an idealism which referred to having ideals and not idealism in the philosophical sense.

Even though this interpretation of Mozi's *jian'ai* was highly sympathetic, there was no doubt that *jian* and *bie* were adjectives describing certain types of people; they could not be used to refer to classes in the Marxist sense. Indeed, even Mozi referred to the *jianshi* and *bieshi* not as actualities, but as hypothetical models: *jian*, like *ren*, was a moral rather than an economic concept. On this point, too, Hou Wailu made no mention of the inheritability of *jian*.

However, no matter how *jian'ai* is analysed, there is no doubt that, compared with the other pre-Qin philosophers, Mozi advocated a love that extended far more to the lower classes. It would thus be difficult to argue directly that his was an ideology of the oppressor class. Instead, those who wanted to eulogize Kongzi and attack Mozi argued that Mozi's philosophy was not really applicable in present-day China, an argument which is, in fact, not very different from traditional thinking. Feng Youlan, for example, voicing the feelings of many on this, agreed that Mozi proposed *jian'ai* as a means to help the weak, the poor, and ignorant people. It was thus a theory which was formulated to help the lower classes, the people that Mozi was close to. Feng also agreed that Mozi therefore represented the standpoint of the exploited classes. However, Feng Youlan argued that Mozi's *jian'ai*, unlike Kongzi's *ren*, was not inheritable:

Mozi's '*jian'ai*' has none of the characteristics of the universal form mentioned in Marx and Engels' *German Ideology*. The thinking [which could be described as having a universal form] Marx and Engels described in this work was intended mainly to replace the ideology of the old ruling class with that of the new one. The handicraft small producer that Mozi represented was not this new kind of class.[54]

Feng Youlan took the prevalent view that the new emerging class at the end of the Spring and Autumn period was the landlord class. Thus, as Mozi was said to have belonged to the artisan class and not the landlord class, Feng was able to deduce that his thinking ought not to be inherited. This 'logic' reaffirmed the traditional antipathy towards the Moists in a novel way. By saying that because the class that Mozi represented was not one which was emerging and becoming dominant his thinking should not be inherited, but that Kongzi's *ren* should be inherited because it represented the thinking of a new class which was to become the new oppressors, Feng Youlan has stood the *German Ideology* on its head.

The attacks on Feng Youlan for his earlier proposals of 'abstract inheritance' and his 'universal form' mainly concentrated on certain aspects of tradition, namely Kongzi's *ren* and Zhuangzi's thinking. His dismissal of Mozi by using the same principles did not meet with any protest. There are several possible reasons for this. One is that Feng Youlan's severest critic was Guan Feng, who did not write on Mozi at all. Because of this, Feng Youlan's negative assessment of Mozi did not encounter the objections of his usual adversary.

For those who wanted to promote traditional values, Feng Youlan's attempt to elevate Kongzi at the expense of Mozi was not in itself objectionable. Mozi had never been popular with the élite, and, in the final analysis, Kongzi's philosophy was much more élitist than Mozi's. In short, those who disagreed with Feng Youlan were not interested in Mozi and those who agreed with him were happy to have the *German Ideology* cited in support of Kongzi compared with other philosophers.

The élitist bias on the part of those who favoured Kongzi was unambiguously spelled out by Liu Jie, who advocated the abandonment of class analysis when discussing Kongzi. In 1963, a year after Mao had announced 'never forget class struggle', Liu Jie still continued to analyse classical philosophy in total contempt of the class analysis. Instead of arguing that the exploiting classes in Chinese history should be denounced, he claimed that sections of these should be eulogized, namely the Confucian sections:

Mozi's *'jian'ai* theory' clearly differed from Kongzi's *'weiren* theory'; Mozi had wanted to look after the concrete interests of the whole people, but Kongzi had wanted to develop a comparatively deep and detailed theoretical system which could care for the people, so he could not but be partial towards those who had a comparatively deep and profound level of thought, that is, those 'wise men' (*xianzhe*) of the Spring and Autumn period.[55]

To Liu Jie, the notion that the whole people could be loved and educated was absurd. He believed that it made more sense to choose a small section of the populace to lead and guide the rest. Thus, Kongzi had 'wanted first to educate a group of politically responsible people, so that they could keep the masses at peace.'[56] The 'group of politically responsible people' Liu Jie claimed Kongzi had wanted to educate sounds very much like the Leninist 'vanguard'. This élitism common to Confucianism and Leninism partly explains why Kongzi, and not Mozi, was 'inheritable' to many Party officials and academic scholars. As well, Liu Jie also agreed with most other writers in dismissing Mozi's notions as impractical because they were idealist and based on concepts such as 'The Will of Heaven'. Thus, while Liu Jie was adamant that he would not use Marxist concepts such as class to analyse classical Chinese philosophy, he was quite happy to use the idealist/materialist dichotomy when it suited his arguments about cultural inheritance.

MOZI'S GHOSTS: SUPERSTITION OR POLITICAL TOOLS?

Mozi was also the only major pre-Qin philosopher who unambiguously and explicitly affirmed the existence of spirits and the supernatural and even tried logically to prove the existence of ghosts.[57] Although Mozi was generally considered one of the most 'scientific' and 'logical' of the classical philosophers, his religious outlook meant that he was normally regarded as an idealist. As with the other philosophers then, the analysis of his metaphysics was often reduced to an analysis of his cosmological and religious theories. This was in line with Guo Moruo's theory that, in the Spring and Autumn period, the deciding factor for determining whether a person was materialist was whether or not he believed in an anthropomorphic god, as that was the most violently debated issue at that time.[58]

Before 1949, when the Zhdanov dichotomy was not so strictly adhered to and when Guo Moruo's influence was not so pervasive, left-wing historians had been much more favourable to Mozi. In his 1946 book *The Thought of Kongzi and Mozi*, for example, Yang Rongguo began the discussion of Mozi's cosmology by saying that his concept of the Will of Heaven was really proposed as a weapon against Kongzi's fatalism. Kongzi, according to Yang, had argued that the Will of Heaven determined unalterably who would be rich and who would be poor. Mozi, by contrast, was against this interpretation of the Will of Heaven, which he saw had been designed to dissuade the people from rising in rebellion.[59]

With this as an introduction to the discussion of Mozi's cosmological outlook, Yang went on to state that, when Mozi talked about god, he was referring to a god that belonged to everybody.[60] Thus, the positing of a god was another way of advocating equality. This had also been true of Mozi's belief in ghosts. Yang Rongguo explained that, before Mozi, people had believed that only the very wealthy had souls and that the lower classes, like animals, had no souls. He quoted a story from the *Zuozhuan* in which the duke of Zheng died and his ghost returned to haunt people. When asked about this, Zichan said that the duke had been wealthy[61] and it was natural that his spirit should return to haunt people.[62] Mozi's belief that everyone had a soul, according to Yang Rongguo, was therefore a progressive step.

Yang Rongguo continued to follow this line of thought in the 1952 and 1973 editions of his book *The History of Ancient Chinese Thought*. This was a very common explanation of why someone as logical and clear-minded as Mozi argued so vehemently for the existence of ghosts and spirits. There were many variations of this theory, concentrating on the view that Mozi had worked out a programme for arousing the peasants to action and that his saying that the Will of Heaven was 'for men to love one another (*jian'ai*) and to be of mutual benefit to one another'[63] was in fact an attempt to use the traditional concept of the Will of Heaven for his own political ends. These arguments were put forward by such influential writers as Lü Zhenyu.[64]

Jian Bozan similarly argued that, by the Warring States period, the authority of the central leadership had declined so much that the vassals no longer feared it, and thus the idea of an omnipotent god above was also similarly discounted. The vassals were thus more and more arbitrary and ruthless in their behaviour. 'The peasants at that time, however, dreamt up a most powerful authority, in order to control the lawlessness of these vassals. And so Mozi's Will of Heaven appeared.'[65] Plausible as these apologetics were in explaining why Mozi had believed in the supernatural, they were really addressed once again to the distinction between means and ends. Even if Mozi had used the Will of Heaven as a means to arouse the peasants to social action, as some commentators had argued, it was still not possible to deduce from this that he was a materialist.

Guo Moruo attacked all these positions in his *Ten Critiques*, although he did not mention by name the authors of these theories except Jian Bozan. After Guo Moruo's onslaught, the general view after Liberation was that Mozi genuinely believed in the supernatural and was thus an idealist. Guo claimed that, even though Jian Bozan's arguments seemed plausible, as both Chinese and foreign peasant leaders had been known to use religion as rallying calls for their movements, the same did not apply to Mozi. According to Guo Moruo, the peasants at that time did not hate the feudal lords or princes but, in fact, cherished them as their recent liberators from slavery.[66] This line of reasoning, of course, was only valid if Guo Moruo's periodization scheme was correct. As Jian Bozan's periodization scheme was not the same,[67] the criticism was not really valid. However, with Guo's scheme gaining wider acceptance, his assessment of Mozi naturally gained more support too.

As to Yang Rongguo's argument that, before Mozi, only the aristocracy were supposed to have had spirits (*gui*), Guo replied that this was simply not true because, in earlier times, the common people had also believed in ghosts. He cited as evidence his interpretation of the character of *gui* as having the shape of a bloated corpse. He also quoted from the *Chuyu*, which mentioned different sacrificial ceremonies for the aristocracy and commoners.[68] To Guo Moruo then, Mozi had genuinely believed in the supernatural and the Will of Heaven. Guo claimed that the Will of Heaven was the backbone of Mozian theory and that Mozi would not be Mozi without it. The ruler in Heaven was just an extension and reflection of the ruler on earth. Thus, Mozi had in fact tried to use the Will of Heaven to keep the slaves in check, so that his ideological position was indefensible, and he was not even a reformist, but a restorationist (*fugu*). The latter theme was later taken up by people like Liu Jie.[69]

The contention that the central core of Mozi's thinking was based on the Will of Heaven became widespread later when it was necessary to argue whether he was idealist or materialist. Almost all writers after 1949 agreed that he could not be discussed without reference to the Will of Heaven, even when they did not take the Will of Heaven or *jian'ai* as the central core of his thinking.[70] Although few people followed the line taken up by Guo Moruo on Kongzi, most agreed with his assessments of Mozi as an idealist. For this reason, it was impossible even to attempt to suggest inheriting his philosophy.

Those who argued that there were aspects of Mozi which were materialist generally concentrated on his epistemology. For example, Zhang Dainian, in his book on the evolution of materialism in China, referred only to Mozi's epistemology in the section on Mozi.[71] Hou Wailu, who tried to argue that Mozi's attitudes to the Will of Heaven and the supernatural were a 'method' and not a metaphysical outlook, could only conclude that one should not therefore label Mozi a 'reactionary'.[72] He, too, concentrated on Mozi's epistemology. Whether Mozi's ghosts were political tools or superstition therefore, the fact that he spoke of them as if they were real certainly meant that even those historians sympathetic to his ideas were obliged to denounce him as an idealist. Because it is universally agreed by contemporary writers that Mozi was an idealist, in terms of the Zhdanov dichotomy and the admonitions by Party theoreticians that idealism equals reactionary politics, it is not surprising that Mozi's ideas were not raised in the inheritance debate. It is a peculiar case where, even when the class credentials of a philosopher fit in with Marxist demands, his failure to meet an arbitrarily defined notion of philosophic progressiveness can be used as an excuse to make sure that his philosophy will continue to be a neglected legacy among Party bureaucrats and academic scholars.

MOZI AND THE LOGICIANS

If there was comparatively little debate on Mozi before the Cultural Revolution, there was even less on the 'Later Moists', Gongsun Long and Hui Shi. Again, this is a continuation of the traditional lack of interest in logic. These philosophers will be grouped together here as 'logicians' because the issues they raised may be seen as logic in the modern sense of the word. These include some paradoxes arising from set theory, semantics, and the relationship between space and infinity.

The modern Chinese word for 'logic' (*luoji*) is itself derived from the English (or Greek to be exact). Traditionally, of course, none of the philosophers mentioned were regarded as 'logicians' as such, and even after 1949, they have been variously referred to as the 'School of Names' (*mingjia*), 'School of Sophistry' (*guibianjia*), or 'School of Rhetoric' (*bianzhe*). In the Chinese, as in the English translations, all the names have connotations of time not profitably spent. This was in keeping with traditional interpretations, expressed most aptly by Xunzi when he referred to Hui Shi and Deng Xi (both logicians):

> they loved to indulge in strange talk and played with curious propositions. What they said seemed profound but did not make sense. They debated much about useless matters, but with few results. What they said could not serve as rules for the affairs of government.[73]

With such interpretations, it is not surprising that very little was said of inheriting the thinking of these philosophers.

Although Mozi was not a 'logician' as such, his writings nevertheless represented some of the first logical and scientific theorizing in pre-Qin philosophy. His style has often been considered lack-lustre, partly because of the meticulous and methodical way in which he made his point. Such a mechanical style may not be inspiring, but it is also characteristic of modern scientific writing.

While there was no debate about his style, his famous criteria for judging the truth of a proposition were the subject of some disagreement. He was the only pre-Qin philosopher who proposed a method, however faulty, for testing the truth of propositions. This was the 'Three Criteria' (*san biao*) test. Briefly, the method stated that, for a proposition to be true, it had to satisfy three tests: (a) the ancient sage kings had to agree with it; (b) the people had to be able to see it as fact; and (c) it had to be useful to the people of the nation. This method was put forward in part I of the chapter 'Against Fatalism' (*feiming*).[74] It was repeated, with slight modifications, in parts II and III of the same chapter. In part II, moreover, he added that the proposition should satisfy the Will of Heaven and spirits as well as the sage kings.[75]

Naturally, this method was far from scientific, as can be seen from the fact that Mozi himself had used it to prove the existence of ghosts. Guo Moruo chose the version given in part II to argue that Mozi was an idealist whose claim to demonstrate truth was in fact a ploy to deceive the people and keep them oppressed.[76] Because Guo Moruo was so totally anti-Mozi, his criticism did not receive much support. Indeed, Zhan Jianfeng, an expert on Moist logic, made the accusation that 'the attitude Mr Guo takes towards "Moist logic" is one of nihilism.'[77]

Most writers argued instead that Mozi's logical thinking had elements of materialism and that his 'Three Criteria' method was a forerunner of scientific thinking in China. Ren Jiyu, for example, remarked that this method was proposed by Mozi to avoid partiality and subjectiveness in epistemological discussions. He added, however, that 'the shortcomings of this method were that Mozi had not implemented materialism right to the end,'[78] a criticism one could level at all philosophers before Marx. Although it was generally agreed that the 'Three Criteria' method was essentially materialist, there was practically no debate about its inheritability, unlike the vast amount of discussion which raged around the inheritability of Kongzi's concept of *ren* and his ideas on education.

Although there was little debate on the 'Three Criteria' method, it was at least acknowledged as having been written by Mozi, coming as it did from the chapter 'Against Fatalism'. The *Moist Canon* (*Mo jing*) had also been traditionally ascribed to Mozi. However, in modern times, beginning with Tan Sitong and Liang Qichao,[79] the *Moist Canon* has been regarded as a work of Moists rather than Mozi himself. Thus, in most modern histories of Chinese philosophy, a special section is normally devoted to the 'Later Moists' (*hou Mojia*). The most representative example is perhaps Hou Wailu's standard work, where he actually tried to demonstrate that Mozi did not write the *Moist Canon*.[80]

Few challenged this widely held idea. The only notable exception was Zhan Jianfeng, whose book *The Formal Logic of the Moists* contains a section dealing with the authorship of the *Moist Canon*. He attempted to refute both Hu Shi and Hou Wailu in some detail.[81] However, even though this was a very substantial book and Zhan's argument was quite compelling, few people took notice of his theory that the *Moist Canon* was in fact by Mozi. This neglect was indicative of the general indifference towards Mozi, and whether Mozi was the author of the *Moist Canon* or not seems to have made little difference to evaluations of him anyway, as there were very few polemical articles on the text.

In contrast to the *Mozi* proper though, which attracted only Ren Jiyu's small book *Mozi*, quite a few substantial and scholarly works were published after 1949 on the *Moist Canon*, mostly in the form of textual annotations. As well as Zhan Jianfeng's book, there are the meticulous studies by Gao Heng and Tan Jiefu.[82] Both Gao and Tan were eminent scholars of classical philosophy. The fact that so many established and careful scholars have worked on the *Moist Canon* shows the prestige which came from being able actually to analyse it, for it is not an easy text to understand. Because of its 'logical and scientific' nature, it was perhaps regarded as a 'safe' project to work on, and there was an almost total lack of polemical essays written about it.

This is not surprising, as the *Moist Canon* is mostly a treatise on logical and scientific matters, unlike most of the other pre-Qin texts, which were concerned with ways of government and conduct. Even Guo Moruo, whose aversion to the Moists was self-declared, found little to attack in the *Moist Canon*, except to say that its contents were very similar to the *Hui Shi* and the *Gongsun Long*.[83] He did, however, manage to conclude his assessment of the Moists by quoting from the *Moist Canon*, 'to kill robbers is not to kill people' (*sha dao fei sha ren*).[84] He claimed on the basis of this that, had the Moists said that to kill robbers was not the same as to kill good people, it would have been all right. But by saying 'to kill robbers is not to kill people,'

they had forced the robbers outside the human species, so that robbers were wild beasts, objects which could be slaughtered without question. This meant that tyrants and ruthless officials had an excuse to treat the people as objects.[85]

This aroused some opposition from those who regarded the *Moist Canon* highly. For example, Zhan Jianfeng claimed that 'to kill robbers is not to kill people' was a misrepresentation of the *Moist Canon* deliberately made by Xunzi, where this quotation could be found attributed to the Moists. The original quotation from the *Moist Canon*, according to Zhan, was 'to kill people who rob is not to kill people' (*sha dao ren fei sha ren*). Zhan argued that the *Moist Canon* thus specifically mentioned that robbers were also people, and that historians, including 'specialists' on the Moists, had been tricked by Xunzi for centuries into thinking that, to the Moists, robbers were not human beings.[86] Thus, what seemed sophistry in the *Moist Canon* was, according to Zhan Jianfeng, very sensible.

To say that the Moists were not sophists is to say that they were different from Gongsun Long and Hui Shi who, most writers considered, had only indulged in sophistry. In fact, many people argued that one of the greatest achievements of the 'later Moists' was their 'scientific' criticisms of Gongsun Long and Hui Shi. The strongest advocate of this view was Yang Rongguo. The chapter in *The History of Ancient Chinese Thought* which deals with the 'later Moists' is in fact entitled 'The Moist School Which Opposed Hui Shi and Gongsun Long.'[87] Just as he had claimed that one of the greatest contributions made by Mozi had been his criticisms of Kongzi, Yang Rongguo now believed that the most important aspect of the Moist school had been its opposition to the 'sophists' Hui Shi and Gongsun Long.

Before the Cultural Revolution, almost all the commentators looked upon Hui Shi and Gongsun Long as having engaged in metaphysical speculations divorced from practical realities. Whenever the idealist/materialist dichotomy was mentioned, they were regarded as idealists. Even those who were favourable to Gongsun Long confined themselves to annotating the text and avoided evaluation of the content.[88] This was because Gongsun Long came up with such propositions as 'a white horse is not a horse'[89] and Hui Shi was famous for seemingly absurd paradoxes like 'I go to the state of Yue today and I arrived there yesterday.'[90] To the historians of early Communist China, who had interpreted materialism as at least something tangible and sensible, such metaphysical propositions could only mean idealism. Hui Shi and Gongsun Long were thus generally condemned as idealists. There was no debate on their relevance to socialist society and no talk of inheritance at all.

Again, this was a continuation of the traditional disdain for Gongsun Long and Hui Shi, most clearly demonstrated in the fact that Hui Shi's pronouncements only survive as cryptic statements in the *Zhuangzi*,[91] and there are no extant texts on how he arrived at his perplexing paradoxes. Similarly, the *Gongsun Long* also only survives as isolated chapters; much of it has simply been lost. It seems that Xunzi's denunciations of Hui Shi were taken literally and few scholars in traditional China indulged in 'strange propositions' that had no practical relevance of a political or moral nature.

Compared to the Confucians and Daoists, Mozi and the Logicians have certainly not aroused much emotion among the conservative or radical intellectuals in post-1949 China. Those who were sympathetic to Mozi, such as Ren Jiyu, wrote only very simple tracts on the subject while those less favourable, such as Feng Youlan, attempted to prove that he was not 'inheritable' in contrast to the teachings of Kongzi. There were no polemics of the sort characteristic of many of the disputes on Kongzi and Zhuangzi. Thus, the traditional neglect of Mozi continues.

It has often been claimed that the *Mozi* displays little philosophical depth and its literary style is pedantic and laborious. These qualities, however, are only consistent with Mozi's pleas for simple living and denunciation of ostentation. Besides, his lack of sophistication is not a reason for not wanting to 'inherit' his thought, because ideologies with much less elegance and profundity have certainly been praised in China. Like the traditional scholar-gentry, contemporary intellectuals and Party officials feel no allegiance to the essence of Mozi's thought because what he advocated in the short term does not benefit them. Being a cultural élite, there is no reason why they would want to 'inherit' a philosophy which, as Zhuangzi observed, 'would make men toil through life, with a bare funeral at death.'

Technicians and scientists may feel some affinity with Mozi because, though he had no time for the arts, he was supposed to have been a brilliant inventor whose approach to intellectual problems was logical and practical. But, traditionally, the artisan class in China has never been in a position of power and, in contemporary China, scientists have joined the élite and, having done so, would naturally not feel inclined towards Mozi's proposals. If Mozi represents the humble man then, as always, Moism will never be popular with writers because, in general, the humble man does not write.

6 Reconstructing Minor Traditions: Mengzi, Xunzi, and Han Feizi

TRADITIONALLY, the schools of thought of Mengzi and Xunzi have been regarded as the two major divergent trends of Confucianism. Mengzi's doctrine of the innate goodness of human nature was diametrically opposed to Xunzi's doctrine of the innate evil of human nature and government by rules and regulations. Although Xunzi's influence was greater throughout the Han dynasty, it was the Mengzi brand of Confucianism which became the orthodox school of thought until modern times. The *Mengzi* has been elevated to a Confucian classic and Mengzi is referred to as the 'second sage', but Xunzi has essentially been neglected and few commentaries have been written on his work. Han Feizi, Xunzi's student, suffered a worse fate than his teacher. Not only did he die a tragic death, but his Legalist teachings, which helped to unify the various Zhou states into the Chinese Empire, had by the latter part of the Han dynasty fallen into disrepute. His open contempt for the Confucian scholars meant that, for nearly two thousand years, his theories of statecraft by the use of power and political manipulation, though utilized by generations of rulers, have never been favourably received.

The traditional views on Mengzi, Xunzi, and Han Feizi did not change markedly after 1949. But in the anti-Kongzi movement of the early 1970s, when Confucianism was completely negated and both Kongzi and Mengzi were vilified, Xunzi and Han Feizi were designated as materialists and Han Feizi's thought was considered the most glorious in China's past. Thus, even at a time when a nation-wide campaign was launched to condemn tradition in the form of Confucianism, another strand of tradition, Legalism, was officially revived and promoted as a philosophy which had a place in present-day China. Although the extraordinary shift in interpretations in the early seventies seemed anomalous, the theoretical justifications for it had in fact already been made before the Cultural Revolution. By grouping these three philosophers together then, the continuing attempts to 'inherit' tradition are brought into sharper focus.

MENGZI

In contrast to Kongzi, there was relatively little written on Mengzi before the Cultural Revolution. Nearly all the major pre-Qin philosophers were the subject of interpretive monographs before the Cultural Revolution, but on Mengzi there were none. The only works on Mengzi were either in the area of annotations or else in translations into modern Chinese. One reason for this is that Kongzi and Mengzi were traditionally linked together so that any discussion of Kongzi automatically reflected on Mengzi. Thus, the term Kong-Meng is still used in discussions of Confucian thought, whereas one rarely sees, for example, Kong-Xun, even though Xunzi was also a prominent figure in the Confucian school. Another reason for the relative lack of interest in Mengzi is that the task of making a positive evaluation of his thinking is formidable. While many have tried to argue that Kongzi was a materialist and that he was progressive politically for his time, Mengzi's explicit statements on the desirability of the division of labour and avowed belief in the Will of Heaven make any favourable descriptions of him in a Zhdanov framework difficult. Because few wrote about him in terms of cultural inheritance, critics such as Guan Feng did not find it necessary to refute anyone. Nevertheless, enough has been written about him to make a brief assessment of the critiques possible.

Mengzi the Philosopher

Although no book-length study of Mengzi was written between 1949 and 1966, the Chinese Department of Lanzhou University published an excellent annotated version of the *Mengzi* in 1960, containing a useful introduction on the dating, reliability, and authenticity of the *Mengzi*. The introduction states that Mengzi was born in the fourth century BC and that he was a follower of the Zisi school of Confucianism, though not necessarily a student of Zisi.[1] This accords with the traditional and still widely accepted account derived from the *Xunzi* and Sima Qian's *History*,[2] although some simplified it by saying that Mengzi was actually Zisi's student.[3]

As to the authorship of the *Mengzi*, the introduction lists three different views. The first is that the *Mengzi* was written by Mengzi himself, as believed by Song philosophers like Zhu Xi.[4] The second view is that the *Mengzi* was written after the death of Mengzi by disciples such as Wan Zhang and Gongsun Chou. Advocates of this view include the Tang philosopher Han Yu.[5] The final view is that the *Mengzi* was written by both Mengzi and his disciples, with the bulk of the writing being by Mengzi himself. This suggestion was first proposed by Sima Qian[6] and was adopted by the Lanzhou University group.[7]

This short introduction was perhaps the most scholarly analysis of the *Mengzi* after 1949. Most other commentators simply took the *Mengzi* as the canonical work of Mengzi the philosopher and proceeded to evaluate Mengzi accordingly. The introduction claims that Mengzi belonged to the *shi* class and that he was an idealist, two attributes which were almost universally agreed upon. Although some people asserted that Mengzi had come from a poor family,[8] the argument is not very plausible. In the *Mengzi* it is stated that, when Mengzi travelled, he had several scores of chariots and several hundred attendants to accompany him.[9] There is no doubt that, in adult life at least, he acquired considerable wealth and privileges, a point almost every writer made. Scholars also compared him in this regard with other pre-Qin thinkers: the Daoists and Moists, for example, were definitely not so conspicuously wealthy.

The popular story of Mengzi's mother having moved three times to gain a good education for her child was still told to children after 1949,[10] but serious scholars could not argue effectively from such tales that Mengzi did not belong to the ruling class. Thus, even those historians most sympathetic to the Confucians had to acknowledge the fact that Mengzi was an adviser to the ruling class. Fan Wenlan, for example, had to concede that 'the fact that Mozi had been seen as an animal [by Mengzi] is because Mozi represented the labouring masses in demanding some political rights'.[11] Like the Lanzhou University group, Fan Wenlan depicted Mengzi as a member of the *shi* class. As indicated earlier, this class was similar to the modern-day intellectual class and most of the pre-Qin philosophers were grouped into it. Being labelled a *shi* was, of course, not so politically derogatory as being called a member of the declining oppressor class, as Zhuangzi was.

Nevertheless, as the debate surrounding the periodization of ancient history developed and Guo Moruo's ideas became more widely accepted by historians of thought, a general class description such as *shi* was regarded as inadequate. Guo's scheme assumed that, by the time Mengzi was teaching, the slave system had all but passed and the landlord class had practically been established in power. It was also generally assumed that the Confucians represented by Mengzi's school and the Legalists were already carrying out an ideological struggle. As both factions were quite obviously members of the ruling classes, the only question for debate was which class exactly they represented. Feng Youlan gave an answer which was to be developed later to extremes:

The newly-arisen landlord class represented by the Legalists was the radical faction of the landlord class ... the landlord class, which had been transformed from the slave-owning aristocracy represented by the Confucianists, was the conservative faction of the landlord class ... Mengzi was a typical representative of the latter.[12]

Given the fact that Fan Wenlan and Feng Youlan were in general very pro-Confucian, their admission that Mengzi had stood on the side of a more conservative wing of the ruling class indicated that, in terms of the historical material available, it was almost impossible to argue otherwise. There was thus no disagreement over the class affiliations of Mengzi. There was also near unanimity of opinion on the question whether Mengzi was an idealist or a materialist, for nearly all the critics agreed that he was an idealist. Traditionally, Mengzi was famous for his advocacy of the innate goodness in man, as opposed to Xunzi's advocacy of the innate evil in man. Statements like 'I possess all the ethical qualities innately and do not acquire them from without myself,' and 'all things are in me,'[13] as distinguishing characteristics of his thought made it difficult to argue otherwise.

Tang Yijie was perhaps typical of those who criticized Mengzi for his idealism. Quoting from the *Mengzi* to substantiate his arguments, Tang said in 1961 that the idealism of Mengzi included his advocacy that political power was bestowed by Heaven. Thus, Mengzi believed that Heaven had a Will, implying that there was an anthropomorphic god. Also, Mengzi's epistemology was against the acquisition of knowledge by experience, claiming instead that knowledge is gained by introspection. Tang therefore concluded that Mengzi's metaphysics was one of subjective idealism and that this directly affected his ethics. Mengzi believed, for example, that man was born with innate qualities and that the character of man was therefore unchanging, which to Tang Yijie was an idealistic belief. Also, to say that there was innate goodness meant that it was possible through introspection to become a moral man, thus strengthening the argument that it was not necessary to seek truth in the objective world.[14]

In many ways, Tang Yijie summarized and systematized the common assessments of Mengzi before the Cultural Revolution. However, this nevertheless provoked a notable defence of Mengzi's philosophy by Zhang Dejun, which appeared in two consecutive issues of the prestigious *Wenhui Daily*. He claimed that Tang Yijie and others were wrong to call Mengzi idealist and that they confused his epistemology with his ethics. For example, one quotation often used to attack the idealism of Mengzi was, 'all things are in me.' Zhang argued that if this quotation was taken out of context, then it was obviously idealist. But if one considered the whole passage, that is, 'all things are in me; reflect and be sincere, then happiness is possible; if actions are forced, then *ren* cannot be achieved,'[15] then the phrase was clearly meant to relate to ethics. To Zhang, this was a dictum on ways of ethical action and not a description of epistemological knowledge.

Numerous other quotations from the *Mengzi* were provided by Zhang Dejun to substantiate his claim that Mengzi was a materialist. One example to show that Mengzi sought truth in the real world was 'Praise the *Book of Poetry*, read the *Book of History*. How else does one know? This way, one can talk about the world.'[16] This example illustrates, in fact, the feeble way in which Zhang Dejun argued. Mengzi was here talking about making virtuous friends, including those already dead. Besides, to equate reading with getting acquainted with the real world is spurious, to say the least. Zhang also gave a rather long quotation to show that Mengzi thought that knowledge could not be achieved without the sense organs:

Therefore, when Heaven wants to give an important task to a particular individual, it will trouble his will, harden his muscles, make him hungry, weaken his body, and make all his actions difficult. In this way, his will will be aroused, his character strengthened and his ability increased...[17]

Zhang concluded from this that 'this attitude of Mengzi was in complete accord with scientific truth,'[18] because only through hard training could one develop one's abilities.

Tang Yijie did not reply to this article. But, in 1964, Wang Zhibang and Feng Guixian wrote a reply attacking Zhang Dejun for 'modernizing' Mengzi. At this stage, the phrase 'modernizing the

ancients' was a common charge against people who tried to interpret the classical philosophers in such a way as to make it possible
to 'inherit' or denounce them in modern Chinese society. In a
sense, Wang and Feng were right in accusing Zhang Dejun of
'modernizing' Mengzi, for the examples he gave did not adequate-
ly substantiate his conclusions. Wang and Feng believed that in
quotations such as 'all things are in me' Mengzi was quite obviously talking about innate qualities of man and not about ethics.[19]

The debate over Mengzi's metaphysics is a good example of the
way in which scholars like Zhang Dejun were prepared to manipulate texts to justify the inheritability of a certain philosopher, for it
is obvious that the *Mengzi* is full of statements which say that man
is endowed with innate qualities. This position had been accepted
as orthodox for centuries and formed the basis of much of traditional education. Claims that Mengzi's epistemology was in complete accordance with scientific truth established nothing more
than the writer's poor grasp of science. Again, it is naive to claim
that Marxist and scientific theories state that knowledge is
achieved only through the senses and that man had no innate qualities whatever. Such weak arguments also reveal the extent to
which historians of thought were using Marxian concepts as value
judgements rather than analytic tools.

Mengzi on Government

As mentioned earlier, Kongzi and Mengzi are normally grouped
together. How is it possible, then, that so much was written about
the inheritability of Kongzi's legacy while the philosophy of Mengzi was rejected as having served the ruling class and idealist? Unlike Kongzi, whose services were often rejected by the rulers,
Mengzi seems to have enjoyed tremendous prestige as an adviser
to the rulers of his time. However, those who were favourable
towards the Confucian tradition were able to salvage Mengzi by
concentrating on the doctrine *renzheng* (roughly translated as 'benevolent government'), much in the same way that they had concentrated on the meaning of *ren* in regard to Kongzi.

The evaluation given to *renzheng* not surprisingly conformed
very closely with the commentators' views of *ren*. According to
Feng Youlan, who had used *ren* as the 'abstract' concept in his
'abstract inheritance' method, *renzheng* was the same as *wang-
zheng*, that is, the kingly way. Feng believed that Mengzi had

defined *ren* as meaning 'not being able to tolerate seeing others' suffering.'[20] On the basis of this interpretation, Feng Youlan gave his own readings of *Mengzi*. For example, 'people cannot tolerate others' [suffering—Feng Youlan's own interpretation], the former kings could not tolerate others' [suffering]; and my government cannot tolerate others' [suffering].'[21] Mengzi's model form of government was thus shown to be based on benevolence.

Feng maintained also that 'the way of loyalty and forgiveness' (*zhongshu zhi dao*) was made into government policy by Mengzi; furthermore, this kingly way was said to have been beyond class. Although Feng routinely pointed out that this was an illusion created by the ruling classes to deceive the people, he went on to say that this idea of government was a 'universal form'. As Feng Youlan had earlier argued that the 'universal form' was inheritable, there seemed little doubt that he wanted to see what he understood as Mengzi's model of a benevolent government inherited.

For those who had interpreted *ren* favourably therefore, *renzheng* took the form of the kind and benevolent ruler who suffered with his people and tried his best to extend the policy of loyalty and forgiveness to his subjects. It was supposed to have been a form of government which restricted the power of tyrants as well, 'placing emphasis on the people, and not on the rulers' (*zhongmin qingjun*).[22] Fan Wenlan similarly believed that *renzheng* was unique in its statement that tyrants should and could be eliminated. He argued that:

In relating the killing of rulers in the *Spring and Autumn Annals* Kongzi admitted that citizens had the right to kill tyrants. Mengzi, following Kongzi's ideas and the ideas of respecting Heaven and protecting the people current in Western Zhou times, boldly developed this thought. It became a most precious political theory during the feudal period.[23]

Whatever *renzheng* might mean, it is true that the *Mengzi* is full of advice to rulers regarding the treatment of their subjects in order to forestall unrest and dissent. But as there is so much that is contradictory in terms of whether it was really the benefit of the ordinary people which was sought, the evaluation depends very much on which aspect the commentator wants to highlight. For example, one other axiom in the *Mengzi* which seems to indicate some degree of democratic thinking is found in the statement that 'the people are the most important' (*min wei gui*).[24] This has been acclaimed by most writers as 'a glorious proposition advocated by Mengzi.'[25] According to writers like Yang Xiangkui and Hou Wailu, although Mengzi emphasized rulers, he also emphasized the people and neglected the feudal lords; that is to say, what he stood for was for the benefit of benevolent sagely kings and the ordinary people and not the real power-holders, the feudal lords.

The fact that Mengzi had stated that 'the people (*min*) are the most important' presented a dilemma for those who wanted to prove that he worked on behalf of the upper class only. This was because, in their discussions on Kongzi, a general agreement had been reached that *min* referred to the class of slaves, so that presumably even by Mengzi's time, they could not suddenly have been transformed into a ruling class. If Mengzi had placed greatest value on the *min*, how was one to attack him?

Yang Rongguo, always critical of the Confucians, sought in 1952 to overcome this problem by arguing that, by Mengzi's time, the *min* or slave class had become freemen, and the term therefore referred to a class of former officials and freed slaves. He argued that, since ancient Zhou times, there had been a distinction between the *baixing* and the *min*, the *baixing* being officials and the *min* slaves. Mengzi, however, had spoken of the *baixing* and the *min* in the same breath.[26] Yang Rongguo argued that Mengzi had used the term *meng* to denote the slaves instead. He gave three quotes from the *Mengzi* to substantiate this view: 'willing to be the *meng* of a single residence'; 'willing to be the *meng* of sages' and 'although one is a freeman, yet one is willing to be a *meng*.'[27] This was simply asserted and Yang's argument was not convincing. *Meng* in the three quotes is dependent on interpretation and does not necessarily mean slaves.

However, Yang Rongguo went further. He equated the *meng* with the *yeren* (translated roughly as 'wild people'), another class of people whose identity was disputed in the discussions on Kongzi. In the same vein as Guan Feng was to argue later, Yang Rongguo held that *yeren* and *meng* were alternative names for slaves. If this were accepted, then it was an easy matter for him to conclude that Mengzi had worked on behalf of the aristocracy, that is, the slave-owners. As clinching proof, Yang and others invariably cited the following quotation: 'There are no gentlemen (*junzi*) who do not rule the slaves (*yeren*), and no slaves who do not serve the gentlemen.'[28]

There is little doubt that Mengzi believed that different classes existed and that certain classes should serve others. What those who were favourable towards Mengzi wanted to show was that the masters were benevolent. Yang Rongguo, however, tried to prove that the oppressed classes were, in fact, slaves. However, the tenuous nature of his arguments meant that, when he reiterated them in 1962 in the journal *Academic Research*,[29] he was rebuked by pro-Confucian scholars such as Li Yinnong. Li quoted a passage from the *Mengzi*:

Wan Zhang said, 'Why don't the *shi* seek the support of the feudal lords?' Mengzi replied, 'They dare not do so. If a feudal lord has lost his country and seeks support elsewhere, it is righteous. If a *shi* seeks support, it is not righteous.' Wan Zhang said, 'But if a ruler bestows grain on him, should he accept it?'
'Yes.'
'Why is this righteous?'
'Because a ruler should look after the *meng*.'[30]

From this passage, Li Yinnong concluded that the *meng* in fact did not refer to slaves but to freemen who were once slaves and who wandered from country to country in search of employment and opportunities. Because the various states had tried to entice these people into joining them in order to increase their manpower, the *meng* were in fact better off than the *min*.[31] This reading of *meng* was derived from the annotations of the Qing scholar Jiao Xun,[32] and it was adopted by the Lanzhou University group. Unfortunately, Li Yinnong's argument was no more convincing than Yang Rongguo's. There really did not seem to have been any concrete evidence to clarify the status of *meng*: interpretations were, on the whole, no better than educated guesses.

Archaeological research offered a possibility of a more scientific hypothesis. Some of the most influential work in this area has again been carried out by Guo Moruo. He did not examine *meng*, but worked on the word *wang*, the left-hand radical for the character *meng*. According to Guo Moruo, in the oracle bones, *wang* was shaped like a person holding a stick, and was read *meng*, meaning blind. This suggested to Guo that the character referred to someone who had been made blind, probably a prisoner of war who had put up resistance and who had become a slave.[33]

On the basis of this research, Peng Yinluo, in answer to Li Yinnong, made the claim that the character *meng* was the same as *wang* and that it was thus reasonable to assume that the *meng* were, in fact, slaves.[34] As to the term *yeren*, Peng Yinluo quoted a passage from *The Yanzi Spring and Autumn Annals* to illustrate the hypothesis that they were slaves who worked in the fields:

When the Duke of Jing went hunting for birds, the *yeren* were frightened. The Duke became angry and ordered his followers to kill the *yeren*. Yanzi said, 'the *yeren* are ignorant. I have heard that to reward the undeserving is chaotic; and to punish the ignorant is tyrannical.'[35]

Interesting as Peng Yinluo's theories were, they were no more than expressions of personal biases. Much of this debate about whether Mengzi had advocated ruling over slaves or freemen seems artificial for it really resulted from the wider periodization debate. It would have been enough simply to say that he was a thinker who defended the oppressor class, as the May Fourth thinkers had done in order to attack him. These semantic analyses, however, seem to have been necessary either to defend or to attack some of the arguments made for 'inheriting' Mengzi. While some of the analyses and arguments are new, most are tedious and repetitive. They are direct results of the periodization debate, which, like Zhdanov's definition of the history of philosophy, was largely artificially generated. It is not surprising then that debates caused by it are also sterile and arbitrary and are often no more than rationalizations to support emotional positions regarding certain aspects of Chinese culture.

Another common attack on Mengzi was based on his advocacy of the use of the well-field system of irrigation (*jingtian*).[36] This system was regarded by Mengzi as an ideal one used in ancient times. The fact that he had wanted to revive it was seen by his critics as a reactionary move to squeeze more from the peasants (or slaves). Critics like Peng Yinluo believed that, at the time, this way of thinking was in direct opposition to progressive steps taken by the Legalist Shang Yang (who lived around the same time), who abolished the *jingtian* system. At this stage, such arguments were only of minor importance, but later in the anti-Kongzi campaign, they became some of the most important themes to be taken up.

The arguments surrounding Mengzi, though not nearly so important or so widespread as those surrounding the other major figures thus had major implications for the debates on cultural inheritance. It can be seen that, although the élitist ideology of Mengzi conflicted quite markedly with the Chinese Marxist one, some critics were still trying to argue that there were aspects that were inheritable, indicating that, given the choice between the élitism of Confucianism or the Marxist egalitarian ideal, many intellectuals would have preferred the former.

XUNZI

The assessments of Xunzi, of all the philosophers examined in this book, illustrate the greatest use of the idealist/materialist dichotomy and the Guo Moruo periodization scheme to provide new frameworks within which traditional classifications can be radically transformed. This section will show that, from being traditionally the one who 'amalgamated classical thought', Xunzi was progressively transformed into the most important pioneer of feudal thought in China in breaking away from the supposedly idealist thinking of pre-Qin philosophy. The evaluations of Xunzi, and later Han Feizi, show quite clearly that in spite of, indeed with the use of, class analysis, it was possible to claim that, within a Marxist framework, a person from the ruling class could at times be progressive and praiseworthy.

Xunzi's Class

In comparison with the other major pre-Qin philosophers, there was very little debate on the class background of Xunzi. He enjoyed the almost unique privilege of actually benefiting from belonging to the ruling class and also from having worked on their behalf. It was agreed that he had wandered from state to state after his sojourn in the famous Jixia Academy in the state of Qi seeking and often obtaining official appointments.[37] The fact that he was highly educated and had been able to obtain office in that period made it impossible to argue that he was of lower class origins. However, compared with the cases of Kongzi, Mengzi, and Mozi, almost no apologetics were devised for Xunzi's having been a member of the ruling class.

All periodization schemes agreed that, by the time of the Warring States, a new social system had essentially been formed. Indeed, the unification of China by the state of Qin was a reality only about twenty years after Xunzi died. As Xunzi was the teacher of Han Feizi and Li Si, who together helped to establish the first empire, it seemed logical to argue that Xunzi therefore was a new kind of thinker who represented the interests of a new progressive ruling class.

According to the Qing historian Wang Zhong, Xunzi lived from 298 to 238 BC.[38] Although some writers argued that the Sima Qian biography of Xunzi stating that he was 50 in 285 BC was correct (thus making him nearly 100 years old by the time he died),[39] most accepted the traditional view that the '50' (*wushi*) in Sima Qian's *History* was a misprint and should read '15' (*shiwu*). Even with the discrepancy of these forty years, however, Xunzi still lived right at the end of the Warring States period, which according to Guo Moruo's periodization scheme was when the feudal system was about to begin its two-thousand-year history. The majority of history books argue that a new class had begun to consolidate its power: the landlord class, according to Guo Moruo's scheme.

This important event marked the difference between Xunzi and all the philosophers before him. It was agreed that Xunzi, as a Confucian (more of this later), had been intensely interested in how to govern, as opposed to the Daoists and Moists whose affiliations with the ruling class were slightly more difficult to establish. However, to say that Xunzi was a thinker of the ruling class was in fact praise, for to say that he worked on behalf of a new ruling class at that time implied that he was progressive historically.

This seemingly contradictory conclusion is a result of the Chinese Marxist belief in the progression of history through different periods, each one better than the last. Not only was the ruling class of each progressive period 'improved', but at the beginning of a period it was historically praiseworthy because it was responsible for overthrowing a more outdated system of the previous period. Whether this faith in the inevitable correctness of historical progress is justified or not is beyond the scope of this book. What had to be established, for the purposes of arguing that Xunzi was progressive whereas the other Confucians were not, was that fundamentally he was different in his philosophy from Kongzi and Mengzi, that is, from the mainstream of Confucian philosophy. This was no easy task as it had been traditionally acknowledged that Xunzi's thought was a development of Kongzi's and he himself had praised Kongzi's thinking and acknowledged Kongzi as a teacher. In order to establish that Xunzi's philosophy was 'inheritable', he was gradually transformed into a Legalist rather than a Confucian, and a materialist rather than an idealist.

The Link between Confucians and Legalists

Traditionally, Xunzi was classified as a Confucian who, like Mengzi, developed Kongzi's thinking and began an important branch of Confucianism. This goes as far back as Sima Qian, who grouped the biographies of Mengzi and Xunzi in one chapter and those of Laozi, Zhuangzi, Shen Buhai, and Han Feizi in another.[40] Since the Han dynasty, Xunzi's position had never been as high as that of Mengzi, and since the Song dynasty the *Mengzi* had been incorporated into the *Four Books (Si Shu)* and was therefore compulsory reading for any educated Chinese.[41] Modern scholars like Liang Qichao and Tan Sitong revised traditional historiography to a certain extent when they claimed that the Confucianism as practised in Chinese tradition was that of Xunzi rather than that of Mengzi.[42] This interpretation influenced contemporary writers like Yang Rongguo profoundly, to such an extent that many of them took Xunzi as the philosopher whose thinking guided traditional China. When modern writers such as Tan Sitong expressed the idea that Xunzi rather than Mengzi was responsible for traditional Confucianism, they were trying to prove that Xunzi had distorted the original goodness of Kongzi's thinking. By the time Yang Rongguo wrote, however, he was attempting to prove that Xunzi rather than Kongzi began feudal thinking in China.

Despite the slight rise in status that Xunzi experienced in contemporary times, his position was still that of a Confucian, and most writers treated him as such. In the influential philosophy book by Huang Zitong, for example, where an attempt was made 'to concentrate on the fundamentals of each school's thought to arrive at the system that it belonged to,'[43] Xunzi was automatically classed as a member of the Confucian school. This classification was also true of books written by left-wing writers published after 1949. A typical example is Jian Bozan's standard history textbook, which was published in 1950, in which Xunzi and Mengzi are simply regarded as representing different strands of Kongzi's thought.[44] The identification of Xunzi as a Confucian continued right up to the early sixties, and his status changed radically only with the changed position of Kongzi himself.

Thus, although Xunzi was the teacher of Han Feizi and Li Si and thus would be viewed as a direct predecessor of the Legalists, he was, prior to the Cultural Revolution, seen more in terms of a Confucian than a Legalist. It was often claimed that:

Although Xunzi's thinking was a reflection of the demands and wishes of the landlord class which had been transformed from the slave-owning aristocracy, it was nevertheless still different from the Legalists which reflected the desires and wishes of the newly arisen landlord class.[45]

At best then, Xunzi's thinking before the Cultural Revolution was seen as a bridge between the Confucians and the Legalists. For example, in the only book-length commentary on Xunzi, which took as its framework post-1949 Communist historical methods, Li Deyong commented that, when Xunzi toured the state of Qin, he found it deficient in that it 'had no Confucians.'[46] He claimed that Xunzi had found the Confucians far superior to the Legalists in activities such as the management of the economy. Also, Xunzi's political outlook was several times more perceptive than that of the Legalists. However, the Qin state did not adopt his ideas.[47]

Li Deyong concluded that Xunzi's ideas were 'wiser' than Han Feizi's dictatorial line (badao luxian). This was because, in addition to his belief in the use of force (li), which the Legalists had favoured, Xunzi had also believed in winning popular support. Also, Xunzi was more enlightened than Mengzi because he did not, like Mengzi, belittle the use of military force.[48] Li Deyong did not hide the fact that he regarded Xunzi as superior to both the Legalists and Mengzi. However, at this stage, there were no comparisons made with Kongzi.

This is not surprising as Xunzi himself in the chapter 'Critique of the Twelve Philosophers' summarized and assessed the founders of the important philosophical schools in the pre-Qin era and criticized them all. However, he remained faithful to Kongzi, whom he regarded as a sage.[49] Most later historians, including those writing in modern and contemporary times, accepted this view of Xunzi as a very learned Confucian, who differed from the Confucians of the Mengzi type in being 'harder' and more 'realistic' about life.

However, as almost all the historians agreed that the Legalists were qualitatively different from the Confucians and Xunzi was a precursor of the Legalists, how was one to explain this qualitative change? In terms of later assessments in the Cultural Revolution era, perhaps the most influential view was that expressed by Yang Rongguo. This was also a view which created some controversy in the pre-Cultural Revolution era. Yang Rongguo followed the Guo Moruo periodization scheme very closely. He pinpointed Xunzi's thinking as standing at the beginning of and forming the basis of feudal thought. Some of the reasons given by Yang Rongguo were later to be adopted during the anti-Kongzi movement as self-evident truths. Here, it should be noted that the main reason given by Yang was that, in a slave society, the most important principle of life was rites (*li*). This has already been discussed in Chapter 3. According to Yang, Xunzi retained the use of the term *li* but changed its meaning.

Yang Rongguo argued that, whereas to Kongzi and Mengzi *li* was designed to maintain the rule of the old slave aristocracy, to Xunzi it was 'to satisfy the desires of the people and meet their demands.'[50] In this, *li* already possessed elements of the *fa* (law) which was designed to eradicate remnants of the slave system. By the time of Han Feizi, a student of Xunzi, *li* had been dispensed with altogether in favour of *fa*.[51] Although this was later taken as an unchallengeable truth, it was at this stage still quite an unorthodox position to adopt. Logically, Guo Moruo's periodization scheme should have suggested that the ancestor of feudal thought was Xunzi, as he lived at the dawn of the feudal age. However, the traditional view that Kongzi was the original sage of Chinese civilization and the modern version that Kongzi was the ancestor of feudal thought in China were taken as self-evident and never questioned. Yang was thus departing from the orthodox view in his proposals.

Yang Rongguo's interpretation, however, raised some difficult problems. Neither he nor those who followed him could deny that, for two thousand years, when people spoke of Confucianism, they meant a Confucianism which was very much in the Kong-Meng tradition. When earlier critics like Tan Sitong and Liang Qichao blamed feudalism on Xunzi instead of Kongzi and Mengzi, they were very much trying to lay the blame of a then backward 'feudal' China on Xunzi. Yang, however, was trying to say that Xunzi represented the progressive element and Mengzi the conservative element. But how then can one explain the phenomenon that, once feudalism had been established, the Xunzi-Han Feizi tradition was overthrown in favour of a lost Kongzi-Mengzi tradition? Had a slave ideology then been used for a feudal system?

These were some of the problems raised in 1957 by Wu Wen, a critic of Yang Rongguo. Wu Wen agreed with Yang that Xunzi was a materialist who did not believe in the Will of Heaven and who wanted greater equality between the rulers and the ruled. Such beliefs were diametrically opposed to those of Zisi and

Mengzi. Wu Wen asked, 'Were these things that feudal rulers welcomed?'[52] He argued that, in fact, the feudal rulers had chosen to adopt the teachings of Zisi and Mengzi rather than those of Xunzi because the former were more useful in intimidating and controlling the masses. Thus, the founders of feudal ideas were Zisi and Mengzi, and not Xunzi as Yang Rongguo had claimed.

In fact, the evaluations of Xunzi by both Yang Rongguo and Wu Wen were essentially the same. They both agreed that Xunzi was a materialist and progressive for his time. Their disagreement lay in their interpretations of the feudal past. Wu Wen observed that, if Yang Rongguo believed that Xunzi was working on behalf of all the oppressed people of his time, then Yang's vision of the struggle between the landlords and the slave-owners was too romantic, for he saw the landlord class as the saviour of mankind.

Yang Rongguo himself probably saw the difficulties of elevating Xunzi to a position which was too high. By saying that Xunzi's thinking was the epitome of feudal ideas, and at the same time arguing that his thinking was designed for the purpose of liberating the oppressed class, Yang Rongguo was risking the danger of eulogizing an ideology which every left-wing intellectual in modern China had tried to denounce. At this stage, however, these objections raised by Wu Wen were ignored. Yang's interpretation, in fact, became so popular that by the anti-Kongzi campaign of the early seventies, it was the interpretation officially adopted as the 'correct' doctrine.

The reason is again political: this interpretation suited the current policies of that time. The Cultural Revolution platform was that the seventeen years prior to 1966 were a betrayal of the original Communist cause of Yan'an times, because almost as soon as the Communists had won power, it was alleged, a system not very different from that of pre-Communist times was established. Thus, it was no surprise that, in the feudal period, as soon as feudal power was established, the slave-owners' thinking on Kongzi and Mengzi was re-established. Of course, this was really talking in ethical terms. In strictly Marxist analysis, it is nonsense to claim that the economic relations of a slave system were no different from those of a feudal one, or that the collectivization of land and other commodities after 1949 created not a socialist system but one which was no different from that which previously existed. Critics were well aware of these difficulties both before and after 1966, as Wu Wen's criticisms of Yang Rongguo reveal. Before 1966, Yang

Rongguo's interpretation was only one of many. But after the Cultural Revolution, when political needs meant it was the only permissible interpretation, the notion that 'history serves politics' became even more extreme. Thus, political judgements of the philosophers once again overrode more historical or philosophical assessments of them.

Xunzi the Materialist

Although after 1949 it was generally agreed that what distinguished Xunzi from Kongzi and Mengzi was his thoroughgoing materialism, the contention that his thinking differed qualitatively from the earlier Confucians and the reasons given by the Communist critics for this were by no means new. In fact, they had been proposed by non-Communist historians of thought in modern times, as stated earlier, with only the terminology being changed. For example, before 1949, one of the most influential works on the history of Chinese philosophy by Hu Shi did not use the idealist/materialist dichotomy to analyse Xunzi's thought, but his conclusions were remarkably similar to later studies using Marxist analysis. Although Hu Shi held that Xunzi had developed the thinking of Kongzi, a point upon which most later critics also agreed, he nevertheless also emphasized that what made Xunzi different from the other pre-Qin philosophers was his attitude towards Heaven: that one should look after the affairs of men rather than be concerned about Heaven.[53] This, according to Hu Shi, was in the same spirit as Kongzi's 'If you don't know human affairs, how can you know about ghosts?'[54] This cosmological outlook attributed to Xunzi was widely used by Communist writers as evidence that he was a materialist.

Feng Youlan, who employed the terminology of materialism/idealism in his pre-1949 work on Xunzi, did so only sparingly. In the beginning of his lengthy analysis of Xunzi, he did say that, in contrast to Mengzi, who had an idealist tendency, Xunzi had materialist tendencies.[55] However, the reasons provided by Feng were very different from the ones to be given by him later. He claimed that Western philosophers on the whole were divided into Platonists or Aristotelians, and that 'Plato was a representative of the soft-minded school and Aristotle was a representative of the hard-minded school.'[56] Using this analogy, he concluded that Mengzi belonged to the 'soft-minded' camp and thus had idealist tendencies, while Xunzi belonged to the 'hard-minded' camp and thus had materialist tendencies!

This use of idealism and materialism, although very prevalent, was very muddle-headed. In English, idealism is sometimes confused with the idealism of being idealistic, which is a non-philosophical use of the term and which has a favourable connotation. The same is true of the Chinese use, where *wei-xin* has been used for idealism. *Xin*, the mind of the heart, has overtones of benevolence or tender-heartedness as in *liangxin*, especially for those sympathetic to neo-Confucianism like Feng Youlan. This use of idealism to describe Mengzi and materialism to describe Xunzi is certainly very different from the use of these terms to describe the philosophers in post-1949 interpretations.

Guo Moruo remarked on this confused usage of the terms 'idealism' and 'materialism' when he wrote on Xunzi before 1949. Like Hu Shi, Guo Moruo pointed out that Xunzi did not believe in the Will of Heaven, but Guo went further and claimed that Mengzi also followed this Confucian tradition, saying that 'it is better to benefit the World than Heaven, and it is better to benefit Man than the Earth.'[57] This denial of fate, Guo Moruo agreed, was in keeping with the modern scientific spirit. However, he did not conclude that Xunzi was a materialist. Instead, Guo claimed that, in his view of human nature, it is acknowledged that Xunzi believed in the innate evil of man, whereas Mengzi believed in the innate goodness of man. While this may have helped someone like Feng Youlan in his view that Mengzi was tender-hearted and Xunzi hard-hearted, Guo remarked that both men perceived only one extreme of man, and both were equally biased: 'Therefore when some people call Mengzi an idealist because he postulated man's natural goodness and Xunzi a materialist because he postulated innate evil in man it seems a bit unfair.'[58] This seems to have been the most balanced statement on the two philosophers but, as time progressed, when the idealism/materialism dichotomy became increasingly more rigid, philosophers had to make a stand on one side or the other. Almost arbitrarily, Xunzi became more and more a materialist. This is most clearly seen in Feng Youlan's changing evaluations. In 1950, he stated that Xunzi's thinking 'was a development of Kongzi's materialism,'[59] and in 1962, Xunzi had become 'the greatest materialist in ancient China.'[60]

This term was actually applied to Xunzi by Zhang Dainian in 1957 in his book *A Short History of Chinese Materialist Thought*.

This book, together with the Russian book on the same topic by Yang Xingshun published in 1956 and then translated into Chinese in 1957, set the tone for later works on the history of Chinese philosophy. It is interesting to note here that, in the section dealing with Xunzi and Han Feizi, only one paragraph is devoted to Han Feizi in a discussion comprising six pages on the two philosophers. At this stage, the materialism of Xunzi was certainly stressed above that of Han Feizi who, as a philosopher, was considered to be less significant.

The reasons given by both Zhang Dainian and Yang Xingshun for the materialism of Xunzi were in fact elaborations of the short essay by Feng Youlan in 1950. Zhang Dainian listed five points which hc claimed Xunzi had advocated:

First, the natural processes do not follow human wishes but their own objective laws. Second, natural phenomena can be classified into four kinds: that which has *qi*, that which has *sheng*, that which has *zhi*, and that which has *yi*. *Qi* is the basis for life and consciousness. Third, the human spirit has as its basis the human physical being. Fourth, ghosts and spirits are only illusions. Fifth, man should not eulogize nature and wait on nature, but should conquer nature and utilize nature.[61]

As the list shows, Xunzi's materialism was quite remarkable, especially for his time. It even comprehended the idea of Man actually transforming Nature, an idea which was developed in detail by Mao Zedong and which became highly influential in the Cultural Revolution.

Zhang Dainian's book was significant because it attempted to trace materialism in China, thus showing that Chinese philosophy was similar to European philosophy in having a materialist stream. The discovery of Xunzi in classical philosophy as a thoroughgoing materialist was thus of the utmost importance. This was shown by the fact that, in the same year, an article by Zhang Dainian on Xunzi also appeared in the influential magazine *Study*, listing almost the same reasons for claiming Xunzi to be a materialist.

In this article, Zhang Dainian also claimed that Xunzi's most important contribution to materialism was his idea that man could conquer nature. He paraphrased into modern Chinese the passage from Xunzi's '*Tianlun pian*', 'It would be better to regard Heaven as an object to mould and control than to admire for its greatness.'[62] Yang Rongguo had actually used the expression 'Man Can Conquer Nature' (*ren ding sheng tian*) as the heading for his section on Xunzi's cosmological view, and it was to become a slogan during the Cultural Revolution period, not only in philosophical circles but also in all other spheres of life.

Thus, although in the fifties some works still pointed to 'defects' in Xunzi,[63] his philosophy was already considered materialist by the majority of writers. Once this had been acknowledged, it became difficult to criticize him and unnecessary to defend him in arguments for inheritance. More and more, his thinking was reinterpreted in such a way as to fit in with Chinese Communist ideas of progressiveness and enlightenment. For example, although in the early sixties accusations were levelled against many writers for 'modernizing' less acceptable pre-Qin philosophers such as Kongzi and Laozi, little was said about the modernization of Xunzi. This occurred despite the fact that Xunzi was increasingly credited with having a philosophy which was remarkably similar to the thinking of those who wanted to prove him a materialist.

On Human Nature

As well as his cosmological outlook, Xunzi's thinking in other areas was also used to prove that he was a materialist. One interesting example is his epistemology. Li Deyong's assessment of this was typical of the many comments on it. Xunzi had used the two concepts *tiangong* (heavenly palace) and *tianjun* (heavenly office) to refer to the mind and the sense organs. Li Deyong claimed that, by pointing to the importance of the sense organs, Xunzi showed himself a materialist by implying that experience was a path to knowledge. And because Xunzi also stressed the role of the mind in analysing the senses, Li Deyong claimed that he therefore had been able to stress the relationship between knowledge (*zhi*) and practice (*xing*).[64] This interpretation of Xunzi's epistemology, which was to become standard, was again not very different from Mao's ideas on knowledge as stated in *On Practice*.

Li Deyong did concede that Xunzi's epistemology was not without fault. He believed that there were three points which showed that it was not completely materialist: first, Xunzi overemphasized the subjective power of the mind, secondly, he overemphasized the power and potential of knowledge as a guide for practice and, lastly, he thought that the highest knowledge was that of a sage or a ruler.[65] Although these points were mentioned in the fifties and early sixties by other writers, they were raised less and less frequently in the course of time.[66] In fact, one of the tenets of the Cultural Revolution slogan 'man controls nature' assumed the first 'defect', that the subjective power of the mind had overall control over other things.[67]

Xunzi's ideas on human nature were also quoted as evidence of his materialism. Traditionally, it was recognized that Xunzi believed human beings to be innately evil (*e*) in direct contrast to Mengzi's belief in innate goodness (*shan*). This difference gave Mengzi rather than Xunzi a place in the mainstream of Confucian thinking. Because Mengzi was seen as idealist, Xunzi by contrast was interpreted as materialist. Despite Guo Moruo's objection to this use of the idealist/materialist method, almost all writers who compared Mengzi and Xunzi concluded that 'this contrast is essentially a contrast between materialism and idealism.'[68]

The reasons for this contrast were not complicated. It was often claimed that Mengzi's concept of innate goodness encompassed knowledge and was thus idealist because it implied that man was born with knowledge. However, when Xunzi talked about innate evil (*e*), the *e* did not carry any connotations of morality or knowledge, but simply meant having sense organs and desires ('when hungry, wishing to eat; when cold, wishing to be clothed; and when tired, wishing for a rest').[69]

However, one difficulty remained. Although it was possible to argue that *e* for Xunzi referred only to simple nature, his use of the term sometimes had definite ethical connotations.[70] In a detailed article, Liang Qixiong in 1963 attempted to clarify this contradiction. He claimed that the inconsistency would not exist if *e* were seen in terms of a crude and unknowing original nature which could become *shan* through *wei* (education, conditioning, or socialization).[71] This would show too that Xunzi did not believe in innate knowledge while Mengzi did. By seeing *e* as an unsophisticated and innocent nature which could be moulded into goodness through education, Xunzi's philosophy could be brought even closer to the Maoist conception of education which believed in the malleability of human nature and consciousness.[72]

There are many passages in the *Xunzi* illustrating the differences between unadulterated nature (*xing*) and educated or conditioned personality (*wei*). In the chapter 'On the Evilness of Human Nature', Xunzi stated:

The emotional nature (*qingxing*) that men are born with comprises phenomena such as the eyes desiring colour, the ears desiring sounds, the mouth desiring flavours, the mind desiring gain and the body desiring pleasure and ease. Such feelings are natural and they occur even when men do nothing to produce them. But that which does not occur naturally but which must wait for some activity before it is brought into being is called the product of education (*wei*). Therefore, unadulterated and educated human nature (*xing* and *wei*) are brought about by different causes.[73]

Such passages were often quoted in attempts to prove that Xunzi's view of human nature was materialistic and that his ideas on education were progressive.

The interpretations of Xunzi's philosophy and his view of human nature as essentially materialist in practical terms were of course relevant to the inheritance question. This is demonstrated most clearly, as in the case of Kongzi, in education. The increasing disenchantment with the Soviet Union during the late fifties and early sixties led to a search for materialist elements within the native tradition. Such elements which could still be significant for the present were more easily found in ideas on education, epistemology, and metaphysics.

While the teaching of the orthodox Kong-Meng classics had been discredited even before 1949, the favourable reception given to Xunzi's philosophy after 1949 made it possible to argue that a particular strain of Confucian education could still be utilized. More was written on Xunzi's educational ideas than any other pre-Qin thinkers apart from Kongzi. In an article which traces the development of materialist educational thought in Chinese history, Qu Junong in 1963 echoed the universally accepted view that Xunzi had absorbed and developed materialist educational thinking that was already evident in Kongzi. On the basis of Xunzi's views of human nature, where *e* was a simple unmoulded human nature that could be changed by education (*wei*), Qu Junong claimed that Xunzi had developed the materialist idea that environmental influences were the determining factors in human development.[74] He quoted Xunzi's 'human nature is *e*, and it becomes *shan* through education (*wei*)'[75] as evidence that the materialist tradition in education in China began with Xunzi, a view held by most writers at that time.[76]

There were several important advantages in recommending Xunzi's educational theory for present-day use. Because he studied for many years in the Jixia Academy, he could be said to have absorbed the thinking of most of the important schools of thought in classical China. Thus, he was in some ways more representative of the 'true China' than Mengzi. Also, by saying that he was the ancestor of materialist education in China, other thinkers such as Wang Chong, Wang Anshi, and Liu Zongyuan could be said to have carried on the tradition he established. This was widely emphasized and utilized in the early seventies.[77]

The time when Xunzi lived was also said to have contributed to his educational ideas. Comparing Mengzi and Xunzi, Li Deyong claimed that, because Mengzi lived at the end of the slave period, his view of human nature was still that innate goodness could be passed from generation to generation. By the time Xunzi was active, however, the slave system had deteriorated and human nature was no longer seen as innately good, but exposed as evil by the changed situation.[78] The interpretation of e here is not just human nature as unadulterated simplicity, but actual evil. Some writers who took this traditional view that e meant innate evil simply ignored Guo Moruo's objection that to say man was innately evil was as 'idealist' as regarding man as innately good. Others argued that, although evil was not innate, it would nevertheless grow in people if it were not restricted. Unlike Mengzi (and the Daoists), whose view was that goodness would flourish in man if left unhampered, in Xunzi's theory, the function of education was to prevent the growth of evil in man.[79]

Although there were some, such as Li Deyong, who distinguished between Xunzi and Han Feizi in regard to education by claiming that Xunzi advocated persuasion to prevent the growth of evil, others such as Zhang Ruifan had already proposed that Xunzi had essentially utilized the Legalist doctrine of rule by law in his educational theories.[80] Zhang also argued that Xunzi's educational theories still had relevance for the present, but modified this view by saying that it was ideal for adults, but had to be carefully analysed before being applied to children.

This admission is an interesting facet of the political use and purpose of such philosophical analysis. If e were really innate in human beings as Zhang Ruifan claimed, then it would make sense to 'educate' (meaning to coerce) young children. By saying that education, as understood by Xunzi, should be applied to adults only, Zhang was quite obviously thinking that the e of Xunzi did not really relate to innate human nature, but to society and man in society. For the relatively young Communist state, where many people probably remained opposed to the new leadership and ideology, a degree of coercion was therefore to be encouraged. It is not surprising then that some articles which were supposedly on Xunzi's educational theory were in fact political essays on contemporary events rather than classical philosophy. They contained phrases such as 'use the proletarian world outlook to teach ourselves ... otherwise we will be captives of bourgeois thinking.'[81] This trend was to continue into the Cultural Revolution.

HAN FEIZI

Traditionally, Han Feizi has been seen as the theoretician whose writings have formed a basis for the rule of tyrants and despots. Sima Qian recorded that Han Feizi's writing inspired the First Emperor so much that when he read 'Solitary Indignation' and 'The Five Vermin', he sighed, 'I would die happy if I could meet the author of these works.'[82] Qin Shihuang has traditionally been interpreted as the archetype tyrant who 'buried Confucians and burnt books.'[83] Han Feizi was similarly blamed for having been anti-Confucian and thus anti-culture.

Of the pre-Qin philosophers, Mozi is well-known as being very critical of the Confucians and, partly because of this, Mozi's teachings were largely ignored for centuries. Han Feizi also attacked Confucian scholars as one of the 'five vermin' in society (though he was not anti-Kongzi as such).[84] As Han Feizi was a student of Xunzi and thus partly attached to the Confucian school, he was traditionally considered a renegade from Confucianism, and so his thinking was even more detested than that of Mozi. However, the fact that his philosophy was an outgrowth of Confucianism is also evident in its preoccupation with how to govern, the concern of all Confucians. The difference between the orthodox Confucians and Han Feizi lay in the 'Machiavellian' way with which Han Feizi described the process.[85] Whereas orthodox Confucians indulged in what Han Feizi referred to as hypocritical and empty talk of benevolent government (*renzheng*), Han Feizi's own concerns were diplomatic strategy, political intrigue, and political power.

Although Han Feizi was detested by orthodox scholars, there is no doubt that his teachings were used by rulers of traditional China. Like Machiavelli, his descriptions and methods for dealing with people earned him an unfavourable reputation, yet among all pre-Qin thinkers, his was really the most systematic and scientific writing on government and diplomacy. As Burton Watson observed:

Generations of Chinese scholars have professed to be shocked by its contents—their rejection of all moral values, the call to harshness and deceit in politics, the assertion that even one's own wife and children are not to be trusted—and have taken up their brushes to denounce it. But there has never been an age when the book was unread, and the text appears to have come down to us complete. It is one of those books that will compel attention in any age, for it deals with a problem of unchanging importance—the nature and use of power.[86]

Even more than other pre-Qin texts then, the *Han Feizi* is a political tract. Yet, although its influence was profound, this was traditionally not acknowledged, and it has been discussed far less than other Confucian and Daoist texts. This trend continued into the Communist period right up to the early seventies.

Han Feizi as a Legalist

As a result of the traditional antipathy towards the Legalists, many general books on philosophy even in the modern period have simply dismissed them as a branch of philosophy not warranting discussion.[87] Hu Shi, for instance, claimed that, although Han Feizi was a Legalist, his predecessors such as Shang Yang and Shen Buhai were not really Legalists in the philosophical sense but mere politicians. One reason he gave was that these 'Legalists' had not written the books attributed to them.[88] Such a reason was indicative of a certain anti-Legalist bias on Hu Shi's part but not a very valid one as the same could be said of the Daoists, Moists, or even the Confucians. Although the legitimacy of Legalism as a proper branch of philosophy before Han Feizi was questioned by some, most writers took it for granted that he was influenced by earlier Legalist thinkers. Some also suggested that he was influenced to varying degrees by other schools of thought such as the Daoists and Moists.

Like the *Xunzi*, much of the *Han Feizi* is concerned with evaluations of the other pre-Qin philosophers. Nevertheless, there are basic differences between the two. Yang Rongguo, whose theories on Han Feizi were to become the most influential during the anti-Kongzi campaign of the seventies, claimed in his book on ancient Chinese philosophy that Xunzi was the 'real representative of feudal thought' whereas Han Feizi was 'the epitome of Legalist thought.'[89] Later on, of course, Xunzi was also seen as a Legalist philosopher but, in the fifties, Han Feizi was seen by the majority of writers as being the most important Legalist thinker in classical times. Instead of stressing that his teacher was Xunzi therefore, some writers emphasized the fact that he was highly influenced by Legalists like Shang Yang. Yang Rongguo in fact singled out Shang Yang above the other Legalists as having exerted a great influence on Han Feizi. Hitherto, Shang Yang had been regarded more as a historical political figure, rather than an important philosopher, but more and more his status as a thinker rose.

Not all historians agreed with Yang. Guo Moruo, for instance, believed that Han Feizi was equally influenced by Shang Yang and Shen Buhai. The *Han Feizi* itself stated that 'Shen Buhai talked about statecraft (*shu*) and Shang Yang advocated laws (*fa*).'[90] Some people thus concluded that he was a specialist in both statecraft and law.[91] Besides this introduction to *fa* and *shu*, most commentators also believed that Han Feizi was influenced by another Legalist, Shen Dao, whose main contribution to Legalism was said to have been the concept of the use of power (*shi*).[92] Thus, even for those critics who thought that Han Feizi was influenced by the Legalists, the branch of Legalism they stressed differed. Shang Yang, Han Feizi, and Wu Qi were taken as the most progressive of the thinkers in the pre-Qin era.[93] The fact that they were all imprisoned and executed by their rulers may explain some of the adulation piled upon them. During the Cultural Revolution, many top cadres who had been in Nationalist prisons in the thirties or forties were attacked for having 'capitulated' to the enemy: the assumption was that, if one had remained true to the cause, execution would have resulted. Thus, Shang Yang and Wu Qi were presented as martyrs in the pre-Qin historiography of the Cultural Revolution period.

Many writers pointed out that Han Feizi had been influenced by several other schools apart from Legalism. Fan Wenlan, for example, stated explicitly that 'Han Fei was a great thinker who lived at the end of the Warring States era, who summarized all the different schools of thought of pre-Qin times.'[94] Thus, he was said to have developed Xunzi's Confucianism even further and to have absorbed and reinterpreted Laozi's thinking as well. Feng Youlan wrote an essay specifically on the influence of Laozi on Han Feizi because Han Feizi had annotated the *Laozi*.[95] Guo Moruo went even further. For Guo, Mozi and Han Feizi had provided the ideological framework for all the tyrants in Chinese history. Prior to 1949, he claimed that 'Han Feizi's thought had its origins in the Daoist school of thought and its roots in the Confucian school of thought. But his affinity with the Moists has seldom been recognized.'[96] Most writers agreed that Han Feizi was influenced by the Moists, and some, like Liang Qixiong, claimed that he had been influenced also by the Logicians.[97] Thus, while the origins of Han Feizi's thinking were attributed to the influences of the other pre-Qin philosophers in varying degrees, there was at least general agreement that he was well-versed in all the different schools of thought existing in pre-Qin times. This point was significant during the early seventies, when there was a great revival of classical philosophy in the movement to criticize Kongzi and to praise the Legalists, because a study of Han Feizi signified in effect some knowledge of the other schools of classical thought. In the fifties and sixties, however, the problem was still to determine which school he was closest to. No matter how one looks at Han Feizi and his relationship with the other thinkers, it cannot be denied that he was very critical of the Confucian scholars, as his popular essay 'The Five Vermin' showed. Han Feizi, as the most virulent critic of the Confucians, became a central theme in the anti-Kongzi campaign in the early seventies but, at this stage, this point was not emphasized, although as early as 1957 Hou Wailu had stated that the Confucian-Legalist struggle began in the middle of the Spring and Autumn period.[98]

Before the Cultural Revolution, Guo Moruo's interpretation was more widely accepted. With his pro-Confucian bias, Guo suggested that, in developing Xunzi's ideas of human nature, Han Feizi had in fact distorted them. Guo Moruo believed that, while Xunzi had proposed that human nature was innately evil, the way to overcome this handicap was through persuasion and education. Han Feizi, by contrast, had been prepared to let this evil nature develop to its fullest, because it could then be used as a defence from others, and perhaps harm others for the benefit of the self.[99] Thus, while Xunzi had opposed Kongzi in stressing the present rather than the past, he was at least progressive in still wanting to retain the rites (li). But, according to Guo Moruo, Han Feizi had also wanted to abolish that last remnant of benevolent rule. Guo Moruo also frowned on Han Feizi's repudiation of the doctrines of his teacher, Xunzi. He said that Han Feizi extended this disrespect

to his other teachers in the statement that 'Shenzi had not developed *shu* and Shang Yang had not developed *fa* enough.'[100]
Guo concluded that Han Feizi was responsible for a system of
tyranny and abuse of power as exemplified in the Qin state.

Ever since Sima Qian's biography of Han Feizi, the judgement
that he assisted the First Emperor in his dictatorship and abuse of
power has been generally accepted. The few who were sympathetic to Han Feizi did not dispute the claim that Qin Shihuang was a
despot. Rather, they tried to excuse Han Feizi by pointing out that
he was put to death by Qin Shihuang, so that he could hardly be
identified with Qin.[101] The general opinion on Han Feizi, however, was still tied closely to the evaluation of the First Emperor.
In the fifties, although some had been sympathetic to the achievements of the First Emperor for having unified China, most still
regarded him with distaste. Li Deyong perhaps summarized the
general feeling on Han Feizi when he said, 'As time passed, the
thinking of Han Feizi became more and more reactionary, so that
it could be said that Han Feizi was the person who contributed
immensely to the ideology of the landlord class.'[102] It is interesting
that, at this stage, the recognition that Han Feizi contributed significantly to the ideology of the landlord class meant that he was
responsible for much of China's autocratic rule in the past. By the
time Guo Moruo's periodization scheme was universally accepted
and its implications understood, the claim that Han Feizi was the
greatest philosopher in ancient China was established by this very
characteristic.

Han Feizi as Philosopher

Because Han Feizi's philosophy was predominantly concerned
with political behaviour, the analysis of his thought must to a large
extent concentrate on this aspect. Even the discussion of the
idealism/materialism dichotomy was based more on his political
and economic thought than his metaphysics, epistemology, or cosmology. Naturally, this did not mean that nothing was written on
these topics, only that there was little debate on them. Just as
scholarly books written on the logic and scientific theories of the
later Moists engendered little controversy, there were also books
written about Han Feizi's logical theories which provoked no
debate.[103] The topic of debates on Han Feizi was invariably his
politics.

Almost all critics agreed that Han Feizi was a materialist, with Feng Youlan proclaiming that he was the 'greatest materialist of the pre-Qin era.'[104] The two most common reasons for his supposed materialism were his twin 'inheritances' of the epistemology of the Moists and Xunzi and the cosmology of Laozi.[105] It was said that he inherited the 'practical' aspect of Xunzi's epistemology as a test for truth. This was derived from his statement that, to test the truth of a proposition, one should test all its different aspects.[106] In cosmology, because of the extensive annotations Han Feizi had made on the *Laozi*, it was claimed not only that he had inherited the materialistic tradition of Laozi in not seeing a god in Heaven, but that he also had reduced the mystery of the *dao* into something more general: the general principles governing the natural world, an interpretation most people agreed on.[107] In fact, most people were in agreement that Han Feizi's cosmology was a materialist one. Those who attacked him did so on other grounds, such as politics or economics.

In politics, the discussions tended to concentrate on his social theories or his refutations of Confucian theory. There was relatively little debate on the class affiliations or interests that he supported, compared with those on the other pre-Qin philosophers. This is not surprising as the other philosophers, though from the upper classes, did not belong to any distinct group and held various positions during their lifetimes. Han Feizi, by contrast, was known to have been a prince of the Han state and, although this later cost him his life, there is no doubt that he was the only prominent pre-Qin philosopher who was definitely a member of the aristocracy. This information about him came from Sima Qian's *History* and it was never questioned.

If it appears ironic that Xunzi, whose thinking was supposed to have embodied the slave mentality of the Zhou, was nevertheless said to have started a progressive trend in feudal thought, the case of Han Feizi is even more so. As the only true member of the aristocratic slave-owning class, his ideas were held responsible for the final break-up of the slave society. Most commentators recognized this ambiguity but were willing to allow it to remain.

To Guo Moruo, of course, who maintained that Han Feizi was a renegade from Xunzi and who believed, as most traditional scholars did, that Han Feizi's thinking was for tyrants anyway, there was no difficulty here. But to others, like Wang Yi, who said that Han Feizi's thinking 'was a reflection of the aristocratic classes and was anti-people,' and in the same breath said that his 'political thought was devised in the interests of the newly arisen landlord classes, so that in the historical conditions of the time, it created a progressive result,'[108] an explanation was certainly necessary. Before the Cultural Revolution, it was never satisfactorily explained why a person could be progressive and yet simultaneously 'mercilessly repressive' towards the common people. Later, it was claimed that Han Feizi's theories were cruel because the old ruling classes had to be repressed, so that the new rulers could establish their positions more quickly and firmly.

Before the Cultural Revolution, the consensus was still that Han Feizi had advocated cruelty and mercilessness in his theories for their own sake. Wang Yi, for example, expressed the view that morally Han Feizi was reprehensible because his cruelty extended to family members, as shown in his matter-of-fact statements in the chapter 'Taking Precautions Within' (*bei nei*) where wives, sons, and other family members were to be distrusted.[109] In other articles which supported Han Feizi, it was argued that his statements on such matters did not show that he himself was cruel, but that he exposed the hypocrisies of Confucianism, with its fine talk of benevolence and rites.[110]

When it later became necessary to denounce tradition as represented by Confucianism, Han Feizi and other Legalists were promoted precisely because it was thought that they were anti-Confucianist. Even then, Han Feizi was seen as a member of the ruling class who was trying to overthrow another faction of the ruling class, the Confucians. Even Yang Rongguo, who had previously praised Han Feizi for his anti-Confucianism in the fifties, agreed that Han Feizi was essentially working on behalf of the landlord classes against the old slave-owning class: that is, a rising power group against a declining power group.[111] This way of interpreting class interests was agreed upon even in the anti-Kongzi movement of the early seventies, when it was alleged that Han Feizi's 'materialism was not thorough enough; he only trusted the rulers and did not trust the people.'[112] The obvious and ostensible reason for this interpretation was undoubtedly because none of the philosophers could have been thoroughly materialist; for that we would have to wait for the rise of Communism. Other, more subtle reasons will be discussed in the concluding chapter of this book.

Han Feizi has also often been contrasted with 'orthodox' Confucians like Mengzi because of his adoption of Xunzi's view that human nature was evil. If human beings were essentially selfish, advancing only their own ends, it was necessary to impose laws and punishments to restrict their freedom of movement. This was consistent with Han Feizi's political theory. Subjects of a state were to be used for the advancement of that state, and not for the needs and desires of the individuals. Although in the fifties Liang Qixiong observed that such an extreme form of utilitarianism on a national level would lead to absolute dictatorships,[113] later interpretations did not question the idea that many people in society had to be subjected to authoritarian rule.

Han Feizi's economic formulations included 'the wealth of a nation depends on its agriculture'[114] and 'an enlightened ruler will decrease the number of merchants and artisans.'[115] Merchants, artisans, and specifically Confucian scholars (by extension, scholars in general as in traditional China all scholars were Confucian) were all denounced as 'vermin' in his writings.[116] These economic policies, stripped of his overt anti-Confucianism, were in fact practised in China for centuries after him, as Li Zongmao pointed out in 1962 in an article in the *Guangming Daily* on Han Feizi's economic thought.[117]

Another famous theory put forward by Han Feizi was that, as the population grew, demand for food supplies would increase and living standards would drop. He argued this point most strongly in the 'The Five Vermin', saying, for example:

In the ancient past, men did not have to work in the fields, for there were enough grain and fruit for people to eat. Women did not have to weave, for the skins of beasts provided enough clothing. No one had to struggle to provide for himself. There were few people and an abundance of goods, so nobody fought ... Nowadays, the number of people has increased, and goods have grown scarce, and men have to struggle for a meagre living.[118]

In his essay on Han Feizi's economic thought, Li Zongmao argued that this theory showed that Han Feizi's viewpoint was materialist. He also saw in Han Feizi's writing a certain 'historical progression', a notion never advanced before Han Feizi's time. Because Han Feizi saw history as essentially 'progressing', Li Zongmao argued that his theory was different from that of Malthus, who viewed society as a static entity. There seems little justification for this argument, and the fact that it was proposed in all seriousness showed that Li Zongmao was very eager to prove the 'progressiveness' and 'Chineseness' of Han Feizi. By 1962, the desire to find materialist strains in Chinese tradition was quite strong. In fact, Han Feizi's population theory was already the centre of a debate in 1957 when the national conferences were held to discuss the treatment of Chinese philosophy and cultural inheritance.

In Chapter 2, reference was made to Feng Youlan's attempt to argue that there were materialist systems before Marx and that, in China, this was manifested in the thinking of Guanzi and Han Feizi: in his *New History of Chinese Philosophy*, Han Feizi was called the 'greatest materialist in ancient China.' This argument was important in 1957 because it was made at the first major national philosophy conference on how to treat Chinese philosophy and how to inherit it. It inevitably had repercussions, as it was made in conjunction with Feng Youlan's theories on the abstract inheritance of Kongzi's *ren* which had created so much controversy.

In support of his claim that Han Feizi could be considered a materialist, Feng Youlan quoted from 'The Five Vermin' the passage on population growth and its relationship to food supply cited above. Feng concluded that

although this was not correct, this theory which attempted to explain history by social and material conditions should still be considered fundamentally different from the idealist theories which attempted to explain history in terms of 'great men' or 'God's Will'.[119]

Although Feng Youlan did not explicitly claim that Han Feizi's theory was as correct as that of Marx, his motive in comparing classical Chinese philosophy to Marx in this conference was clear, and several articles were published attacking this.

Some critics directly disagreed with the claim that Han Feizi could be considered a materialist, saying that because he proclaimed innate evil his idealism was as obvious as that of Mengzi, who promoted the innate goodness of man.[120] Others said that to explain social development by using either geography or population growth was not materialist because the two factors had to be taken together. Taken individually, they did not really explain social development properly at all.[121] The most common complaint, however, was the argument that, although Han Feizi's theories had some elements of materialism in their use of population growth to explain social development, this materialism was not thoroughgoing and ultimately resulted in idealism because Han Feizi overestimated the value of laws (*fa*) in historical change. It was claimed that, by making *fa* absolute, Han Feizi neglected the importance of economics.[122]

However, many people also supported Feng Youlan, and in fact the criticisms did not really refute his ideas, as he did not state explicitly that Han Feizi's materialism was systematic or thoroughgoing, or that it was as good as that of Marx. Indeed, unless Han Feizi was, as Li Zhikui claimed, an idealist, the criticism that he only had some elements of materialism was part of Feng Youlan's argument anyway. Most scholars did not believe that Han Feizi was simply an idealist. As one defender of Feng Youlan concluded, 'Therefore I believe that, although Han Feizi's historical outlook has areas which were not scientific, systematic, or thorough, its tendency on the whole was towards materialism. It was a simple materialism.'[123] The idea that Han Feizi was a materialist was accepted by most writers. The fact that Feng Youlan had, as early as 1957, tried to use it as a means of advocating the revival of Chinese classical philosophy may partly explain why he was later willing to put his name to the anti-Kongzi movement. For, although one traditional thought was to be abolished, another was to take its place.

The tendency to substitute the Kong-Meng tradition with the Xunzi tradition was already noticeable in the fifties and sixties. By the early seventies, when slogans like 'dictatorship of the proletariat' were fashionable and when political control was authoritarian and total, Han Feizi's philosophy was 'inherited' above all else. This chapter has clearly shown that the unorthodox interpretations of Han Feizi's political doctrines in the early seventies did not appear by sudden fiat from the 'Gang of Four'. They had already gained some popularity before the Cultural Revolution and, it seems, for reasons which were similar to the favourable evaluations made on Kongzi: the desire on the part of many intellectuals to claim that aspects of Chinese tradition were 'inheritable'.

This chapter has also shown the random way in which scholars argued when writing about the classical philosophers. The terms 'idealist' and 'materialist' were often used, but they never really meant anything definite: as Guo Moruo pointed out, Mengzi and Xunzi both believed in an original human nature, but one was declared idealist and the other materialist, depending on the prejudice of the historian rather than well-founded evidence and reasoning. The writings of any scholar working on any topic anywhere must necessarily be limited by the environment in which that work is produced. The fact that most of the debates considered in this chapter lack variety and sophistication reflects a scholarship reduced to a political tool, one which was used by both politicians and scholars alike to manipulate the Chinese perception of their past.

Conclusion

IN their insistence that only the 'good' aspects of tradition should be salvaged for present-day use, Chinese intellectuals and politicians have, like their predecessors in Imperial times, taken a very conservative and élitist approach to history and philosophy. The 'abstract inheritance method' has in effect symbolized and intensified this approach. As Benjamin Schwartz observed, people who want to justify established tradition normally do so in terms of universal norms,[1] and, as Feng Youlan himself has indicated, the 'abstract' in his method was meant to be a universal norm. Many people, especially scholars who have studied traditional Chinese philosophy, would applaud the belief that this philosophy has universal significance but, in thus providing a rationale for the preservation of tradition in the name of Marxism, Feng Youlan and his supporters have opted for a brand of Marxism which is both conservative and élitist.

The huge amount of time and energy spent on the questions of periodization and the struggle between idealism and materialism is justified by the Leninist doctrine that society is propelled forwards by a select vanguard. The received opinion seems to be that, in the Spring and Autumn period, there was a tremendous social upheaval and that the philosophers of that time both reflected and guided that social change. Modern intellectuals saw themselves as heirs to and performing the same social roles as those early thinkers. The political leadership also welcomed such a view because they saw themselves as interpreters and engineers of the rapid changes in today's China. Thus, both the politicians and the intellectuals gladly embraced a Leninist-Stalinist interpretation of history rather than a more egalitarian Marxist one.

The result is that many of the proposals to abstract and inherit the culture of the labouring masses in ancient China are reduced to platitudes. The mere fact that scholars base their evidence almost solely on the written word already determines the scope of the debates on 'inheriting tradition'. The labouring masses simply did not write. The tenets of historical materialism do force writers to consider the class composition and economic and political conditions under which the pre-Qin philosophers lived, but the bulk of their writing only parrots the crude theories put forward by historians such as Guo Moruo and Fan Wenlan before 1949. More 'mass-based' theses such as those by Yang Rongguo and Cai Shangsi, which considered the effects of the major philosophies on 'minorities' such as women and ordinary workers, were largely ignored.

The more liberal expressions by left-wing writers were in fact very similar to those voiced by May Fourth iconoclasts such as Chen Duxiu and Lu Xun, who perceived traditional morality as a man-eat-man one.[2] As they were not obliged to defer to the Stalinist dogmas of periodization and the struggle between idealism and materialism, radicals of the May Fourth mould were able to condemn Chinese tradition much more easily and thoroughly than Communist writers after 1949.[3] Tradition to the May Fourth mind referred mainly to Confucianism, and Chapter 3 has shown that it is doubtful if Communist intellectuals would have wished to denounce Kongzi and his ideas even if they had been allowed to do so.

The only period in the Communist era when Kongzi's philosophy was attacked with the vehemence of the May Fourth period was during the anti-Kongzi campaign of the early 1970s. This was when Lu Xun's 'eat people' was echoed in writings about Kongzi and when issues such as the position of women in Confucian society were raised. With few exceptions, however, this was also the period when scholars as a whole stopped writing. True, the anti-Kongzi campaign was a movement with ulterior motives engineered by politicians, but very few academics in China are unaware that nearly all intellectual activity has been politically motivated since 1949. It was a question of choice: which policies they felt more comfortable with to express themselves. The ephemeral nature of both the May Fourth and Cultural Revolution iconoclastic attempts to revise perceptions of Chinese history points to the desire on the part of most intellectuals to 'inherit' tradition, especially that represented by Kongzi's *ren* and his educational theories. Feng Youlan's 'abstract inheritance method' was really framed for this purpose. It had support before the Cultural Revolution and, after 'normality' was restored, it was again being proposed as a reasonable method.[4]

Whether the adulations and denunciations of Kongzi's thought were politically inspired or not, the truth is that there has never been any period when he was ignored. He has always been discussed as if he were still alive. Indeed, his legacy is still very much a part of Chinese reality. The continual controversies surrounding Kongzi since 1949 testify to the intense commitment Chinese intellectuals seem to have made to Confucianism.[5] Even when he is not supposed to matter, he matters very much.

There are good reasons why Chinese intellectuals remain enamoured of Confucianism. Many of them have spent a lifetime studying this philosophy, and most have 'inherited' their predecessors' belief that Kongzi was 'the paragon of teachers' and the epitome of wisdom and learning. Moreover, the orthodox Kong-Meng stream of Confucianism which stresses respect for the aged and the learned is a highly élitist philosophy which established intellectuals in particular find very attractive as they often see themselves as the enlightened core who would lead the ignorant masses. For example, Liu Jie's Mengzi-inspired assertion that, even in a Communist society, only a small group of individuals should and can be educated to guide the majority is now given a Marxist philosophical respectability. It was claimed in 1980 that Mengzi was a materialist because he argued against Mozi, Yang Zhu, and Xu Xing. Mozi's 'universality' was said to represent the interests of the small producers, Yang Zhu's 'egoism' the landlords, and Xu Xing's 'egalitarianism' the peasants.[6] It is significant that, although all three philosophers were influential in Mengzi's time, only Mozi's works are extant. The present distaste for extreme individualism and egalitarianism is really a continuation of traditional attitudes. Individualism and egalitarianism, of course, are anathema not only to orthodox Confucianism but to Leninism as well.

As well as its inherent élitism, another aspect of Confucianism which would appeal to politicians and scholars is its statism. More than most of the world's great philosophies, Confucianism occupies itself with qualities of good statesmanship, methods for producing social harmony, and ways of making the state wealthier and mightier. These are concerns which modern intellectuals share with their counterparts in Imperial times. The scholar-gentry of old, of course, benefited from the Confucian order because in it they were the powerful and the privileged. To them, only the Confucian civilization was normal and moral; all else was foreign and barbaric. Although established Chinese scholars after 1949 have had to question this assumption, they have followed their predecessors by redefining being Chinese as essentially being Confucian. Even when talking about modernization and importing foreign

ideas, political leaders and university professors alike are careful to qualify modernization as 'Chinese-style' modernization. In
almost every field, this means keeping traditional Confucian
values.[7] In an unpublished paper for the Taiyuan Conference in
1978, Feng Youlan made the point that it is Confucianism which
gives coherence to and which has sustained Chinese civilization for
so long. The implication, which most intellectuals would agree
with, is that without Confucianism China would no longer be
Chinese.

By contrast, Daoism, which has also sustained Chinese civilization for over two thousand years, has not been so explicitly called
on as a legacy which needs to be observed in present-day China for
the continuance of the civilization. Daoism has always acted as an
escape-valve for the frustrated scholar-official. There is no reason
why politicians would want openly to call for its 'inheritance'. Of
all the pre-Qin philosophers considered in this book (with the
possible exception of the Logicians), Zhuangzi's is the only truly
apolitical philosophy, and Laozi is more often than not interpreted
in a non-political way. This anti-statist tendency in Daoism stands
in sharp contrast to Confucianism. When the state feels secure,
Daoists are tolerated,[8] but the non-compliance implicit in Daoist
philosophy makes it particularly unwelcome when the state wants
to assert itself.

The Confucian abhorrence of the non-participation advocated
by Daoists is 'inherited' to a large extent by the more zealous
Communist writers. Guan Feng's bitter diatribe against Zhuangzi and the 'modern-day Zhuangzi', Feng Youlan, testifies to the
hatred those who stand for the state feel towards those who want
to find avenues for opting out. Though Guan Feng's accusations
reached fanatical and slanderous proportions at times,[9] he was
quite accurate in his perceptions. Feng Youlan, in his self-
criticism, admitted that he had only wanted to 'escape' into
Zhuangzi because he was not satisfied with certain periods of
Communist rule. The application of Daoism in this case is thus no
different from the way in which the traditional frustrated Confucian literati used it.

Guan Feng's reflections on Zhuangzi as he languished in gaol for
over ten years would be fascinating and would tell much about the
workings of the Chinese mind. However, even though he has been
freed now, he will probably still never fully reveal what his
thoughts were then. Nevertheless, some idea of the thought pro-

cesses of the disgruntled intellectual can be gauged from the many stories written by the former 'educated youth', some of whom were social activists in the Cultural Revolution, but later became disillusioned. Many were said to have become so alienated that they 'saw through the vanity of the world' (*kan po hongchen*) and led dissolute lives. Many, however, turned to religion and Daoism for meaning in an otherwise chaotic and absurd existence.[10] In stories such as 'The Chess King',[11] written in 1984, the author's descriptions of how Cultural Revolution youth used Daoist methods to escape into their own minds is reminiscent of Feng Youlan's descriptions of the way in which university professors sought to 'run away' from the advance of the Communists in the late forties and early fifties. The point about using mental avenues for escape, however, is that this is only open to those who use their minds, that is, an intellectual élite.

Because the social impact of Daoism is not conscious or active, its influence is not as easily discernible as Confucianism, which has traditionally been a respected creed which its adherents openly preached. The manifestations of Daoism are found rather more in creative pursuits such as painting, calligraphy, and poetry. These activities are generally no less élitist than the morality and politics inherent in Confucianism. No wonder, then, that Chinese culture—at least the refined one presented in books—is so often seen as walking on the two legs of Confucianism and Daoism. True, not all artistic pursuits are snobbish. Many of the Huxian peasant paintings,[12] for example, are works by and about labouring people but, like the Cultural Revolution itself, such art pieces enjoyed but a brief moment of popularity and prestige. The seemingly contradictory trend whereby both Confucianism and philosophic Daoism experienced a certain revival after the Cultural Revolution is thus easy to explain when viewed in the light of the shared élitism of the two philosophies. Present Chinese policies openly welcome a more hierarchical society. Aspects of Chinese philosophy which were previously denounced as having served the upper classes have thus been reassessed to show that they are materialist and thus 'inheritable'. Both Laozi and Zhuangzi have in fact been labelled as materialists in recent years.[13]

The writers' concern with only 'high culture' when they discuss 'inheriting tradition' is further shown by the relative silence on popular Daoism. With only a few exceptions, the majority of

essays on Daoism have been on the philosophy as espoused by
Laozi and Zhuangzi and very little has been written on the more
massed-based aspects such as Daoist alchemy, Daoist-inspired
tales of the supernatural, and Daoist shamanism. It is true that
Feng Youlan, in the fifties, did quote the legendary figure Bandit
Zhi from the *Zhuangzi* to support his theory that the 'abstract inheritance method' could be used to include the morality of the
lower classes, and during the anti-Kongzi movement of the early
seventies, the Bandit Zhi legend and the alleged execution of
Shaozheng Mao by Kongzi were highlighted to emphasize the fact
that a people's philosophy did exist in pre-Qin times. In practice,
however, a 'people's philosophy' was interpreted to mean one
which served the interest of the general populace rather than one
created by them.

If there had been a philosophy which was close to 'the people' in
pre-Qin times, then it must surely be that of Mozi. Historically,
Moism has never been popular among the literati. Although it is
generally agreed that Mozi's ideas have been absorbed into the
ideology of the ever-popular 'knights-errant' (*xia*),[14] the assumption has been that the influence of Moism on Chinese culture has
been minor, with Guo Moruo even doubting the claim that it had
affected the 'knights-errant' concept.[15] The unstated scorn shown
towards Moism has continued into the present; it is apparent in the
relative scarcity of calls to 'inherit' from him. This is particularly
conspicuous when seen against the May Fourth attempts to uphold
Mozi as the true sage of Chinese tradition. That nobody has proposed salvaging Mozi's thought in the way that Feng Youlan or
Liu Jie wanted to 'inherit' Kongzi's *ren* or that the 'Gang of
Four' wanted to adopt Legalism reveals further the élitist bias of
the proponents of 'inheriting tradition' in the People's Republic of
China. Even left-wing historians such as Yang Rongguo and Cai
Shangsi, who before 1949 argued strongly that Mozi was a better
alternative to Kongzi, had by the fifties moderated their tone.

The egalitarian principles embodied in Mozi's thought, though
seemingly 'communist', were precisely what made it unacceptable
to intellectuals and politicans alike. Mozi's philosophy was simply
not designed for the powerful and privileged. After 1949, the only
national 'debate' held on Mozi was conducted through a daily
newspaper, and by writers who were little known, and even then
the editors of the newspaper put a stop to the discussion after only
a couple of articles. This contrasts sharply with the many academic

conferences, collections of articles in books and journals, and controversies involving top scholars and politicians which were devoted to the Confucians, Daoists, and Legalists. Not only was there no interest in 'inheriting' Mozi's thought, but Feng Youlan claimed explicitly that *jian'ai* could not be inherited because it lacked a 'universal form' in the *German Ideology* sense.[16] There is little logic in such claims, just as the desire to make sure that the Confucian *ren* has a place in socialist China or the need to use Daoist attitudes in times of despair in the modern world are based more on personal preferences than rational argument.

The emotional attachment or aversion to Confucianism and Daoism, as indicated above, was based on the feeling that intellectuals were above the ordinary people. Why, then, was Mozi's philosophy completely ignored during the Cultural Revolution period when so much attention was paid to destroying the class system and when intellectuals were classed as 'the stinking ninth category' (*chou laojiu*)? Curiously, Mozi's philosophy also directly contradicted Cultural Revolution policies. Mozi's basic premise of *jian'ai* ran counter to Mao Zedong's directive that there was no such thing as universal love. Other important ingredients of Mozi's philosophy such as anti-militarism were also diametrically opposed to Cultural Revolution concerns, in this case the hysteria of preparing for war. Even the idea that only the worthy should be elevated (*shang xian*) was inconsistent with the Cultural Revolution educational principles of nurturing and promoting only the working classes. Thus, Mozi did not stir much emotion among Chinese intellectuals (neither Guan Feng nor Feng Youlan said very much about him), and his philosophy has received little praise or abuse in any period in the history of the People's Republic. It seems that Moism, with its utilitarian rather than 'moral' emphasis, is almost alien to Chinese culture. This is further indicated by the fact that suggestions have been made by scholars that Mozi may have been Indian,[17] because his thinking was so un-Chinese. It is inconceivable that anyone should make the same allegations about Kongzi or Zhuangzi.

The traditional scholars' distaste for the artisan class and technical knowledge in general may partly explain why Mozi and his way of thinking suffered such a setback after the Qin dynasty. Mozi himself was said to have been the inventor of sophisticated machines, a fame which would not have impressed the Confucian scholar who was more immersed in questions of moral rectitude

and government. The Later Moists in particular were very sci-
entifically-minded, with the *Moist Canon* devoting much space
to principles of physics and mathematics. Although the traditional
bias against the technically qualified was sustained right into the
Cultural Revolution, the present calls for the 'four moderniza-
tions' may make the Moist tradition more acceptable in China.
There have certainly been many serious studies of the *Moist
Canon* and the *Mozi* itself since 1976.[18] With the recent prestige
and privilege accorded the élite scientific community, perhaps the
'Chinese-style modernization' which the present leadership is aim-
ing for may include Moist aspects of Chineseness.

If Moism is seemingly the most 'communist' of the pre-Qin philosophies in its advocacy of working for the benefit of the common
people and preventing imperialistic wars by any means including
civil disobedience, then Legalism must be the least Marxist philosophy considered in this book. Conceived by the ruling aristocracy of its time, it stressed ruthless and brutal dictatorship over the
masses. It is a philosophy which might suit a politician who wanted
to establish a controlled state quickly and securely. This may explain why it is the Xunzi-Han Feizi tradition that has since 1949
steadily been given a more favourable interpretation by the use of
the idealist/materialist dichotomy and why this was the philosophy
which was chosen by the 'Gang of Four' as the most glorious of the
Chinese traditions.

The apparent contradiction of praising a non-Communist philosophy in a Communist state is not difficult to explain when seen
in the context of the inherent Sinocentric bias of Chinese intellectuals and politicians. In terms of 'inheriting tradition', the elevation of Xunzi and Han Feizi in fact meant the preservation of nearly all the pre-Qin philosophies, for these two, of all the classical
philosophers, have summarized the thinking of all the other major
schools of thought. By claiming, as the 'Gang of Four' writers have
done, that the Confucian-Legalist conflict was a 'two-line struggle'
which lasted into the present, the writings of over half the Chinese
philosophers in the past have been praised. As most of these
'Legalist' writings were also attacks on the 'Confucians', the study
of Confucian texts was also seen to be imperative. In fact, in terms
of publication of the Confucian classics, the anti-Kongzi campaign in the early seventies saw the greatest revival of Confucianism in modern times. This phenomenon only reflects the simple
truth that Legalism is an integral part of the overall Chinese tradi-

tion. To the average Chinese intellectual, this makes it eminently more preferable as a vehicle for the path towards wealth and power than any foreign ideology.[19]

Legalism would appeal to politicians too because it is even more statist than Confucianism. The Legalists stood for a single and united nation. Qin Shihuang is, after all, remembered for being the first unifier of China. His position after 1949 thus experienced a complete reversal from traditional evaluations which have judged him a tyrant and megalomaniac.[20] The same was true of other Legalists such as Shang Yang, who were also reinterpreted in very glowing terms.[21] The Chinese political scene in this century has been a series of violent inter- and intra-party struggles for control, and it is fairly certain that the *Han Feizi*, in its emphasis on the centralization and merciless execution of power, has provided much inspiration for this process. When Mao Zedong declared that the Communists had surpassed Qin Shihuang's 'burning of books and burying of scholars', he was emphasizing the use of power rather than showing his distaste for the Confucians.[22]

Although national unity and the authority of the central leadership were probably ideals the orthodox Confucians also agreed with, the teachings of Xunzi and Han Feizi had one element which was different from all the other pre-Qin schools of thought, namely, their belief that the ancient past might not have been a utopia as suggested by the other philosophers. This was an important idea which accorded well with Cultural Revolution thinking as expressed in the attacks on the belief that 'each generation is not as good as the one before' (*yi dai bu ru yi dai*). Although the idea of historical progression tallied well with the Marxist periodization schemes, it certainly ran counter to the conservative element found in the thinking of established Chinese intellectuals.

The Legalist hostility towards scholars, shown in their unambiguous naming of them as 'vermin', moreover, meant that any co-operation between politicians and intellectuals in attempting to replace Confucianism with Legalism could only be a temporary affair. Furthermore, although the Legalists emphasized government control, their insistence on legal codes and the 'Gang of Four' interpretations of this as meaning government without distinction of classes stripped the Legalist doctrine of its élitist origins. To intellectuals accustomed to thinking in terms of the Confucian morally superior man (*junzi*), this further lessened its appeal. It is hardly surprising then that, as soon as the political faction which briefly made the Legalists popular fell, interest in this philosophy immediately waned too.[23]

China in the wake of Mao is more prepared to have foreign contacts but, in its perceptions of itself, many of the attitudes of the pre-Cultural Revolution era have been resurrected. Certainly, the agonizing questions of what and how to salvage from the Chinese past are once more major topics for discussion in academic conferences.[24] In the fifties and early sixties, some of the older scholars and politicians expressed the fear that the advent of Marxism would spell doom to Chinese civilization. In the same way, many people in China now are alarmed at the possibility of 'cultural pollution' if China opens its doors wider. Thus, instead of talking about modernizing China, the Chinese are adamant that they are heading for a 'Chinese-style modernization', lest modernization lead to Westernization. Such fears stem from a mentality dating from a 'semi-feudal, semi-colonialist' past which saw Chinese culture as a mere passive lump responding to outside stimuli.[25] It does not take into account the fact that, whatever China takes from the outside world it will actively mould to suit its needs with or without exhortations from politicians and intellectuals. Whether the Chinese leadership aims for a 'Chinese-style modernization' or not, China when it modernizes will inevitably be Chinese, and continued insistence on this only suggests a slight case of a cultural inferiority complex.

Any fears that Western culture will swamp Chinese culture are groundless. The history of the People's Republic of China shows that, despite thirty odd years of intensive Communist indoctrination, what has emerged is still very much Chinese. Confucianism and Daoism have certainly continued to be highly revered, whereas Marxism has been interpreted and reinterpreted so often that in practice it is now more Chinese than German.[26] Works by Marx and Lenin are still referred to as the 'Marxist Scriptures' (*jingdian*) but, like all sacred gospels, words are taken from them only to suit the readers' needs. China now feels that it needs to train and establish quickly an educated leadership in all fields. Present indications are that the more élitist Chinese traditions will again be called upon to help to promote that goal.

Notes

NOTES TO THE PREFACE

1. Mao Zedong, 'The Role of the Chinese Communist Party in the National War', *Selected Works of Mao Tse-tung* (Beijing, Foreign Languages Press), Vol. II (1967), p. 209.
2. Kam Louie, *Critiques of Confucius in Contemporary China* (Hong Kong, Chinese University Press, 1980).
3. Terms such as 'conservative' and 'radical' are used to describe the attitudes of intellectuals towards tradition rather than their political affiliations, although the two often coincide.
4. 'Manifesto of the Communist Party', in Karl Marx and Frederick Engels, *Selected Works* (Moscow, Progress Publishers, 1969), Vol. 1, p. 126.
5. Despite the importance of this topic, there is surprisingly little research on it. Donald J. Munro's 'Chinese Communist Treatment of the Thinkers of the Hundred Schools Period', in Albert Feuerwerker (ed.), *History in Communist China* (Cambridge, Mass., MIT Press, 1968), pp. 74–95, is still one of the best accounts today.

NOTES TO CHAPTER 1

1. For example, Charlotte Furth (ed.), *The Limits of Change* (Cambridge, Mass., Harvard University Press, 1976) has excellent essays on the intellectuals who are considered conservatives in the Republican era. A general history of the thinking and the times of intellectuals in modern China is narrated in Jerome B. Grieder, *Intellectuals and the State in Modern China* (New York, The Free Press, 1981).
2. The formation of intellectuals in Eastern Europe as a class is argued persuasively by Gyorgy Konrad and Istvan Szelenyi in *The Intellectuals on the Road to Class Power*, translated by Andrew Arato and Richard Allen (Brighton, Harvester Press, 1979). Although this book is about intellectuals in Eastern Europe, parallels can be drawn for other socialist countries.
3. Almost any general history text to come out of China begins with such a statement. For example, 'Obviously, an important path which we cannot do without is to study history and to absorb correctly the rich historical heritage of our country', Wu Han, *Zhongguo lishi changshi* (*General Knowledge in Chinese History*) (Beijing, Zhongguo qingnian chubanshe, 1964), p. 1.
4. In Mao Zedong's accounts of the campaign, for example, there is no mention of intellectuals. See Mao Zedong, 'On the Struggle Against the "Three Evils" and the "Five Evils"', *Selected Works of Mao Tse-tung*, Vol. V, pp. 64–70.
5. Although the main thrust of this campaign was literary, it had obvious repercussions for historical studies, especially for the evaluation of historical figures.
6. Whoever initiated it, the campaign had the backing of Mao. See Mao Zedong, 'Pay Serious Attention to the Discussion of the Film *The Life of Wu Hsun*', *Selected Works of Mao Tse-tung*, Vol. V, pp. 53–6.
7. For a summary of the arguments against the film, see Merle Goldman, *Literary Dissent in Communist China* (Cambridge, Mass., Harvard University Press, 1967), pp. 89–93.
8. New China News Agency, 'Ideological Reform among Peking and Tientsin

Professors Enters Second Stage', *Survey of China Mainland Press* (Hong Kong, American Consulate General, 1952), pp. 9–10.

9. Liang Souming, *Zhongguo wenhua yaoyi (The Essentials of Chinese Culture)* (Hong Kong, Jicheng tushu gongsi, 1963), reprint edition.

10. See, for example, the contrast in the prefaces of Zhou Gucheng, *Zhongguo tongshi (General History of China)*, 1939 reprint edition (Hong Kong, Wenluo chubanshe, n.d.), Vol. 1, pp. 2–23 and *Zhongguo tongshi* (Shanghai, Shanghai renmin chubanshe, 1957), Vol. 1, pp. 1–19.

11. Many of these articles are collected in Jian Bozan, *Lishi wenti luncong (Collected Essays on Historical Problems)* (Beijing, Renmin chubanshe, 1962).

12. Ai's ideas are later outlined more fully in Ai Siqi, *Bianzheng weiwuzhuyi, lishi weiwuzhuyi (Dialectical Materialism and Historical Materialism)* (Beijing, Renmin chubanshe, 1961).

13. Liu Guojun, *Zhongguo shushi jianbian (A Brief History of Chinese Books)* (Beijing, Gaodeng jiaoyu chubanshe, 1958), p. 143.

14. Ridannuofu, (Zhdanov), *Ridannuofu tongzhi guanyu xifang zhexueshi de fayan (Comrade Zhdanov's Speech Regarding the History of Western Philosophy)*, translated by Li Lisan (Harbin, Dongbei shudian, 1948).

15. Figures from *Renmin ribao (People's Daily)*, 19 April 1957.

16. *Zhexue yanjiu (Philosophical Research)*, No. 1, 1955, p. 1.

17. See Jerome B. Grieder, *Hu Shih and the Chinese Renaissance: Liberalism in the Chinese Revolution 1917–1937* (Cambridge, Mass., Harvard University Press, 1970).

18. Hou Wailu, 'Cong duidai zhexue yichan de guandian fangfa he lichang pipan Hu Shi zenyang tumo he wumie Zhongguo zhexueshi' ('From the Methods and Standpoint of Treating the Philosophical Legacy to Criticizing Hu Shi's Smearing and Slandering the History of Chinese Philosophy'), *Zhexue yanjiu (Philosophical Research)*, No. 2, 1955, pp. 92–116.

19. Quite apart from the ideological differences, Khrushchev and Mao did not like each other even on a personal level. See the descriptions of Mao in Nikita Khrushchev, *Khrushchev Remembers: The Last Testament*, translated and edited by Strobe Talbott (London, Deutsch, 1974).

20. Mao's speech was not published, but the main ideas were incorporated in a report by Lu Dingyi. The official translation of this report is reprinted in *Communist China, 1955–59: Policy Documents with Analysis* (Cambridge, Mass., Harvard University Press, 1962), pp. 151–63.

21. Yang Yongzhi, 'Weile jianshe shehuizhuyi wenhua bixu pipan di jieshou zuguo wenhua yichan' ('The Critical Assimilation of Our Country's Cultural Heritage is Necessary for Socialist Cultural Reconstruction'), *Zhexue yanjiu (Philosophical Research)*, No. 1, 1956, pp. 52–70.

22. Mao Zedong, 'Talks at the Yenan Forum on Literature and Art', *Selected Works of Mao Tse-tung*, Vol. III, p. 81. The quotations used here are from the official post-1949 texts. Bonnie McDougall observes that, in the 1943 text, Mao was considerably more critical of tradition, partly because after 1949 'the Communist Party was no longer a band of rebels, opposing the ruling classes and the culture that supported them, but the ruling group and therefore themselves heir to that culture.' See her 'Introduction', to *Mao Zedong's 'Talks at the Yan'an Conference on Literature and Art': A Translation of the 1943 Text with Commentary* (Ann Arbor, University of Michigan, Center for Chinese Studies, 1980), p. 20.

23. Mao Zedong, 'The Role of the Chinese Communist Party in the National War', *Selected Works of Mao Tse-tung*, Vol. II, p. 209.

24. I have used the translation 'to inherit' here for *jicheng*, although the Chinese usage of the term is wider than the English. *Jicheng* refers to the appropriateness or profitability of something, whether concrete or abstract, being passed on. Chapter 2 will deal with one definition of this process in more detail.

25. Feng Youlan, 'Zhongguo zhexue yichan de jicheng wenti' ('On the Question of Inheriting the Chinese Philosophical Heritage'), in Zhexue yanjiu bianjibu (ed.), *Zhongguo zhexueshi wenti taolun zhuanji (A Symposium on the Problems of the History of Chinese Philosophy)* (Beijing, Kexue chubanshe, 1957), hereafter *Symposium on Chinese Philosophy*, pp. 273–80.

26. Quoted in 'History of Chinese Philosophy', *China News Analysis*, No. 219, 1958, p. 3.

27. Some of these stories are translated in W.J.F. Jenner (ed.), *Fragrant Weeds* (Hong Kong, Joint Publishing Co., 1983).

28. See the extracts reprinted in Roderick MacFarquhar, *The Hundred Flowers* (London, Stevens and Sons, 1960).

29. In the last few years, for example, there have been numerous stories written about injustices committed against intellectuals at this time. They reveal the bitterness with which some people still remember that period.

30. For a discussion of the Yan'an model, see Mark Selden, *The Yenan Way in Revolutionary China* (Cambridge, Mass., Harvard University Press, 1971).

31. Guan Feng, 'Huo shengsheng de bianzhengfa' ('The Living Dialectics'), *Zhexue yanjiu (Philosophical Research)*, No. 4, 1958, pp. 7–9.

32. 'Only Through Showing Real Repentance can Rightists have a Bright Future: Labels of Another Group of Rightists in Shansi Province who have shown Real Repentance are Removed', *Shansi Daily*, 30 September 1960. Translated in *Survey of China Mainland Press* (Supplement), No. 53, 1960, p. 17.

33. Mao had already made the decision to step down in 1958. 'Decision approving Comrade Mao Tse-tung's Proposal that he will not Stand as Candidate for Chairman of the People's Republic of China for the Next Term of Office', adopted by the 8th Central Committee of the Chinese Communist Party at its 6th Plenary Session, 10 December 1958, in *Documents of Chinese Communist Party Central Committee September 1956–April 1969* (Hong Kong, Union Research Institute, 1971), Vol. 1, pp. 121–2.

34. For a discussion of the differences between Mao and Liu in their styles of work, see Lowell Dittmer, *Liu Shao-ch'i and the Chinese Cultural Revolution: The Politics of Mass Criticism* (Berkeley, University of California Press, 1974).

35. R.V Vyatkin and S.L. Tikhvinsky, 'Some Questions of Historical Science in the People's Republic', in Albert Feuerwerker (ed.), *History in Communist China* (Cambridge, Mass., MIT Press, 1968), pp. 331–55.

36. Chen Yi, 'Dui Beijing shi gaodeng yuanxiao yingjie biye xuesheng de jianghua' ('Speech to This Year's Graduates from Beijing's Higher Institutions'), *Zhongguo qingnian (China Youth)*, No. 17, 1961, pp. 2–5.

37. 'Zai xueshu yanjiu zhong jianchi baihua qifang baijia zhengming de fangzhen' ('Stand Firm on the Policy of Letting a Hundred Flowers Blossom and a Hundred Schools of Thought Contend in Academic Research'), *Hongqi (Red Flag)*, No. 5, 1961, pp. 1–5.

38. I Wo-sheng, 'Education in Communist China during 1962 and a Comparison with Education in the Soviet Union', *Communist China 1962* (Hong Kong, Union Research Institute, 1963), Vol. I, p. 180.

39. Some of the major papers from this conference are collected in Zhongguo kexueyuan Shandong fenyuan lishi yanjiusuo (ed.), *Kongzi taolun wenji (Collected Papers on Kongzi)* (Jinan, Shandong renmin chubanshe, 1962), Vol. 1.

40. Liu Shaoqi, *Lun gongchandang yuan de xiuyang (How To Be a Good Communist)* (Beijing, Renmin chubanshe, 1962). Sixty million copies of this revised edition were printed in 1962. The original Chinese actually translates as 'On the Self-Cultivation of a Communist Party Member'.

41. See, for example, Wu Qibing, 'Guchui chongyang fugu, jiu shi maiguo, jiu shi fubi—bo Zhou Yang "quanpan xihua" "quanpan jicheng" de fandong lilun' ('To Advocate Worship of Foreign Things and Return to Old Things is Treason and

Restoration: in Refutation of Zhou Yang's Reactionary Doctrine of "Total Westernization" and "Total Inheritance"'), *Guangming ribao (Guangming Daily)*, 28 August 1970.

42. Mao Zedong, 'Speech at the Tenth Plenum', 24 September 1962, in Stuart Schram (ed.), *Mao Tse-tung Unrehearsed* (Harmondsworth, Penguin Books, 1974), pp. 188–9.

43. Meng Dengjin and Niu Xinfang, '"Wu shi" jiaoyu de renshi lun yiyi' ('The Epistemological Significance of the "Five Histories" Education') *Zhexue yanjiu (Philosophical Research)*, No. 4, 1964, pp. 17–23. This was sometimes referred to as the Four Histories, sometimes as Five, with a division of family histories into worker and peasant families.

44. Yao Wenyuan, 'Ping xinbian lishi ju "Hai Rui ba guan"' ('A Critique of the New Historical Play *Hai Rui Dismissed from Office*'), *Wenhui bao (Wenhui Daily)*, 10 November 1965.

45. See *The Case of Peng Teh-huai 1959–1968* (Hong Kong, Union Research Institute, 1968).

46. Mao Zedong, 'Criticize P'eng Chen', *Miscellany of Mao Tse-tung Thought (1949–1968)*, Part II (Arlington, Joint Publications Research Service, 1974), p. 383.

47. Mao Zedong, 'Speech at Hangchow', in Stuart Schram (ed.), *Mao Tse-tung Unrehearsed*, p. 237. Some scholars claim that Wu Han, in writing the play, only mirrored the concerns of the cultural élite at that time and that it was questionable whether he had Peng Dehuai in mind when he wrote the play. See, for example, Tom Fisher, '"The Play's the Thing": Wu Han and Hai Rui Revisited', *The Australian Journal of Chinese Affairs*, No. 7, 1982, pp. 1–35.

48. Wu Han, 'Guanyu "*Hai Rui ba guan*" de ziwo pipan' ('A Self-criticism relating to *Hai Rui Dismissed from Office*') *Renmin ribao (People's Daily)*, 30 December 1965.

49. Fang Cheng, 'Education in Communist China 1966', *Communist China 1966* (Hong Kong, Union Research Institute, 1968), Vol. II, p. 46.

50. Mao Zedong, 'Speech to the Albanian Military Delegation', *Miscellany of Mao Tse-tung Thought (1949–1968)*, Part II, p. 457.

51. Mao Zedong, '*Pao da silingbu*' ('Bombard the Headquarters'), *Hongqi (Red Flag)*, No. 3, 1967, p. 3.

52. 'Decision of the Central Committee of the Chinese Communist Party concerning the Great Proletarian Cultural Revolution (Adopted on August 8, 1966)', in *Carry the Great Proletarian Cultural Revolution Through to the End* (Beijing, Foreign Languages Press, 1966), pp. 1–14.

53. 'Workers, Peasants and Soldiers in Changsha Unite with "Red Guards" to Smash all Old Ideas, Old Cultures, Old Customs and Old Habits', *Yangcheng wanbao (Canton Evening News)*, 25 August 1966, translated in *Survey of China Mainland Press*, No. 3774, 1966, pp. 17–19.

54. 'Philosophy is No Mystery' (Beijing, Foreign Languages Press, 1972).

55. Mao Zedong, *Quotations from Chairman Mao Tse-tung* (Beijing, Foreign Languages Press, 1966).

56. These are collected in *Mao Tse-tung, Four Essays on Philosophy* (Beijing, Foreign Languages Press, 1968).

57. Duan Chunzuo, 'Yunyong "shijianlun" zongjie minjian cetian jingyan' ('Using "On Practice" to Summarize Folk Experiences in Weather Forecasting') *Hongqi (Red Flag)*, No. 2, 1966, pp. 20–7. Liu Peishun '"*Maodun lun*" de sixiang jinle shuiniyao' ('The Thinking of "On Contradiction" Has Entered the Cement Kiln'), *Hongqi (Red Flag)*, No. 2, 1966, pp. 28–32.

58. See, for example, the deeds supposedly performed under the influence of Mao Zedong thought collected in George Urban (ed.), *The Miracles of Chairman Mao* (London, Stacey, 1971).

59. Zhou Yang was only one of a number of officials who had been in Shanghai in the 1930s who became the object of a personal vendetta by Jiang Qing. See Roxanne Witke, *Comrade Chiang Ch'ing* (London, Weidenfeld and Nicolson, 1977), p. 122.

60. Jean Daubier, *A History of the Chinese Cultural Revolution* (New York, Random House, 1974), pp. 205-10.

61. See, for example, Deng Aimin and Wei Changhai, 'Lun Guan Feng zai zhexue yichan jicheng wentishang de xingershang xue sixiang' ('On Guan Feng's Metaphysical Thinking relating to the Problem of Philosophical Inheritance'), in Zhongguo shehui kexueyuan zhexue yanjiusuo, Zhongguo zhexueshi yanjiushi (ed.), *Zhongguo zhexueshi fangfa lun taolun ji (Collected Papers on the Methodology of the History of Chinese Philosophy)* (Beijing, Zhongguo shehui kexue chubanshe, 1980), pp. 153-68.

62. The Cultural Revolution period refers to 1966-76 for the sake of brevity.

63. The amount of research carried out on Marx would fill a library. Furthermore, much of Western analysis of Marxism has been largely neglected in China. For example, the notion of alienation, which many Western critics see as the central concern of Marx (see, for instance, Bertell Ollman, *Alienation: Marx's Conception of Man in Capitalist Society* (London, Cambridge University Press, 1971) has only been studied very recently.

64. This contention was made by Engels as soon as Marx died, and Marxists ever since have regarded it as true. Frederick Engels, 'Speech at the Graveside of Karl Marx', in K. Marx and F. Engels, *Selected Works* (Moscow, Progress Publishers, 1970), Vol. 3, p. 162.

65. K. Marx and F. Engels, 'The German Ideology', in K. Marx and F. Engels, *Selected Works*, Vol. 1, p. 43.

66. K. Marx, 'Theses on Feuerbach', in T.B. Bottomore and M. Rubel (eds.), *Karl Marx: Selected Writings in Sociology and Social Philosophy* (Harmondsworth, Penguin Books, 1963), p. 83.

67. Mao Zedong, 'On Practice', *Four Essays on Philosophy*, p. 8.

68. Karl Marx and Frederick Engels, 'Manifesto of the Communist Party', *Selected Works*, Vol. 1, p. 108.

69. Zhou Gucheng, 1939 edition, p. 35; 1957 edition, p. 21.

70. Although the term *taishi* came from the official post (*taishiling*) which Sima Qian held and had no connotation of greatness then, there is nevertheless no doubt that, in the minds of many, he was China's greatest historian.

71. K. Marx and F. Engels, 'Manifesto of the Communist Party', p. 117.

72. Karl Marx, 'Preface to *A Contribution to the Critique of Political Economy*', in K. Marx and F. Engels, *Selected Works*, Vol. 1, p. 504.

73. See Maurice Meisner, 'Li Ta-chao and the Chinese Communist Treatment of the Materialist Conception of History', in Albert Feuerwerker (ed.), *History in Communist China* (Cambridge, Mass., MIT Press, 1968), pp. 296-7.

74. Frederick Engels, *The Origin of the Family, Private Property and the State* (New York, International Publishers, 1968).

75. Guo Moruo, *Zhongguo gudai shehui yanjiu (A Study of Ancient Chinese Society)* (Shanghai, Xiandai shuju, 1931), p. 6.

76. See the essays reprinted in Deng Tuo, *Lun Zhongguo lishi de jige wenti (Several Problems in Chinese History)* (Beijing, Sanlian shudian, 1963) and Li Maimai, *Zhongguo gudai zhengzhi zhexue pipan (Critique of Ancient Chinese Political Philosophy)* (Shanghai, Xin shengming shuju, 1933).

77. Guo Moruo, 'Gudai yanjiu de ziwo pipan' ('A Self-criticism of my Research into Ancient Chinese Society'), in *Shi pipan shu (Ten Critiques)* (Beijing, Kexue chubanshe, 1956), pp. 1-70. This was first published in 1945. Even in the 1956 revised edition, however, Guo mentions on page 61 that slaves were truly liberated in Qin times.

78. Guo Moruo, 'Zhongguo nuli shehui' ('Slave Society in China'), *Xin jianshe (New Construction)*, Vol. 3, No. 1, 1950, p. 83.

79. Guo Baojun, 'Ji Yin-Zhou xunren zhi shishi' ('Historical Facts about Human Sacrifices in the Yin and Zhou Dynasties'), reprinted in Lishi yanjiu bianjibu (ed.), *Zhongguo de nulizhi yu fengjianzhi fenqi wenti lunwen xuanji (Selected Essays on the Problems of the Periodization of Chinese Slave and Feudal Systems)* (Beijing, Sanlian shudian, 1956), hereafter *Selected Essays on Periodization*, p. 60.

80. Guo Moruo, 'Dule "Ji Yin-Zhou xunren zhi shishi"' ('After Reading "Historical Facts about Human Sacrifices in the Yin and Zhou Dynasties"'), *Selected Essays on Periodization*, p. 57.

81. Guo Moruo, *Nulizhi shidai (Period of the Slave System)* (Beijing, Renmin chubanshe, 1973), p. 16.

82. Deng Guangming *et al.*, 'Shinian lai de Zhongguo shi yanjiu gaishu' ('A Brief Outline of Chinese Historical Studies of the Past Ten Years'), *Guangming ribao (Guangming Daily)*, 29 October 1959.

83. Fan Wenlan, 'Chuqi fengjian shehui kaishi yu XiZhou' ('The Early Feudal Society Began in the Western Zhou'), *Selected Essays on Periodization*, pp. 359–73.

84. Jian Bozan, *Zhongguo shi gangyao (Outline of Chinese History)* (Beijing, Renmin chubanshe, 1979), Vol. 1. This book was published after Jian Bozan's death. Deng Guangming, the current Head of the History Deparment at Beijing University, relates in the preface that in rewriting the book the editors had originally used Guo Moruo's periodization but after some debate reverted to Jian's original scheme.

85. Translation by James Legge, *The Four Books* (Hong Kong, The Chinese Book Co., no date), p. 442.

86. Guo Moruo, 'Guanyu Zhoudai shehui de shangtao' ('A Discussion of Society in the Zhou Period'), *Selected Essays on Periodization*, p. 88.

87. See Lanzhou daxue zhongwenxi Mengzi yizhu xiaozu (ed.), *Mengzi yizhu (Mengzi Translated and Annotated)* (Beijing, Zhonghua shuju, 1960), hereafter *Mengzi yizhu*, pp. 113–19.

88. Guo Moruo, *Nulizhi shidai*, p. 20.

89. Fan Wenlan, 'Chuqi fengjian shehui kaishi yu XiZhou', p. 361.

90. Wu Dakun, 'Yu Fan Wenlan tongzhi lun huafen Zhongguo nuli shehui yu fengjian shehui de biaozhun wenti' ('Discussing with Comrade Fan Wenlan the Problem of the Criterion for Differentiating Slave and Feudal Societies'), *Selected Essays on Periodization*, p. 122.

91. For example, Zhou Gucheng, 'Zhongguo nuli shehui lun' ('On Slave Society in China'), *Selected Essays on Periodization*, pp. 61–7 and Tong Shuye, 'Zhongguo gushi fenqi wenti de taolun' ('A Discussion of the Problem of Periodization of Ancient Chinese History'), *Selected Essays on Periodization*, pp. 130–61.

92. See, for example, Xie Hua, *Lun XiZhou fengjian (On the Feudalism of Western Zhou)* (Hunan, Hunan renmin chubanshe, 1979).

93. Wu Han, 'A Few Problems in the Teaching Materials of History in History Study', *Renmin jiaoyu (People's Education)*, No. 9, 1961. Translated by Chung Wah-min in 'Criticism of Academic Theories in Communist China, 1966', *Communist China 1966*, Vol. II, p. 132.

94. Jian Bozan, 'Yanjiu ruogan lishi wenti de yixie yijian' ('Preliminary Opinions concerning the Handling of Certain Historical Questions), *Guangming ribao (Guangming Daily)*, 22 December 1961. Translated by Chung Wah-min in 'Criticism of Academic Theories', p. 134.

95. Ning Ke, 'Lun lishizhuyi de jieji guandian' ('On Historicism and Class Viewpoint'), *Lishi yanjiu (Historical Research)*, No. 4, 1963, pp. 1–26.

96. Yuan Liangyi, 'Guanyu lishizhuyi yu jieji guandian' ('On Historicism and Class Viewpoint'), *Guangming ribao (Guangming Daily)*, 6 November 1963.

97. Ning Ke, 'Lun Makesizhuyi de lishizhuyi' ('On Marxist Historicism'), *Lishi yanjiu (Historical Research)*, No. 3, 1964, p. 12.

98. See, for example, Li Wen, 'Zenyang kandai lishizhuyi: yu Ning Ke tongzhi shangque' ('How Historicism Should be Treated: A Debate with Comrade Ning Ke'), *Guangming ribao (Guangming Daily)*, 18 November 1964.

99. Chi Shiwu, 'Chexia Jian Bozan de "lishizhuyi" de heiqi' ('Tear Down Jian Bozan's Black Flag of "Historicism"'), *Guangming ribao (Guangming Daily)*, 1 June 1966.

100. Mao Zedong, 'Speech at Hangchow', in Stuart Schram (ed.), *Mao Tse-tung Unrehearsed*, p. 234.

101. Mao Zedong, 'Report on an Investigation of the Peasant Movement in Hunan', *Selected Works of Mao Tse-tung*, Vol. I, pp. 23-59. Ever since Mao wrote this report in 1927, where he called the peasants the 'vanguards of revolution' (p. 30), the way was opened for peasants to be interpreted in the way that the proletariat was interpreted in Marx.

102. Jian Bozan, 'Preliminary Opinions concerning the Handling of Certain Historical Questions', in Chung Wah-min, 'Criticism of Academic Theories', p. 136.

103. Qi Benyu, Lin Jie, and Yan Changgui, 'Jian Bozan tongzhi de lishi guandian yingdang pipan' ('Comrade Jian Bozan's Historical Outlook Should be Criticized'), *Hongqi (Red Flag)*, No. 4, 1966, p. 26.

104. Hong Jianbin, 'Jian Bozan "rangbu zhengce" lun de fandong shizhi' ('The Reactionary Nature of Jian Bozan's "Policy of Concessions"'), *Guangming ribao (Guangming Daily)*, 26 August 1967.

105. See Wang Gungwu, 'Juxtaposing Past and Present in China Today', *China Quarterly*, No. 61, 1975, pp. 1-24.

106. Mao Zedong, 'Speech at Hangchow', p. 237.

107. See, for example, Zhou Zhenfu, 'Cong "sirenbang" de jia piKong kan yingshe shixue de pochan' ('Looking at the Bankruptcy of Reflective History from the Angle of the "Gang of Four's" False Criticism of Kongzi'), *Lishi yanjiu (Historical Research)*, No. 3, 1978, pp. 28-34.

108. K. Marx, 'Theses on Feuerbach', p. 82.

109. V.I. Lenin, *Materialism and Empirio-Criticism* (Beijing, Foreign Languages Press, 1972), pp. 38-9.

110. The subtitle for *Materialism and Empirio-Criticism*, for example, is 'Critical Comments on a Reactionary Philosophy'.

111. See, in particular, Joseph Stalin, 'Dialectical and Historical Materialism', in Bruce Franklin, *The Essential Stalin* (New York, Anchor Books, 1972), pp. 300-33.

112. Ridannuofu, (Zhdanov), *Zai guanyu Yalishandaluofu zhu 'XiOu zhexueshi' yishu taolunhui shang de fayan (Speech delivered at the Discussion Meeting on Alexandrov's 'History of Western Philosophy')*, translated by Li Lisan (Beijing, Renmin chubanshe, 1954), p. 4.

113. Ai Siqi, *Bianzheng weiwuzhuyi, lishi weiwuzhuyi*.

114. Yang Xianzhen, *Shenme shi weiwuzhuyi (What Is Materialism?)* (Shijiazhuang, Renmin chubanshe, 1980), p. 1. This book is based on lectures given by Yang in the Party School in 1955.

115. V.I. Lenin, *Materialism and Empirio-Criticism*, pp. 45-6.

116. Mao Zedong, 'On Contradiction', *Four Essays on Philosophy*, p. 24.

117. Ai Hengwu and Lin Qingshan, 'Yi fen wei er yu he er er yi' ('One Divides Into Two and Combining Two into One'), *Guangming ribao (Guangming Daily)*, 29 May 1964.

118. Quoted in Xiao Shu, '"He er er yi" lun de fan bianzhengfa shizi' (The Anti-dialectical Nature of "Combining Two into One"'), *Renmin ribao (People's Daily)*, 14 August 1964.

119. Mao Zedong, "On the Correct Handling of Contradictions among the People', *Four Essays on Philosophy*, p. 91.

120. Ha De Er and Yue Li Da Xi, 'Bu tongyi yong "he er er yi" lai qujie duili tongyi guilü' ('A Disagreement with Using "Combining Two into One" to Distort the Law of the Unity of Opposites'), *Renmin ribao* (*People's Daily*), 19 July 1964.

121. Huabeiju honglian fanxiu zhandoudui, 'Chedi pipan Zhongguo Heluxiaofu de touxiangzhuyi zhexue—"he er er yi" lun' (Thoroughly Repudiate China's Khrushchev's Philosophy of Capitulationism—the Theory of "Combining Two into One"'), *Renmin ribao* (*People's Daily*), 1 November 1967.

122. Fan Xiubing, 'Chedi pipan "jieji douzheng ximie" lun de fandong miulun' ('Thoroughly Repudiate the Reactionary Absurdity of the Theory of the Extinction of Class Struggle'), *Renmin ribao* (*People's Daily*), 20 August 1967.

123. The relationship between Yang Xianzhen's theory and the classical philosophers is discussed in Donald J. Munro, 'The Yang Hsien-chen Affair', *China Quarterly*, No. 22, 1965, pp. 75–82.

124. See, for example, Ai Hengwu, *Guanyu 'he er er yi' de lunzhan* (*On the Controversies Surrounding 'Combining Two Into One'*) (Hubei, Hubei renmin chubanshe, 1981).

NOTES TO CHAPTER 2

1. K. Marx and F. Engels, 'Manifesto of the Communist Party', p. 126.

2. K. Marx and F. Engels, 'Manifesto of the Communist Party', p. 125.

3. See Joseph R. Levenson, *Liang Ch'i-ch'ao and the Mind of Modern China* (Berkeley, University of California Press, 1970).

4. See, for example, the discussions in Leo Ou-fan Lee, *The Romantic Generation* (Cambridge, Mass., Harvard University Press, 1974) and Merle Goldman (ed.), *Modern Chinese Literature in the May Fourth Era* (Cambridge, Mass., Harvard University Press, 1977).

5. For a portrayal of Liang in the context of a changing China, see Guy S. Alitto, *The Last Confucian* (Berkeley, University of California Press, 1979).

6. The expression 'to lean to one side' as a description of the policy to learn from the Soviet Union was coined by Mao in 'On the People's Democratic Dictatorship', *Selected Works of Mao Tse-tung*, Vol. IV, p. 415.

7. This article was later reprinted as 'Zhongguo zhexue de fazhan' ('The Development of Chinese Philosophy'), in Feng Youlan, *Zhongguo zhexueshi lunwen chuji* (*Essays on the History of Chinese Philosophy*) (Shanghai, Shanghai renmin chubanshe, 1958), Vol. 1, pp. 1–63.

8. Zheng Xin, 'Kaifang weixinzhuyi' ('Liberate Idealism'), *Symposium on Chinese Philosophy*, p. 2.

9. Ren Hua, 'Tantan zhexueshi yanjiuzhong de jiaotiaozhuyi qingxiang' ('On the Tendency towards Dogmatism in the Study of the History of Philosophy'), *Symposium on Chinese Philosophy*, p. 261.

10. Wang Yi, 'Yige wenti, yidian yijian' ('A Problem, A Suggestion'), *Symposium on Chinese Philosophy*, pp. 55–6.

11. Zhang Dainian, 'Guanyu Zhongguo zhexueshi de fanwei wenti' ('On the Scope of the History of Chinese Philosophy'), *Symposium on Chinese Philosophy*, pp. 79–86.

12. The respected historian Zhu Qianzhi even argued that Marxism was derived from Song Confucianism on the grounds that the introduction of Chinese thought into Europe in the seventeenth and eighteenth centuries had influenced the development of materialist thinking in France and of dialectics in Germany. See Zhu Qianzhi, 'Shiba shiji Zhongguo zhexue dui Ouzhou zhexue de yingxiang' ('The Influence of Chinese Philosophy on European Philosophy in the Eighteenth Century'), *Zhexue yanjiu* (*Philosophical Research*), No. 4, 1957, pp. 48–57.

13. Ren Jiyu, 'Zhongguo zhexueshi de duixiang he fanwei' ('The Object and Scope of the History of Chinese Philosophy'), *Symposium on Chinese Philosophy*, p. 53.

14. Zheng Xin, 'Kaifang weixinzhuyi'.

15. He Lin, 'Duiyu zhexueshi yanjiuzhong liangge zhenglun wenti de yijian' ('Some Suggestions on the Two Controversies in the Study of the History of Philosophy'), *Symposium on Chinese Philosophy*, p. 187.

16. He Lin, 'Duiyu zhexueshi yanjiuzhong liangge zhenglun wenti de yijian', p. 188.

17. Guan Feng, 'Guanyu zhexueshi shang de weiwuzhuyi he weixinzhuyi de douzheng wenti' ('On the Question of the Struggle between Materialism and Idealism in the History of Philosophy'), *Symposium on Chinese Philosophy*, p. 207.

18. Deng Chumin, 'Dule Guan Feng xiansheng "Guanyu zhexueshi shang de weiwuzhuyi he weixinzhuyi de douzheng wenti" yihou' ('After Reading Mr Guan Feng's "On the Question of the Struggle between Materialism and Idealism in the History of Philosophy"'), *Symposium on Chinese Philosophy*, p. 266.

19. Deng Chumin, 'Dule Guan Feng xiansheng "Guanyu zhexueshi shang de weiwuzhuyi he weixinzhuyi de douzheng wenti" yihou', p. 266.

20. Zhu Bokun, 'Women zai Zhongguo zhexueshi yanjiu zhong suo yudao de yixie wenti' ('Some Problems We Have Encountered in the Study of the History of Chinese Philosophy'), *Symposium on Chinese Philosophy*, p. 30.

21. See, for example, Zhang Dainian, *Zhongguo weiwuzhuyi sixiang jianshi* (*A Short History of Chinese Materialist Thought*) (Beijing, Zhongguo qingnian chubanshe, 1957).

22. Hu Shi, *The Development of the Logical Method in Ancient China* (New York, Paragon Book Reprint Corporation, 1963), second edition.

23. Yang Xianzhen, *Shenme shi weiwuzhuyi?*, p. 1.

24. See, for example, Zhu Bokun, '*Women zai Zhongguo zhexueshi yanjiu zhong suo yudao de yixie wenti*', pp. 30-1.

25. Ren Jiyu's assessments of the Daoists is examined in Chapter 5. He has, in fact, changed his evaluations twice since the 1950s, once in the Cultural Revolution period, when he agreed that the Daoists were idealists, and again after the Cultural Revolution, when he reverted to his original claim that the Daoists were materialists.

26. Ren Jiyu, 'Zai Zhongguo zhexueshi de yanjiu zhong suo yudao de jige kunnan wenti' ('A Few Difficult Problems Encountered in the Study of the History of Chinese Philosophy'), *Symposium on Chinese Philosophy*, p. 140.

27. Feng Youlan, 'Guanyu Zhongguo zhexueshi yanjiu de liangge wenti' ('Two Problems concerning the Study of the History of Chinese Philosophy'), *Renmin ribao* (*People's Daily*), 23 October 1956. Reprinted in *Symposium on Chinese Philosophy*, p. 12.

28. *Symposium on Chinese Philosophy*, p. 13.

29. *Symposium on Chinese Philosophy*, p. 16.

30. See Etienne Balazs, *Chinese Civilization and Bureaucracy*, edited by Arthur F. Wright and translated by H.M. Wright (New Haven, Yale University Press, 1964).

31. See Feng Youlan, 'Guanyu lun Kongzi "ren" de sixiang de yixie buchong lunzheng' ('Some Supplementary Remarks on the Discussion of Kongzi's Idea of "ren"'), *Xueshu yuekan* (*Academic Monthly*), No. 8, 1963, pp. 43-7.

32. Tang Yijie et al., 'Lun "zhitong" yu "daotong"' ('On "Rule by Administration" and "Rule by dao"'), *Beijing daxue xuebao* (*Beijing University Journal*), No. 2, 1964, pp. 1-38.

33. This is, in fact, the first sentence of the *Analects*. See Yang Bojun (ed.), *Lunyu yizhu* (*The Analects Translated and Annotated*) (Beijing, Zhonghua shuju, 1980), hereafter *Lunyu yizhu*.

34. Feng Youlan, 'Zhongguo zhexue yichan de jicheng wenti' ('On the Question

of Inheriting the Chinese Philosophical Heritage'), *Guangming ribao* (*Guangming Daily*), 8 January 1957, reprinted in *Symposium on Chinese Philosophy*, pp. 273–80.

35. *Symposium on Chinese Philosophy*, p. 273.

36. *Symposium on Chinese Philosophy*, p. 274.

37. *Lunyu yizhu*, p. 1.

38. *Lunyu yizhu*, p. 4.

39. *Mengzi yizhu*, p. 276.

40. Wang Yangming (also known as Wang Shouren), 1472–1528. He advocated the idea of innate goodness (*liangzhi*), from which came the idea of self-cultivation. He is generally considered an idealist by Communist writers.

41. Li Zhi (1527–1602), a Ming philosopher who wrote critiques of the Confucian classics. Huang Zongxi (1610–1695), criticized the Song neo-Confucians for their mystification of the concept *li*. Both Li and Huang are considered materialists.

42. Feng Youlan, 'Zhongguo zhexue yichan de jicheng wenti', p. 277.

43. Feng Youlan could not foresee that his alleged debt to tradition was precisely what would get Liu Shaoqi into trouble later on.

44. Feng Youlan, 'Zhongguo zhexue yichan de jicheng wenti', p. 279.

45. Liu Wendian (ed.), *Zhuangzi buzheng* (*Zhuangzi with Supplementary Explanations*) (Kunming, Yunnan renmin chubanshe, 1980), 2 Vols, hereafter *Zhuangzi buzheng*, p. 319.

46. Feng Youlan, *Xin lixue* (*New Rational Philosophy*) (Changsha, Shangwu yinshuguan, 1939).

47. Cai Shangsi, *Zhongguo chuantong sixiang zong pipan, bubian* (*A Total Criticism of Traditional Chinese Thought, A Supplement*) (Shanghai, Tangdai chubanshe, 1950), pp. 63–95.

48. Mao stated that 'A splendid culture was created during the long period of Chinese feudal society. To study the development of this old culture, to reject its feudal dross and assimilate its democratic essence is a necessary condition for developing our new national culture and increasing our national self-confidence, but we should never swallow anything and everything uncritically.' Mao Zedong, 'On New Democracy', *Selected Works of Mao Tse-tung*, Vol. II, p. 381.

49. Ai Siqi, 'Dui "Zhongguo zhexue yichan de jicheng wenti" de yixie yijian' ('Some Objections to the Essay "On the Question of Inheriting the Chinese Philosophical Heritage"'), *Symposium on Chinese Philosophy*, p. 440.

50. Hu Sheng, 'Guanyu zhexueshi de yanjiu' ('On the Study of the History of Philosophy'), *Symposium on Chinese Philosophy*, p. 522.

51. Yang Zhengdian, 'Guanyu Zhongguo zhexue yichan jicheng wenti de jidian yijian' ('A Few Objections to the Problem of the Inheritance of China's Philosophical Heritage'), *Symposium on Chinese Philosophy*, p. 322.

52. Feng Youlan, 'Zai lun Zhongguo zhexue yichan di jicheng wenti' ('Again on the Problem of Inheriting the Chinese Philosophical Heritage'), reprinted in Feng Youlan, *Zhongguo zhexueshi lunwen chuji*, p. 130.

53. Zhang Dainian, 'Guanyu zhexue yichan de jicheng wenti ('On the Problem of Inheriting the Philosophical Heritage'), *Symposium on Chinese Philosophy*, p. 345.

54. *Symposium on Chinese Philosophy*, p. 344.

55. Zhang Dainian, 'Daode de jiejixing he jichengxing' ('On the Class Nature and Inheritability of Ethics'), *Symposium on Chinese Philosophy*, p. 296.

56. Tang Yijie, 'Tantan zhexue yichan de jicheng wenti' ('On the Problem of Inheritance of Philosophy'), *Symposium on Chinese Philosophy*, p. 364.

57. See, for example, Ding Si, '*Zhongguo zhexueshi zhong de jichengxing wenti*' ('The Problem of Inheritability in the History of Chinese Philosophy'), *Symposium on Chinese Philosophy*, p. 347.

58. Guan Feng, 'Guanyu jicheng zhexue yichan de yige wenti' ('A Problem con-

cerning the Inheritance of Philosophy'), *Symposium on Chinese Philosophy*, p. 370.

59. Xiao Jiefu, 'Zenyang lijie Makesizhuyi zhexue de jichengxing' ('How Inheritance in Marxist Philosophy Should Be Understood'), *Symposium on Chinese Philosophy*, p. 413.

60. In 1958, numerous articles were published in scholarly journals on the Yan'an experience, so that the Yan'an model was consciously promoted in opposition to the Soviet model, which had been so meticulously followed until that time.

61. Guan Feng, 'Fandui zhexueshi gongzuo zhong de xiuzhengzhuyi' ('Oppose Revisionism in the Work on the History of Philosophy'), *Zhexue yanjiu (Philosophical Research)*, No. 1, 1958, p. 1–24.

62. Guan Feng, *Fandui zhexueshi fangfalun shang de xiuzhengzhuyi (Oppose Revisionism in the Methodology of the History of Philosophy)* (Beijing, Renmin chubanshe, 1958). This book became the focus of attack by people like Deng Aimin, Wei Changhai, and Zeng Leshan in the Taiyuan conference on Chinese philosophy in 1979.

63. Guan Feng, 'Fandui zhexueshi gongzuo zhong de xiuzhengzhuyi', p. 1.

64. He Lin's article has already been discussed above. See also Chen Xiuzhai, 'Dui weixinzhuyi zhexue gujia wenti de yixie yijian' ('A Few Suggestions on the Problem of Evaluating Idealist Philosophy'), *Symposium on Chinese Philosophy*, pp. 225–36.

65. Guan Feng, 'Fandui zhexueshi gongzuo zhong de xiuzhengzhuyi', p. 2.

66. Guan Feng, 'Fandui zhexueshi gongzuo zhong de xiuzhengzhuyi', p. 3.

67. Guan Feng, 'Fandui zhexueshi gongzuo zhong de xiuzhengzhuyi', p. 12.

68. Guan Feng, 'Fandui zhexueshi gongzuo zhong de xiuzhengzhuyi', p. 16.

69. Guan Feng, 'Fandui zhexueshi gongzuo zhong de xiuzhengzhuyi', p. 17.

70. Guan Feng, 'Fandui zhexueshi gongzuo zhong de xiuzhengzhuyi', p. 19.

71. Guan Feng, 'Fandui zhexueshi gongzuo zhong de xiuzhengzhuyi', p. 22.

72. Guan Feng, 'Pipan Feng Youlan xiansheng de "chouxiang jichengfa"' ('A Criticism of Mr Feng Youlan's "Method of Abstract Inheritance"'), *Zhexue yanjiu (Philosophical Research)*, No. 3, 1958, p. 64.

73. Wu Chuanqi, 'Cong Feng Youlan xiansheng de chouxiang jichengfa kan tade zhexue guandian' ('Looking at Mr Feng Youlan's Philosophical Viewpoint from the Perspective of His Abstract Inheritance Method'), *Zhexue yanjiu (Philosophical Research)*, No. 2, 1958, p. 87.

74. Feng Youlan, *Xin lixue*, p. 10.

75. Wu Chuanqi, 'Cong Feng Youlan xiansheng de chouxiang jichengfa kan tade zhexue guandian', p. 87.

76. Tang Yijie, 'Beida zhexuexi he zhexue yanjiusuo pipan Feng Youlan de weixinzhuyi zhexue sixiang' ('The Philosophy Department of Beijing University and the Institute for Philosophical Research Criticize Feng Youlan's Idealist Philosophical Thought'), *Zhexue yanjiu (Philosophical Research)*, No. 5, 1958, p. 23.

77. Lu Junzhong, 'Jiechuan Feng Youlan zai Zhongguo zhexue yichan jicheng wenti shang de weikexue' ('Expose the Pseudo-scientific Nature of Feng Youlan's Treatment of the Problem of Inheriting the Chinese Philosophical Heritage'), *Zhexue yanjiu (Philosophical Research)*, No. 5, 1958, p. 39.

78. Liu Gefa *et al.*, 'Feng Youlan xiansheng yao ba zhexuexi yindao shenme daolu shang qu' ('What Path Does Mr Feng Youlan Want to Lead the Philosophy Department Along?'), *Guangming ribao (Guangming Daily)*, 31 August 1958.

79. Feng Youlan, 'Pipan wodi "chouxiang jichengfa"' ('Criticizing My Own "Abstract Inheritance Method"'), *Zhexue yanjiu (Philosophical Research)*, No. 5, 1958, p. 42.

80. Feng Youlan, 'Sishi nian de huigu' ('Reviewing the Past Forty Years'), reprinted in *Feng Youlan de daolu (The Path of Feng Youlan)* (Hong Kong, Pangu zazhi, 1974), p. 68.

81. Forty years before 1959, of course, was the official beginning of the May Fourth Movement. This document was translated into English by guest editor William A. Wycoff, 'Reflections on the Past Forty Years by Feng Youlan', *Chinese Studies in Philosophy*, Vol. XIII, Nos. 2–3, 1981–2, pp. 9–126.

82. Feng Youlan, 'Sishi nian de huigu', p. 78.

83. The *New Treatise on the Nature of Man* is the title of another of Feng's pre-1949 works where he outlined his philosophy. Feng Youlan, *Xin yuanren* (*New Treatise on the Nature of Man*) (Shanghai, Shangwu yinshuguan, 1946).

84. Feng Youlan, 'Sishi nian de huigu', p. 79.

85. Feng Youlan, 'Sishi nian de huigu', p. 83.

86. Feng Youlan, 'Xin lixue de yuanxing' ('The Real Nature of the New Rational Philosophy'), *Zhexue yanjiu* (*Philosophical Research*), No. 1, 1959, pp. 37–49.

87. Guan Feng, *'Jielu "Xin yuanren" de yuanxing* ('Exposing the Real Nature of the New Treatise on the Nature of Man'), in Guan Feng, *Zhuangzi neipian yijie he pipan* (*The Inner Chapters of Zhuangzi with Annotations and Criticisms*) (Beijing, Zhonghua shuju, 1961), p. 291.

88. Feng Youlan, 'Lun Kongzi guanyu "ren" de sixiang' ('On Kongzi's Idea of "ren"'), *Zhexue yanjiu* (*Philosophical Research*), No. 5, 1961, pp. 63–72 and 31.

89. Karl Marx and Frederick Engels, 'The German Ideology', *Selected Works*, Vol. 1, p. 48.

90. Feng Youlan, 'Lun Kongzi guanyu "ren" de sixiang'.

91. Feng Youlan, *Zhongguo zhexue xinbian* (*New History of Chinese Philosophy*) (Beijing, Renmin chubanshe, 1962), Vol. 1.

92. Guan Feng and Lin Yushi, 'Guanyu Kongzi sixiang taolun zhong de jieji fenxi de jige wenti' ('A Few Questions of Class Analysis relating to the Discussion of Kongzi's Thinking'), *Wen shi zhe* (*Literature, History and Philosophy*), No. 1, 1963, pp. 5–19.

93. Lin Jie, 'Kongzi "airen" de sixiang shizhi' ('The Real Nature of Kongzi's "Love Men"'), *Wenhui bao* (*Wenhui Daily*), 22 February 1963.

94. Sima Wen, 'Yansu duidai Makesizhuyi jingdian wenxian de yinzheng' ('The Marxist Classics Should Be Cited with a Serious Attitude'), *Guangming ribao* (*Guangming Daily*), 29 June 1963.

95. Fang Keli, 'Guanyu Kongzi "ren" de yanjiu zhong de yige fangfalun wenti' ('On the Problem of Methodology in the Study of Kongzi's Theory of *ren*'), *Zhexue yanjiu* (*Philosophical Research*), No. 4, 1963, p. 25, quoting from Karl Marx and Frederick Engels, 'The German Ideology', p. 48.

96. Tang Yijie and Sun Changjiang, 'Du Feng Youlan zhu "*Zhongguo zhexueshi xinbian*" (diyi ce)' ('On Reading Feng Youlan's *New History of Chinese Philosophy*, Vol. 1'), *Jiaoxue yu yanjiu* (*Teaching and Research*), No. 1, 1963, pp. 59–61, No. 2, pp. 55–62, and No. 3, pp. 62–5.

97. Zhao Fu, 'Guanyu "pupianxing de xingshi"—yu Feng Youlan xiansheng shangque' ('On the "Form of Universality"—a Debate with Mr Feng Youlan'), *Zhexue yanjiu* (*Philosophical Research*), No. 5, 1963, p. 48.

98. Liu Jie, 'Zhongguo sixiangshi shang de "tian ren he yi" wenti' ('The Problem of "Unity Between Heaven and Man" in the History of Chinese Thought'), *Xueshu yanjiu* (*Academic Research*), No. 1, 1962, pp. 42–53.

99. He must be referring to Hou Wailu *et al.* (eds.), *Zhongguo sixiang tongshi* (*A General History of Chinese Thought*) (Beijing, Renmin chubanshe, 1957), 6 Vols.

100. Liu Jie, 'Zhongguo sixiangshi shang de "tian ren he yi" wenti,' p. 42.

101. Liu Jie, 'Kongzi de "weiren lun"' ('Kongzi's *ren* Only Theory'), *Xueshu yanjiu* (*Academic Research*), No. 3, 1962, pp. 40–53.

102. Liu Jie, 'Kongzi de "weiren lun"', p. 41.

103. 'Pipan Liu Jie xiansheng cuowu de lishi guandian he fangfalun' ('Criticize Mr Liu Jie's Wrong Historical Viewpoint and Methodology'), *Guangming ribao* (*Guangming Daily*), 20 August 1963.

104. Karl Marx, 'Theses on Feuerbach', in K. Marx and F. Engels, *Selected Works*, Vol. 1, p. 15.

105. Dong Fangming, 'Zhexueshi gongzuo zhong de yizhong ji youhai de fangfa' ('An Extremely Harmful Methodology in the History of Philosophy Work'), *Zhexue yanjiu (Philosophical Research)*, No. 1, 1963, p. 33.

106. Wu Han, 'Shuo daode' ('On Morality'), reprinted in Wu Nanxing, *Sanjiacun zhaji (Notes from a Three Family Village)* (Beijing, Renmin wenxue chubanshe, 1979), p. 49. Wu Nanxing is the pseudonym used by Wu Han, Deng Tuo, and Liao Mosha. All three were denounced during the Cultural Revolution. The contention that Confucian ethics and Communist ethics are not very different is not a new one. Even Western scholars have tried to point to similarities between traditional values such as loyalty to the family and the new loyalty to the state. See, for example, David Nivison, 'Communist Ethics in Chinese Tradition', in John Harrison (ed.), *China: Enduring Scholarship Selected from the Far Eastern Quarterly— The Journal of Asian Studies 1941–1971* (Arizona, The University of Arizona Press, 1972), Vol. 1, pp. 207–30.

107. Wu Han, 'Shuo daode', p. 51.

108. Wu Han, 'Zai shuo daode' ('Again on Morality'), in Wu Nanxing, *Sanjiacun zhaji*, p. 67.

109. Chung Wah-min, 'Criticism of Academic Theories in Communist China', p. 128.

110. Guan Feng and Wu Fuqi, 'Ping Wu Han tongzhi de daodelun' ('A Critique of Comrade Wu Han's Theory of Morality'), *Zhexue yanjiu (Philosophical Research)*, No. 1, 1966, pp. 28–45.

111. For an account of the political fortunes of some of the writers described in this book, see Merle Goldman, *China's Intellectuals: Advise and Dissent* (Cambridge, Mass., Harvard University Press, 1981). Goldman's division of intellectuals and officials into 'liberal' and 'radical', however, has major flaws. For example, it is often difficult to see how people like Feng Youlan, Liu Jie, Peng Zhen, and Zhou Yang can be seen as 'liberal'.

NOTES TO CHAPTER 3

1. This famous phrase was coined by Hu Shi in 'Wu Yu wenlu xu' ('Preface to the Collected Essays of Wu Yu'), in Wu Yu, *Wu Yu wenlu (Collected Essays of Wu Yu)* (Shanghai, Yatong tushuguan, 1921), p. vii. It was the slogan which guided May Fourth thinking on tradition.

2. An English translation of Sima Qian's account can be found in Sima Qian, 'Confucius', *Records of the Historian*, translated by Yang Hsien-yi and Gladys Yang (Hong Kong, Commercial Press, 1974), pp. 1–27.

3. D.C. Lau believes that Kongzi may not have been a prime minister at all, but that this was a later invention. See D.C. Lau (trans.), *Confucius: The Analects* (Harmondsworth, Penguin Books, 1979), pp. 180–94. If Lau's theory is correct, it would invalidate much of the justification for attacks against Zhou Enlai in the anti-Kongzi campaign of the early seventies. Zhou was attacked through the use of Kongzi because both were said to have been prime ministers.

4. Yang Xiangkui, 'Guanyu XiZhou de shehui xingzhi wenti' ('On the Problem of the Nature of the Western Zhou Society'), *Selected Essays on Periodization*, p. 333.

5. Guo Moruo, 'Kong-Mo de pipan' ('A Critique of Kongzi and Mozi'), *Shi pipan shu (Ten Critiques)* (Beijing, Kexue chubanshe, 1956), pp. 71–122.

6. Fan Wenlan, 'Chuqi fengjian shehui kaishi yu XiZhou', pp. 359–73.

7. Mao Zedong, 'Analysis of the Classes in Chinese Society', *Selected Works of Mao Tse-tung*, Vol. I, pp. 13–21.

8. This argument was made by the influential historian Lü Zhenyu, *Zhongguo zhengzhi sixiangshi* (*A History of Chinese Political Thought*) (Beijing, Sanlian shudian, 1955).

9. See Ji Wenfu, 'Guanyu Kongzi de lishi pingjia wenti' ('On the Problem of Appraising Kongzi's Position in History'), *Lishi jiaoxue* (*History Teaching*), No. 8, 1953, pp. 2–4.

10. Feng Youlan *et al.*, 'Kongzi sixiang yanjiu' ('A Study of Kongzi's Thinking'), *Xin jianshe* (*New Construction*), No. 4, 1954, pp. 35–42.

11. Feng Youlan, 'Lun Kongzi' ('On Kongzi'), *Guangming ribao* (*Guangming Daily*), 22 and 29 July 1960.

12. K. Marx and F. Engels, 'Manifesto of the Communist Party', p. 117.

13. Yang Rongguo, *Kong-Mo de sixiang* (*The Thinking of Kongzi and Mozi*) (Shanghai, Shenghuo shudian, 1946) and Zhao Jibin, *Gudai rujia zhexue pipan* (*A Criticism of Ancient Confucian Philosophy*) (Shanghai, Zhonghua shuju, 1950).

14. Yang Rongguo, *Zhongguo gudai sixiangshi* (*History of Ancient Chinese Thought*) (Beijing, Renmin chubanshe, 1973), second edition, pp. 81–106.

15. Zhao Jibin, 'Shi ren min' ('On *ren* and *min*'), *Lun yu xin tan* (*A New Exploration of the Analects*) (Beijing, Renmin chubanshe, 1962), pp. 7–28.

16. Ren Jiyu, 'Kongzi zhengzhi shang de baoshou lichang he zhexue shang de weixinzhuyi' ('Kongzi's Political Conservative Stance and Philosophical Idealism'), in Zhexue yanjiu bianjibu (ed.), *Kongzi zhexue taolun ji* (*Collected Papers on Kongzi's Philosophy*) (Beijing, Zhonghua shuju, 1963), hereafter *Kongzi zhexue taolun ji*, p. 151.

17. Albert Feuerwerker, 'China's History in Marxian Dress', in A. Feuerwerker (ed.), *History in Communist China* (Cambridge, Mass., MIT Press, 1968), pp. 14–44.

18. Zhong Zhaopeng, 'Lüe lun Kongzi sixiang de jieji xing' ('A Brief Discussion on the Class Nature of Kongzi's Thought'), *Kongzi zhexue taolun ji*, pp. 182–95.

19. *Lunyu yizhu*, p. 182.

20. Guan Feng and Lin Yushi, 'Lun Kongzi' ('On Kongzi'), *Kongzi zhexue taolun ji*, pp. 255–8.

21. Sima Qian, 'Confucius', p. 2.

22. Chao Songting, 'Duiyu Guan Feng, Lin Yushi tongzhi "Zai lun Kongzi" de shangque' ('Comments on "A Further Discussion on Kongzi" by Comrades Guan Feng and Lin Yushi'), *Kongzi zhexue taolun ji*, p. 456.

23. Tang Yijie, 'Kongzi sixiang zai Chunqiu moqi de zuoyong' ('The Function of Kongzi's Thought at the End of the Spring and Autumn Period'), *Kongzi zhexue taolun ji*, p. 54.

24. Feng Youlan, 'Lun Kongzi guanyu "ren" de sixiang' pp. 288–9.

25. Feng Youlan, 'Lun Kongzi guanyu "ren" de sixiang' pp. 288–9.

26. Guan Feng and Lin Yushi, 'Zai lun Kongzi' ('A Further Discussion on Kongzi'), *Kongzi zhexue taolun ji*, p. 320.

27. This is especially true in literature. During the Hundred Flowers period many stories were written criticizing negative aspects of the new society such as the inefficiency of the bureaucracy. See, for example, *Chongfang de xianhua* (*The Second Blossoming*) (Shanghai, Shanghai wenyi chubanshe, 1979).

28. Tang Lan, 'Pinglun Kongzi shouxian yinggai bianming Kongzi suochu de shi shenmeyang xingzhi de shehui' ('To Evaluate Kongzi, it is first Necessary to Clearly Understand the Nature of the Society he Lived in'), *Kongzi zhexue taolun ji*, pp. 341–53.

29. Xiong Shili, *Yuan ru* (*The Original Confucianism*), first published in 1956; reprint edition (Hong Kong, Longmen shudian, 1970).

30. Li Kan, 'Bo xin zunKong lun' ('Refuting a New Theory of Kongzi-worship'), *Guangming ribao* (*Guangming Daily*), 17 August 1963.

31. Fan Wenlan, *Zhongguo tongshi jianbian* (*A Concise General History of China*) (Beijing, Renmin chubanshe, 1964), Vol. 1, fourth edition, p. 203.

32. See, for example, Tang Yijie, 'Kongzi sixiang zai Chunqiu moqi de zuoyong', p. 56.

33. Ren Jiyu, 'Kongzi zhengzhi shang de baoshou lichang he zhexue shang de weixinzhuyi', p. 157.

34. Guo Moruo, 'Kong-Mo de pipan'.

35. Du Guoxiang, *XianQin zhuzi sixiang gaiyao* (*An Outline of the Thoughts of the pre-Qin Philosophers*) (Beijing, Sanlian shudian, 1955), second edition.

36. Ji Wenfu, 'Guanyu Kongzi de lishi pingjia wenti', p. 4.

37. Ji Wenfu, *Chunqiu Zhanguo sixiang shihua* (*Comments on the History of Thought in the Spring and Autumn and Warring States Periods*) (Beijing, Zhongguo qingnian chubanshe, 1958), p. 22.

38. Dou Zhongguang, 'Cong rujia de lunli xueshuo zhong kan daode de jicheng wenti' ('The Problem of Inheriting Ethics Viewed from the Moral Doctrines of Confucianism'), *Guangming ribao* (*Guangming Daily*), 10 April 1957.

39. Zhu Qianzhi, 'Shiqiba shiji Xifang zhexuejia de Kongzi guan' ('Western Philosophers' Views of Kongzi in the Seventeenth and Eighteenth Centuries'), *Renmin ribao* (*People's Daily*), 9 March 1962.

40. Feng Youlan et al., 'Kongzi sixiang yanjiu'.

41. See the discussion in Chapter 2.

42. See, for example, Liu Jieren, 'Kongzi sixiang tixi chutan' ('A Preliminary Investigation of Kongzi's System of Thought'), *Guangming ribao* (*Guangming Daily*), 1 November 1959.

43. Liu was criticized by Zhang Shifeng, 'Kongzi de renxue bushi nuli jiefang de lilun' ('Kongzi's Philosophy of ren is not a Theory for the Emancipation of Slaves'), *Guangming ribao* (*Guangming Daily*), 27 March 1960. Feng was criticized by Li Qiqian, 'Dui Feng Youlan xiansheng "Lun Kongzi" de jidian yijian' ('A Few Comments on Mr Feng Youlan's "On Kongzi"'), *Guangming ribao* (*Guangming Daily*), 5 August 1960.

44. Mao Zedong, 'Talks at the Yenan Forum on Literature and Art', p. 91.

45. Feng Youlan, 'Zai lun Kongzi "ren" de sixiang' ('A Further Discussion of Kongzi's Thinking Concerning ren'), *Kongzi zhexue taolun ji*, p. 472.

46. Feng Youlan, 'Lun Kongzi guanyu "ren" de sixiang', p. 292. Feng had quoted from the *German Ideology* to back up this statement.

47. Zhao Jibin, 'Ren li jiegu' ('The Original Meanings of ren and li Explained'), *Lunyu xin tan* (*A New Exploration of the Analects*) (Beijing, Renmin chubanshe, 1962), p. 179.

48. Zhao Jibin, 'Ren li jiegu', p. 179.

49. Zhao Jibin, 'Ren li jiegu', p. 200.

50. Guan Feng and Lin Yushi, 'Lun Kongzi', pp. 218–19.

51. Guan Feng and Lin Yushi, 'Lun Kongzi', p. 226.

52. Feng Youlan, 'Lun Kongzi guanyu "ren" de sixiang', pp. 287–90.

53. See Guan Feng and Lin Yushi, 'Zai lun Kongzi' and 'San lun Kongzi' ('A Third Discussion on Kongzi'), *Kongzi zhexue taolun ji*, pp. 401–11.

54. Some of the people most critical of Chinese tradition, such as Yang Rongguo, Cai Shangsi, and Guan Feng, were based in the provinces rather than at Beijing University, which was the centre of most philosophical controversies.

55. Yang Rongguo, 'Lun Kongzi sixiang' ('On Kongzi's Thinking'), *Kongzi zhexue taolun ji*, p. 384.

56. *Kongzi zhexue taolun ji*, pp. 393–400.

57. Quoted in John H. Hawkins, *Mao Tse-tung and Education: His Thoughts and Teachings* (Hamden, Shoe-string Press, 1974), p. 4.

58. For example, Chan Wing-tsit, *Chinese Philosophy 1949–1963: An Annotated Bibliography of Mainland China Publications* (Honolulu, East-West Center Press, 1967), pp. 107–10, does not list anything on Kongzi and education before 1954.

59. For criticism directed against Hu Shi, see *Hu Shi sixiang pipan (Critiques of Hu Shi's Thought)* (Beijing, Sanlian shudian, 1955), 8 Vols.

60. William Fraser, 'The Traditional and Distinctive in Soviet Education', in Edmund J. King (ed.), *Communist Education* (London, Methuen and Co., 1963), pp. 78–96.

61. Xu Mengying, 'Kongzi de jiaoyu sixiang' ('Kongzi's Educational Thought'), *Guangming ribao (Guangming Daily)*, 14 June 1954.

62. Xu Mengying, 'Kongzi de jiaoyu sixiang'.

63. Shen Yi, 'Du "Kongzi de jiaoyu sixiang" yihou' ('After Reading "Kongzi's Educational Thought"'), *Guangming ribao (Guangming Daily)*, 28 June 1954.

64. Shen Yi, 'Du "Kongzi de jiaoyu sixiang" yihou'.

65. Chu Shusen, 'Dui yanjiu Kongzi jiaoyu sixiang de jidian yijian' ('A Few Suggestions on the Study of Kongzi's Educational Thought'), *Guangming ribao (Guangming Daily)*, 9 August 1954.

66. Chu Shusen, 'Dui yanjiu Kongzi jiaoyu sixiang de jidian yijian'.

67. Chu Shusen, 'Dui "Kongzi de jiaoyu sixiang" yiwen de yijian' ('Comments on the Article "Kongzi's Educational Thought"'), *Guangming ribao (Guangming Daily)*, 4 October 1954.

68. *Lunyu yizhu*, p. 65.

69. O.B. Borisov and B.T. Koloskov, *Soviet-Chinese Relations 1945–1970* (Bloomington and London, Indiana University Press, 1975), p. 104.

70. See the criticisms quoted in R. MacFarquhar, *The Hundred Flowers*.

71. Mao Zedong, 'A Talk with Heads of Education Departments or Bureaus of Seven Provinces and Municipalities', *Unselected Works of Mao Tse-tung 1957* (Hong Kong, Union Research Institute, 1976), p. 91.

72. Huyan Hechi, 'Jieshao "Kongzi de gushi"' ('Introducing *The Story of Kongzi*'), *Renmin jiaoyu (People's Education)*, No. 1, 1957, p. 63. Anton Makarenko was a Soviet educator who came into prominence under Stalin. His complete works were translated and published in China in the fifties. *The Story of Kongzi* was written by Li Changzhi in 1956.

73. Xu Mengying, 'Lüetan Kongzi de jiaoxuefa sixiang' ('A Brief Discussion of Kongzi's Ideas on Teaching Methods'), *Renmin jiaoyu (People's Education)*, No. 2, 1957, pp. 27–9.

74. Xu Mengying, 'Lüetan Kongzi de jiaoxuefa sixiang', p. 27.

75. Huyan Hechi, 'Jieshao "Kongzi de gushi"', pp. 40 and 63.

76. Mao Lirui, 'Shen zhu "Zhongguo gudai jiaoyu he jiaoyu sixiang" pingjie' ('A Critical Introduction to Shen's *Ancient Chinese Education and Educational Thought*'), *Renmin jiaoyu (People's Education)*, No. 6, 1957, pp. 58–61.

77. For example, Shen Guanqun, 'Weida de jiaoyujia Kongzi' ('Kongzi the Great Educationalist'), *Huadong shida xuebao (East China Teachers' University Journal)*, No. 3, 1957, pp. 76–86.

78. Chen Jingpan, *Kongzi de jiaoyu sixiang (Kongzi's Educational Thought)* (Wuhan, Hubei renmin chubanshe, 1957).

79. Chen Jingpan, *Kongzi de jiaoyu sixiang*, pp. 19–24.

80. Chen Jingpan, *Kongzi de jiaoyu sixiang*, p. 27.

81. Chen Jingpan, *Kongzi de jiaoyu sixiang*, p. 27.

82. Chen Jingpan, *Kongzi de jiaoyu sixiang*, p. 62. The quotation comes from Mao Zedong, 'The Role of the Chinese Communist Party in the National War', *Selected Works of Mao Tse-tung*, Vol. II, p. 209.

83. Chen Jingpan, *Kongzi de jiaoyu sixiang*, pp. 60–3.

84. Kang Youwei, *Kongzi gaizhi kao (A Study of Kongzi as a Reformer)* (Taibei, Taiwan shangwu yinshuguan, 1968), p. 5.

85. Chan Wing-tsit, *Chinese Philosophy*, pp. 107–10.

86. Chen Yi, 'Dui Beijing shi gaodeng yuanxiao yingjie biye xuesheng de jianghua', p. 3.

87. Gu Weijin, 'Kongzi tan xuexi' ('Kongzi Talks about Study'), *Guangming ribao (Guangming Daily)*, 27 October 1961.

88. *Lunyu yizhu*, p. 19.

89. Wu Tianshi and Ma Yingbo, *Tantan woguo gudai xuezhe de xuexi jingshen he xuexi fangfa* (*On the Spirit and Method of Learning of Our Country's Ancient Scholars*) (Beijing, Zhongguo qingnian chubanshe, 1964).

90. These quotations, which were to be the source of very fierce controversies in the anti-Kongzi movement of the early seventies, can be found in *Lunyu yizhu*, pp. 170 and 67.

91. See, for example, Zhong Zhaopeng, 'Lüe lun Kongzi sixiang de jieji xing', p. 128.

92. Wang Xianjin, 'Kongzi zai Zhongguo lishi shang de diwei' ('The Place of Kongzi in Chinese History'), *Kongzi zhexue taolun ji*, p. 128.

93. Tang Yijie, 'Kongzi sixiang zai Chunqiu moqi de zuoyong', p. 47.

94. Wang Xianjin, 'Kongzi zai Zhongguo lishi shang de diwei', pp. 128–9.

95. Kuang Yaming, 'Lüe lun shisheng guanxi' ('A Brief Discussion on the Teacher-Student Relationship'), *Hongqi* (*Red Flag*), No. 17, 1961, p. 25.

96. See Agnes Smedley, *The Great Road: The Life and Times of Chu Teh* (New York, Monthly Review Press, 1956), p. 78.

97. Xin Lan, 'Kongzi zai tiyu fangmian de shijian he zhuzhang' ('Kongzi's Actual Practice and Proposals concerning Sports'), *Xin tiyu* (*New Sports*), No. 8, 1962.

98. Zhang Daoyang, 'Cong "she" "yu" lunzheng Kongzi tiyu sixiang' ('Kongzi's Ideas on Sports Discussed and Demonstrated using Archery and Charioteering'), *Guangming ribao* (*Guangming Daily*), 27 March 1962.

99. Xin Lan, 'Kongzi zai tiyu fangmian de shijian he zhuzhang', p. 16.

100. Mao Zedong, 'The Orientation of the Youth Movement', *Selected Works of Mao Tse-tung*, Vol. II, p. 248.

101. Li Yinnong, 'Lun Kongzi dui laodong de taidu', ('On Kongzi's Attitudes towards Labour'), *Yangcheng wanbao* (*Canton Evening News*), 22 March 1962.

102. These stories are from the *Analects*, see *Lunyu yizhu*, pp. 193–6.

103. Li Yinnong, 'Lun Kongzi dui laodong de taidu'.

104. Ren Jiyu, 'Kongzi zhengzhi shang de baoshou lichang he zhexue shang de weixinzhuyi', p. 159.

105. See *Lunyu yizhu*, p. 181.

106. Guan Feng and Lin Yushi, 'Lun Kongzi', p. 250.

107. Yang Rongguo, 'Lun Kongzi sixiang', p. 395.

108. Joseph R. Levenson, 'The Problem of Historical Significance', *Confucian China and Its Modern Fate: A Trilogy* (Berkeley, University of California Press, 1965), p. 82.

109. See Kam Louie, *Critiques of Confucius in Contemporary China*, pp. 5–12.

110. Cai Shangsi, *Zhongguo chuantong sixiang zong pipan* (*A Total Criticism of Traditional Chinese Thought*) (Shanghai, Tangdai chubanshe, 1950). After 1976, however, Cai Shangsi again wrote on this topic, taking very much the same line he took in the fifties. See, for example, Cai Shangsi, '*Kongzi he lidai Kongzi chongbaizhe de guanxi wenti*' ('On the Relationship between Kongzi and the Kongzi-worshippers in History'), *Zhonghua wenshi luncong* (*Selected Essays on Chinese Literature and History*), No. 1, 1979, pp. 19–24.

NOTES TO CHAPTER 4

1. This image of Laozi is popularized in many art objects. See, for example, the painting 'Laozi Riding on an Ox' by the Song painter Chao Buzhi in Chiang Yee, *The Chinese Eye* (Bloomington, Indiana University Press, 1964), p. 32.

2. Sima Qian, *Shiji* (*Records of the Historian*) (Beijing, Zhonghua shuju, 1959), Vol. 7, p. 2139.

3. This theory is still current today. See, for example, the 'Laozi' entry in *Cihai* (*Dictionary of Phrases*) (Shanghai, Shanghai cishu chubanshe, 1980), p. 1235.

4. Guo Moruo, 'Lao Dan, Guan Yin, Huan Yuan' ('Lao Dan, Guan Yin, and Huan Yuan'), in *Qingtong shidai* (*The Bronze Age*) (Beijing, Renmin chubanshe, 1954), p. 235.

5. Lü Zhenyu, *Zhongguo zhengzhi sixiangshi*, p. 53.

6. Feng Youlan, *Zhongguo zhexueshi xinbian*, Vol. 1, pp. 249-56.

7. Apart from Feng Youlan, other scholars who subscribe to this theory include Gu Jiegang, Tang Lan, and Yang Rongguo. Many Western scholars such as Herrlee Creel and D.C. Lau also agree with this view.

8. For a partial list of the hundreds of annotations and translations of the Laozi, see Yan Lingfeng, *Zhongwai Laozi zhushu mulu* (*An Index to Works on Laozi in China and Abroad*) (Taibei, Zhonghua congshu weiyuanhui, 1957).

9. Chen Qiyou (ed.), *Han Feizi jishi* (*The Han Feizi Collated and Explained*) (Shanghai, Shanghai renmin chubanshe, 1974), 2 Vols, hereafter *Han Feizi jishi*, pp. 326-86.

10. R.B. Blakney, *The Way of Life: Lao Tzu* (New York, Mentor Books, 1955).

11. Fan Wenlan, *Zhongguo tongshi jianbian*, Vol. 1, p. 272.

12. Tang Yijie, 'Laozi sixiang de jieji benzhi' ('The Class Nature of Laozi's Thought'), originally in *Guangming ribao* (*Guangming Daily*), 28 June 1959, reprinted in Zhexue yanjiu bianjibu (ed.), *Laozi zhexue taolun ji* (*Collected Papers on Laozi's Philosophy*) (Beijing, Zhonghua shuju, 1959), hereafter *Laozi zhexue taolun ji*, p. 127.

13. Tang Yijie, 'Laozi yuzhouguan de weiwuzhuyi benzhi' ('The Materialist Nature of Laozi's Cosmological Outlook'), *Laozi zhexue taolun ji*, pp. 134-53.

14. Tang Yijie, 'Laozi yuzhouguan de weiwuzhuyi benzhi', p. 134. Both Wang Chong and Fan Zhen (450-510 AD) have been described by Chinese writers as materialist philosophers.

15. Tang Yijie, 'Laozi yuzhouguan de weiwuzhuyi benzhi', p. 137.

16. Fan Wenlan, *Zhongguo tongshi jianbian*, Vol. 1, p. 273.

17. Gao Heng, *Chongding Laozi zhenggu* (*Revised Collation of the Laozi*) (Beijing, Guji chubanshe, 1956), p. 9.

18. Yang Xingshun, *Zhongguo gudai zhexuejia Laozi ji qi xueshuo* (*China's Ancient Philosopher Laozi and His Doctrines*), translated by Yang Chao (Beijing, Kexue chubanshe, 1957), p. 70.

19. Ren Jiyu, *Zhongguo zhexueshi* (*History of Chinese Philosophy*) (Beijing, Renmin chubanshe, 1963), third edition 1979, pp. 57-60.

20. Ren Jiyu (ed.), *Laozi jinyi* (*Laozi Translated into Modern Chinese*) (Beijing, Guji chubanshe, 1956).

21. See, for example, Yang Xiangkui, *Zhongguo gudai shehui yu gudai sixiang yanjiu* (*Study of Ancient Chinese Society and Ancient Thought*) (Shanghai, Shanghai renmin chubanshe, 1962), Vol. 1, p. 423.

22. That is, 'xian' 仙. Herrlee G. Creel, *What is Taoism?* (Chicago, University of Chicago Press, 1970), p. 7.

23. Yang Chao, 'Laozi zhexue de weiwuzhuyi benzhi' ('The Materialist Basis of Laozi's Philosophy'), *Zhexue yanjiu* (*Philosophical Research*), No. 4, 1955, p. 136.

24. Chen Boda, 'Laozi de zhexue sixiang' ('Laozi's Philosophical Thought'), *Jiefang* (*Liberation*), Nos. 63 and 64, 1939, pp. 27-30 and 'Cong mingshi wenti lun Zhongguo gudai zhexue de jiben fenye' ('Using the Problem of Naming and Matter to Discuss the Basic Dividing Line in Ancient Chinese Philosophy'), *Wenshi* (*Literature and History*), Vol. 1, No. 2, 1934, pp. 33-50.

25. Ren Jiyu (ed.), *Laozi xinyi* (*A New Translation of the Laozi*) (Shanghai, Shanghai guji chubanshe, 1978), p. 81. The *Laozi xinyi* is a revised version of the *Laozi jinyi*. This revision follows Mao's assessment of Laozi as an idealist. See

Selected Works of Mao Tse-tung, Vol. V, p. 346. Ren later changed his views yet again.

26. Yang Xingshun, *Zhongguo gudai zhexuejia Laozi ji qi xueshuo*, pp. 37–41.
27. Especially Lenin, Stalin, or other Soviet authorities. At this stage, the Soviet verdicts on scholarly matters were very closely followed.
28. Ren Jiyu and Feng Jingyuan, 'Laozi de yanjiu' ('Studies of Laozi'), *Laozi zhexue taolun ji*, p. 19.
29. Yan Mingxuan, 'Guanyu Laozi zhexue taolun zhong de yixie wenti' ('A Few Problems on the Discussions on Laozi'), *Xin jianshe (New Construction)*, No. 9, 1957, p. 55.
30. Yang Xingshun, *Zhongguo gudai zhexuejia Laozi ji qi xueshuo*, p. 50. For an analysis of the origin and meaning of the word *de*, see Donald J. Munro, *The Concept of Man in Early China* (Stanford, Stanford University Press, 1969), pp. 185–97.
31. Ren Jiyu, *Laozi jinyi*, p. 62.
32. Yang Liuqiao, 'Laozi de zhexue shi weiwuzhuyi de ma?' ('Is Laozi's Philosophy Materialist?'), *Zhexue yanjiu (Philosophical Research)*, No. 4, 1955, pp. 144–8.
33. Ren Jiyu, *Laozi jinyi*, pp. 77–9.
34. Ren Jiyu, *Laozi jinyi*, p. 89.
35. Yang Chao, 'Laozi zhexue de weiwuzhuyi benzhi', pp. 137–8.
36. Guo Moruo, 'XianQin tiandaoguan zhi jinzhan' ('The Development of the pre-Qin Cosmological Outlook', *Qingtong shidai (The Bronze Age)*, pp. 1–42.
37. Ren Jiyu, *Laozi xinyi*, pp. 31 and 57.
38. Hou Wailu *et al.* (eds.), *Zhongguo sixiang tongshi*, Vol. 1, pp. 267–8. In fact, this book does not say definitely that Laozi was idealist. Instead, it makes the point that the *Daodejing* is so full of contradictions that examples can be found in it to illustrate both idealism and materialism.
39. Feng Youlan, *Zhongguo zhexueshi xinbian*, Vol. 1, pp. 261–4.
40. Guan Feng and Lin Yushi, 'Lun Laozi zhexue tixi de weixinzhuyi benzhi' ('On the Idealist Basis of Laozi's Philosophical System'), originally in *Zhexue yanjiu (Philosophical Research)*, No. 6, 1959, reprinted in *Laozi zhexue taolun ji*, p. 177.
41. See, for example, Feng Youlan, 'Guanyu Laozi zhexue de liangge wenti' ('Two Problems on Laozi'), originally in *Renmin ribao (People's Daily)*, 12 and 13 June 1959, reprinted in *Laozi zhexue taolun ji*, p. 58. Although this article appeared after the article by Guan and Lin quoted above, Feng had in fact been aware of their views because they had presented their paper on Laozi at a conference in May 1959.
42. Guan Feng and Lin Yushi, 'Zai tan Laozi zhexue' ('A Further Discussion on Laozi's Philosophy'), originally in *Guangming ribao (Guangming Daily)*, 20 June 1959, reprinted in *Laozi zhexue taolun ji*, pp. 238–9.
43. *Zhuangzi buzheng*, p. 996. In Chinese characters, this expression is 建之以常无, 有; 主之以太一. The Chinese characters will be given here for quotations from the *Laozi* and the *Zhuangzi* as interpreted by Guan Feng and Lin Yushi; they can be quite unorthodox.
44. Guan Feng and Lin Yushi, 'Lun Laozi zhexue tixi de weixinzhuyi benzhi', p. 178.
45. Guan Feng and Lin Yushi, 'Lun Laozi zhexue tixi de weixinzhuyi benzhi', p. 178.
46. Guan Feng and Lin Yushi, 'Lun Laozi zhexue tixi de weixinzhuyi benzhi', p. 179.
47. Ren Jiyu, *Laozi xinyi*, p. 26. 道可道,非常道; 名可名,非常名.
48. Ren Jiyu, *Laozi xinyi*, p. 26. 无,名天地之始; 有,名万物之母.

49. Ren Jiyu, *Laozi xinyi*, p. 27. 故常无欲以观其妙, 常有欲以观其徼.

50. Ren Jiyu, *Laozi xinyi*, p. 27. 此两者同出而异名, 同谓之玄, 玄之又玄, 众妙之门.

51. Guan Feng and Lin Yushi, 'Lun Laozi zhexue tixi de weixinzhuyi benzhi', p. 179.

52. Guan Feng and Lin Yushi, 'Lun Laozi zhexue tixi de weixinzhuyi benzhi', p. 181–4.

53. Ren Jiyu, *Laozi xinyi*, p. 78. 天下万物生于有, 有生于无.

54. Ren Jiyu, *Laozi xinyi*, p. 58. 独立而不改, 周行而不殆, 可以为天下母. The text used by Ren Jiyu here has left out the *'er'* 而 between *'duli'* and *'bugai'*.

55. Ren Jiyu, *Laozi xinyi*, p. 57. 有物混成, 先天地生.

56. Ren Jiyu, *Laozi xinyi*, p. 92. 天下有始, 以为天下母.

57. Guan Feng and Lin Yushi, 'Lun Laozi zhexue tixi de weixinzhuyi benzhi', pp. 190–1.

58. Guan Feng and Lin Yushi, 'Lun Laozi zhexue tixi de weixinzhuyi benzhi', p. 191.

59. Guan Feng and Lin Yushi, 'Lun Laozi zhexue tixi de weixinzhuyi benzhi', pp. 210–11. 塞其兑, 闭其门. The quotation comes from Ren Jiyu, *Laozi xinyi*, p. 93.

60. Guo Moruo, 'XianQin tiandaoguan zhi jinzhan'.

61. Guan Feng and Lin Yushi, 'Lun Laozi zhexue tixi de weixinzhuyi benzhi', p. 222.

62. Ren Jiyu, 'Lun Laozi zhexue de weiwuzhuyi benzhi' ('On the Materialist Basis of Laozi's Philosophy'), originally in *Zhexue yanjiu* (*Philosophical Research*), No. 7, 1959, reprinted in *Laozi zhexue taolun ji*, p. 37.

63. Quoted in *Laozi zhexue taolun ji*, p. 29.

64. *Laozi zhexue taolun ji*, p. 45.

65. Feng Youlan, 'Guanyu Laozi zhexue de liangge wenti', p. 58.

66. Guan Feng and Lin Yushi, 'Zai tan Laozi zhexue', pp. 237–40.

67. Ren Jiyu, 'Lun Laozi zhexue de weiwuzhuyi benzhi', p. 46. The use of modern terminology and modern thinking to explain the ancient philosophers in many ways seems inescapable. In English commentaries on the *Daodejing*, this method is very common. For example, Chang Chung-yuan, *Tao: A New Way of Thinking* (n.p., 1975) uses Heidegger to explain *dao*.

68. Zhan Jianfeng, 'Laozi de "dao" jishi juedui jingshen ma? ('Is Laozi's *dao* an Absolute Spirit?'), *Laozi zhexue taolun ji*, pp. 154–61.

69. Zhan Jianfeng, 'Laozi de "dao" jishi juedui jingshen ma?' p. 155.

70. Zhan Jianfeng, 'Laozi de "dao" jishi juedui jingshen ma?' p. 155.

71. Hu Quyuan, 'Lun Laozi de "dao"' ('On Laozi's "dao"'), originally in *Fudan*, No. 10, 1959, reprinted in *Laozi zhexue taolun ji*, pp. 164–75.

72. Zhou Jianren, 'Laozi de "dao" shi weiwuzhuyi haishi weixinzhuyi?' ('Is Laozi's "dao" Materialist or Idealist?'), *Laozi zhexue taolun ji*, pp. 298–302.

73. Ren Jiyu, *Laozi jinyi*, p. 62.

74. Guan Feng and Lin Yushi, 'Lun Laozi zhexue tixi de weixinzhuyi benzhi', p. 179.

75. Xiang Xiu (AD 227–72) and Guo Xiang (*circa* AD 300) were two of the most famous interpreters of the *Zhuangzi*. Xiang Xiu's annotations are now lost, but it is widely accepted that the standard annotated version used now, though under the name of Guo Xiang, is a joint product of them both.

76. Lü Zhenyu, *Zhongguo zhengzhi sixiangshi*, p. 175.

77. Guo Moruo, 'Zhuangzi de pipan' ('Criticism of Zhuangzi'), *Shi pipan shu*, p. 202.

78. Feng Youlan, 'Xin lixue de yuanxing' ('The Real Nature of the New Rational Philosophy'), *Zhexue yanjiu* (*Philosophical Research*), No. 1, 1959, pp. 37–49.

79. Guan Feng, 'Jielu "Xin yuanren" de yuanxing', pp. 295–6.

80. Feng Youlan, 'Zhiyi he qingjiao' ('Queries and Seeking Advice'), *Zhexue yanjiu* (*Philosophical Research*), No. 3, 1959, pp. 8–13.

81. Guan Feng, 'Da Feng Youlan xiansheng' ('Answering Mr Feng Youlan'), *Xin jianshe* (*New Construction*), No. 5, 1959, pp. 50–8.

82. Feng Youlan, 'Zhiyi he qingjiao' reprinted in postscript to Feng Youlan, 'Sishi nian de huigu', in *Feng Youlan de daolu* (*The Path of Feng Youlan*) (Hong Kong, Pangu zazhi, 1974), pp. 78–90.

83. Guo Xiaochuan, 'Wang xingkong' ('Gazing at the Starry Sky'), *Renmin wenxue* (*People's Literature*), No. 11, 1959, pp. 90–3.

84. For example, see Xiao San, 'Tan "Wang xingkong"' ('On "Gazing at the Starry Sky"'), *Renmin wenxue* (*People's Literature*), No. 1, 1960, pp. 11–12.

85. Guan Feng, 'Tan "Wang xingkong" de linghun' ('On the Soul of "Gazing at the Starry Sky"'), in *Zhuangzi neipian yijie he pipan*, p. 310.

86. An exception is Ma Xulun, *Zhuangzi tianxia pian shuyi* (*The 'Under Heaven' Chapter Explained*) (Shanghai, Longmen lianhe shuju, 1958). Ma regarded the 'Under Heaven' chapter as having also been Zhuangzi's work.

87. Guan Feng, 'Zhuangzi waiza pian chutan' ('A Preliminary Investigation on the Outer and Miscellaneous Chapters of the Zhuangzi'), originally in *Zhexue yanjiu* (*Philosophical Research*), No. 2, 1961, reprinted in *Zhuangzi neipian yijie he pipan*, pp. 319–22.

88. Sima Qian, *Shiji*, Vol. 7, pp. 2143–4.

89. Guan Feng, 'Zhuangzi waiza pian chutan', pp. 322–3.

90. Guan Feng, 'Zhuangzi waiza pian chutan', pp. 324–58.

91. Guan Feng himself wrote an article about this school. See Guan Feng, 'Lun SongYin xuepai' ('On the Song Yin school), *Zhexue yanjiu* (*Philosophical Research*), No. 5, 1959, pp. 28–45.

92. Tan Jiefu, 'Xiancun Zhuangzi "Tianxiapian" de yanjiu' ('A Study of the "Under the Heavens" Chapter of the Existing *Zhuangzi*'), in Zhexue yanjiu bianjibu (ed.), *Zhongguo zhexueshi lunwen chuji* (*Collected Essays on the History of Chinese Philosophy*) (Beijing, Kexue chubanshe, 1959), Vol. 1, pp. 50–78. Quoted in Guan Feng, 'Zhuangzi waiza pian chutan', p. 358.

93. Tan Jiefu, 'Xiancun Zhuangzi "Tianxiapian" de yanjiu', pp. 50–78.

94. Feng Youlan, 'Lun Zhuangzi' ('On Zhuangzi'), originally in *Renmin ribao* (*People's Daily*), 26 February 1961, reprinted in Zhexue yanjiu bianjibu (ed.), *Zhuangzi zhexue taolun ji* (*Collected Papers on Zhuangzi's Philosophy*) (Beijing, Zhonghua shuju, 1962), hereafter *Zhuangzi zhexue taolun ji*, p. 116.

95. Feng Youlan, 'Zai lun Zhuangzi' ('A Further Discussion on Zhuangzi'), originally in *Zhexue yanjiu* (*Philosophical Research*), No. 3, 1961, reprinted in *Zhuangzi zhexue taolun ji*, p. 130. For Qin Shihuang's comment, see Sima Qian, *Shiji*, p. 2155.

96. Feng Youlan, 'Lun Zhuangzi', p. 117. The quotation comes from *Zhuangzi buzheng*, p. 1001.

97. *Zhuangzi buzheng*, p. 16.

98. Ren Jiyu, 'Zhuangzi tanyuan' ('An Investigation into the *Zhuangzi*'), originally in *Zhexue yanjiu* (*Philosophical Research*), No. 2, 1961, reprinted in *Zhuangzi zhexue taolun ji*, pp. 179–80.

99. Ren Jiyu, 'Zhuangzi tanyuan', p. 180.

100. Ren Jiyu, 'Zhuangzi tanyuan', p. 180.

101. Zhang Shitong (ed.), *Xunzi jianzhu* (*A Simple Annotation of Xunzi*) (Shanghai, Shanghai renmin chubanshe, 1974), hereafter *Xunzi jianzhu*, p. 231.

102. Ren Jiyu, 'Zhuangzi tanyuan', p. 184.

103. Ren Jiyu, 'Zhuangzi tanyuan', pp. 185–8.

104. Zhang Dejun, '"Zhuangzi" neipian shi XiHan churen de zhuzuo ma?'

('Were the Inner Chapters of the *Zhuangzi* Written in the Early Western Han Dynasty?'), originally in *Zhexue yanjiu* (*Philosophical Research*), No. 5, 1961, reprinted in *Zhuangzi zhexue taolun ji*, pp. 245-83.

105. Guan Feng, 'Zhuangzi zhexue pipan' ('A Criticism of Zhuangzi's Philosophy'), originally in *Zhexue yanjiu* (*Philosophical Research*), Nos. 7 and 8, 1960, reprinted in *Zhuangzi zhexue taolun ji*, pp. 1-60. Translated into English in *Chinese Studies in History and Philosophy*, No. 1, 1967.

106. Guan Feng, 'Zhuangzi zhexue pipan', p. 16.

107. Guan Feng, 'Zhuangzi zhexue pipan', p. 13, footnote 2.

108. Feng Youlan, 'Lun Zhuangzi', p. 115.

109. Feng Youlan, 'Lun Zhuangzi', p. 125.

110. Feng Youlan, 'Lun Zhuangzi', p. 127.

111. The Huang-Lao school was a Daoist school of thought current in the Warring States period and early in the Han dynasty. It saw both Huangdi (the mythical Heavenly Emperor) and Laozi as co-founders of Daoism; hence the name of the school.

112. Tang Yijie, 'Guanyu Zhuangzi zhexue sixiang de jige wenti' ('A Few Questions on the Philosophical Thought of Zhuangzi'), *Zhuangzi zhexue taolun ji*, p. 313.

113. Ren Jiyu, 'Zhuangzi de weiwuzhuyi shijieguan' ('Zhuangzi's Materialist World Outlook'), *Zhuangzi zhexue taolun ji*, p. 160.

114. Ren Jiyu, 'Zhuangzi tanyuan', p. 190.

115. Ren Jiyu, 'Zhuangzi tanyuan', p. 193. The quotation comes from *Zhuangzi buzheng*, p. 904.

116. Ren Jiyu, 'Zhuangzi tanyuan', p. 194.

117. Ge Feng, 'Zhuangzi zhexue xiangduizhuyi de shizhi' ('The Real Nature of Relativism in Zhuangzi's Philosophy'), originally in *Guangming ribao* (*Guangming Daily*), 17 March 1961, reprinted in *Zhuangzi zhexue taolun ji*, p. 326.

118. Ren Jiyu, 'Zhuangzi tanyuan zhi san' ('A Third Investigation into the *Zhuangzi*'), originally in *Beijing daxue xuebao* (*Beijing University Journal*), No. 5, 1961, reprinted in *Zhuangzi zhexue taolun ji*, p. 237.

119. Ren Jiyu, 'Zhuangzi de weiwuzhuyi shijieguan', pp. 161-2. The quotation comes from *Zhuangzi buzheng*, pp. 225-6.

120. Ren Jiyu, 'Zhuangzi de weiwuzhuyi shijieguan', p. 162.

121. Ren Jiyu, 'Zhuangzi de weiwuzhuyi shijieguan', p. 165.

122. Ren Jiyu, 'Zhuangzi de weiwuzhuyi shijieguan', p. 171.

123. For example, see Tang Yijie, 'Guanyu Zhuangzi zhexue sixiang de jige wenti'.

124. Guan Feng, *Zhuangzi neipian yijie he pipan*.

125. Yang Xiangkui, 'Zhuangzi de sixiang' ('Zhuangzi's Thinking'), originally in *Wen shi zhe*, No. 8, 1957, reprinted in *Zhuangzi zhexue taolun ji*, pp. 329-46.

126. Guan Feng, 'Zhuangzi zhexue pipan'.

127. See, for example, *Zhuangzi buzheng*, pp. 2 and 8.

128. *Zhuangzi buzheng*, pp. 101-2.

129. See, for example, Ren Jiyu, 'Zhuangzi tanyuan', p. 199.

130. In China, this is most widely known in the form of Mao Zedong's essay 'On Practice'.

131. *Zhuangzi buzheng*, p. 283.

132. Guan Feng, *Zhuangzi neipian yijie he pipan*, p. 264.

133. Feng Youlan, 'San lun Zhuangzi' ('A Third Essay on Zhuangzi'), originally in *Beijing daxue xuebao*, No. 4, 1961, reprinted in *Zhuangzi zhexue taolun ji*, p. 147.

134. Feng Youlan, 'San lun Zhuangzi', p. 157.

135. Ren Jiyu, like everybody else after 1962, agreed that both Laozi and Zhuangzi were idealists. See, for example, Ren Jiyu (ed.), *Zhongguo zhexueshi*

jianbian (*A Brief History of Chinese Philosophy*) (Beijing, Renmin chubanshe, 1973), pp. 124–55.

136. Feng Youlan, 'Lun Zhuangzi', p. 127.
137. Feng Youlan, 'Lun Zhuangzi', p. 127.
138. Thomas A. Metzger's thesis that the modern Chinese 'escapes' from the intolerable situation in which he finds himself by embracing foreign ideas is an interesting one. In the context of this chapter though, Metzger's claim is debatable because it would mean that Guan Feng is doing the 'escaping' and not Feng Youlan. Thomas A. Metzger, *Escape from Predicament* (New York, Columbia University Press, 1977).

NOTES TO CHAPTER 5

1. Guo Moruo, 'Kong-Mo de pipan', Yang Rongguo, *Kong-Mo de sixiang*, and Hou Wailu *et al.* (eds.), 'Zhongpian: Kong-Mo xianxue' ('Middle Section: The Illustrious Schools of Kongzi and Mozi'), in *Zhongguo sixiang tongshi*, Vol. 1, pp. 131–256.
2. See Hou Wailu *et al.* (eds.), *Zhongguo sixiang tongshi*, p. 193.
3. 'Fei ru xia' ('Against Confucians Part 2'), in Zhang Chunyi (ed.), *Mozi jijie* (*Mozi Collated and Explained*) (Shanghai, Shijie shuju, 1936), hereafter *Mozi jijie*, pp. 247–63. According to Zhang Chunyi, Part 1 is lost.
4. *Han Feizi jishi*, p. 1080.
5. Sima Qian, *Shiji*, Vol. 7, p. 2350.
6. Sima Qian, *Shiji*, Vol. 7, p. 2350.
7. Ren Jiyu, *Mozi* (*Mozi*) (Shanghai, Shanghai renmin chubanshe, 1956), p. 6.
8. Compare Chapter 5.
9. *Mozi jijie*, p. 426.
10. Yang Rongguo, *Kong-Mo de sixiang*, p. 57.
11. Yang Rongguo, *Kong-Mo de sixiang*, p. 58 and Qian Mu, *Mozi* (Shanghai, Shangwu yinshuguan, 1930), pp. 2–3. Qian Mu was a famous scholar who left China when the People's Republic was established. He continued writing outside China after 1949 when he was denounced.
12. Yang Rongguo, *Zhongguo gudai sixiangshi* (Beijing, Renmin chubanshe, 1954), p. 112.
13. Ren Jiyu, *Mozi*, p. 5.
14. *Mengzi yizhu*, p. 145.
15. *Mozi jijie*, p. 430.
16. *Mozi jijie*, pp. 459–60.
17. Zhang Dainian, 'Mozi de jieji lichang yu zhongxin sixiang' ('The Class Stance and Central Core of Mozi's Thinking'), *Guangming ribao* (*Guangming Daily*), 24 March 1954.
18. Zhang Dainian, 'Mozi de jieji lichang yu zhongxin sixiang'.
19. Hou Wailu *et al.* (eds.), *Zhongguo sixiang tongshi*, p. 198.
20. Zhao Jibin, *Gudai rujia zhexue pipan*.
21. 述而不作;述而且作.
22. Zhao Jibin, 'Kong-Mo xianxue duili de jieji he luoji yiyi' ('The Significance of the Contrast of Class and Logic between the Illustrious Schools of Kongzi and Mozi'), *Xueshu yuekan* (*Academic Monthly*), No. 11, 1963, pp. 34–50.
23. Yang Xiangkui, *Zhongguo gudai shehui yu gudai sixiang yanjiu* (*A Study of Ancient Chinese Society and Ancient Thought*) (Shanghai, Shanghai renmin chubanshe, 1962), Vol. 1, p. 392.
24. Yang Rongguo, *Kong-Mo de sixiang*.
25. Yang Rongguo, *Zhongguo gudai sixiangshi*, p. 114.
26. Guo Moruo, '*Kong-Mo de pipan*', p. 117.

27. Jin Zhong, 'Mozi de meixue guandian he "fei yue" lilun' ('Mozi's Aesthetic Outlook and His "Anti-music" Theory'), *Guangming ribao* (*Guangming Daily*), 7 July 1961. The quotation comes from 'Fei yue' ('Against Music'), *Mozi jijie*, p. 219.

28. Li Chunyi, 'Mozi "fei yue" lilun de yixie wenti' ('A Few Problems on the "Anti-music" Theory of Mozi'), *Guangming ribao* (*Guangming Daily*), 15 December 1961.

29. Li Chunyi, 'Mozi "fei yue" lilun de yixie wenti'.

30. It is of course difficult to determine whether this demarcation is true or not, but writers have on the whole worked from this assumption.

31. From the *Huainanzi*. Quoted in Yang Rongguo, *Kong-Mo de sixiang*, p. 62.

32. This episode, from the *Lüshi chunqiu*, was used very frequently by those who favoured Mozi. It is quoted in Yang Rongguo, *Kong-Mo de sixiang*, p. 63.

33. 'Gongshu' ('Gongshu'), *Mozi jijie*, pp. 460–3.

34. Lu Xun, 'Fei gong' ('Against Offensive Warfare'), in *Lu Xun quanji* (*Complete Works of Lu Xun*) (Beijing, Renmin chubanshe, 1973), Vol. 2, pp. 576–92.

35. Ren Jiyu, *Mozi*, p. 1.

36. Feng Youlan, *Zhongguo zhexueshi xinbian*, p. 155.

37. 'Fei gong' ('Against Offensive Warfare'), *Mozi jijie*, pp. 123–46.

38. Guo Moruo, 'Kong-Mo de pipan', pp. 111–5.

39. Zhong Lei, 'Mozi "fei gong" "jian'ai" de fandong shizhi' ('The Reactionary Nature of Mozi's "Against Offensive Warfare" and "Universal Love"'), *Guangming ribao* (*Guangming Daily*), 1 December 1961.

40. *Guangming ribao* (*Guangming Daily*), 26 January 1962.

41. Zhang Dehong, 'Mozi de "fei gong" "jian'ai" shi fandong de ma?' ('Are Mozi's "Against Offensive Warfare" and "Universal Love" Reactionary?'), *Guangming ribao* (*Guangming Daily*), 16 January 1962.

42. These quotations, which have for centuries been accepted judgements on Mozi, are found in *Mengzi yizhu*, p. 155.

43. Zhang Dehong, 'Mozi de "fei gong" "jian'ai" shi fandong de ma?'

44. Lü Lizhuo, 'Cong "Gongshu" tanqi' ('Starting with "Gongshu"'), *Guangming ribao* (*Guangming Daily*), 26 January 1962.

45. Yang Rongguo, *Kong-Mo de sixiang*.

46. Yang Rongguo, *Kong-Mo de sixiang*, p. 89.

47. Burton Watson (trans. and ed.), *Mo Tzu: Basic Writings* (New York, Columbia University Press, 1963), pp. 9–10.

48. In 1954, Yang Rongguo still insisted that *jian'ai* was proposed as an alternative by the lower class to Kongzi's *ren*. See Yang Rongguo, *Zhongguo gudai sixiangshi* (*History of Ancient Chinese Thought*) (Beijing, Sanlian shudian chubanshe, 1954), pp. 123–6. In 1973, however, the new edition included the idea of 'class compromise'. See his *Zhongguo gudai sixiangshi* (*History of Ancient Chinese Thought*) (Beijing, Renmin chubanshe, 1973), p. 119.

49. Ren Jiyu, *Mozi*, p. 28.

50. Hou Wailu *et al.* (eds.), *Zhongguo sixiang tongshi*, Vol. 1, pp. 202–6.

51. In Chinese characters, these terms are 兼君 (*jianjun*), 兼士 (*jianshi*), 别君 (*biejun*), and 别士 (*bieshi*).

52. This is related in the *Mozi jijie*, pp. 110–11.

53. Hou Wailu *et al.* (eds.), *Zhongguo sixiang tongshi*, Vol. 1, p. 204.

54. Feng Youlan, *Zhongguo zhexueshi xinbian*, p. 150.

55. Liu Jie, 'Mozi de "jian'ai" he shili sixiang' ('Mozi's Theory of "Universal Love" and Material Benefits'), *Xueshu yanjiu* (*Guangzhou*) (*Academic Research (Canton)*), No. 1, 1963, p. 57.

56. Liu Jie, 'Mozi de "jian'ai" he shili sixiang', p. 64.

57. See 'Ming gui xia' ('Clarifying Ghosts Part III'), *Mozi jijie*, pp. 197–218. According to Zhang Chunyi, Parts I and II are lost.

58. This theory proposed by Guo Moruo was the basis for many arguments on the metaphysics of the pre-Qin philosophers. Guo Moruo, 'XianQin tiandaoguan

zhi jinzhan' ('The Development of the pre-Qin Cosmological Outlook'), *Qingtong shidai* (*The Bronze Age*) (Beijing, Renmin chubanshe, 1954), pp. 1–42.

59. Yang Rongguo, *Kong-Mo de sixiang*, p. 96.

60. Yang Rongguo, *Kong-Mo de sixiang*, p. 99.

61. Zichan (*circa* 500) was a reformer in the Zheng state during the Spring and Autumn period. He is credited with having legal codes inscribed on bronze tripods.

62. This incident from the *Zuozhuan* is quoted in Yang Rongguo, *Kong-Mo de sixiang*, p. 103.

63. This definition of the 'Will of Heaven' is expressed in many different forms in the *Mozi jijie*. They are listed in Lü Zhenyu, *Zhongguo zhengzhi sixiangshi*, pp. 123–4.

64. Lü Zhenyu, *Zhongguo zhengzhi sixiangshi*, pp. 123–4.

65. Jian Bozan, *Zhongguo shigang*.

66. Guo Moruo, *Shi pipan shu*, p. 106.

67. The scheme adopted by Jian Bozan was the same as Fan Wenlan's. See Chapter 1.

68. Guo Moruo, *Shi pipan shu*, p. 107.

69. Liu Jie, 'Mozi de "jian'ai" he shili sixiang', p. 52.

70. Du Guoxiang, for example, who was generally very favourable towards Mozi, argued that, although the central core of the *Mozi* was *yi*, this concept was expressed by the Will of Heaven. Du Guoxiang, 'XianQin zhuzi sixiang gaiyao' ('An Outline of the Thoughts of the pre-Qin Philosophers'), *Du Guoxiang wenji* (*Collected Articles by Du Guoxiang*) (Beijing, Renmin chubanshe, 1962).

71. Zhang Dainian, *Zhongguo weiwuzhuyi sixiang jianshi*, pp. 41–4.

72. Hou Wailu *et al.* (eds.), *Zhongguo sixiang tongshi*, p. 222.

73. 'Fei shi'er zi' ('Critique of the Twelve Philosophers'), *Xunzi jianzhu*, p. 47.

74. *Mozi jijie*, pp. 229–36.

75. *Mozi jijie*, pp. 236–40.

76. Guo Moruo, *Shi pipan shu*, pp. 119–22.

77. Zhan Jianfeng, 'Guanyu Mojia he Mojia bianzhe de pipan wenti' ('On The Criticism of the Moists and the Moist Rhetoricians'), *Xueshu yuekan* (*Academic Monthly*), No. 4, 1957, p. 15.

78. Ren Jiyu, *Mozi*, p. 71.

79. For the attitudes of Tan Sitong and Liang Qichao on Mozi, see the quotations in Yang Rongguo, 'Xuyan' ('Preface'), *Zhongguo gudai sixiangshi*, p. 2.

80. Hou Wailu *et al.* (eds.), *Zhongguo sixiang tongshi*, pp. 472–85.

81. Zhan Jianfeng, *Mojia de xingshi luoji* (*The Formal Logic of the Moists*) (Hubei, Hubei renmin chubanshe, 1956, second edition 1979), pp. 202–29.

82. Gao Heng, *Mojing jiaoquan* (*The Moist Canon Collated and Explained*) (Beijing, Kexue chubanshe, 1958) and Tan Jiefu, *Mobian fawei* (*The Moist Rhetorics Explained*) (Beijing, Kexue chubanshe, 1958).

83. Guo Moruo, *Shi pipan shu*, pp. 280–99.

84. *Mozi jijie*, p. 409.

85. Guo Moruo, *Shi pipan shu*, p. 299.

86. Zhan Jianfeng, 'Guanyu Mojia he Mojia bianzhe de pipan wenti', p. 15. In the Zhang Chunyi edition of the *Mozi*, used in this book, the word 'ren' does not appear. However, Zhang Chunyi in his notes acknowledged that, in old editions, 'ren' did appear and that it had been deleted because it was thought superfluous. So, it seems that Zhan Jianfeng did make a valid objection to Guo Moruo.

87. Yang Rongguo, *Zhongguo gudai sixiangshi*, p. 294.

88. For example, Gao Heng and Tan Jiefu.

89. Pang Pu, *Gongsun Longzi yanjiu* (*Study of the Gongsun Longzi*) (Beijing, Zhonghua shuju, 1979), p. 11.

90. Quoted in 'Tianxia pian' ('Under the Heaven Chapter'), *Zhuangzi buzheng*, p. 1005.

91. *Zhuangzi buzheng*, pp. 1003–11.

NOTES TO CHAPTER 6

1. Zisi (483–402 BC) was said to have been Kongzi's grandson. He made 'the golden mean' (*zhongyong*) the central concept in Confucianism. He and Mengzi represented the orthodox stream of Confucianism (*ZiMeng xuepai*).

2. Sima Qian, *Shiji*, Vol. 7, p. 2343.

3. See, for example, Fan Wenlan, *Zhongguo tongshi jianbian*, Vol. 1, p. 263.

4. Zhu Xi (1130–1200). Together with the Cheng Brothers (also Song philosophers), Zhu Xi founded the neo-Confucianist school (*lixue*) which stressed the *li* 理 over the *qi* 气. This was the philosophy which influenced later thinkers like Feng Youlan.

5. Han Yu (768–824 AD), a prolific essayist who defended the orthodox Kong-Meng stream of Confucianism.

6. Sima Qian, *Shiji*, Vol. 7, p. 2343.

7. *Mengzi yizhu*, pp. 6–8.

8. See, for example, Li Yinnong, 'Guanyu Mengzi de jieji huafen lun' ('On Mengzi's Theory of Class Distinction'), *Xueshu yanjiu* (*Academic Research*), No. 3, 1962, p. 56.

9. *Mengzi yizhu*, p. 145.

10. It was told to me in the late 1950s when I was at primary school in China.

11. Fan Wenlan, *Zhongguo tongshi jianbian*, Vol. 1, p. 264.

12. Feng Youlan, *Zhongguo zhexueshi xinbian*, Vol. 1, p. 214.

13. *Mengzi yizhu*, pp. 259 and 302.

14. Tang Yijie, 'Mengzi de zhexue sixiang' ('Mengzi's Philosophical Thought'), *Xin jianshe* (*New Construction*), No. 7, 1961, pp. 24–35.

15. *Mengzi yizhu*, p. 302.

16. *Mengzi yizhu*, p. 251.

17. *Mengzi yizhu*, p. 298.

18. Zhang Dejun, 'Mengzi de renshi lun' ('Mengzi's Epistemology'), *Wenhui bao*, 15 and 16 February 1962.

19. Wang Zhibang and Feng Guixian, 'Mengzi renshi lun de weixinzhuyi benzhi' ('The Idealist Basis of Mengzi's Epistemology'), *Wenhui bao* (*Wenhui Daily*), 23 April 1964.

20. Feng Youlan, *Zhongguo zhexueshi xinbian*, Vol. 1, p. 226.

21. Feng Youlan, *Zhongguo zhexueshi xinbian*, Vol. 1, p. 226. The original quotation comes from *Mengzi yizhu*, p. 79.

22. The original quotation in the Mengzi is '*min wei gui, sheji ci zhi, jun wei qing*', *Mengzi yizhu*, p. 328.

23. Fan Wenlan, *Zhongguo tongshi jianbian*, Vol. 1, p. 265.

24. *Mengzi yizhu*, p. 328.

25. Hou Wailu *et al.* (eds.), *Zhongguo sixiang tongshi*, Vol. 1, p. 392.

26. Yang Rongguo, *Zhongguo gudai sixiangshi*, 1954 edition, pp. 172–5.

27. Yang Rongguo, *Zhongguo gudai sixiangshi*, p. 174. The quotations are from *Mengzi yizhu*, pp. 123 and 77.

28. *Mengzi yizhu*, pp. 118–9.

29. Yang Rongguo, 'Lun Kongzi sixiang', p. 39.

30. *Mengzi yizhu*, pp. 244.

31. Li Yinnong, 'Guanyu Mengzi de jieji huafen lun', p. 56.

32. See *Mengzi yizhu*, pp. 246–7, footnote 2. Jiao Xun (1763–1820), a scholar of diverse talents, wrote on various subjects, including the classics, plays, and mathematics. His *Mengzi zhengyi* (*Annotated Mengzi*) is still used today as a standard reference.

33. Discussed in Peng Yinluo, 'Lun "minmeng", "yeren", "caomang zhi chen" de jieji diwei ji Mengzi zhengzhi sixiang' ('On the Class Positions of the "*minmeng*", "*yeren*", "*caomang zhi chen*" and Mengzi's Political Thought'), *Xueshu yanjiu* (*Academic Research*), No. 4, 1962, p. 65.

34. Peng Yinluo, 'Lun "minmeng", "yeren", "caomang zhi chen" de jieji diwei ji Mengzi zhengzhi sixiang'.

35. Peng Yinluo, 'Lun "minmeng", "yeren", "caomang zhi chen" de jieji diwei ji Mengzi zhengzhi sixiang', p. 69.

36. See Mengzi's descriptions of this system in *Mengzi yizhu*, pp. 117–19.

37. Jixia was the name of a place near the capital city of the state of Qi. Around 300 BC, thousands of scholars from different states gathered there to lecture and to learn, including some of the most famous such as Shen Dao, Yin Wen, Huan Yuan, and Xunzi.

38. Quoted in Hou Wailu *et al.* (eds.), *Zhongguo sixiang tongshi*, Vol. 1, p. 529.

39. See, for example, Yang Xiangkui, *Zhongguo gudai shehui yu gudai sixiang yanjiu*, Vol. 1, p. 221.

40. Sima Qian, *Shiji*, pp. 2139–56 and pp. 2343–50.

41. The *Si Shu* (*Four Books*), which included the *Lunyu*, the *Da xue*, the *Zhongyong*, and the *Mengzi*, were compiled and annotated by Zhu Xi in the Song dynasty, and subsequently became required reading.

42. See Yang Rongguo's discussion of this and his disagreements with Tan and Liang in Yang Rongguo, 'Xuyan', *Zhongguo gudai sixiangshi*, p. 3.

43. Huang Zitong, *Ru dao liang jia zhexue xitong* (*The Confucian and Daoist Philosophical Systems*) (Changsha, Yuzhou shuju, 1946), second edition, p. 1.

44. Jian Bozan, *Zhongguo shigang*, Vol. 1, pp. 397–8.

45. Feng Youlan, *Zhongguo zhexueshi xinbian*, Vol. 1, p. 548.

46. This comes from the statement in *Xunzi jianzhu*, p. 61, where King Zhao of Qin remarked that Confucians do not benefit the people of a state.

47. Li Deyong, *Xunzi* (*Xunzi*) (Shanghai, Shanghai renmin chubanshe, 1961), p. 5.

48. Li Deyong, *Xunzi*, pp. 6–7.

49. 'Fei shi'er zi' ('Critique of the Twelve Philosophers'), *Xunzi jianzhu*, pp. 45–53.

50. *Xunzi jianzhu*, p. 203.

51. Yang Rongguo, *Zhongguo gudai sixiangshi*, p. 371.

52. Wu Wen, 'Xunzi shi Zhongguo fengjianzhuyi sixiang de kaishanzhe ma?' ('Was Xunzi the Founder of Feudal Thought in China?'), *Zhexue yanjiu* (*Philosophical Research*), No. 4, 1957, p. 143.

53. Hu Shi, *Zhongguo zhexueshi dagang* (*Outline of the History of Chinese Philosophy*) (Shanghai, Shangwu yinshuguan, 1919), p. 309.

54. *Lunyu yizhu*, p. 113.

55. Feng Youlan, *Zhongguo zhexue shi* (*History of Chinese Philosophy*), originally published in 1930, reprinted in Hong Kong by the Taipingyang tushu gongsi in 1970, p. 352.

56. Feng Youlan, *Zhongguo zhexue shi*.

57. Quoted in Guo Moruo, 'Xunzi de pipan' ('Critique of Xunzi'), *Shi pipan shu*, p. 212.

58. Guo Moruo, 'Xunzi de pipan', p. 219.

59. Feng Youlan, 'Zhongguo zhexue de fazhan', p. 20.

60. Feng Youlan, *Zhongguo zhexueshi xinbian*, Vol. 1, p. 512.

61. Zhang Dainian, *Zhongguo weiwuzhuyi sixiang jianshi*, p. 45.

62. Zhang Dainian, 'Xunzi de weiwuzhuyi sixiang' ('Xunzi's Materialist Thinking'), *Xuexi* (*Study*), No. 1, 1957, p. 6. The quotation comes from *Xunzi jianzhu*, pp. 183–4.

63. In most cases, pointing out the 'defects' of a person was just a routine part of writing about any historical figure before Marx.

64. Zhang Dainian, 'Xunzi de weiwuzhuyi sixiang', p. 29.

65. Zhang Dainian, 'Xunzi de weiwuzhuyi sixiang', pp. 43–4.

66. For example, Feng Youlan, *Zhongguo zhexueshi xinbian*, Vol. 1, pp. 531–2.

67. The question of man's will versus determination in history is a complicated

one. Mao Zedong himself has often been seen as subscribing to the view that human will triumphs over nature. See, in particular, 'The Foolish Old Man Who Removed the Mountains', *Selected Works of Mao Tse-tung*, Vol. III, pp. 271–5, which was essential reading in the Cultural Revolution.

68. See, for example, Hou Wailu *et al.* (eds.), *Zhongguo sixiang tongshi*, Vol. 1, p. 573.

69. *Xunzi jianzhu*, p. 260.

70. See, for example, his statement 'All people desire to be good, but they have evil natures', in *Xunzi jianzhu*, p. 261.

71. Liang Qixiong, 'Xunzi sixiang shuping' ('A Critical Outline of Xunzi's Thought'), *Zhexue yanjiu (Philosophical Research)*, No. 4, 1963, pp. 48–63.

72. On the contemporary Chinese conception of the malleability of the human mind, see Donald J. Munro, *The Concept of Man in Contemporary China* (Ann Arbor, University of Michigan Press, 1979).

73. *Xunzi jianzhu*, pp. 260–1.

74. Qu Junong, 'Zhongguo gudai de weiwuzhuyi jiaoyu sixiang' ('Materialist Educational Thought in Ancient China'), *Xin jianshe (New Construction)*, No. 7, 1963, pp. 47–57.

75. *Xunzi jianzhu*, p. 258.

76. See, for example, Li Qingsong, 'Xunzi jiaoyu lun de sixiang jichu he jiji yinsu' ('The Basis of Xunzi's Education Thought and the Factors for Its Activeness'), *Wenhui bao (Wenhui Daily)*, 6 March 1962. This was one of a number of articles published in the early sixties on the merits of Xunzi's educational thought. They were the predecessors of the many articles in the early seventies elevating Xunzi as an educationalist over Kongzi.

77. For example, Qu Junong, 'Zhongguo gudai de weiwuzhuyi jiaoyu sixiang'. Wang Chong (AD 27–97), Wang Anshi (1021–1086), and Liu Zongyan (773–819) are all considered materialist philosophers.

78. Li Deyong, *Xunzi*, pp. 78–9.

79. See, for example, Zhang Ruifan, 'Xunzi de jiaoyu sixiang' ('Xunzi's Educational Thought'), *Huadong shida xuebao (East China Teachers' University Journal)*, No. 3, 1957, p. 91.

80. Zhang Ruifan, 'Xunzi de jiaoyu sixiang', p. 93.

81. Zhong Kui, 'Du Xunzi "quan xue" zhaji' ('Notes on Xunzi's "Exhortation to Learning"'), *Guangming ribao (Guangming Daily)*, 29 September 1961.

82. Sima Qian, *Shiji*, Vol. 7, p. 2155.

83. These events are related in Sima Qian, 'Qin Shihuang benji' ('Annals of Qin Shihuang'), *Shiji*, Vol. 1, pp. 255 and 258.

84. See, for example, *Han Feizi jishi*, p. 1057.

85. Many writers have compared Han Feizi with Machiavelli. See, for example, Wang Teh-chao, 'Majiyafuli yu Han Fei sixiang de yitong' ('A Comparison between the Thinking of Machiavelli and Han Feizi'), *Xinya xueshu niankan (New Asia Academic Annual)*, No. 9, 1967, pp. 163–95.

86. Burton Watson, 'Introduction', in Burton Watson (trans.), *Han Fei Tzu* (New York, Columbia University Press, 1964), p. 14.

87. For example, Huang Zitong in *Ru dao liang jia zhexue xitong* discusses only Confucians and Daoists and does not mention Han Feizi at all.

88. Hu Shi, *Zhongguo zhexueshi dagang*, Vol. 1, pp. 360–4.

89. Yang Rongguo, *Zhongguo gudai sixiangshi*, pp. 2 and 375.

90. *Han Feizi jishi*, p. 906.

91. For example, Guo Moruo, 'Han Feizi de pipan' ('Critique of Han Feizi'), *Shi pipan shu*, p. 340.

92. Feng Youlan, *Zhongguo zhexueshi xinbian*, Vol. 1, p. 587.

93. See, for example, Yang Rongguo, *Zhongguo gudai sixiangshi*, p. 377.

94. Fan Wenlan, *Zhongguo tongshi jianbian*, Vol. 1, p. 280.

95. Feng Youlan, 'Han Fei "jie Lao", "yu Lao" pian xin shi' ('A New Explana-

tion of Han Feizi's "Explaining Laozi" and "Clarifying Laozi"), originally in *Beijing daxue xuebao* (*Beijing University Journal*), No. 2, 1961; reprinted in *Zhongguo zhexueshi lunwen erji* (*Essays on the History of Chinese Philosophy*) reprint edition (Macau, Xinfeng tushushe, no date), pp. 375–82.

96. Guo Moruo, 'Han Feizi de pipan', p. 347.

97. Liang Qixiong, *Hanzi qianjie* (*A Simple Explanation of Han Feizi*) (Beijing, Zhonghua shuju, 1960), p. 11.

98. Hou Wailu *et al.* (eds.), *Zhongguo sixiang tongshi*, Vol. 1, p. 605.

99. Guo Moruo, 'Han Feizi de pipan', p. 372.

100. Guo Moruo, 'Han Feizi de pipan', p. 373. Guo Moruo in this quotation used the Gu Guangqi edition of the *Han Feizi*. In the more reliable Chen Qiyou edition used in this book, this statement does not appear. See *Han Feizi jishi*, pp. 906–8.

101. Wang Hsien-ch'ien, 'Preface to the Complete Works of Han Fei Tzu' (1897), in W.K. Liao (trans.), *The Complete Works of Han Fei Tzu* (London, Arthur Probsthain, 1939), Vol. 1, p. xxxiii.

102. Li Deyong, 'Han Fei de shehui zhengzhi sixiang' ('Han Feizi's Social Political Thought'), *Xin jianshe* (*New Construction*), No. 12, 1956, p. 38.

103. See, for example, Zhou Zhongling, *Han Feizi de luoji* (*Han Feizi's Logic*), (Beijing, Renmin chubanshe, 1958).

104. Feng Youlan, *Zhongguo zhexueshi xinbian*, Vol. 1, p. 512.

105. As well as Feng Youlan, other authorities such as Hou Wailu also put forward this argument. Hou Wailu *et al.* (eds.), *Zhongguo sixiang tongshi*, Vol. 1, p. 625.

106. *Han Feizi jishi*, p. 290. Paraphrased in Feng Youlan, *Zhongguo zhexueshi xinbian*, Vol. 1, p. 576.

107. Ren Jiyu, *Han Fei* (Shanghai, Shanghai renmin chubanshe, 1964), p. 55.

108. Wang Yi, 'Han Fei', *Zhongguo qingnian* (*China Youth*), No. 3, 1957, p. 28.

109. *Han Feizi jishi*, p. 289.

110. Geng Ye, 'Dui Wang Yi tongzhi "Han Fei de sixiang" yi wen de jidian yijian' ('A Few Objections to Comrade Wang Yi's Essay "Han Feizi's Thought"'), *Guangming ribao* (*Guangming Daily*), 23 February 1955. This article is a comment on an earlier article by Wang Yi, 'Han Fei de sixiang' ('Han Feizi's Thought'), *Guangming ribao* (*Guangming Daily*), 5 May 1954.

111. Yang Rongguo, *Zhongguo gudai sixiangshi*, p. 354.

112. *Fajia renwu gushi* (*Stories about the Legalists*) (Shanghai, Shanghai renmin chubanshe, 1975), p. 76.

113. Liang Qixiong, *Hanzi qianjie*, p. 19.

114. *Han Feizi jishi*, p. 1058.

115. *Han Feizi jishi*, p. 1075.

116. 'Wu du' ('Five Vermin'), *Han Feizi jishi*, pp. 1040–79.

117. Li Zongmao, 'Tan Han Feizi de ruogan jingji guandian' ('On a Few of Han Feizi's Economic Viewpoints'), *Guangming ribao* (*Guangming Daily*), 30 July 1962.

118. *Han Feizi jishi*, pp. 1040–1.

119. Feng Youlan, 'Guanyu Zhongguo zhexueshi yanjiu de liangge wenti,' p. 13.

120. Li Zhikui, 'Du Feng Youlan xiansheng "Guanyu Zhongguo zhexueshi yanjiu de liangge wenti" de yidian yijian' ('A Suggestion on Mr Feng Youlan's "Two Problems on the Study of the History of Chinese Philosophy"'), *Symposium on Chinese Philosophy*, p. 449.

121. Sun Changjiang, 'Makesizhuyi chuxian yiqian shehui lishi lilun zhong you mei you weiwuzhuyi he weixinzhuyi de douzheng' ('Were There Struggles between Materialism and Idealism in the Theories of Social History before the Appearance of Marxism?'), *Symposium on Chinese Philosophy*, p. 457.

122. Dai Qingliang and Lin Keji, 'Dui Makesizhuyi yiqian lishiguan de pingjia

de yixie yijian' ('A Few Comments on the Evaluation of Historical Outlooks before the Appearance of Marxism'), *Symposium on Chinese Philosophy*, pp. 480–2.

123. Yang Huarong, 'Wo zancheng Feng Youlan xiansheng de kanfa' ('I agree with Mr Feng Youlan's Viewpoint'), *Symposium on Chinese Philosophy*, p. 472.

NOTES TO THE CONCLUSION

1. Benjamin I. Schwartz, 'Notes on Conservatism in General and in China in Particular', in Charlotte Furth (ed.), *The Limits of Change* (Cambridge, Mass., Harvard University Press, 1976), p. 4.

2. See Lu Xun's famous story, 'Kuangren riji' ('Madman's Dairy'), in *Lu Xun quanji*, Vol. 1, pp. 277–91.

3. For an account of the anti-Confucian movement in the May Fourth era, see Kam Louie, *Critiques of Confucius in Contemporary China*, pp. 1–16.

4. See, for example, Xu Kangsheng, 'Tantan guanyu pipan jicheng yu "chouxiang jicheng" de wenti' ('On the Problem of Critical Inheritance and "Abstract Inheritance"'), in *Zhongguo zhexueshi fangfa lun taolun ji*, pp. 210–214.

5. As Daniel Overmyer observed in his review of *Critiques of Confucius in Contemporary China*, the discussions on Kongzi were carried out 'as if the majority of American intellectuals were still passionately debating the divinity of Christ'. *Religious Studies Review*, Vol. 7, No. 2. 1981, p. 185.

6. See Liu Yichun, 'Mengzi zai pingjia' ('Further Evaluations of Mengzi'), in Zhongguo shehuikexue yuan (ed.), *Zhexue zhenglun yijiubaling-yijiubaer chu* (*Controversies in Philosophy 1980 to Early 1982*) (Xian, Shanxi renmin chubanshe, 1984), p. 330.

7. Even in industrial management, administrators with Confucian morals are made into models. See Kam Louie, 'In Search of Socialist Capitalism and Chinese Modernisation', *The Australian Journal of Chinese Affairs*, No. 12, 1984, pp. 87–96.

8. An interesting example in post-1976 literature is found in Liu Xinwu's 'The Young Man in the Yellow Overcoat'. See the discussion in Kam Louie, 'Youth and Education in the Short Stories of Liu Xinwu', *Westerly*, No. 3, 1981, pp. 115–20.

9. This 'blind faith in the power of abstract doctrine' typical of the Guan Feng-type intellectual had parallels in the Russian intelligentsia. See Tibor Szamuely, *The Russian Tradition* (London, Secker & Warburg, 1974), p. 160.

10. A good example of this kind of story is found in Li Ping, 'Wanxia xiaoshi de shihou' ('At the Time of the Vanishing Twilight'), *Shiyue* (*October*), No. 1, 1981, pp. 77–134.

11. Ah Cheng, 'Qi wang' ('Chess King'), *Shanghai wenxue* (*Shanghai Literature*), No. 7, 1984, pp. 15–35.

12. *Huxian nongmin hua xuanji* (*Peasant Paintings from Huxian*) (Xian, Shanxi renmin chubanshe, 1974).

13. See some of the arguments presented in Zhou Longhua, 'Guanyu Laozi zhexue' ('On Laozi's Philosophy'), in Zhongguo shehuikexue yuan (ed.), *Zhexue zhenglun yijiubaling–yijiubaer chu*, pp. 320–8 and Ren Jiyu (ed.), *Zhongguo zhexue fazhanshi* (*History of the Development of Chinese Philosophy*) (Beijing, Renmin chubanshe, 1983), pp. 379–421.

14. See a summary of the arguments advanced by Feng Youlan in James Liu, *The Chinese Knight-Errant* (Chicago, University of Chicago Press, 1967), pp. 10–12.

15. Guo Moruo, *Shi pipan shu*, p. 81.

16. Feng Youlan, *Zhongguo zhexueshi xinbian*, Vol. 1, p. 150.

17. Hu Huaichen, 'Modi wei Yinduren bian' ('On Mozi as an Indian'), *Dongfang zazhi* (*Eastern Miscellany*), Vol. 25, No. 8, 1928, pp. 79–82.

18. As well as the many annotations of the *Moist Canon*, there is even a new annotated *Mozi*: Wang Huanbiao (ed.), *Mozi jiaoshi* (*Mozi Collated and Explained*) (Hangzhou, Zhejiang wenyi chubanshe, 1984).

19. As Benjamin Schwartz commented about the 'self-strengthening' efforts in the late Qing dynasty, 'What was being emphasized was not, of course, a frank commitment to Legalism, but that quasi-Legalist vein of Confucian thought which had stressed the compatibility of wealth and power with Confucian values.' B.I. Schwartz, *In Search of Wealth and Power* (Cambridge, Mass., Harvard University Press, 1964), p. 17.

20. For changing evaluations made on Qin Shihuang, see the translations in Li Yu-ning (ed.), *The First Emperor of China: The Politics of Historiography* (New York, M.E. Sharpe, 1975).

21. See the translations in Li Yu-ning (ed.), *Shang Yang's Reforms and State Control in China* (New York, M.E. Sharpe, 1977), 2 Vols.

22. Mao Zedong, 'Zai ba da erci huiyi shang de jianghua' ('Speech at the Second Session of the Eighth Congress of the Communist Party of China'), *Mao Zedong sixiang wansui* (*Long Live Mao Zedong Thought*) (n.p., 1969), p. 195.

23. After 1976, there have been few studies of the Legalists. The two volume *Zhexue zhenglun*, which summarizes philosophical debates from 1977 to 1982, for example, does not discuss the Legalists at all.

24. In the first academic convention of the Chinese Society of History, which opened in Beijing on 11 April 1983, for example, the major item discussed was the 'relations between cultural heritage and socialist ethics' (Beijing, Xinhua News Agency, 16 April 1983).

25. This 'response' model was popular among Western historians too, but it has been discredited for a more China-centred one. See the discussion in Paul A. Cohen, *Discovering History in China* (New York, Columbia University Press, 1984).

26. A.A. Zhdanov had performed the same deed in the Soviet Union. In a legislative statement that he made in 1944, for example, 'the names of Belinsky, Chernyshevsky, and Dobrolyubov are mentioned nineteen times, Lenin seven times, Stalin six times and Marx not at all.' Rufus Mathewson Jr., *The Positive Hero in Russian Literature* (Stanford, Stanford University Press, 1975), p. 21.

Bibliography

ENGLISH LANGUAGE WORKS AND TRANSLATIONS FROM OTHER LANGUAGES

Alitto, Guy S., *The Last Confucian* (Berkeley, University of California Press, 1979).

Balazs, Etienne, *Chinese Civilization and Bureaucracy*, edited by Arthur F. Wright and translated by H.M. Wright (New Haven, Yale University Press, 1964).

Blakney, R.B., *The Way of Life: Lao Tzu* (New York, Mentor Books, 1955).

Borisov, O.B. and Koloskov, B.T., *Soviet-Chinese Relations 1945–1970* (Bloomington and London, Indiana University Press, 1975).

Bottomore, T.B. and Rubel, M. (eds.), *Karl Marx: Selected Writings in Sociology and Social Philosophy* (Harmondsworth, Penguin Books, 1963).

The Case of Peng Teh-huai 1959–1968 (Hong Kong, Union Research Institute, 1968).

Chan Wing-tsit, *Chinese Philosophy 1949–1963: An Annotated Bibliography of Mainland China Publications* (Honolulu, East-West Center Press, 1967).

Chang Chung-yuan, *Tao: A New Way of Thinking* (no publication details, 1975).

Chiang Yee, *The Chinese Eye* (Bloomington, Indiana University Press, 1964).

Chow Tse-tsung, *The May Fourth Movement* (Stanford, Stanford University Press, 1960).

Chung Wah-min, 'Criticism of Academic Theories in Communist China, 1966', *Communist China 1966* (Hong Kong, Union Research Institute, 1967), Vol. 2, pp. 118–50.

Cohen, Paul A., *Discovering History in China* (New York, Columbia University Press, 1984).

Communist China, 1955–59: Policy Documents with Analysis (Cambridge, Mass., Harvard University Press, 1962).

Creel, Herrlee G., *What Is Taoism?* (Chicago, University of Chicago Press, 1970).

Daubier, Jean, *A History of the Chinese Cultural Revolution* (New York, Random House, 1974).

'Decision of the Central Committee of the Chinese Communist Party concerning the Great Proletarian Cultural Revolution (Adopted on August 8, 1966)', in *Carry the Great Proletarian Cultural Revolution through to the End* (Beijing, Foreign Languages Press, 1966), pp. 1–14.

Dittmer, Lowell, *Liu Shao-ch'i and the Chinese Cultural Revolution: The Politics of Mass Criticism* (Berkeley, University of California Press, 1974).

Documents of Chinese Communist Party Central Committee, September 1956–April 1969 (Hong Kong, Union Research Institute, 1971), Vol. 1.

Engels, Frederick, *The Origin of the Family, Private Property and the State* (New York, International Publishers, 1968).

—— 'Speech at the Graveside of Karl Marx', in K. Marx and F. Engels, *Selected Works* (Moscow, Progress Publishers, 1970), Vol. 3, pp. 162–3.

Fang Cheng, 'Education in Communist China 1966', *Communist China 1966* (Hong Kong, Union Research Institute, 1968), Vol. II, pp. 40–62.

Feuerwerker, Albert, 'China's History in Marxian Dress', in Albert Feuerwerker (ed.), *History in Communist China* (Cambridge, Mass., MIT Press, 1968), pp. 14–44.

—— (ed.), *History in Communist China* (Cambridge, Mass., MIT Press, 1968).

Fisher, Tom, ' "The Play's the Thing": Wu Han and Hai Rui Revisited', *The Australian Journal of Chinese Affairs*, No. 7, 1982, pp. 1–35.

Fraser, William, 'The Traditional and Distinctive in Soviet Education', in Edmund J. King (ed.), *Communist Education* (London, Methuen and Co., 1963), pp. 78–96.

Furth, Charlotte (ed.), *The Limits of Change* (Cambridge, Mass., Harvard University Press, 1976).

Goldman, Merle, *China's Intellectuals: Advise and Dissent* (Cambridge, Mass., Harvard University Press, 1981).

—— *Literary Dissent in Communist China* (Cambridge, Mass., Harvard University Press, 1967).

—— (ed.), *Modern Chinese Literature in the May Fourth Era* (Cambridge, Mass., Harvard University Press, 1977).

Grieder, Jerome B., *Hu Shih and the Chinese Renaissance: Liberalism in the Chinese Revolution 1917–1937* (Cambridge, Mass., Harvard University Press, 1970).

—— *Intellectuals and the State in Modern China* (New York, The Free Press, 1981).

Hawkins, John H., *Mao Tse-tung and Education: His Thoughts and Teachings* (Hamden, Shoe-string Press, 1974).

Hu Shih, *The Development of the Logical Method in Ancient China* (New York, Paragon Book Reprint Corporation, 1963), second edition.

I Wo-sheng, 'Education in Communist China during 1962 and a Comparison with Education in the Soviet Union', *Communist China 1962* (Hong Kong, Union Research Institue, 1963), Vol. 1, pp. 176–203.

Jenner, W.J.F. (ed.), *Fragrant Weeds* (Hong Kong, Joint Publishing Co., 1983).

Johnson, Chalmers, *Communist Politics Towards the Intellectual Class* (Hong Kong, Union Research Institute, 1959).

Khrushchev, Nikita, *Khrushchev Remembers: The Last Testament*, translated and edited by Strobe Talbott (London, Deutsch, 1974).

Konrad, Gyorgy, and Szelenyi, Istvan, *The Intellectuals on the Road to Class Power*, translated by Andrew Arato and Richard Allen (Brighton, Harvester Press, 1979).

Lau, D.C. (trans.), *Confucius: The Analects* (Harmondsworth, Penguin Books, 1979).

Lee, Leo Ou-fan, *The Romantic Generation* (Cambridge, Mass., Harvard University Press, 1974).

Legge, James (trans.), *The Four Books* (Hong Kong, The Chinese Book Co., no date).

Lenin, V.I., *Materialism and Empirio-Criticism* (Beijing, Foreign Languages Press, 1972).

Levenson, Joseph R., *Confucian China and Its Modern Fate: A Trilogy* (Berkeley, University of California Press, 1965).

——— *Liang Ch'i-ch'ao and the Mind of Modern China* (Berkeley, University of California Press, 1970).

Li Yu-ning (ed.), *The First Emperor of China: The Politics of Historiography* (New York, M.E. Sharpe, 1975).

——— (ed.), *Shang Yang's Reforms and State Control in China* (New York, M.E. Sharpe, 1977), 2 Vols.

Liu, James J.Y., *The Chinese Knight-Errant* (Chicago, University of Chicago Press, 1967).

Louie, Kam, *Critiques of Confucius in Contemporary China* (Hong Kong, Chinese University Press, 1980).

———'In Search of Socialist Capitalism and Chinese Modernisation', *The Australian Journal of Chinese Affairs*, No. 12, 1984, pp. 87–96.

——— 'Youth and Education in the Short Stories of Liu Xinwu', *Westerly*, No. 3, 1981, pp. 115–20.

MacFarquhar, Roderick, *The Hundred Flowers* (London, Stevens and Sons, 1960).

McDougall, Bonnie S. (trans.), *Mao Zedong's 'Talks at the Yan'an Conference on Literature and Art': A Translation of the 1943 Text with Commentary* (Ann Arbor, University of Michigan, Centre for Chinese Studies, 1980).

Mao Tse-tung, 'Analysis of the Classes in Chinese Society', *Selected Works of Mao Tse-tung* (Beijing, Foreign Languages Press, 1967), Vol. I, pp. 13–21.

———'Criticize P'eng Chen', *Miscellany of Mao Tse-tung Thought (1949–1968)* (Arlington, Joint Publications Research Service, 1974), Part II, p. 383.

—— 'The Foolish Old Man Who Removed the Mountains', *Selected Works of Mao Tse-tung* (Beijing, Foreign Languages Press, 1967), Vol. III, pp. 271–5.

—— *Mao Tse-tung, Four Essays on Philosophy* (Beijing, Foreign Languages Press, 1968).

—— 'On Contradiction', *Mao Tse-tung, Four Essays on Philosophy* (Beijing, Foreign Languages Press, 1968), pp. 23–78.

—— 'On the Correct Handling of Contradictions among the People', *Mao Tse-tung, Four Essays in Philosophy* (Beijing, Foreign Languages Press, 1968), pp. 79–133.

—— 'On New Democracy', *Selected Works of Mao Tse-tung* (Beijing, Foreign Languages Press, 1967), Vol. II, pp. 339–84.

—— 'On Practice', *Mao Tse-tung, Four Essays on Philosophy* (Beijing, Foreign Languages Press, 1968), pp. 1–22.

—— 'On the People's Democratic Dictatorship', *Selected Works of Mao Tse-tung* (Beijing, Foreign Languages Press, 1969), Vol. IV, pp. 411–24.

—— 'On the Struggle Against the "Three Evils" and the "Five Evils"', *Selected Works of Mao Tse-tung* (Beijing, Foreign Languages Press, 1977), Vol. V, pp. 64–70.

—— 'The Orientation of the Youth Movement', *Selected Works of Mao Tse-tung* (Beijing, Foreign Languages Press, 1967), Vol. II, pp. 241–50.

—— 'Pay Serious Attention to the Discussion of the Film *The Life of Wu Hsun*', *Selected Works of Mao Tse-tung* (Beijing, Foreign Languages Press, 1977), Vol. V, pp. 53–6.

—— *Quotations from Chairman Mao Tse-tung* (Beijing, Foreign Languages Press, 1966).

—— 'Report on an Investigation of the Peasant Movement in Hunan', *Selected Works of Mao Tse-tung* (Beijing, Foreign Languages Press, 1967), Vol. I, pp. 23–59.

—— 'The Role of the Chinese Communist Party in the National War', *Selected Works of Mao Tse-tung* (Beijing, Foreign Languages Press, 1967), Vol II, pp. 195–212.

—— *Selected Works of Mao Tse-tung* (Beijing, Foreign Languages Press), 5 Vols; Vols. I, II, III, 1967, Vol. IV, 1969, Vol. V, 1977).

—— 'Speech at Hangchow', in Stuart Schram (ed.), *Mao Tse-tung Unrehearsed* (Harmondsworth, Penguin Books, 1974), pp. 232–43.

—— 'Speech at the Tenth Plenum', 24 September 1962, in Stuart Schram (ed.), *Mao Tse-tung Unrehearsed* (Harmondsworth, Penguin Books, 1974), pp. 188–96.

—— 'Speech to the Albanian Military Delegation', *Miscellany of Mao Tse-tung Thought (1949–1968)* (Arlington, Joint Publications Research Service, 1974), Part II, pp. 453–61.

—— 'A Talk with Heads of Education Departments or Bureaus of

Seven Provinces and Municipalities', *Unselected Works of Mao Tse-tung 1957* (Hong Kong, Union Research Institute, 1976), p. 91.
—— 'Talks at the Yenan Forum on Literature and Art', *Selected Works of Mao Tse-tung* (Beijing, Foreign Languages Press, 1967), Vol. III, pp. 69–98.
Marx, Karl, 'Preface to *A Contribution to the Critique of Political Economy*', in K. Marx and F. Engels, *Selected Works* (Moscow, Progress Publishers, 1969), Vol. 1, pp. 502–6.
—— 'Theses on Feuerbach', in K. Marx and F. Engels, *Selected Works* (Moscow, Progress Publishers, 1969), Vol. 1, pp. 13–15.
—— and Engels, Frederick, 'The German Ideology', *Selected Works* (Moscow, Progress Publishers, 1969), Vol. 1, pp. 16–80.
—— 'Manifesto of the Communist Party', *Selected Works* (Moscow, Progress Publishers, 1969), Vol. 1, pp. 98–138.
—— *Selected Works* (Moscow, Progress Publishers, 1969–70), 3 Vols.
Mathewson, Rufus Jr., *The Positive Hero in Russian Literature* (Stanford, Stanford University Press, 1975).
Meisner, Maurice, 'Li Ta-chao and the Chinese Communist Treatment of the Materialist Conception of History', in Albert Feuerwerker (ed.), *History in Communist China* (Cambridge, Mass., MIT Press, 1968), pp. 277–305.
Metzger, Thomas A., *Escape from Predicament* (New York, Columbia University Press, 1977).
Munro, Donald J., 'Chinese Communist Treatment of the Thinkers of the Hundred Schools Period', in Albert Feuerwerker (ed.), *History in Communist China* (Cambridge, Mass., MIT Press, 1968), pp. 74–95.
—— *The Concept of Man in Contemporary China* (Ann Arbor, University of Michigan Press, 1979).
—— *The Concept of Man in Early China* (Stanford, Stanford University Press, 1969).
—— 'The Yang Hsien-chen Affair', *China Quarterly*, No. 22, 1965, pp. 75–82.
New China News Agency, 'Ideological Reform among Peking and Tientsin Professors Enters Second Stage', *Survey of China Mainland Press* (Hong Kong, American Consulate General, 1952), pp. 9–10.
Nivison, David, 'Communist Ethics in Chinese Tradition', in John Harrison (ed.), *China: Enduring Scholarship Selected from the Far Eastern Quarterly—The Journal of Asian Studies 1941–1971* (Arizona, The University of Arizona Press, 1972), Vol. I, pp. 207–30.
Ollman, Bertell, *Alienation: Marx's Conception of Man in Capitalist Society* (London, Cambridge University Press, 1971).
'Only through Showing Real Repentance can Rightists have a Bright Future: Labels of Another Group of Rightists in Shansi Province who have Shown Real Repentance are Removed', *Shansi Daily*, 30 September 1960. Translated in *Survey of China Mainland Press* (Supplement), No. 53, 1960, pp. 16–19.

Philosophy Is No Mystery (Beijing, Foreign Languages Press, 1972).

Schram, Stuart (ed.), *Mao Tse-tung Unrehearsed* (Harmondsworth, Penguin Books, 1974).

Schwartz, Benjamin I., *In Search of Wealth and Power* (Cambridge, Mass., Harvard University Press, 1964).

—— 'Notes on Conservatism in General and in China in Particular', in Charlotte Furth (ed.), *The Limits of Change* (Cambridge, Mass., Harvard University Press, 1976), pp. 3–21.

Selden, Mark, *The Yenan Way in Revolutionary China* (Cambridge, Mass., Harvard University Press, 1971).

Sima, Qian, 'Confucius', *Records of the Historian*, translated by Yang Hsien-yi and Gladys Yang (Hong Kong, Commercial Press, 1970), pp. 1–27.

Smedley, Agnes, *The Great Road: The Life and Times of Chu Teh* (New York, Monthly Review Press, 1956).

Stalin, Joseph, 'Dialectical and Historical Materialism', in Bruce Franklin, *The Essential Stalin* (New York, Anchor Books, 1972), pp. 300–33.

Szamuely, Tibor, *The Russian Tradition* (London, Secker & Warburg, 1974).

Urban, George (ed.), *The Miracles of Chairman Mao* (London, Stacey, 1971).

Vyatkin, R.V., and Tikhvinsky, S.L., 'Some Questions of Historical Science in the People's Republic', in Albert Feuerwerker (ed.), *History in Communist China* (Cambridge, Mass., MIT Press, 1968), pp. 331–55.

Waley, Arthur (trans.), *The Way and its Power* (London, George Allen & Unwin, 1934).

Wang Gungwu, 'Juxtaposing Past and Present in China Today', *China Quarterly*, No. 61, 1975, pp. 1–24.

Wang Hsien-ch'ien, '*Preface to the Complete Works of Han Fei Tzu*', in W.K. Liao (trans.), *The Complete Works of Han Fei Tzu* (London, Arthur Probsthain, 1939), Vol. I, p. xxxiii.

Watson, Burton (trans.), *Han Fei Tzu* (New York, Columbia University Press, 1964).

—— (trans. and ed.), *Mo Tzu: Basic Writings* (New York, Columbia University Press, 1963).

Witke, Roxanne, *Comrade Chiang Ch'ing* (London, Weidenfeld and Nicolson, 1977).

Wittfogel, Karl, *Oriental Despotism* (New Haven, Yale University Press, 1957).

'Workers, Peasants and Soldiers in Changsha Unite with "Red Guards" to Smash All Old Ideas, Old Cultures, Old Customs and Old Habits', *Yangcheng wanbao (Canton Evening News)*, 25 August 1966, translated in *Survey of China Mainland Press*, No. 3774, 1966, pp. 17–19.

Wycoff, William A. (guest ed.), 'Reflections on the Past Forty Years by Feng Youlan', *Chinese Studies in Philosophy*, Vol. XIII, Nos. 2–3, 1981–2, pp. 9–126.

CHINESE LANGUAGE SOURCES

Ah Cheng 阿城, *'Qi Wang'* 棋王 ('Chess King'), *Shanghai wenxue* 上海文学 (*Shanghai Literature*), No. 7, 1984, pp. 15–35.

Ai Hengwu 艾恒武, *Guanyu 'he er er yi' de lunzhan* 关于"合二而一" 的论战 (*On the Controversies Surrounding 'Combining Two Into One'*) (Hubei, Hubei renmin chubanshe, 1981).

—— and Lin Qingshan 林青山, 'Yi fen wei er yu he er er yi' 一分为二与合二而一 ('One Divides into Two and Combining Two into One'), *Guangming ribao* 光明日报 (*Guangming Daily*), 29 May 1964.

Ai Siqi 艾思奇, *Bianzheng weiwuzhuyi lishi weiwuzhuyi* 辩证唯物 主义,历史唯物主义 (*Dialectical Materialism and Historical Materialism*) (Beijing, Renmin chubanshe, 1961).

—— 'Dui "Zhongguo zhexue yichan de jicheng wenti" de yixie yijian' 对"中国哲学遗产的继承问题"的一些意见 ('Some Objections to the Essay "On the Question of Inheriting the Chinese Philosophical Heritage"'), Zhexue yanjiu bianjibu 哲学研究编辑部 (ed.), *Zhongguo zhexueshi wenti taolun zhuanji* 中国哲学史 问题讨论专辑 (*A Symposium on the Problems of the History of Chinese Philosophy*) (Beijing, Kexue chubanshe, 1957), hereafter *Symposium on Chinese Philosophy*, pp. 437–41.

Beijing shifandaxue Mao Zedong sixiang hongweibing Jinggangshan zhandoutuan 北京师范大学毛泽东思想红卫兵井冈山战斗团, 'Niu gui she shen zai Kongzi taolunhui shang fangle xie shenmo du?' 牛鬼蛇神在孔子讨论会上放了些甚么毒 ('What Poisons Were Spread by the Monsters and Demons at the Forum on Kongzi?'), *Renmin ribao* 人民日报 (*People's Daily*), 10 January 1967.

Cai Shangsi 蔡尚思, 'Kongzi he lidai Kongzi chongbaizhe de guanxi wenti' 孔子和历代孔子崇拜者的关系问题 ('On the Relationship between Kongzi and Kongzi-worshippers in History'), *Zhonghua wenshi luncong* 中华文史论丛 (*Selected Essays on Chinese Literature and History*), No. 1, 1979, pp. 19–24.

—— *Zhongguo chuantong sixiang zong pipan* 中国传统思想总批判 (*A Total Criticism of Traditional Chinese Thought*) (Shanghai, Tangdai chubanshe, 1950).

—— *Zhongguo chuantong sixiang zong pipan, bubian* 中国传统思想 总批判,补编 (*A Total Criticism of Traditional Chinese Thought, A Supplement*) (Shanghai, Tangdai chubanshe, 1950).

Chao Songting 晁松亭, 'Duiyu Guan Feng, Lin Yushi tongzhi "Zai lun

Kongzi" de shangque' 对于关锋, 林聿时同志《再论孔子》的商榷 ('Comments on Comrades Guan Feng's and Lin Yushi's "A Further Discussion on Kongzi"'), Zhexue yanjiu bianjibu 哲学研究编辑部 (ed.), *Kongzi zhexue taolun ji* 孔子哲学讨论集 (*Collected Papers On Kongzi's Philosophy*) (Beijing, Zhonghua shuju, 1963), hereafter *Kongzi zhexue taolun ji*, pp. 455–69.

Chen Boda 陈伯达, 'Cong mingshi wenti lun Zhongguo gudai zhexue de jiben fenye' 从名实问题论中国古代哲学的基本分野 ('Using the Problem of Naming and Matter to Discuss the Basic Dividing Line in Ancient Chinese Philosophy') *Wenshi* 文史 (*Literature and History*), Vol. 1, No. 2, 1934, pp. 33–50.

——— 'Laozi de zhexue sixiang' 老子的哲学思想 ('Laozi's Philosophical Thought'), *Jiefang* 解放 (*Liberation*), Nos. 63 and 64, 1939, pp. 27–30.

Chen Jingpan 陈景磐, *Kongzi de jiaoyu sixiang* 孔子的教育思想 (*Kongzi's Educational Thought*) (Wuhan, Hubei renmin chubanshe, 1957).

Chen Qiyou 陈奇猷 (ed.), *Han Feizi jishi* 韩非子集释 (*The Han Feizi Collated and Explained*) (Shanghai, Shanghai renmin chubanshe, 1974), 2 Vols.

Chen Xiuzhai 陈修斋, 'Dui weixinzhuyi zhexue gujia wenti de yixie yijian' 对唯心主义哲学估价问题的一些意见 ('A Few Suggestions on the Problem of Evaluating Idealist Philosophy'), *Symposium on Chinese Philosophy*, pp. 225–36.

Chen Yi 陈毅, 'Dui Beijing shi gaodeng yuanxiao yingjie biye xuesheng de jianghua' 对北京市高等院校应届毕业学生的讲话 ('Speech to This Year's Graduates from Beijing's Higher Institutions'). *Zhongguo qingnian* 中国青年 (*China Youth*), No. 17, 1961, pp. 2–5.

Chi Shiwu 迟世武, 'Chexia Jian Bozan de "lishizhuyi" de heiqi' 扯下翦伯赞的「历史主义」的黑旗 ('Tear Down Jian Bozan's Black Flag of "Historicism"'), *Guangming ribao* (*Guangming Daily*), 1 June 1966.

Chongfang de xianhua 重放的鲜花 (*The Second Blossoming*) (Shanghai, Shanghai wenyi chubanshe, 1979).

Chu Shusen 褚树森, 'Dui "Kongzi de jiaoyu sixiang" yiwen de yijian' 对《孔子的教育思想》一文的意见 ('Comments on the Article "Kongzi's Educational Thought"'), *Guangming ribao* (*Guangming Daily*), 4 October 1954.

——— 'Dui yanjiu Kongzi jiaoyu sixiang de jidian yijian' 对研究孔子教育思想的几点意见 ('A Few Suggestions on the Study of Kongzi's Educational Thought'), *Guangming ribao* (*Guangming Daily*), 9 August 1954.

Dai Qingliang 戴清亮 and Lin Keji 林可济, 'Dui Makesizhuyi yiqian lishiguan de pingjia de yixie yijian' 对马克思主义以前历史观的

评价的一些意见 ('A Few Comments on the Evaluation of Historical Outlooks before the Appearance of Marxism'), *Symposium on Chinese Philosophy*, pp. 480–2.

Deng Aimin 邓艾民 and Wei Changhai 魏常海, 'Lun Guan Feng zai zhexue yichan jicheng wenti shang de xingershang xue sixiang' 论关锋在哲学遗产继承问题上的形而上学思想 ('On Guan Feng's Metaphysical Thinking relating to the Problem of Philosophical Inheritance'), in Zhongguo shehui kexueyuan zhexue yanjiusuo, Zhongguo zhexueshi yanjiushi 中国社会科学院哲学研究所,中国哲学史研究室 (ed.), *Zhongguo zhexueshi fangfa lun taolun ji* 中国哲学史方法论讨论集 (*Collected Papers on the Methodology of the History of Chinese Philosophy*) (Beijing, Zhongguo shehui kexue chubanshe, 1980), hereafter *Zhongguo zhexueshi fangfa lun taolun ji*, pp. 153–68.

Deng Chumin 邓初民, 'Dule Guan Feng xiansheng "Guanyu zhexueshi shang de weiwuzhuyi he weixinzhuyi de douzheng wenti" yihou' 读了关锋先生"关于哲学史上的唯物主义和唯心主义的斗争问题"以后 ('After Reading Mr Guan Feng's "On the Question of the Struggle between Materialism and Idealism in the History of Philosophy"'), *Symposium on Chinese Philosophy*, pp. 265–72.

Deng Guangming 邓广铭 *et al.*, 'Shinian lai de Zhongguo shi yanjiu gaishu' 十年来的中国史研究概述 ('A Brief Outline of Chinese Historical Studies of the Past Ten Years'), *Guangming ribao* (*Guangming Daily*), 29 October 1959.

Deng Tuo 邓拓, *Lun Zhongguo lishi de jige wenti* 论中国历史的几个问题 (*Several Problems in Chinese History*) (Beijing, Sanlian shudian, 1963).

Ding Si 定思, 'Zhongguo zhexueshi zhong de jichengxing wenti' 中国哲学史中的继承性问题 ('The Problem of Inheritability in the History of Chinese Philosophy'), *Symposium on Chinese Philosophy*, pp. 346–50.

Dong Fangming 东方明, 'Zhexueshi gongzuo zhong de yizhong ji youhai de fangfa' 哲学史工作中的一种极有害的方法 ('An Extremely Harmful Methodology in the History of Philosophical Work'), *Zhexue yanjiu* 哲学研究 (*Philosophical Research*), No. 1, 1963, pp. 33–7.

Dou Zhongguang 窦重光, 'Cong rujia de lunli xueshuo zhong kan daode de jicheng wenti' 从儒家的伦理学说中看道德的继承问题 ('The Problem of Inheriting Ethics Viewed From the Moral Doctrines of Confucianism'), *Guangming ribao* (*Guangming Daily*), 19 April 1957.

Du Guoxiang 杜国庠, *Du Guoxiang wenji* 杜国庠文集 (*Collected Articles by Du Guoxiang*) (Beijing, Renmin chubanshe, 1962).

—— *XianQin zhuzi sixiang gaiyao* 先秦诸子思想概要 (*An Outline of the Thoughts of the pre-Qin Philosophers*) (Beijing, Sanlian shudian, 1955), second edition. Reprinted in *Du Guoxiang wenji* (*Col-*

lected Articles by Du Guoxiang) (Beijing, Renmin chubanshe, 1962).

Duan Chunzuo 段春作, 'Yunyong "shijianlun" zongjie minjian cetian jingyan' 运用《实践论》总结民间测天经验 ('Using "On Practice" to Summarize Folk Experiences in Weather Forecasting') *Hongqi* 红旗 (Red Flag), No. 2, 1966, pp. 20–7.

Fajia renwu gushi 法家人物故事 (*Stories about the Legalists*) (Shanghai, Shanghai renmin chubanshe, 1975).

Fan Wenlan 范文兰, 'Chuqi fengjian shehui kaishi yu XiZhou' 初期封建杜会开始于西周 ('The Early Feudal Society Began in the Western Zhou'), Lishi yanjiu bianjibu 历史研究编辑部 (ed.), *Zhongguo de nulizhi yu fengjianzhi fenqi wenti lunwen xuanji* 中国的奴隶制与封建制分期问题论文选集 (*Selected Essays on the Problem of the Periodization of Chinese Slave and Feudal Systems*) (Beijing, Sanlian shudian, 1956), hereafter *Selected Essays on Periodization*, pp. 359–73.

—— *Zhongguo tongshi jianbian* 中国通史简编 (*A Concise General History of China*) (Beijing, Renmin chubanshe, 1964), Vol. I, fourth edition.

Fan Xiubing 反修兵, 'Chedi pipan "jieji douzheng ximie lun" de fandong miulun' 彻底批判「阶级斗争熄灭论」的反动谬论 ('Thoroughly Repudiate the Reactionary Absurdity of the Theory of the Extinction of Class Struggle', *Renmin ribao* (*People's Daily*), 20 August 1967.

Fang Keli 方克立, 'Guanyu Kongzi 'ren' de yanjiu zhong de yige fangfalun wenti' 关于孔子"仁"的研究中的一个方法论问题 ('On the Problem of Methodology in the Study of Kongzi's Theory of *ren*), *Zhexue yanjiu* (*Philosophical Research*), No. 4, 1963, pp. 23–32.

Feng Youlan 冯友兰, 'Guanyu Laozi zhexue de liangge wenti' 关于老子哲学的两个问题 ('Two Problems on Laozi's philosophy'), originally in *Renmin ribao* (*People's Daily*), 12 and 13 June 1959, reprinted in Zhexue yanjiu bianjibu (ed.), *Laozi zhexue taolun ji* 老子哲学讨论集 (*Collected Papers on Laozi's Philosophy*) (Beijing, Zhonghua shuju, 1959), hereafter *Laozi zhexue taolun ji*, pp. 48–66.

—— 'Guanyu lun Kongzi "ren" de sixiang de yixie buchong lunzheng' 关于论孔子"仁"的思想的一些补充论证 ('Some Supplementary Remarks on the Discussion of Kongzi's Idea of *ren*), *Xueshu yuekan* 学术月刊 (*Academic Monthly*), No. 8, 1963, pp. 43–7.

—— 'Guanyu Zhongguo zhexueshi yanjiu de liangge wenti' 关于中国哲学史研究的两个问题 ('Two Problems concerning the Study of the History of Chinese Philosophy'), *Renmin ribao* (*People's Daily*), 23 October 1956.

—— 'Han Fei "jie Lao", "yu Lao" pian xin shi' 韩非"解老""喻老"篇新释 ('A New Explanation of Han Feizi's "Explaining Laozi" and "Clarifying Laozi"'), originally in *Beijing daxue xuebao*

北京大学学报 (*Beijing University Journal*), No. 2, 1961; reprinted in *Zhongguo zhexueshi lunwen erji* 中国哲学史论文二集 (*Essays on the History of Chinese Philosophy*), reprint edition (Macau, Xinfeng tushushe, no date), pp. 375–82.

—— 'Lun Kongzi' 论孔子 ('On Kongzi'), *Guangming ribao* (*Guangming Daily*), 22 and 29 July 1960, reprinted in *Kongzi zhexue taolun ji*, pp. 78–95.

—— 'Lun Kongzi guanyu "ren" de sixiang 论孔子关于"仁"的思想 ('On Kongzi's Idea of *"ren"'*), *Zhexue yanjiu* (*Philosophical Research*) No. 5, 1961, pp. 63–72 and 31.

—— 'Lun Zhuangzi' 论庄子 ('On Zhuangzi'), originally in *Renmin ribao* (*People's Daily*), 26 February 1961, reprinted in Zhexue yanjiu bianjibu (ed.), *Zhuangzi zhexue taolun ji* 庄子哲学讨论集 (*Collected Papers on Zhuangzi's Philosophy*) (Beijing, Zhonghua shuju, 1962), hereafter *Zhuangzi zhexue taolun ji*, pp. 115–28.

—— '*Pipan wodi "chouxiang jichengfa*"' 批判我底"抽象继承法" ('Criticizing My Own "Abstract Inheritance Method"'), *Zhexue yanjiu* (*Philosophical Research*), No. 5, 1958, pp. 41–5.

—— 'San lun Zhuangzi' 三论庄子 ('A Third Essay on Zhuangzi'), originally in *Beijing daxue xuebao*, No. 4, 1961, reprinted in *Zhuangzi zhexue taolun ji*, pp. 147–59.

—— 'Sishi nian de huigu' 四十年的回顾 ('Reviewing the Past Forty Years'), reprinted in *Feng Youlan de daolu* 冯友兰的道路 (*The Path of Feng Youlan*) (Hong Kong, Pangu zazhi, 1974).

—— *Xin lixue* 新理学 (*New Rational Philosophy*) (Changsha, Shangwu yinshuguan, 1939).

—— 'Xin lixue de yuanxing' 新理学的原形 ('The Real Nature of the *New Rational Philosophy*'), *Zhexue yanjiu* (*Philosophical Research*), No. 1, 1959, pp. 37–49.

—— *Xin yuanren* 新原人 (*New Treatise on the Nature of Man*) (Shanghai, Shangwu yinshuguan, 1946).

—— 'Zai lun Kongzi ren de sixiang' 再论孔子仁的思想, ('A Further Discussion of Kongzi's Thinking Concerning *ren*'), *Kongzi zhexue taolun ji*, pp. 470–3.

—— 'Zai lun Zhongguo zhexue yichan di jicheng wenti' 再论中国哲学遗产底继承问题 ('Again on the Problem of Inheriting the Chinese Philosophical Heritage'), reprinted in Feng Youlan, *Zhongguo zhexueshi lunwen chuji* (*Essays on the History of Chinese Philosophy*) (Shanghai, Shanghai renmin chubanshe, 1958), Vol. 1, pp. 126–41.

—— 'Zai lun Zhuangzi' 再论庄子 ('A Further Discussion on Zhuangzi'), originally in *Zhexue yanjiu* (*Philosophical Research*), No. 3, 1961, reprinted in *Zhuangzi zhexue taolun ji*, pp. 129–46.

—— 'Zhiyi he qingjiao' 质疑和请教 ('Queries and Seeking Advice'), *Zhexue yanjiu* (*Philosophical Research*), 1959, No. 3, pp. 8–13.

—— 'Zhongguo zhexue de fazhan' 中国哲学的发展 ('The Development of Chinese Philosophy'), in *Zhongguo zhexueshi lunwen chuji* (*Essays on the History of Chinese Philosophy*) (Shanghai, Shanghai renmin chubanshe, 1958), pp. 1–63.

—— 'Zhongguo zhexue yichan de jicheng wenti' 中国哲学遗产的继承问题 ('On the Question of Inheriting the Chinese Philosophical Heritage') *Guangming ribao* (*Guangming Daily*), 8 January 1957, reprinted in *Symposium on Chinese Philosophy*, pp. 273–80.

—— *Zhongguo zhexueshi* 中国哲学史 (*History of Chinese Philosophy*), originally published in 1930, reprinted in Hong Kong by Taipingyang tushu gongsi in 1970.

—— *Zhongguo zhexueshi lunwen chuji* 中国哲学史论文初集 (*Essays on the History of Chinese Philosophy*) (Shanghai, Shanghai renmin chubanshe, 1958), Vol. 1.

—— *Zhongguo zhexueshi xinbian* 中国哲学史新编 (*New History of Chinese Philosophy*) (Beijing, Renmin chubanshe, 1962), 2 Vols.

—— *et al.*, 'Kongzi sixiang yanjiu' 孔子思想研究 (A Study of Kongzi's Thinking), *Xin jianshe* 新建设 (*New Construction*), No. 4, 1954, pp. 35–42.

Gao Heng 高享, *Chongding Laozi zhenggu* 重订老子正诂 (*Revised Collation of the Laozi*) (Beijing, Guji chubanshe, 1956).

—— *Mojing jiaoquan* 墨经校诠 (*The Moist Canon Collated and Explained*) (Beijing, Kexue chubanshe, 1958).

Ge Feng 革锋, 'Zhuangzi zhexue xiangduizhuyi de shizhi' 庄子哲学相对主义的实质 ('The Real Nature of Relativism in Zhuangzi's Philosophy'), originally in *Guangming ribao* (*Guangming Daily*), 17 March 1961, reprinted in *Zhuangzi zhexue taolun ji*, pp. 322–8.

Geng Ye 耕野, 'Dui Wang Yi tongzhi "Han Fei de sixiang" yi wen de jidian yijian' 对汪毅同志"韩非的思想"一文的几点意见 ('A Few Objections to Comrade Wang Yi's Essay "Han Feizi's Thought"'), *Guangming ribao* (*Guangming Daily*), 23 February 1955.

Gu Weijin 顾卫今, 'Kongzi tan xuexi' 孔子谈学习 ('Kongzi Talks about Study'), *Guangming ribao* (*Guangming Daily*), 27 October 1961.

Guan Feng 关锋, 'Da Feng Youlan xiansheng' 答冯友兰先生 ('Answering Mr Feng Youlan'), *Xin jianshe* (*New Construction*), No. 5, 1959, pp. 50–8.

—— *Fandui zhexueshi fangfalun shang de xiuzhengzhuyi* 反对哲学史方法论上的修正主义 (*Oppose Revisionism in the Methodology of the History of Philosophy*) (Beijing, Renmin chubanshe, 1958).

—— 'Fandui zhexueshi gongzuo zhong de xiuzhengzhuyi' 反对哲学史工作中的修正主义 ('Oppose Revisionism in the Work on the History of Philosophy'), *Zhexue yanjiu* (*Philosophical Research*), No. 1, 1958, pp. 1–24.

—— 'Guanyu jicheng zhexue yichan de yige wenti' 关于继承哲学

遗产的一个问题 ('A Problem concerning the Inheritance of Philosophy'), *Symposium on Chinese Philosophy*, pp. 369–82.

—— 'Guanyu zhexueshi shang de weiwuzhuyi he weixinzhuyi de douzheng wenti' 关于哲学史上唯物主义和唯心主义的斗争问题 ('On the Question of the Struggle between Materialism and Idealism in the History of Philosophy'), *Symposium on Chinese Philosophy*, pp. 205–15.

—— 'Huo shengsheng de bianzhengfa' 活生生的辩证法 ('Living Dialectics') *Zhexue yanjiu* (*Philosophical Research*), No. 4, 1958, pp. 7–9.

—— 'Jielu "Xin yuanren" de yuanxing' 揭露《新原人》的原形 ('Exposing the Real Nature of *A New Treatise on the Nature of Man*'), originally in *Zhexue yanjiu* (*Philosophical Research*), No. 2, 1959, reprinted in *Zhuangzi neipian yijie he pipan* (*Translations, Explanations, and Critiques of Zhuangzi's Inner Chapters*) (Beijing, Zhonghua shuju, 1961), pp. 267–308.

—— 'Lun SongYin xuepai' 论宋尹学派 ('On the SongYin school'), *Zhexue yanjiu* (*Philosophical Research*), No. 5, 1959, pp. 28–45.

—— 'Pipan Feng Youlan xiansheng de "chouxiang jichengfa"' 批判冯友兰先生的"抽象继承法" ('A Criticism of Mr Feng Youlan's "Method of Abstract Inheritance"'), *Zhexue yanjiu* (*Philosophical Research*), No. 3, 1958, pp. 63–81.

—— 'Tan "Wang xingkong" de linghun' 谈《望星空》的灵魂 ('On the Soul of "Gazing at the Starry Sky"') in *Zhuangzi neipian yijie he pipan* (*Translations, Explanations, and Critiques of Zhuangzi's Inner Chapters*) (Beijing, Zhonghua shuju, 1961), pp. 309–13.

—— *Zhuangzi neipian yijie he pipan* 庄子内篇译解和批判 (*Translations, Explanations, and Critiques of Zhuangzi's Inner Chapters*) (Beijing, Zhonghua shuju, 1961).

—— 'Zhuangzi waiza pian chutan' 庄子外杂篇初探 ('A Preliminary Investigation on the Outer and Miscellaneous Chapters of the Zhuangzi'), originally in *Zhexue yanjiu* (*Philosophical Research*), No. 2, 1961, reprinted in *Zhuangzi neipian yijie he pipan* (*Translation, Explanations, and Critiques of Zhuangzi's Inner Chapters*) (Beijing, Zhonghua shuju, 1961).

—— 'Zhuangzi zhexue pipan' 庄子哲学批判 ('A Criticism of Zhuangzi's Philosophy'), originally in *Zhexue yanjiu* (*Philosophical Research*), Nos. 7 and 8, 1960, reprinted in *Zhuangzi zhexue taolun ji*, pp. 1–60. Translated into English in *Chinese Studies in History and Philosophy*, No. 1, 1967.

Guan Feng and Lin Yushi 林聿时, 'Guanyu Kongzi sixiang taolun zhong de jieji fenxi de jige wenti' 关于孔子思想讨论中的阶级分析的几个问题 ('A Few Questions of Class Analysis relating to the Discussion of Kongzi's Thinking'), *Wen shi zhe* 文史哲 (*Literature, History and Philosophy*), No. 1, 1963, pp. 5–19.

—— 'Lun Kongzi' 论孔子 ('On Kongzi'), *Kongzi zhexue taolun ji*, pp. 255–8.

—— 'Lun Laozi zhexue tixi de weixinzhuyi benzhi' 论老子哲学体系 的唯心主义本质 ('On the Idealist Basis of Laozi's Philosophical System'), originally in *Zhexue yanjiu* (*Philosophical Research*), No. 6, 1959, reprinted in *Laozi zhexue taolun ji*, pp. 176–227.

—— 'San lun Kongzi' 三论孔子 ('A Third Discussion on Kongzi'), *Kongzi zhexue taolun ji*, pp. 401–11.

—— 'Zai lun Kongzi' 再论孔子 ('A Further Discussion on Kongzi'), *Kongzi zhexue taolun ji*, pp. 303–27.

—— 'Zai tan Laozi zhexue' 再谈老子哲学 ('A Further Discussion on Laozi's Philosophy'), originally in *Guangming ribao* (*Guangming Daily*), 20 June 1959, reprinted in *Laozi zhexue taolun ji*, pp. 228–40.

Guan Feng and Wu Fuqi 吴傅启, 'Ping Wu Han tongzhi de daodelun' 评吴晗同志的道德论 ('A Critique of Comrade Wu Han's Theory of Morality'), *Zhexue yanjiu*, No. 1, 1966, pp. 28–45.

Guo Baojun 郭宝钧, 'Ji Yin-Zhou xunren zhi shishi' 记殷周殉人之史实 ('Historical Facts about Human Sacrifices in the Yin and Zhou Dynasties'), reprinted in *Selected Essays on Periodization*, pp. 58–60.

Guo Moruo 郭沫若, 'Dule "Ji Yin-Zhou xunren zhi shishi"' 读了《记殷周殉人之史实》 ('After Reading "Historical Facts about Human Sacrifices in the Yin and Zhou Dynasties"'), *Selected Essays on Periodization*, pp. 54–7.

—— 'Guanyu Zhoudai shehui de shangtao' 关于周代社会的商讨 ('A Discussion of Society in the Zhou Period'), *Selected Essays on Periodization*, pp. 85–100.

—— 'Gudai yanjiu de ziwo pipan' 古代研究的自我批判 ('A Self-criticism of my Research into Ancient Chinese Society'), *Shi pipan shu* (*Ten Critiques*) (Beijing, Kexue chubanshe, 1956), pp. 1–70.

—— 'Han Feizi de pipan' 韩非子的批判 ('Critique of Han Feizi'), *Shi pipan shu* (*Ten Critiques*) (Beijing, Kexue chubanshe, 1956), pp. 340–86.

—— 'Kong-Mo de pipan' 孔墨的批判 ('A Critique of Kongzi and Mozi'), *Shi pipan shu* (*Ten Critiques*) (Beijing, Kexue chubanshe, 1956), pp. 71–122.

—— 'Lao Dan, Guan Yin, Huan Yuan' 老聃, 关尹, 环渊 ('Lao Dan, Guan Yin and Huan Yuan'), *Qingtong shidai* 青铜时代 (*The Bronze Age*) (Beijing, Renmin chubanshe, 1954).

—— *Nulizhi shidai* 奴隶制时代 (*Period of the Slave System*) (Beijing, Renmin chubanshe, 1973).

—— *Qingtong shidai* 青铜时代 (*The Bronze Age*) (Beijing, Renmin chubanshe, 1954).

—— *Shi pipan shu* 十批判书 (*Ten Critiques*) (Beijing, Kexue chubanshe, 1956).

—— 'XianQin tiandaoguan zhi jinzhan' 先秦天道观之进展 ('The Development of the pre-Qin Cosmological Outlook'), *Qingtong shidai* (*The Bronze Age*) (Beijing, Renmin chubanshe, 1954), pp. 1–42.

—— 'Xunzi de pipan' 荀子的批判 ('Critique of Xunzi'), *Shi pipan shu* (*Ten Critiques*) (Beijing, Kexue chubanshe, 1956), pp. 209–47.

—— *Zhongguo gudai shehui yangjiu* 中国古代社会研究 (*A Study of Ancient Chinese Society*) (Shanghai, Xiandai shuju, 1931).

—— 'Zhongguo nuli shehui' 中国奴隶社会 ('Slave Society in China'), *Xin jianshe* 新建设 (*New Construction*), Vol. 3, No. 1, 1950, pp. 83–4.

—— 'Zhuangzi de pipan' 庄子的批判 ('Criticism of Zhuangzi'), *Shi pipan shu* (*Ten Critiques*) (Beijing, Kexue chubanshe, 1956), pp. 185–208.

Guo Xiaochuan 郭小川, 'Wang xingkong' 望星空 ('Gazing at the Starry Sky'), *Renmin wenxue* 人民文学 (*People's Literature*), No. 11, 1959, pp. 90–3.

Ha De Er 哈的尔 and Yue Li Da Xi 约里达西, 'Bu tongyi yong "he er er yi" lai qujie duili tongyi guilü 不同意用「合二而一」来曲解对立统一规律 ('A Disagreement with Using "Combining Two into One" to Distort the Law of the Unity of Opposites'), *Renmin ribao* (*People's Daily*), 19 July 1964.

He Lin 贺麟, 'Duiyu zhexueshi yanjiu zhong liangge zhenglun wenti de yijian' 对于哲学史研究中两个争论问题的意见 ('Some Suggestions on the Two Controversies in the Study of the History of Philosophy'), *Symposium on Chinese Philosophy*, pp. 186–95.

Hong Jianbin 洪坚斌, 'Jian Bozan "rangbu zhengce" lun de fandong shizhi' 翦伯赞「让步政策」论的反动实质 ('The Reactionary Nature of Jian Bozan's "Policy of Concessions"'), *Guangming ribao* (*Guangming Daily*), 26 August 1967.

Hou Wailu 侯外庐, 'Cong duidai zhexue yichan de guandian fangfa he lichang pipan Hu Shi zenyang tumo he wumie Zhongguo zhexueshi' 从对待哲学遗产的观点和立场批判胡适怎样涂抹和诬蔑中国哲学史 ('From the Methods and Standpoint of Treating the Philosophical Legacy to Criticizing Hu Shi's Smearing and Slandering the History of Chinese Philosophy'), *Zhexue yanjiu* (Philosophical Research) No. 2, 1955, pp. 92–116.

Hou Wailu *et al.* (eds.), *Zhongguo sixiang tongshi* 中国思想通史 (A General History of Chinese Thought) (Beijing, Renmin chubanshe, 1957), 6 Vols.

—— 'Zhongpian: Kong-Mo xianxue' 中篇: 孔墨显学 ('Middle Section: The Illustrious Schools of Kongzi and Mozi'), in *Zhongguo sixiang tongshi* 中国思想通史 (*A General History of Chinese Thought*) (Beijing, Renmin chubanshe, 1957), Vol. 1, pp. 131–256.

Hu Huaichen 胡怀琛, 'Modi wei Yinduren bian' 墨翟为印度人辨 ('On

Mozi as an Indian'), *Dongfang zazhi* 东方杂志 (*Eastern Miscellany*), Vol. 25, No. 8, 1928, pp. 79–82.

Hu Quyuan 胡曲园, 'Lun Laozi de "dao"' 论老子的道 ('On Laozi's "dao"'), originally in *Fudan* 复旦, No. 10, 1959, reprinted in *Laozi zhexue taolun ji*, pp. 164–75.

Hu Sheng 胡绳, 'Guanyu zhexueshi de yanjiu' 关于哲学史的研究 ('On the Study of the History of Philosophy'), *Symposium on Chinese Philosophy*, pp. 504–22.

Hu Shi 胡适, 'Chongfen shijiehua yu quanpan xihua' 充分世界化与全盘西化 ('On Full Universalization and Complete Westernization') in *Hu Shi yu ZhongXi wenhua* 胡适与中西文化 (*Hu Shi and Chinese and Western Civilizations*) (Hong Kong, Lianyi shudian, 1974), pp. 35–52.

—— 'Wu Yu wenlu xu' 吴虞文序 ('Preface to the Collected Essays of Wu Yu'), in Wu Yu 吴虞, *Wu Yu wenlu* 吴虞文录 (*Collected Essays of Wu Yu*) (Shanghai, Yatong tushuguan, 1921), p. vii.

—— *Zhongguo zhexueshi dagang* 中国哲学史大纲 (*Outline of the History of Chinese Philosophy*) (Shanghai, Shangwu yinshuguan, 1919).

Hu Shi sixiang pipan 胡适思想批判 (*Critiques of Hu Shi's Thought*) (Beijing, Sanlian shudian, 1955), 8 Vols.

Huabeiju honglian fanxiu zhandoudui 华北局红联反修战斗队, 'Chedi pipan Zhongguo Heluxiaofu de touxiang zhuyi zhexue—"he er er yi" lun' 彻底批判中国赫鲁晓夫的投降主义哲学—「合二而一」论 ('Thoroughly Repudiate China's Khrushchev Philosophy of Capitulationism—the Theory of "Combining Two into One"'), *Renmin ribao* (*People's Daily*), 1 November 1967.

Huang Zitong 黄子通, *Ru dao liang jia zhexue xitong* 儒道两家哲学系统 (*The Confucian and Daoist Philosophical Systems*) (Changsha, Yuzhou shuju, 1946), second edition.

Huxian nongmin hua xuanji 户县农民画选集 (*Peasant Paintings from Huxian*) (Xian, Shanxi renmin chubanshe, 1974).

Huyan Hechi 呼延河池, 'Jieshao "Kongzi de gushi"' 介绍《孔子的故事》 ('Introducing "The Story of Kongzi"'), *Renmin jiaoyu* 人民教育 (*People's Education*), No. 1, 1957, p. 63.

Ji Wenfu 嵇文甫, *Chunqiu Zhanguo sixiang shihua* 春秋战国思想史话 (*Comments on the History of Thought in the Spring and Autumn and Warring States Periods*) (Beijing, Zhongguo qingnian chubanshe, 1958).

—— 'Guanyu Kongzi de lishi pingjia wenti' 关于孔子的历史评价问题 ('On the Problem of Appraising Kongzi's Position in History'), *Lishi jiaoxue* 历史教学 (*History Teaching*), No. 8, 1953, pp. 2–4.

Jian Bozan 翦伯赞, *Lishi wenti luncong* 历史问题论丛 (*Collected Essays on Historical Problems*) (Beijing, Renmin chubanshe, 1962).

—— 'Yanjiu ruogan lishi wenti de yixie yijian' 研究若干历史问题

的一些意见 ('Preliminary Opinions concerning the Handling of Certain Historical Questions') *Guangming ribao* (*Guangming Daily*), 22 December 1961.

—— *Zhongguo shi gangyao* 中国史纲要 (*An Outline of Chinese History*) (Beijing, Renmin chubanshe, 1979), Vol. 1.

—— *Zhongguo shigang* 中国史纲 (*A Historical Outline of China*) (Beijing, Sanlian shudian, 1950).

Jin Zhong 金钟, 'Mozi de meixue guandian he "fei yue" lilun' 墨子的美学观点和"非乐"理论 ('Mozi's Aesthetic Outlook and His "Anti-music" Theory'), *Guangming ribao* (*Guangming Daily*), 7 July 1961.

Kang Youwei 康有为, *Kongzi gaizhi kao* 孔子改制考 (*A Study of Kongzi as a Reformer*) (Taibei, Taiwan shangwu yinshuguan, 1968).

Kuang Yaming 匡亚明, 'Lüe lun shisheng guanxi' 略论师生关系 ('A Brief Discussion on the Teacher-Student Relationship'), *Hongqi* (*Red Flag*), No. 17, 1961, pp. 25–9.

Lanzhou daxue zhongwenxi Mengzi yizhu xiaozu 兰州大学中文系孟子译注小组 (ed.), *Mengzi yizhu* 孟子译注 (*Mengzi Translated and Annotated*) (Beijing, Zhonghua shuju, 1960).

Li Chunyi 李纯一, 'Mozi "fei yue" lilun de yixie wenti' 墨子"非乐"理论的一些问题 ('A Few Problems on the "Anti-music" Theory of Mozi'), *Guangming ribao* (*Guangming Daily*), 15 December 1961.

Li Deyong 李德永, 'Han Fei de shehui zhengzhi sixiang' 韩非的社会政治思想 ('Han Feizi's Social Political Thought'), *Xin jianshe* (*New Construction*), No. 12, 1956, pp. 33–41.

—— *Xunzi* 荀子 (*Xunzi*) (Shanghai, Shanghai renmin chubanshe, 1961).

Li Kan 李侃, 'Bo xin zunKong lun' 驳新尊孔论 ('Refuting a New Theory of Kongzi-worship'), *Guangming ribao* (*Guangming Daily*), 17 August 1963.

Li Maimai 李麦麦, *Zhongguo gudai zhengzhi zhexue pipan* 中国古代政治哲学批判 (*Critique of Ancient Chinese Political Philosophy*) (Shanghai, Xin shengming shuju, 1933).

Li Ping 礼平, 'Wanxia xiaoshi de shihou' 晚霞消失的时候 ('At the Time of the Vanishing Twilight'), *Shiyue* 十月 (*October*), No. 1, 1981, pp. 77–134.

Li Qingsong 李清悚, 'Xunzi jiaoyu lun de sixiang jichu he jiji yinsu' 荀子教育论的思想基础和积极因素 ('The Basis of Xunzi's Educational Thought and the Factors for its Activeness'), *Wenhui bao* 文汇报 (*Wenhui Daily*), 6 March 1962.

Li Qiqian 李启谦, 'Dui Feng Youlan xiansheng "Lun Kongzi" de jidian yijian' 对冯友兰先生"论孔子"的几点意见 ('A Few Comments on Mr Feng Youlan's "On Kongzi"'), *Guangming ribao* (*Guangming Daily*), 5 August 1960.

Li Wen 力文, 'Zenyang kandai lishizhuyi: yu Ning Ke tongzhi shangque' 怎样看待历史主义: 与宁可同志商榷 ('How Historicism Should Be Treated: A Debate with Comrade Ning Ke'), *Guangming ribao* (*Guangming Daily*), 18 November 1964.

Li Yinnong 李荫农, *'Guanyu Mengzi de jieji huafen lun'* 关于孟子的阶级划分论 ('On Mengzi's Theory of Class Distinction'), *Xueshu yanjiu* (*Academic Research*), No. 3, 1962, pp. 54–64.

—— *'Lun Kongzi dui laodong de taidu'* 论孔子对劳动的态度 ('On Kongzi's Attitudes towards Labour'), *Yangcheng wanbao* 羊城晚报 (*Canton Evening News*), 22 March 1962.

Li Zhikui 李志逵, 'Du Feng Youlan xiansheng "Guanyu Zhongguo zhexueshi yanjiu de liangge wenti" de yidian yijian' 读冯友兰先生"关于中国哲学史研究的两个问题"的一点意见 ('A Suggestion on Mr Feng Youlan's "Two Problems on the Study of the History of Chinese Philosophy"'), *Symposium on Chinese Philosophy*, pp. 442–51.

Li Zongmao 李宗茂, 'Tan Han Feizi de ruogan jingji guandian' 谈韩非子的若干经济观点 ('On a Few of Han Feizi's Economic Viewpoints'), *Guangming ribao* (*Guangming Daily*), 30 July 1962.

Liang Qixiong 梁启雄, *Hanzi qianjie* 韩子浅解 (*A Simple Explanation of Han Feizi*) (Beijing, Zhonghua shuju, 1960).

—— 'Xunzi sixiang shuping' 荀子思想述评 ('A Critical Outline of Xunzi's Thought'), *Zhexue yanjiu* (*Philosophical Research*), No. 4, 1963, pp. 48–63.

Liang Souming 梁漱溟, *DongXi wenhua ji qi zhexue* 东西文化及其哲学 (*Eastern and Western Civilizations and their Philosophies*) (Shanghai, Shangwu yinshuguan, 1922).

—— *Zhongguo wenhua yaoyi* 中国文化要义 (*The Essentials of Chinese Culture*) (Hong Kong, Jicheng tushu gongsi, 1963) reprint edition.

Lin Jie 林杰, 'Kongzi "airen" de sixiang shizhi' 孔子"爱人"的思想实质 ('The Real Nature of Kongzi's "Love Men"'), *Wenhui bao* (*Wenhui Daily*), 22 February 1963.

Lishi yanjiu bianjibu 历史研究编辑部 (ed.), *Zhongguo de nulizhi yu fengjianzhi fenqi wenti lunwen xuanji* 中国的奴隶制与封建制分期问题论文选集 (*Selected Essays on the Problem of the Periodization of Slave and Feudal Systems in China*) (Beijing, Sanlian shudian, 1956).

Liu Gefa 刘谔法 *et al.*, 'Feng Youlan xiansheng yao ba zhexuexi yindao shenme daolu shang qu' 冯友兰先生要把哲学系引到什么道路上去 ('What Path Does Mr Feng Youlan Want to Lead the Philosophy Department Along?') *Guangming ribao* (*Guangming Daily*), 31 August 1958.

Liu Guojun 刘国钧, *Zhongguo shushi jianbian* 中国书史简编 (*A Brief History of Chinese Books*) (Beijing, Gaodeng jiaoyu chubanshe, 1958).

Liu Jie 刘节, 'Kongzi de "weiren lun"' 孔子的唯仁论 ('Kongzi's *ren* only Theory'), *Xueshu yanjiu* (*Academic Research*), No. 3, 1962, pp. 40–53.

—— 'Mozi de "jian'ai" he shili sixiang' 墨子的"兼爱"和实利思想 ('Mozi's Theory of "Universal Love" and Material Benefits'), *Xueshu yanjiu* (*Guangzhou*) 学术研究(广州) (*Academic Research* (*Canton*)), No. 1, 1963, pp. 52–64.

—— 'Zhongguo sixiangshi shang de "tian ren he yi" wenti' 中国思想史上的"天人合一"问题 ('The Problem of the "Unity between Heaven and Man" in the History of Chinese Thought'), *Xueshu yanjiu* (*Academic Research*), No. 1, 1962, pp. 42–53.

Liu Jieren 刘介人, 'Kongzi sixiang tixi chutan' 孔子思想体系初探 ('A Preliminary Investigation of Kongzi's System of Thought'), *Guangming ribao* (*Guangming Daily*), 1 November 1959.

Liu Peishun 刘培顺, '"Maodun lun" de sixiang jinle shuiniyao' 《矛盾论》的思想进了水泥窑 ('The Thinking of "On Contradiction" Has Entered the Cement Kiln'), *Hongqi* (*Red Flag*), No. 2, 1966, pp. 28–32.

Liu Shaoqi 刘少奇, *Lun gongchandang yuan de xiuyang* 论共产党员的修养 (*How To Be A Good Communist*) (Beijing, Renmin chubanshe, 1962).

Liu Wendian 刘文典 (ed.), *Zhuangzi buzheng* 庄子补正 (*Zhuangzi with Supplementary Explanations*) (Kunming, Yunnan renmin chubanshe, 1980), 2 Vols.

Liu Yichun 刘一春, 'Mengzi zai pingjia' 孟子再评价 ('Further Evaluations of Mengzi'), in Zhongguo shehuikexue yuan (ed.), *Zhexue zhenglun yijiubaling–yijiubaer chu* 哲学争论1980—1982初 (*Controversies in Philosophy 1980 to Early 1982*) (Xian, Shanxi renmin chubanshe, 1984), pp. 329–37.

Lu Junzhong 卢俊忠, 'Jiechuan Feng Youlan zai Zhongguo zhexue yichan jicheng wenti shang de weikexue' 揭穿冯友兰在中国哲学遗产继承问题上的伪科学 ('Expose the Pseudo-scientific Nature of Feng Youlan's Treatment of the Problem of Inheriting the Chinese Philosophical Heritage'), *Zhexue yanjiu* (*Philosophical Research*), No. 5, 1958, pp. 39–40.

Lü Lizhuo 吕立琢, 'Cong "Gongshu" tanqi' 从"公输"谈起 ('Starting with "Gongshu"') *Guangming ribao* (*Guangming Daily*), 26 January 1962.

Lu Xun 鲁迅, 'Fei gong' 非攻 ('Against Offensive Warfare'), *in Lu Xun quanji* 鲁迅全集 (*Complete Works of Lu Xun*) (Beijing, Renmin chubanshe, 1973), Vol. 2, pp. 576–92.

—— 'Kuangren riji' 狂人日记 ('Madman's Diary'), in *Lu Xun quanji* (*Complete Works of Lu Xun*) (Beijing, Renmin chubanshe, 1973), Vol. 1, pp. 277–91.

Lü Zhenyu 吕振羽, *Zhongguo zhengzhi sixiangshi* 中国政治思想史 (*A*

History of Chinese Political Thought) (Beijing, Sanlian shudian, 1955).

Ma Xulun 马叙伦, *Zhuangzi "Tianxiapian" shuyi* 庄子天下篇述义 (*The 'Under Heaven' Chapter Explained*) (Shanghai, Longmen lianhe shuju, 1958).

Mao Lirui 毛礼锐, 'Shen zhu "Zhongguo Gudai jiaoyu he jiaoyu sixiang" pingjie' 沈著《中国古代教育和教育思想》评介 ('A Critical Introduction to Shen's *Ancient Chinese Education and Educational Thought*'), *Renmin jiaoyu*, No. 6, 1957 人民教育 (*People's Education*), pp. 58–61.

Mao Zedong 毛泽东, 'Pao da silingbu' 炮打司令部 ('Bombard the Headquarters'), *Hongqi* (*Red Flag*), No. 3, 1967, p. 3.

—— 'Zai ba da erci huiyi shang de jianghua' 在八大二次会议上的讲话 ('Speech at the Second Session of the Eighth Congress of the Communist Party of China'), *Mao Zedong sixiang wansui* 毛泽东思想万岁 (*Long Live Mao Zedong Thought*) (no publication details, 1969), pp. 186–96.

Meng Dengjin 蒙登进 and Niu Xinfang 牛欣芳, '"Wu shi" jiaoyu de renshi lun yiyi' 「五史」教育的认识论意义 ('The Epistemological Significance of the "Five Histories" Education'), *Zhexue yanjiu* (*Philosophical Research*), No. 4, 1964, pp. 17–23.

Mozi 墨子, 'Fei gong' 非攻 ('Against Offensive Warfare'), in Zhang Chunyi 张纯一 (ed.), *Mozi jijie* 墨子集解 (*Mozi Collated and Explained*), (Shanghai, Shijie shuju, 1936), hereafter *Mozi jijie*, pp. 123–46. According to Zhang Chunyi, Part 1 is lost.

—— 'Fei ru xia' 非儒下 ('Against Confucians, Part 2'), *Mozi jijie*, pp. 247–63.

—— 'Fei yue' 非乐 ('Against Music'), *Mozi jijie*, pp. 219–32.

—— 'Gongshu' 公输 ('Gongshu'), *Mozi jijie*, pp. 460–63.

—— 'Ming gui xia' 明鬼下 ('Clarifying Ghosts Part III'), *Mozi jijie*, pp. 197–218. According to Zhang Chunyi, Parts I and II are lost.

Ning Ke 宁可, 'Lun lishizhuyi de jieji guandian' 论历史主义的阶级观点 ('On Historicism and Class Viewpoint'), *Lishi yanjiu* (*Historical Research*), No. 4, 1963, pp. 1–26.

—— 'Lun Makesizhuyi de lishizhuyi' 论马克思主义的历史主义 ('On Marxist Historicism'), *Lishi yanjiu* (*Historical Research*), No. 3, 1964, pp. 1–37.

Pang Pu 庞朴, *Gongsun Longzi yanjiu* 公孙龙子研究 (*Study of the Gongsun Longzi*) (Beijing, Zhonghua shuju, 1979).

Peng Yinluo 彭殷雒, 'Lun "minmeng", "yeren", "caomang zhi chen" de jieji diwei ji Mengzi zhengzhi sixiang' 论"民氓""野人""草莽之臣"的阶级地位及孟子政治思想 ('On the Class Positions of the "minmeng", "yeren", "caomang zhi chen" and Mengzi's Political Thought'), *Xueshu yanjiu* (*Academic Research*), No. 4, 1962, pp. 64–74.

'Pipan Liu Jie xiansheng cuowu de lishi guandian he fangfalun' 批判刘节先生错误的历史观点和方法论 ('Criticize Mr Liu Jie's Wrong Historical Viewpoint and Methodology'), *Guangming ribao* (*Guangming Daily*), 20 August 1963.

Qi Benyu 戚本禹, Lin Jie 林杰, and Yan Changgui 阎长贵, 'Jian Bozan tongzhi de lishi guandian yingdang pipan' 翦伯赞同志的历史观点应当批判 ('Comrade Jian Bozan's Historical Outlook Should Be Criticized'), *Hongqi* (*Red Flag*), No. 4, 1966, pp. 19–30.

Qian Mu 钱穆, *Mozi* 墨子 (Shanghai, Shangwu yinshuguan, 1930).

'Qin Shihuang benji' 秦始皇本纪 ('Annals of Qin Shihuang'), in Sima Qian 司马迁, *Shiji* 史记 (*Records of the Historian*) (Beijing, Zhonghua shuju, 1959), Vol. 1, pp. 223–94.

Qu Junong 瞿菊农, 'Zhongguo gudai de weiwuzhuyi jiaoyu sixiang' 中国古代的唯物主义教育思想 ('Materialist Educational Thought in Ancient China'), *Xin jianshe*, No. 7, 1963, pp. 47–57.

Ren Hua 任华, 'Tantan zhexueshi yanjiu zhong de jiaotiaozhuyiqingxiang' 谈谈哲学史研究中的教条主义倾向 ('On the Tendency towards Dogmatism in the Study of the History of Philosophy'), *Symposium on Chinese Philosophy*, pp. 261–4.

Ren Jiyu 任继愈, *Han Fei* 韩非 (Shanghai, Shanghai renmin chubanshe, 1964).

—— 'Kongzi zhengzhi shang de baoshou lichang he zhexue shang de weixinzhuyi' 孔子政治上的保守立场和哲学上的唯心主义 ('Kongzi's Political Conservative Stance and Philosophical Idealism'), *Kongzi zhexue taolun ji*, pp. 147–61.

—— 'Lun Laozi zhexue de weiwuzhuyi benzhi' 论老子哲学的唯物主义本质 ('On the Materialist Basis of Laozi's Philosophy') originally in *Zhexue yanjiu* (*Philosophical Research*), No. 7, 1959, reprinted in *Laozi zhexue taolun ji*, pp. 28–47.

—— *Mozi* 墨子 (*Mozi*) (Shanghai, Shanghai renmin chubanshe, 1956).

—— 'Zai Zhongguo zhexueshi de yanjiu zhong suo yudao de jige kunnan wenti' 在中国哲学史的研究中所遇到的几个困难问题 ('A Few Difficult Problems Encountered in the Study of the History of Chinese Philosophy'), *Symposium on Chinese Philosophy*, pp. 139–45.

—— *Zhongguo zhexueshi* 中国哲学史 (*History of Chinese Philosophy*) (Beijing, Renmin chubanshe, 1963), 4 Vols, third edition 1979.

—— 'Zhongguo zhexueshi de duixiang he fanwei' 中国哲学史的对象和范围 ('The Object and Scope of the History of Chinese Philosophy'), *Symposium on Chinese Philosophy*, pp. 46–53.

—— 'Zhuangzi de weiwuzhuyi shijieguan' 庄子的唯物主义世界观 ('Zhuangzi's Materialist World Outlook'), *Zhuangzi zhexue taolun ji*, pp. 160–77.

—— 'Zhuangzi tanyuan' 庄子探源 ('An Investigation into the *Zhuang-*

zi'), originally in *Zhexue yanjiu* (*Philosophical Research*), No. 2, 1961, reprinted in *Zhuangzi zhexue taolun ji*, pp. 178–209.

—— 'Zhuangzi tanyuan zhi san' 庄子探源之三 ('A Third Investigation into the *Zhuangzi*'), originally in *Beijing daxue xuebao* 北京大学学报 (*Beijing University Journal*), No. 5, 1961, reprinted in *Zhuangzi zhexue taolun ji*, pp. 228–44.

—— (ed.), *Laozi jinyi* 老子今译 (*Laozi Translated into Modern Chinese*) (Beijing, Guji chubanshe, 1956).

—— (ed.), *Laozi xinyi* 老子新译 (*A New Translation of Laozi*) (Shanghai, Shanghai guji chubanshe, 1978).

—— (ed.), *Zhongguo zhexue fazhanshi* 中国哲学发展史 (*History of the Development of Chinese Philosophy*) (Beijing, Renmin chubanshe, 1983).

—— (ed.), *Zhongguo zhexueshi jianbian* 中国哲学史简编 (*A Brief History of Chinese Philosophy*) (Beijing, Renmin chubanshe, 1973).

—— and Feng Jingyuan 冯憬远, 'Laozi de yanjiu' 老子的研究 ('Studies of Laozi'), *Laozi zhexue taolun ji*, pp. 1–27.

Ridannuofu 日丹诺夫 (Zhdanov), *Ridannuofu tongzhi guanyu xifang zhexueshi de fayan* 日丹诺夫同志关于西方哲学史的发言 (*Comrade Zhdanov's Speech Regarding the History of Western Philosophy*), translated by Li Lisan 李立三 (Harbin, Dongbei shudian, 1948).

—— *Zai guanyu Yalishandaluofu zhu 'XiOu zhexueshi' yishu taolunhui shang de fayan* 在关于亚历山大洛夫著《西欧哲学史》一书讨论会上的发言 (*Speech delivered at the Discussion Meeting on Alexandrov's Book 'History of Western Philosophy'*), translated by Li Lisan (Beijing, Renmin chubanshe, 1954).

Shen Guanqun 沈灌群, 'Weida de jiaoyujia Kongzi' 伟大的教育家孔子 ('Kongzi the Great Educationalist'), *Huadong shida xuebao* 华东师大学报 (*East China Teachers' University Journal*), No. 3, 1957, pp. 76–86.

Shen Yi 沈沂, 'Du "Kongzi de jiaoyu sixiang" yihou' ('After Reading "Kongzi's Educational Thought"'), *Guangming ribao* (*Guangming Daily*), 28 June 1954.

Sima Qian 司马迁, *Shiji* 史记 (*Records of the Historian*) (Beijing, Zhonghua shuju, 1959), 10 Vols.

Sima Wen 司马文, 'Yansu duidai Makesizhuyi jingdian wenxian de yinzheng' 严肃对待马克思主义经典文献的引证 ('The Marxist Classics Should Be Cited with a Serious Attitude'), *Guangming ribao* (*Guangming Daily*), 29 June 1963.

Sun Changjiang 孙长江, 'Makesizhuyi chuxian yiqian shehui lishi lilun zhong you mei you weiwuzhuyi he weixinzhuyi de douzheng' 马克思主义出现以前社会历史理论中有没有唯物主义和唯心主

义的斗争 ('Were There Struggles between Materialism and Idealism in the Theories of Social History before the Appearance of Marxism?'), *Symposium on Chinese Philosophy*, pp. 452–62.

Tan Jiefu 谭戒甫, *Mobian fawei* 墨辩发微 (*Moist Rhetoric Explained*) (Beijing, Kexue chubanshe, 1958).

—— '*Xiancun Zhuangzi "Tianxiapian" de yanjiu*' 现存庄子"天下篇"的研究 ('A Study of the "Under the Heavens" Chapter of the Existing *Zhuangzi*'), in Zhexue yanjiu bianjibu (ed.), *Zhongguo zhexueshi lunwen chuji* 中国哲学史论文初集 (*Collected Essays on the History of Chinese Philosophy*) (Beijing, Kexue chubanshe, 1959), Vol. 1, pp. 50–78.

Tang Lan 唐兰, 'Pinglun Kongzi shouxian yinggai bianming Kongzi suochu de shi shenmeyang xingzhi de shehui' 评论孔子首先应该辨明孔子所处的是什么样性质的社会 ('To Evaluate Kongzi, it is first Necessary to Clearly Understand the Nature of the Society he Lived in'), *Kongzi zhexue taolun ji*, pp. 341–53.

Tang Yijie 汤一介, 'Beida zhexucxi he zhexue yanjiusuo pipan Feng Youlan de weixinzhuyi zhexue sixiang' 北大哲学系和哲学研究所批判冯友兰的唯心主义哲学思想 ('The Philosophy Department of Beijing University and the Institute for Philosophical Research Criticize Feng Youlan's Idealist Philosophical Thought'), *Zhexue yanjiu* (*Philosophical Research*), No. 5, 1958, p. 23.

—— 'Guanyu Zhuangzi zhexue sixiang de jige wenti' 关于庄子哲学思想的几个问题 ('A Few Questions on the Philosophical Thought of Zhuangzi'), *Zhuangzi zhexue taolun ji*, pp. 298–317.

—— 'Kongzi sixiang zai Chunqiu moqi de zuoyong' 孔子思想在春秋末期的作用 ('The Function of Kongzi's Thought at the End of the Spring and Autumn Period'), *Kongzi zhexue taolun ji*, pp. 43–77.

—— 'Laozi sixiang de jieji benzhi' 老子思想的阶级本质 ('The Class Nature of Laozi's Thought'), originally in *Guangming ribao* (*Guangming Daily*), 28 June 1959, reprinted in *Laozi zhexue taolun ji*, pp. 125–33.

—— 'Laozi yuzhouguan de weiwuzhuyi benzhi' 老子宇宙观的唯物主义本质 ('The Materialist Nature of Laozi's Cosmological Outlook'), *Laozi zhexue taolun ji*, pp. 134–53.

—— 'Mengzi de zhexue sixiang' 孟子的哲学思想 ('Mengzi's Philosophical Thought'), *Xin jianshe* (*New Construction*), No. 7, 1961, pp. 24–35.

—— 'Tantan zhexue yichan de jicheng wenti' 谈谈哲学遗产的继承问题 ('On the Problem of Inheritance of Philosophy'), *Symposium on Chinese Philosophy*, pp. 359–68.

Tang Yijie and Sun Changjiang 孙长江, 'Du Feng Youlan zhu "Zhongguo zhexueshi xinbian (diyi ce)"' 读冯友兰著《中国哲学史新编（第一册）》 ('On Reading Feng Youlan's *New History of*

Chinese Philosophy, Vol. 1'), *Jiaoxue yu yanjiu* 教学与研究 (*Teaching and Research*), No. 1, 1963, pp. 59–61; No. 2, 1963, pp. 55–62; No. 3, 1963, pp. 62–5.

Tang Yijie *et al.*, 'Lun "zhitong" yu "daotong"' 论"治统"与"道统" ('On "Rule by Administration" and "Rule by *dao*"'), *Beijing daxue xuebao* 北京大学学报 (*Beijing University Journal*), No. 2, 1964, pp. 1–38.

Tong Shuye 童书业 'Zhongguo gushi fenqi wenti de taolun' 中国古史分期问题的讨论 ('A Discussion of the Problem of Periodization of Ancient Chinese History'), *Selected Essays on Periodization*, pp. 130–61.

Wang Huanbiao 王焕镳, *Mozi jiaoshi* 墨子校释 (*Mozi Collated and Explained*) (Hangzhou, Zhejiang wenyi chubanshe, 1984).

Wang Ming 王明, 'Cong Mozi dao Taiping jing de sixiang yanbian' 从墨子到太平经的思想演变 ('The Ideological Transformations from *Mozi* to the *Taiping Canon*'), *Guangming ribao* (*Guangming Daily*), 1 December 1961.

Wang Teh-chao 王德昭, 'Majiyafuli yu Han Fei sixiang de yitong' 马基雅弗里与韩非思想的异同 ('A Comparison between the Thinking of Machiavelli and Han Feizi'), *Xinya xueshu niankan* 新亚学术年刊(*New Asia Academic Annual*), No. 9, 1967, pp. 163–95.

Wang Xianjin 王先进, 'Kongzi zai Zhongguo lishi shang de diwei' 孔子在中国历史上的地位 ('The Place of Kongzi in Chinese History'), *Kongzi zhexue taolun ji*, pp. 102–34.

Wang Yi 汪毅, 'Han Fei' 韩非 *Zhongguo qingnian* 中国青年 (*China Youth*), No. 3, 1957, pp. 26–8.

—— 'Han Fei de sixiang' 韩非的思想 ('Han Feizi's Thought'), *Guangming ribao* (*Guangming Daily*), 5 May 1954.

—— 'Yige wenti, yidian yijian' 一个问题，一点意见 ('A Problem, A Suggestion'), *Symposium on Chinese Philosophy*, pp. 54–60.

Wang Zhibang 王之榜 and Feng Guixian 冯贵贤, 'Mengzi renshilun de weixinzhuyi benzhi' 孟子认识论的唯心主义本质 ('The Idealist Basis of Mengzi's Epistemology'), *Wenhui bao* (*Wenhui Daily*), 23 April 1964.

Wu Chuanqi 吴传启, 'Cong Feng Youlan xiansheng de chouxiang jichengfa kan tade zhexue guandian' 从冯友兰先生的抽象继承法看他的哲学观点 ('Looking at Mr Feng Youlan's Philosophical Viewpoint from the Perspective of His Abstract Inheritance Method'), *Zhexue yanjiu* (*Philosophical Research*), No. 2, 1958, pp. 83–96.

Wu Dakun 吴大琨, 'Yu Fan Wenlan tongzhi lun huafen Zhongguo nuli shehui yu fengjian shehui de biaozhun wenti' 与范文兰同志论划分中国奴隶社会与封建社会的标准问题 ('Discussing with Comrade Fan Wenlan the Problem of the Criterion for Differentiat-

254   BIBLIOGRAPHY

ing Slave and Feudal Societies'), *Selected Essays on Periodization*, pp. 116–29.

Wu Han 吴晗, 'Guanyu "Hai Rui ba guan" de ziwo pipan' 关于《海瑞罢官》的自我批判 ('A Self-criticism relating to *Hai Rui Dismissed from Office*'), *Renmin ribao* (*People's Daily*), 30 December 1965.

—— 'Shuo daode' 说道德 ('On Morality'), reprinted in Wu Nanxing 吴南星, *Sanjiacun zhaji* 三家村札记 (*Notes from a Three Family Village*) (Beijing, Renmin wenxue chubanshe, 1979).

—— 'Zai shuo daode' 再说道德 ('Again on Morality'), in Wu Nanxing, *Sanjiacun zhaji* (*Notes from a Three Family Village*) (Beijing, Renmin wenxue chubanshe, 1979), p. 67.

—— *Zhongguo lishi changshi* 中国历史常识 (*General Knowledge in Chinese History*) (Beijing, Zhongguo qingnian chubanshe, 1964).

Wu Qibing 吴齐兵, 'Guchui chongyang fugu, jiu shi maiguo, jiu shi fubi—bo Zhou Yang "quanpan xihua" "quanpan jicheng" de fandong lilun' 鼓吹崇洋复古, 就是卖国, 就是复辟 — 驳周杨「全盘西化」「全盘继承」的反动理论 ('To Advocate Worship of Foreign Things and Return to Old Things is Treason and Restoration: in Refutation of Zhou Yang's Reactionary Doctrine of "Total Westernization" and "Total Inheritance"'), *Guangming ribao* (*Guangming Daily*), 28 August 1970.

Wu Tianshi 吴天石 and Ma Yingbo 马莹伯, *Tantan woguo gudai xuezhe de xuexi jingshen he xuexi fangfa* 谈谈我国古代学者的学习精神和学习方法 (*On the Spirit and Method of Learning of Our Country's Ancient Scholars*) (Beijing, Zhongguo qingnian chubanshe, 1964).

Wu Wen 伍文, 'Xunzi shi Zhongguo fengjianzhuyi sixiang de kaishanzhe ma?' 荀子是中国封建主义思想的开山者吗 ('Was Xunzi the Founder of Feudal Thought in China?'), *Zhexue yanjiu* (*Philosophical Research*), No. 4, 1957, pp. 136–45.

Xiao Jiefu 肖萐父, 'Zenyang lijie Makesizhuyi zhexue de jichengxing' 怎样理解马克思哲学的继承性 ('How Inheritance in Marxist Philosophy Should Be Understood'), *Symposium on Chinese Philosophy*, pp. 413–22.

Xiao San 萧三, 'Tan "Wang xingkong"' 谈《望星空》('On "Gazing at the Starry Sky"'), *Renmin wenxue* (*People's Literature*), No. 1, 1960, pp. 11–12.

Xiao Shu 萧述, '"He er er yi" lun de fan bianzhengfa shizhi' 「合二而一」论的反辩证法实质 ('The Anti-dialectical Nature of "Combining Two into One"'), *Renmin ribao* (*People's Daily*), 14 August 1964.

Xie Hua 谢华, *Lun XiZhou fengjian* 论西周封建 (*On the Feudalism of Western Zhou*) (Hunan, Hunan renmin chubanshe, 1979).

Xin Lan 辛兰, 'Kongzi zai tiyu fangmian de shijian he zhuzhang' 孔子在体育方面的实践和主张 ('Kongzi's Actual Practice and

Proposals concerning Sports'), *Xin tiyu* 新体育 (*New Sports*), No. 8, 1962, pp. 13–16.

Xiong Shili 熊十力, *Yuan ru* 原儒 (*The Original Confucianism*), first published in 1956, reprint edition (Hong Kong, Longmen shudian, 1970).

Xu Kangsheng 许抗生, 'Tantan guanyu pipan jicheng yu "chouxiang jicheng" de wenti' 谈谈关于批判继承与"抽象继承"的问题 ('On the Problem of Critical Inheritance and "Abstract Inheritance"'), in *Zhongguo zhexueshi fangfalun taolun ji*, pp. 210–14.

Xu Mengying 许梦瀛, 'Kongzi de jiaoyu sixiang' 孔子的教育思想 ('Kongzi's Educational Thought'), *Guangming ribao* (*Guangming Daily*), 14 June 1954.

—— 'Lüetan Kongzi de jiaoxuefa sixiang' 略谈孔子的教学法思想 ('A Brief Discussion of Kongzi's Ideas of Teaching Methods'), *Renmin jiaoyu* (*People's Education*), No. 2, 1957, pp. 27–9.

Xunzi 荀子, 'Fei shi'er zi' 非十二子 ('Critique of the Twelve Philosophers'), in Zhang Shitong 章诗同 (ed.), *Xunzi jianzhu* 荀子简注 (*A Simple Annotation of Xunzi*) (Shanghai, Shanghai renmin chubanshe, 1974), pp. 45–53.

Yan Lingfeng 严灵峯, *Zhongwai Laozi zhushu mulu* 中外老子著述目录 (*An Index to Works on Laozi in China and Abroad*) (Taibei, Zhonghua congshu weiyuanhui, 1957).

Yan Mingxuan 燕鸣轩, 'Guanyu Laozi zhexue taolun zhong de yixie wenti' 关于老子哲学讨论中的一些问题 ('A Few Problems on the Discussions on Laozi'), *Xin jianshe* (*New Construction*), No. 9, 1957, pp. 53–6.

Yang Bojun 杨伯峻 (ed.), *Lunyu yizhu* 论语译注 (*The Analects Translated and Annotated*) (Beijing, Zhonghua shuju, 1980).

Yang Chao 杨超, '*Laozi zhexue de weiwuzhuyi benzhi*' 老子哲学的唯物主义本质 ('The Materialist Basis of Laozi's Philosophy'), *Zhexue yanjiu* (*Philosophical Research*), No. 4, 1955, pp. 135–8.

Yang Huarong 羊华荣, 'Wo zancheng Feng Youlan xiansheng de kanfa' 我赞成冯友兰先生的看法 ('I Agree with Mr Feng Youlan's Viewpoint'), *Symposium on Chinese Philosophy*, pp. 463–72.

Yang Liuqiao 杨柳桥, 'Laozi de zhexue shi weiwuzhuyi de ma?' 老子的哲学是唯物主义的吗? ('Is Laozi's Philosophy Materialist?'), *Zhexue yanjiu* (*Philosophical Research*), No. 4, 1955, pp. 144–8.

Yang Rongguo 杨荣国, *Kong-Mo de sixiang* 孔墨的思想 (*The Thought of Kongzi and Mozi*) (Shanghai, Shenghuo shudian, 1946).

—— 'Lun Kongzi sixiang' 论孔子思想 ('On Kongzi's Thought'), *Xueshu yanjiu* (*Academic Research*), No. 1, 1962, pp. 24–41, reprinted in *Kongzi zhexue taolun ji*, pp. 373–400.

—— *Zhongguo gudai sixiangshi* 中国古代思想史 (*History of Ancient Chinese Thought*) (Beijing, Sanlian shudian chubanshe, 1954).

—— *Zhongguo gudai sixiangshi* 中国古代思想史 (*History of Ancient*

Chinese Thought) (Beijing, Renmin chubanshe, 1973), second edition.

Yang Xiangkui 杨向奎, 'Guanyu XiZhou de shehui xingzhi wenti' 关于西周的社会性质问题 ('On the Problem of the Nature of the Western Zhou Society'), *Selected Essays on Periodization*, pp. 331–58.

────── *Zhongguo gudai shehui yu gudai sixiang yanjiu* 中国古代社会与古代思想研究 (*A Study of Ancient Chinese Society and Ancient Thought*) (Shanghai, Shanghai renmin chubanshe, 1962), Vol. 1.

────── 'Zhuangzi de sixiang' 庄子的思想 ('Zhuangzi's Thinking'), originally in *Wen shi zhe* (*Literature, History, and Philosophy*), No. 8, 1957, reprinted in *Zhuangzi zhexue taolun ji*, pp. 329–46.

Yang Xianzhen 杨献珍, *Shenme shi weiwuzhuyi* 什么是唯物主义 (*What Is Materialism?*) (Shijiazhuang, Renmin chubanshe, 1980).

Yang Xingshun 杨兴顺, *Zhongguo gudai zhexuejia Laozi ji qi zhexue* 中国古代哲学家老子及其哲学 (*China's Ancient Philosopher Laozi and His Philosophy*), translated by Yang Chao (Beijing, Kexue chubanshe, 1957).

Yang Yongzhi 杨永志, 'Weile jianshe shehui zhuyi wenhua bixu pipan di jieshou zuguo wenhua yichan' 为了建设社会主义文化必须批判地接受祖国文化遗产 ('The Critical Assimilation of Our Country's Cultural Heritage is Necessary for Socialist Cultural Reconstruction'), *Zhexue yanjiu* (*Philosophical Research*), No. 1, 1956, pp. 52–70.

Yang Zhengdian 杨正典, 'Guanyu Zhongguo zhexue yichan jicheng wenti de jidian yijian' 关于中国哲学遗产继承问题的几点意见 ('A Few Objections to the Problem of the Inheritance of China's Philosophical Heritage'), *Symposium on Chinese Philosophy*, pp. 322–32.

Yao Wenyuan 姚文元, 'Ping xinbian lishi ju "*Hai Rui ba guan*"' 评新编历史剧《海瑞罢官》('A Critique of the New Historical Play *Hai Rui Dismissed from Office*'), *Wenhui bao* (*Wenhui Daily*), 10 November 1965.

Yi Baisha 易白沙, 'Kongzi pingyi' 孔子平议 ('Commentary on Kongzi'), Part 1, *Xin qingnian* 新青年 (*New Youth*), Vol. 1, No. 6 (February 1916).

────── 'Shu Mo' 述墨 ('On Mozi'), *Xin qingnian* (*New Youth*), Vol. 1, No. 2 (October 1915).

Yuan Liangyi 袁良义, 'Guanyu lishizhuyi yu jieji guandian' 关于历史主义与阶级观点 ('On Historicism and Class Viewpoint'), *Guangming ribao* (*Guangming Daily*), 6 November 1963.

'Zai xueshu yanjiu zhong jianchi baihua qifang baijia zhengming de fangzhen' 在学术研究中坚持百花齐放百家争鸣的方针 ('Stand Firm on the Policy of Letting a Hundred Flowers Blossom and a Hundred Schools of Thought Contend in Academic Research'), *Hongqi* (*Red Flag*), No. 5, 1961, pp. 1–5.

Zhan Jianfeng詹剑峰, 'Guanyu Mojia he Mojia bianzhe de pipan wenti' 关于墨家和墨家辩者的批判问题('On The Criticism of the Moists and the Moist Rhetoricians'), *Xueshu yuekan (Academic Monthly)*, No. 4, 1957, pp. 14–17.

—— 'Laozi de "dao" jishi juedui jingshen ma?' 老子的"道"即是绝对精神吗? ('Is Laozi's *dao* an Absolute Spirit?'), *Laozi zhexue taolun ji*, pp. 154–61.

—— *Mojia de xingshi luoji* 墨家的形式逻辑 (*The Formal Logic of the Moists*) (Hubei, Hubei renmin chubanshe, 1956), second edition 1979, pp. 202–29.

Zhang Chunyi 张纯一 (ed.), *Mozi jijie* 墨子集解 (*Mozi Collated and Explained*) (Shanghai, Shijie shuju, 1936).

Zhang Dainian 张岱年, 'Daode de jiejixing he jichengxing' 道德的阶级性和继承性 ('On the Class Nature and Inheritability of Ethics'), *Symposium on Chinese Philosophy*, pp. 295–6.

—— 'Guanyu zhexue yichan de jicheng wenti' 关于哲学遗产的继承问题 ('On the Problem of Inheriting the Philosophical Heritage'), *Symposium on Chinese Philosophy*, pp. 342–5.

—— 'Guanyu Zhongguo zhexueshi de fanwei wenti' 关于中国哲学史的范围问题('On the Scope of the History of Chinese Philosophy'), *Symposium on Chinese Philosophy*, pp. 79–86.

—— 'Mozi de jieji lichang yu zhongxin sixiang' 墨子的阶级立场与中心思想 ('The Class Stance and Central Core of Mozi's Thinking'), *Guangming ribao (Guangming Daily)*, 24 March 1954.

—— 'Xunzi de weiwuzhuyi sixiang' 荀子的唯物主义思想 ('Xunzi's Materialist Thinking'), *Xuexi* 学习 (*Study*), No. 1, 1957, pp. 5–6.

—— *Zhongguo weiwuzhuyi sixiang jianshi* 中国唯物主义思想简史(*A Short History of Chinese Materialist Thought*) (Beijing, Zhongguo qingnian chubanshe, 1957).

Zhang Daoyang 张道杨, 'Cong "she" "yu" lunzheng Kongzi tiyu sixiang' 从"射""御"论证孔子体育思想 ('Kongzi's Ideas on Sports Discussed and Demonstrated using Archery and Charioteering'), *Guangming ribao (Guangming Daily)*, 27 March 1962.

Zhang Dehong 张德鸿, 'Mozi de "fei gong" "jian'ai" shi fandong de ma?' 墨子的"非攻""兼爱"是反动的吗? ('Are Mozi's "Against Offensive Warfare" and "Universal Love" Reactionary?'), *Guangming ribao (Guangming Daily)*, 26 January 1962.

Zhang Dejun 张德钧, 'Mengzi de renshi lun' 孟子的认识论 ('Mengzi's Epistemology'), *Wenhui bao (Wenhui Daily)*, 15 and 16 February 1962.

—— '"Zhuangzi" neipian shi XiHan churen de zhuzuo ma?' 《庄子》内篇是西汉初人的著作吗? ('Were the Inner Chapters of the *Zhuangzi* Written in the Early Western Han Dynasty?"), originally in *Zhexue yanjiu (Philosophical Research)*, No. 5, 1961, reprinted in *Zhuangzi shexue taolun ji*, pp. 245–83.

Zhang Ruifan 张瑞璠, 'Xunzi de jiaoyu sixiang' 荀子的教育思想 ('Xunzi's Educational Thought'), *Huadong shida xuebao* 华东师大学报 (*East China Teachers' University Journal*), No. 3, 1957, pp. 87–100.

Zhang Shifeng 章士风, 'Kongzi de renxue bushi nuli jiefang de lilun' 孔子的仁学不是奴隶解放的理论 ('Kongzi's Philosophy of *ren* is not a Theory for the Emancipation of Slaves'), *Guangming ribao* (*Guangming Daily*), 27 March 1960.

Zhang Shitong 章诗同 (ed.), *Xunzi jianzhu* 荀子简注 (*A Simple Annotation of Xunzi*) (Shanghai, Shanghai renmin chubanshe, 1974).

Zhao Fu 昭父, 'Guanyu "pupianxing de xingshi"—yu Feng Youlan xiansheng shangque' 关于"普遍性的形式"—与冯友兰先生商榷('On the "Form of Universality"—A Debate with Mr Feng Youlan'), *Zhexue yanjiu* (*Philosophical Research*), No. 5, 1963, pp. 47–56.

Zhao Jibin 赵纪彬, *Gudai rujia zhexue pipan* 古代儒家哲学批判 (*A Criticism of Ancient Confucian Philosophy* (Shanghai, Zhonghua shuju, 1950).

—— 'Kong-Mo xianxue duili de jieji he luoji yiyi' 孔墨显学对立的阶级和逻辑意义 ('The Significance of the Contrast of Class and Logic between the Illustrious Schools of Kongzi and Mozi'), *Xueshu yuekan* (*Academic Monthly*), No. 11, 1963, pp. 34–50.

—— *Lunyu xin tan* 论语新探 (*A New Exploration of the Analects*) (Beijing, Renmin chubanshe, 1962).

—— 'Ren li jiegu' 仁礼解故('The Original Meanings of *ren* and *li* Explained'), *Lunyu xin tan* (*A New Exploration of the Analects*) (Beijing, Renmin chubanshe, 1962), pp. 166–200.

—— 'Shi ren min' 释人民 ('On *ren* and *min*'), *Lunyu xin tan* (*A New Exploration of the Analects*) (Beijing, Renmin chubanshe, 1962), pp. 7–28.

Zheng Xin 郑昕, 'Kaifang weixinzhuyi' 开放唯心主义 ('Liberate Idealism'), *Symposium on Chinese Philosophy*, pp. 1–10.

Zhexue yanjiu bianjibu 哲学研究编辑部 (ed.), *Kongzi zhexue taolun ji* 孔子哲学讨论集 (*Collected Papers on Kongzi's Philosophy*) (Beijing, Zhonghua shuju, 1963).

—— (ed.), *Laozi zhexue taolun ji* 老子哲学讨论集 (*Collected Papers on Laozi's Philosophy*) (Beijing, Zhonghua shuju, 1959).

—— (ed.), *Zhongguo zhexueshi lunwen chuji* 中国哲学史论文初集 (*Collected Essays on the History of Chinese Philosophy, Vol. 1*) (Beijing, Kexue chubanshe, 1959).

—— (ed.), *Zhongguo zhexueshi wenti taolun zhuanji* 中国哲学史问题讨论专辑 (*A Symposium on the Problems of the History of Chinese Philosophy*) (Beijing, Kexue chubanshe, 1957).

—— (ed.), *Zhuangzi zhexue taolun ji* 庄子哲学讨论集 (*Collected Papers on Zhuangzi's Philosophy*) (Beijing, Zhonghua shuju, 1962).

Zhong Kui 钟奎, 'Du Xunzi "quan xue" zhaji' 读荀子《劝学》札记 ('Notes on Xunzi's "Exhortation to Learning"'), *Guangming ribao* (*Guangming Daily*), 29 September 1961.

Zhong Lei 钟蕾, 'Mozi "fei gong" "jian'ai" de fandong shizhi' 墨子"非攻""兼爱"的反动实质 ('The Reactionary Nature of Mozi's "Against Offensive Warfare" and "Universal Love"'), *Guangming ribao* (*Guangming Daily*), 1 December 1961.

Zhong Zhaopeng 钟肇鹏, 'Lüelun Kongzi sixiang de jieji xing' 略论孔子思想的阶级性 ('A Brief Discussion on the Class Nature of Kongzi's Thought'), *Kongzi zhexue taolun ji*, pp. 182–95.

Zhongguo kexueyuan Shandong fenyuan lishi yanjiusuo 中国科学院山东分院历史研究所 (ed.), *Kongzi taolun wenji* 孔子讨论文集 (*Collected Papers on Kongzi*) (Jinan, Shandong renmin chubanshe, 1962), Vol. 1.

Zhongguo shehui kexueyuan zhexue yanjiusuo, Zhongguo zhexueshi yanjiushi (ed.) 中国社会科学院哲学研究所, 中国哲学史研究室, *Zhongguo zhexueshi fangfa lun taolun ji* 中国哲学史方法论讨论集 (*Collected Papers on the Methodology of the History of Chinese Philosophy*) (Beijing, Zhongguo shehui kexue chubanshe, 1980).

Zhongguo shehuikexue yuan 中国社会科学院 (ed.), *Zhexue zhenglun yijiubaling-yijiubaer chu* 哲学争论1980 1982初 (*Controversies in Philosophy 1980 to Early 1982*) (Xian, Shanxi renmin chubanshe, 1984).

Zhou Gucheng 周谷城'Zhongguo nuli shehui lun'中国奴隶社会论('On Slave Society in China'), *Selected Essays on Periodization*, pp. 61–7.

—— *Zhongguo tongshi* 中国通史 (*General History of China*) (Hong Kong, Wenluo chubanshe, 1939), reprint edition, and *Zhongguo tongshi* (Shanghai, Shanghai renmin chubanshe, 1957).

Zhou Jianren 周建人, 'Laozi de "dao" shi weiwuzhuyi haishi weixinzhuyi?' 老子的"道"是唯物主义还是唯心主义 ('Is Laozi's "dao" Materialist or Idealist?'), *Laozi zhexue taolun ji*, pp. 298–302.

Zhou Longhua 周龙华, 'Guanyu Laozi zhexue' 关于老子哲学 ('On Laozi's Philosophy'), in Zhongguo shehuikexue yuan (ed.), *Zhexue zhenglun yijiubaling-yijiubaer chu* 1980–1982 (*Controversies in Philosophy 1980 to Early 1982*) (Xian, Shanxi renmin chubanshe, 1984), pp. 320–8.

Zhou Zhenfu 周振甫, 'Cong "sirenbang" de jia piKong kan yingshe shixue de pochan' 从"四人帮"的假批孔看影射史学的破产 ('Looking at the Bankruptcy of Reflective History From the Angle of the "Gang of Four's" False Criticism of Kongzi'), *Lishi yanjiu* (*Historical Research*), No. 3, 1978, pp. 28–34.

Zhou Zhongling 周钟灵, *Han Feizi de luoji* 韩非子的逻辑 (*Han Feizi's Logic*) (Beijing, Renmin chubanshe, 1958).

Zhu Bokun 朱伯昆, 'Women zai Zhongguo zhexueshi yanjiu zhong suo yudao de yixie wenti' 我们在中国哲学史研究中所遇到的一些问题 ('Some Problems we have Encountered in the Study of the

History of Chinese Philosophy'), *Symposium on Chinese Philosophy*, pp. 29–36.

Zhu Qianzhi 朱谦之, 'Shiba shiji Zhongguo zhexue dui Ouzhou zhexue de yingxiang' 十八世纪中国哲学对欧洲哲学的影响 ('The Influence of Chinese Philosophy on European Philosophy in the Eighteenth Century'), *Zhexue yanjiu* (*Philosophical Research*), No. 4, 1957, pp. 48–57.

—— 'Shiqiba shiji Xifang zhexuejia de Kongzi guan' 十七八世纪西方哲学家的孔子观 ('Western Philosophers' Views of Kongzi in the Seventeenth and Eighteenth Centuries'), *Renmin ribao* (*People's Daily*), 9 March 1962.

Index